Working Families

Working Families

The Transformation of the American Home

EDITED BY

Rosanna Hertz and
Nancy L. Marshall

UNIVERSITY OF CALIFORNIA PRESS
Berkeley · *Los Angeles* · *London*

University of California Press
Berkeley and Los Angeles, California

University of California Press, Ltd.
London, England

© 2001 by the Regents of the University of California

"Getting Younger While Getting Older: Family-
Building at Midlife" © 2001 by Lillian B. Rubin

Library of Congress Cataloging-in-Publication Data

Working families : the transformation of the
American home / edited by Rosanna Hertz and
Nancy L. Marshall.
    p.   cm.
  Includes bibliographical references and index.
  ISBN 0-520-22222-9 (alk. paper)—ISBN 0-520-
22649-6 (pbk. : alk. paper)
    1. Dual-career families—United States. 2. Work
and family—United States. 3. Children
of working parents—United States. I. Hertz,
Rosanna. II. Marshall, Nancy L.

HQ536 .W6215 2001
306.3'6'0973—dc21   2001027445

Manufactured in the United States of America

10 09 08 07 06 05 04 03 02 01

10 9 8 7 6 5 4 3 2 1

Contents

Sub for other ?? No - See
'father' piece . conclusion
but too technical

Preface

This book grew out of a faculty seminar we co-organized at Wellesley College to discuss emerging research in multiple disciplines on work and family as the beginning of a new century approached. Our colleagues in that seminar identified the incredible complexity of work and family scholarship that is shifting the intersection of these two fields from a simple dichotomy to a multifaceted arena. When the seminar ended, we decided to expand this work and were fortunate to establish a joint partnership with the Alfred P. Sloan Foundation and the Business and Professional Women's Foundation to cosponsor, in 1998, a national conference entitled "Work and Family: Today's Realities and Tomorrow's Visions."

The conference attempted to link academics and the business community to examine current issues involving work and family. The sponsors brought different but compatible interests to the planning of the conference. The Alfred P. Sloan Foundation program on Working Families was interested in the issues faced by dual-career families as they coped with the competing demands of work and family. The Business and Professional Women's (BPW) Foundation was interested in research that supports its mission to promote equity for working women. To this we added our interest in the diversity of experiences across multiple social locations, including social class, race or ethnicity, and gender. This partnership produced a rich and varied conference, with over 100 papers and presentations.

Based for the most part on talks given at this conference, the chapters in this volume admittedly represent only a part of the cutting-edge research presented there. They were chosen to provide an interdisciplinary perspective, including voices from academia as well as the business community. The goal of this volume is to argue that the intersection of family and work is much more complex than is commonly thought and to provide examples of the cutting-edge work that continues to ask interesting questions and generate new scholarship, policies, and practices.

We wish to thank Naomi Schneider, our editor at the University of California Press, for her continuous enthusiasm and support of our work. We also thank Kathleen Christensen of the Alfred P. Sloan Foundation for her intellectual support and the Business and Professional Women's Foundation for its commitment to an atypical partnership between business and academia. Our thanks also to Mary O'Neill and the other staff at the BPW Foundation for making the conference happen. We are very much indebted to Susan Bailey, executive director of the Wellesley Centers for Women, for her support and contributions to the conference and to our work. We thank Susan Wellington and Elizabeth Starr for their able assistance with the conference and in producing this volume, including library work and the creation of a seamless manuscript out of myriad chapters.

Introduction

Rosanna Hertz and Nancy L. Marshall

The family remains a controversial topic in American political life. Alarming stories of family dissolution, teenage mothers, and children abandoned by employed mothers and absentee fathers take center stage on talk shows and in glitzy promos for the eleven o'clock news. But controversy, like a magician, often misdirects our attention from the real action. In this case, the real action lies in the rise of dual-earner families and employed single mothers, not in imagined fears of the death of the family, loss of masculinity, or domination by women. The story that needs to be told involves a different kind of drama, one that centers on the development of new patterns of relationships among individuals, families, workplaces, and the larger social context.

Despite the enduring 1950s image of the happy suburban middle-class family with Dad as the breadwinner and Mom as the homemaker, not all U.S. families at the time lived in that world (Coontz 1992). As we enter the twenty-first century, family structure has become quite diverse, even for the white middle class. Not only is Mom more likely to be employed outside the home, but among married couples, dual-earner couples are now the modal family type. Families with same-sex parents have become more visible. More women are having their first child after the age of thirty. As a result, the life course is no longer standard: mothers of two-year-olds may be of different generations, live in different family structures, have different employment histories, and have conceived their children through different reproductive methods. Fathers'

I

lives have also become more diverse. Some fathers are involved in the nurturing care of their children, while others have minimal contact with the children they father. One out of three children born in the late 1990s had mothers who were not married at the time of the birth (U.S. Bureau of the Census 1998). While the vast majority of children currently live with married parents (including stepparents), divorce and single parenthood have changed the experiences of many children, a considerable number of whom live for a period of time with only one parent. Not only are families diverse, but mothers, fathers, and children experience family life and parental employment from different vantage points.

This volume focuses primarily on the extraordinary sea change that has occurred with women's entry into the labor force. In fact, there has been a quiet but steady increase in the percentage of women entering and staying in the labor force after becoming mothers. Today 61 percent of married couples include two earners. In both working-class and middle-class couples employment has become the norm for both women and men, even when children are very young. In addition, among children living with single parents, 69 percent have an employed parent (Waite and Nielsen, chapter 1). The women in these families are not selfish careerists, as they have often been (and still are) characterized. Women seek employment for the same reasons men do: they need a paycheck, they want personal rewards, and they wish to do meaningful work.

The rise in women's employment has taken place in the context of a dramatically changing economy, which has brought new players and new rules to the workplace. This shift has raised serious issues about equity in the workplace (Pitt-Catsouphes and Googins 1999), the meshing of families and workplaces, and the involvement of nonfamily and outside institutions in the raising of the next generation.

We as editors share the growing academic consensus that "work" and "family" should not be portrayed or understood as separate worlds. Rather, we view paid work and family as interrelated expressions of the ways we ensure the continuity of and reproduce our society.[1]

The objective of this volume is to better grasp the intricately interwoven fabric of work and family by shedding new light on the ways we

---

1. Throughout this volume "paid work" or "employment" has generally been used to refer to marketplace labor. "Home work" refers to labor that occurs within the household. Although we have used the phrase "work and family" because this is still in common usage, we have also used the term "work/family" in our introduction to indicate that we, the editors, do not view paid work and family as separate spheres.

organize our lives. To that end, the essays in this volume explore how families and workplaces are embedded in local, national, and global contexts and are stitched together by institutions, such as schools, community organizations, and government. In addition, they emphasize that families and their members are not monolithic: they occupy differing socioeconomic, cultural, regional, and other social positions. Similarly, workplaces vary along many dimensions, including size, composition, structure, and whether they are local or multinational. These are the issues that need to be addressed as families and workplaces move into the twenty-first century. We have not been able to cover every aspect of these issues in this volume. In particular, we do not adequately speak to the issues of same-sex families, nor to the experiences of those caring for aging parents or disabled family members. We wish we had been able to include more material on families of different race or ethnic backgrounds and migration histories. These topics alone would make for a second compelling volume (cf. Baca Zinn and Dill 1994; Coontz 1999; Taylor 1998).

We have organized the essays in this volume to address four key assumptions about families and workplaces. The first part of the book refutes the assumption that there is one normative model for "the family" by chronicling the major changes of the twentieth century: historical shifts in family structure, life course variations, living longer and having children later, and the changing character of men's family work.

The second part challenges the assumption that there is one normative model for employment: a white-collar, nine-to-five career in a Fortune 500 company. Instead, the changing economy, with the increasingly diverse labor force, the pressures of globalization, the rise in contingent labor, and the growth of small businesses, requires a reconceptualization of variations in work and family in specific locations or contexts. The chapters in this section contribute to such a rethinking of workplace practices and policies.

The third part counters both the assumption that individuals, not families, are the unit of family decision-making and should be the unit of scholarly analysis and the assumption that the relation of work and family is "only a women's issue." The chapters in this section talk about the gendered experiences of families in different sociocultural locations in the United States. They also address the contradictions and paradoxes inherent in gendering both caring work and paid employment.

The fourth part focuses on children and the impact of parental employment on children's lives. Children are not passive players in the family. While the vast majority of literature on work and family has either ignored children or has examined children only as objects of parents' decision-making, this section positions the children as subjects in their own lives. The authors explore the ways children make sense of their parents' decisions and behavior.

This volume is interdisciplinary in nature, reflecting the development of the field of work and family out of concerns that any single field could provide only one perspective on a complex system. Further, scholars have recognized for over two decades that to understand the historical separation of home and work, we needed to relink intellectually what have been spatially separate spheres. As a result, over time and in a range of disciplines, scholarship has emerged that not only addresses the complex interrelationship of work and family, but also begins to examine the differences by race or ethnicity, social class, and gender in the expression and experience of these issues. Not all of the chapters in this volume do all of these things, partly because of the specific theoretical concerns and the nature of the data available to the different authors. As editors of this volume, we have selected papers that collectively illustrate the kinds of variables and concerns that need to be addressed. We hope that other researchers will note the missing pieces and develop new ways to provide a more complete picture of work and family.

This collection presents not only basic research by academics but also applied research from the private sector. We have included pieces by people who are located outside of traditional academic institutions because they have been able to bring to bear perspectives and data that academics do not always have. They also provide a more applied understanding of how research is related to practice and suggest how organizations may be changed by experts who focus on human resources and corporate cultures. There are rigorous quantitative chapters and elegant qualitative ones. We have deliberately included papers from a broad range of theoretical perspectives that do not always agree with each other. The issues raised by the various chapters should contribute to discussions in the classroom as well as in the field at large.

The beginning of this new century should witness the growth of scholarship that attempts to contend with a flourishing array of work cultures and family constellations as the United States becomes increasingly involved in the global economy.

CHANGING FAMILIES

At the beginning of the twenty-first century women have become full-time and continuous participants in the labor force. This is in contrast to the experiences of their mothers and grandmothers, who often were less educated and may have moved in and out of the labor force, depending on their social location and family circumstances. Waite and Nielsen (chapter 1) document the dramatic historical changes in women's employment, including the rise in the prevalence of dual-earner couples and the growth in women's full-time employment. The proportion of U.S. married couples with two incomes grew from 36 percent in 1963 to 68 percent in 1997; the proportion of married couples in which both work *full-time* rose from 21 percent in 1963 to 44 percent in 1997.

But to describe these changes as only about gender would obscure the multiplicity of women's experiences; specifically, gender is experienced *through* race and class (among other identities) (Gerstel and Gerson 1999). Reflecting the economic position of Black families, 51 percent of Black married couples were two-earner couples in 1965, compared to 42 percent of White married couples (Waite and Nielsen, chapter 1). By 1997, 66 percent of Black married couples were two-earner couples, with both spouses employed full-time in 49 percent of all Black married couples. And given the already high level of employment for Black women, having children does not change the rate of employment among married couples.

We also see variations in the experiences of working-class and middle-class women and men. Among working-class married couples of all races, 64 percent were dual-earners in 1997. Parenthood had little or no impact on the rates of employment for working-class couples. The same pattern holds when we consider only working-class couples with two full-time earners: 42 percent of parents and 48 percent of all married couples include two full-time earners. However, for middle-class married couples, the effects of parenthood are more dramatically evident, reflecting the greater incomes of middle-class men *and* women: almost half of all middle-class married couples include two full-time earners, yet only one in three middle-class married couples with children includes two full-time earners. But middle-class married women with children do not return to the home and breadwinner/homemaker family; rather, they reduce their hours to part-time. Finally, gender is also experienced through marital status. Single parents (most of whom are women) are more likely to be employed than are women in married couples and, when employed, are more likely to be employed full-time. This is most evident among White families and middle-class families, but it is also true among Black families and working-class families.

Waite and Nielsen report that household income adjusted for needs is greater for dual-earner couples than for comparable single-earner households. We would add that gender inequality remains alive and well in both the workplace and the couple. In 1995, women earned 71 cents for every dollar a man earned (U.S. Bureau of the Census 1998). Further, in the majority of dual-earner couples, women continue to earn less than their husbands. In 1981, 16 percent of women earned more than their husbands, and in another 2 percent of couples they earned the same (within $1 of each other) (Bianchi and Spain 1983). By 1997, these figures had risen only slightly; just 23 percent of wives earned more than their husbands in two-earner couples (U.S. Bureau of the Census 1999) (figures were not available for 1997 couples where both partners earned the same amount). The importance of each partner's contribution to the overall household finances and this interplay with the gender dynamics in the family are discussed in several chapters in this volume.

More Equal than Others (Hertz 1986, 32) quotes a husband who, groping for words to describe his dual-career marriage, struck on what he felt was an apt metaphor: "It's two separate lives in some ways. It's like a dual carriage way, and we're both going down those carriage ways at more or less the same speed, I would say. While those carriage ways don't cross one another, if something happens on one of them, something necessarily happens on the other one."

His understanding is not simply the product of a faulty metaphor; it is also the result of being taught to think in individual terms, rather than to see his employment decisions as made within the context of a couple. The emphasis on the individual as the unit of analysis in linking work and family is critiqued by Moen and Han (chapter 2). By using the couple as the unit of analysis, the authors provide a more holistic account of work and family by considering them not parallel tracks but parts of one unified life. The links between the employment of partners are particularly evident in those couples who work tandem shifts or who coordinate their work hours to manage time with children. But all dual-earner couples make employment decisions conjointly, even though they may not be conscious of the links and accommodations each makes to the other. This construction of independent careers is no accident: the hegemonic culture of the workplace presumes the independence of each employee, rarely acknowledging either the invisible work of a spouse on behalf of the other's career or the possibility that the individual is part of a dual-earner couple (e.g., Gerstel and Gross 1984; Lewis and Lewis 1996; Papanek 1975).

Moen and Han also document the ways in which occupational work patterns have diversified from the masculine prototype (one employer with upward advancement through positions of increasing greater responsibility, authority, and reward) to a range of paths that incorporate continuities and discontinuities in the occupational and family careers. Their use of the term "career" is generic, that is, it refers to occupational work histories or family pathways. They are among the first scholars to acknowledge how occupational paths are gendered. The gendered nature of specific paths has meant that only certain kinds of trajectories (e.g., the masculine prototype just described) have been acknowledged as appropriate ways for advancement in the workplace. The authors document the newer career paths that, we suggest, have been ignored because they are typically associated with women.

Rubin (chapter 3) points out another major demographic shift: life expectancy at birth rose from 47 years of age at the dawn of the twentieth century to nearly 80 at the century's end. This longer life span, combined with new reproductive technology and women's increased employment, has contributed to rising numbers of children born to parents at midlife. Age is no longer a predictor of life stage. This revolutionary social change has no recent historical precedent: earlier generations cannot serve as models for current midlifers with young children. As a result, individuals are left to revise their own life plans, with little support or understanding from the larger community. Rubin identifies important consequences of this upending of the usual pathways through employment and parenthood. We find Rubin's observation of the disparity between the "young" lives these parents are living and their aging bodies particularly compelling.

There have also been subtle, and not so subtle, changes in men's lives. Coltrane and Adams (chapter 4) raise questions about the definition of fatherhood and men's family work in the context of changing behavior and expectations for women and men. While many studies of the division of labor report that men are doing more in the home, Coltrane and Adams argue that men's increased time at home does not always challenge the hegemony of masculinity in the home. Men who participate in more companionate activities with their children (such as play, leisure activities, and TV watching) are no more likely to take on other household chores than less-involved fathers. It is only the men who participate in nurturing, child-centered fathering activities (such as helping with homework or having private talks) who are more nearly full partners in family work. Men are also more likely to be involved in housework when women's occupational resources are similar to men's. In this way, gender equity in the workplace is linked to gender equity in the home.

CHANGING WORKPLACES

The U.S. economy has changed greatly since the beginning of the twentieth century. Today it is a powerful but interdependent element of an increasingly global economy. The paid labor force has diversified from predominantly white males to include a growing proportion of women and people of color. The nature of employment has also changed, with a shift from manufacturing to service industries, with the majority of new jobs created in the service sector. There has been a concomitant shift from employment in the primary sector (with standard hours and core benefits) to a two-tiered market. Many employees are in secondary labor markets with fewer benefits and/or are in contingent employment (temporary work, contract work, and part-time work). Under the old economy, unions won many benefits and improved working conditions for the (predominantly male) workforce; the new economy is much less unionized. Finally, much of our thinking about the economy and the labor force assumes that employees work in large firms. In reality, more than four out of five businesses have fewer than 20 employees.

These changes call for a new understanding of the changing workplace and of workplace-based efforts to address work/family and gender equity issues. These efforts can be seen as grounded in one or more of several perspectives on work and family. One perspective views work/family tensions as an individual issue, usually a women's issue. From this perspective, workplaces either declare that work/family tensions are not their problem or develop individualized solutions for individual women. Those solutions tend to be limited to women who have some negotiating power and/or have skills that are valued by employers (Glass and Estes 1997; Deitch and Huffman, chapter 5).

Another view, responding to women's growing presence in the labor force, maintains that work/family tensions are something that must be addressed to foster gender equity in the workplace or to allow employers to reap the benefits of women's contributions to the workplace. Workplaces that hold this perspective see the solution as the provision of family-friendly benefits that make it easier for women to function at work in the same way that men do. However, the current interest in family-friendly benefits comes at a time when the changing economy is less conducive to expanding employee benefits.

Several key changes in the economy are examined in this volume, including the rise of contingent workers (including part-time employees), the decline in the power of unions, the growing number of small businesses, and the increasing cultural and gender diversity of the labor force. Contingent workers are less likely to receive fringe benefits. Deitch and Huffman (chapter 5) demonstrate that, paradoxically, firms that rely heavily on contingent workers tend to offer more family-friendly benefits, but not necessarily to their contingent employees. The use of contingent labor allows employers to invest more heavily in their "real" employees by financing good benefits for this core group out of the savings on contingent workers.

The increasing diversity of the labor force also has an impact on family-responsive benefits. While increasing numbers of men report work/family tensions and the need for family-friendly benefits, the realities of the workplace and the family still leave women more at risk than men for work/family tensions. It is sometimes expected that the growing numbers of women in the labor force will increase the demand for family benefits and that employers will be forced to respond to maintain their workforce. Consistent with this line of reasoning, Deitch and Huffman report that firms with few women are not likely to offer family-friendly benefits. However, for some employers it is cheaper to replace employees who quit for family reasons than to incur the anticipated costs associated with family benefits. And other employers *expect* high turnover among their low-wage, female workforce and perceive women workers as easily replaceable. These are at least partial explanations of Deitch and Huffman's finding that employers with predominantly female employees are also less likely to offer family-friendly benefits. As Kanter (1977) argued, in these gender-imbalanced settings (too few women or too many women), women have limited power to get the family-responsive benefits they need.

Consistent with this power explanation is Galinsky's finding (chapter 8) that when women are evident in executive positions in a company, the company is more likely to offer specific family benefits. However, this appears to be a two-tiered system. Both the Deitch and Huffman study and the Galinsky study found that employers who paid their core employees more—that is, invested in more highly skilled or educated labor—offered more family-friendly benefits. Similarly, Deitch and

Huffman report that employers with a greater investment in training their workforce offer more family-friendly benefits: the social class of the employee continues to filter the experience of gender in the workplace. In the past, unions were effective negotiators of conventional benefits, such as paid health insurance, for lower-waged employees. Galinsky found that the presence of unions continues to be associated with paid health insurance, paid maternity leave, and leave when children are mildly ill, but not with other family benefits, such as child care assistance or part-time jobs. Overall, Deitch and Huffman found that the presence of unions was associated with greater availability of conventional benefits, but not with more family-responsive benefits.

Another significant change in the economy is the rise of small businesses. In 1997, 87 percent of all business establishments in the United States had fewer than 20 employees (U.S. Bureau of the Census 1997). Smaller businesses are less likely to have separate personnel or human resources departments and are less likely to have formal personnel policies (Pitt-Catsouphes and Litchfield, chapter 6); not surprisingly, they also have fewer formal benefits. Smaller employers are less likely to offer both conventional benefits and family-friendly benefits (Deitch and Huffman, chapter 5; Galinsky, chapter 8) and are exempt from compliance with the Family and Medical Leave Act. However, Pitt-Catsouphes and Litchfield found that small businesses put a greater priority on having flexible policies to respond to individual needs and on helping employees with work/family balance than did medium or large businesses. Their chapter highlights the gaps in our knowledge about the experiences of women and men working in small businesses: models and expectations built on Fortune 500 companies will not necessarily apply.

While family-friendly benefits are an important part of the response needed from the workplace, they do not challenge the hegemony of workplace culture, which is still predicated on the view of employees as individuals rather than as members of families and of communities, and on the separation of "work" and "family." Even when benefits are available, many employees do not take advantage of them because of a workplace culture that may exact costs in job security, work assignments, or promotions (Glass and Estes 1997). In addition, workplace culture is gendered: men risk being seen as not conforming to the masculine-dominant norm if they use family-friendly benefits, while women are judged not able to compete in a "man's world" if they cannot manage family responsibilities quietly (Starrels 1992). Kropf (chapter 7) documents the ways in which these workplace assumptions translate into barriers to employees' well-being. What is needed is a significant change in our understanding of the fact that individuals are embedded in larger social groups—families, communities—and that the work that takes place in the family is as valuable to society as the work that takes place in the workplace. Incorporating this understanding would change not only the availability of family-responsive benefits, but also the dynamics within the workplace and family.

Gross (chapter 9) calls our attention to the corporate hegemony that has accompanied globalization of the economy. The social contract crafted under the old economy offered some protections to lower-waged employees and supported the development of a middle class. That social contract is no longer tenable. Transnational corporations in their thirst for profit have eliminated or destabilized paid jobs and undermined kin ties and communities. The social impact of these changes is felt around the world, most strongly in the Third World but also in the First World, particularly among minorities. Gross argues that Third World women have become "maids to the world economy," consigned to harsh work conditions that "enable" multinational corporations to profit hand-somely. The social and economic pressures of globalization serve as the new context for existing tensions between the workplace and family life and demand a new social contract that protects families and individuals from the worst excesses. That new social contract would include higher wages and job security (Glass and Estes 1997; Raabe 1990; Rayman and Bookman 1999; Gross, chapter 9).

THE VIEW WITHIN FAMILIES

The organization of paid work is predicated on the erroneous assumption that employees are individuals, supported by a homemaker/wife. Even when workplaces offer services to replace the home work traditionally assigned to wives, the basic assumption of how paid work is structured is not challenged. Put differently, families remain the "dependent variable," shaped by the demands and constraints of the workplace. While women have made great strides in labor force participation, their presence has not altered the way organizations operate or how they structure individual jobs and careers. This is not simply a women's issue. Both men and women are participants in a workplace culture that has yet to take into account the fact that individuals are members of families and that many of these families include two wage earners. The rise in women's employment and two-earner couples has not been able to challenge significantly the hegemony of the workplace culture. In fact, competitive pressures have led to increased hours at work for certain employees—an increase that is compounded for two-earner couples. One of the critical debates at present, as the European Union discusses reducing paid-work time, concerns the length of the workweek in the United States. We have become known as a culture of workaholics whose priorities are misplaced as work lives have become increasingly out of control.

Gerson and Jacobs (chapter 10) argue that the average time spent at paid work has not increased over the past few decades, but the *dispersion* of hours at paid work has increased—some workers are working more; other workers are working less, and less than they would like. Like Moen and Han (chapter 2), Gerson and Jacobs shift our focus to the couple and away from the individual. Here is where the most dramatic changes have occurred, with the added effects of longer workweeks for both members in dual-earner couples. Most provocative among the findings in this chapter is that both men and women would prefer to spend fewer hours at paid work and to devote more of their time to family and personal leisure than they currently do. Those who are on the job more than 40 hours a week do so not out of personal preference but because of the demands of the workplace.

Yet a focus on hours does not adequately describe the work/family conflicts that dual-earner couples experience. An equally important factor is the culture of the workplace, including flexibility in the scheduling of paid work hours, and worker autonomy on the job. For both women and men working fewer hours contributes to greater flexibility. At the opposite end of the spectrum, men who work long hours also tend to have greater flexibility and control over their work schedule. However, women working more than 40 hours a week are not in positions that offer them the compensating increase in flexibility and control that men experience. Therefore gender inequality persists in the workplace. It is not surprising, then, that the desire for flexibility and the willingness to trade other benefits or change jobs to get greater flexibility are highest among professional women with preschool children (Gerson and Jacobs, chapter 10).

Families must often choose between "heartstrings and pursestrings"—weighing the love, labor, and desires of family members against the monetary needs of the family and the demands of the workplace. Sometimes there is no choice for families, who are pulled by fears of job loss, and pursestrings must reign over heartstrings. The birth of a first child highlights this tension and brings to the forefront the question of the workplace culture's response to the needs of families. Organizational support, supervisor support, and coworker support are all crucial to the adjustment of the working-class couples studied by Haley, Perry-Jenkins, and Armenia (chapter 11). This chapter also highlights the limitations of structural policies available to working-class employees. Haley and colleagues reveal the underbelly of supposedly family-friendly benefits, detailing the ways women patch together sick leave and vacation time to create what the women themselves refer to as "paid maternity leaves" in the absence of formal paid leaves offered by their employers. Similarly, they point out the gap between employee reports of occasional flexibility granted by their supervisors and a formal policy of flexible scheduling. In spite of these limitations, Haley and colleagues found that women whose employers offered child care benefits were less anxious, compared to women without access to child care benefits, after returning to paid employment.

Ironically, women who take longer maternity leaves report greater role overload when they return to paid employment, and men report greater depression and anxiety after their wives or partners return to paid work. The authors speculate that when women take longer maternity leaves, either the longer absence from paid employment depletes the couple's financial resources or the longer leave shifts the couple's division of labor to a more traditional one, and the transition back to employment—without a parallel shift in home division of labor—is thereby more difficult.

Lundgren, Fleischer-Cooperman, Schneider, and Fitzgerald (chapter 12) argue that gender also matters when couples in which both partners are medical doctors decide who is to reduce their paid work hours (in a field where 40 to 50 hours per week is "part-time"). Ironically, even among these couples with two high-powered careers, decisions about reduced hours reflect an acceptance of traditional external norms and constraints. While they might individually reject the traditional roles of breadwinner and homemaker, these couples nevertheless believe that the costs of reduced hours (and therefore a different career track within medicine) would be greater to men's careers than to women's (see also Potuchek 1997). The authors note that the ability to reduce work hours is predicated upon the high income that both partners enjoy. Physician couples' decisions are made against the backdrop of a field that remains the quintessential example of an unyielding work culture predicated upon the belief that individuals (that is, men) are married to careers and

ideology of careerism

families are little more than ornaments of success. Choosing to work part-time under such structural conditions does little to alter the omni-present ideology of careerism.

Families like those described in the preceding paragraphs are not ne-gotiating their employment and family arrangements on their own, how-ever; other family members and child care providers are key players as well. In 1991, 52 percent of preschool children with employed mothers were cared for by relatives (including parents) during their mothers' paid work hours. Of the children in non-relative care, 37 percent were cared for by a family child care provider (Casper, Hawkins, and O'Connell 1994). These providers are often themselves negotiating paid-work and family responsibilities. Fitz Gibbon (chapter 13) argues that family child care providers are placed between the family and the traditional world of paid work, and as "outsiders within" (Collins 1990) are in a unique position to shed light on the status and power inequalities evident in families. Fitz Gibbon documents the shift in women's consciousness from a view of child-minding as an extension of their own family work to recognition that what they are doing is not only a job, it is essential work that allows other women and men to engage in paid employment. In the process, these women come to see the power imbalances and gender inequalities in their own families and in the families of the chil-dren in their care. In redefining care as not a labor of love but a job that contributes to a greater good, they also elevate their own status as com-parable to that of other employed women. In this way, their traditional caring work becomes politicized and the women themselves begin to challenge the status quo, with calls for stronger child care regulations and the inclusion of funding for child care in welfare reform. They come to see themselves not as the invisible handmaidens of either their hus-bands or their wealthier clients, but as women staking a claim to making visible their paid work and their contributions. In this regard, this kind of home work blurs the physical boundaries between paid and unpaid work.

CHILDREN'S EXPERIENCES

Most research on family and work starts from the vantage point of the adult, as employee or parent. Rarely does research start from the daily experiences of children or consider their perspective. Yet children's ex-periences reflect the same multiplicity that adults' experiences do. They also vary according to social, cultural, and historical location. The meaning of childhood is not universal: in other times and other cultures children have been expected to contribute to productive labor and have been seen as "miniature adults" (Ariès 1962). Ariès argued that childhood is socially constructed, not biologically determined, and that it is historically changing. The passage of child labor laws and the establishment of universal schooling in the United States around the beginning of the twentieth century (Zelizer 1985) gave rise to a new construction of childhood as a period of intensive parental investment, guided by experts who argued that children have distinctive needs. Now, a hundred years later, we find ourselves again rethinking the nature of childhood, only now placing emphasis on children as agents in their own lives. This is not to say that parents are no longer influential in their children's lives, but rather to recognize the active role that children play in making sense of the locales around them and the social worlds they face daily.

Ehrensaft (chapter 15) proposes that the new definition of childhood incorporates both aspects of the child: innocent cherub and miniature adult. She points out that the child who is expected to be independent at school or child care while parents are employed is the same child who is indulged by parents at night, out of parental guilt or a desire to provide a sense of balance in the child's life. Interestingly, when children were asked what they would most like changed in their relationships with their parents, they identified the hurried parent who comes home from work stressed as the problem. Ehrensaft argues that while parental guilt plays a role, the genesis of the "kinderdult" is also rooted in the need of (middle-class) parents to provide their children with a résumé that guarantees them a successful future. We would further add that this reflects a growing concern with the widening social class division in the United States. That is, middle-class parents are anxious for their children to be accepted into the best schools so they can enter topflight careers. Universities and colleges, in turn, select students not simply on the basis of grades, but also on the basis of these résumés. However, the middle-class experience of childhood is only one of a multiplicity of experiences of childhood at this point in time.

Ehrensaft also argues that the myth of the self-centered, work-focused parent is as erroneous as the myth of the child as a miniature adult. She views parenthood as bifurcated, for women and men, encompassing both the nurturing caretaker and the labor force participant. In her words, "the changing definition of parenthood leaves us not with a bunch of raving narcissists but with a whole generation of fragmented parents who cannot fathom how they will do it all."

As Garey and Arendell warn us (chapter 14), we need not repeat with children the shortsightedness of our earlier attempts at studies of women and motherhood. Learning from that experience, the authors offer critical advice, which includes placing children at the center stage of our research and taking into account the diversity of meaning children may bring to their activities. In her study of children's games, Lever (1976) provides a marvelous example of the potential pitfalls of ignoring this counsel; in her research she notes that an adult observer sees a child delivering newspapers and calls it work, while the child views it as a game of target practice.

Much of children's negative behavior has been laid at the door of feminism. Every woman who entered the labor force was cause for alarm as questions were raised about her place in her family and whether her employment would threaten her marriage and damage her children. Blaming mothers for all our cultural ills is a popular sport, used to provide explanations for problems ranging from the rising rates of hyperactive children to teenage violence and sexuality, and childhood stress and burnout. Garey and Arendell take mother-blame to task by emphasizing that while structural changes in the family may coexist with children's problems, the evidence indicates that divorce, single parenthood, maternal employment, and child care are not the cause of any difficulties children may experience.

The picture of idyllic childhoods of the past, with unstructured play time to explore nature and the greater world with other children, whether during long summers or on lazy school-day afternoons, has come to symbolize the lost childhood for the present generation. In stark contrast, structured after-school programs, lesson after lesson to attend, and camps designed to give children an edge in whatever area their parents desire have come to symbolize the experience of children today. But these two images capture only particular children in particular times and places. That is, the child who played leisurely in pastures and fields was a rural child (who might also have risen early to feed the chickens), and the "hurried child," the offspring of the baby boom generation (likely to be the topic of a cover story) lives in the suburbs where organized sports and a computer in every home are affordable "necessities." The low-income child, whether urban or rural, is less likely to have the same structures that organize afternoons and summers as the middle-class child in the suburbs. Children's experiences vary with time, with geography, with social class, and with other differences in social location.

Thorne (chapter 18) and Romero (chapter 16) each provide a context-rich, empirical study of children's experiences of work and family. Their analyses connect particular local situations and institutions with larger cultural and structural dynamics. Thorne selects an important moment of the day—the after-school hours—as a lens through which to view children's vantage points. She is interested in the multiplicity of experiences that come out of specific locations and institutional settings. By focusing on children and the processes of care, Thorne generates insights into the juxtaposition of multiple childhoods in a diverse geographic area: there is no one model for providing care when school is out. Thorne highlights the different views of what constitutes "good" care among individuals who vary by class, immigration, and race. While there is no consensus in this diverse community (about either good care or the developmental milestones of childhood), each child is continually monitored by multiple caregivers—including parents, teachers, other school personnel, paid and unpaid child caregivers, and family members—looking for clues about the child's well-being and daily experiences.

Romero (chapter 16) recounts a woman's life that is embedded in passing across social class and race/ethnic lines. In so doing, she also tells a story from the perspective of a girl of Mexican heritage raised by a single mother while the mother is working as a maid in the United States. The daughter, Olivia, deals on a daily basis with the contradictions of trying to "pass" while retaining links to her extended family and heritage. She is also the "outsider within" (Collins 1990), with a bird's-eye view of the worlds of both the upper middle class and that of the maids, gardeners, and other domestic employees. Olivia's experiences are potentially comparable to those of other children whose mothers are employed in "private household occupations," one of the top ten occupational categories for women in the United States. Moreover, Olivia's account illustrates how children's views of the intersection of paid work and family work may differ from the perspective of adults. Further, it illustrates the ways in which a mother may attempt to interpret the meaning of her employment to her child, but in the end the child makes her own meaning. As an adult, Olivia believes she must choose between racial authenticity and personal success.

Hochschild (chapter 17) also explores the ways in which children make meaning of the various cultures of care that their parents arrange. She focuses on the accounts of two young children: Janey King, from a

White middle-class family, and Hunter Escala, from a White working-class family. Hochschild astutely describes children's searches for clues, through eavesdropping and observation, that will help them to frame an understanding of their social world and the norms that govern the relationships in that world. Children pick up not only factual information but also the affective load attached to that information—whether parents are happy with or upset about the caregiver—and interpret parental affect in the context of what they already know about the structure of their social world.

These three empirical chapters by Thorne, Romero, and Hochschild differ from prior studies in this field, which focused on children as the *objects* of parental decision-making. Each chapter examines children's relationships to caregivers (including parents) with children as active agents in the construction and understanding of their surroundings. They provide contextualized illustrations of the multiplicity of children's experiences and are excellent examples of the kind of research that is needed if we are to fully understand the links between children and the social systems they experience.

CONCLUSION

Initial scholarship on work/family was based on a model of two separate spheres competing for limited resources and thus in conflict with each other. These two separate worlds, where all men were "workers" and all women were wives, were connected only by "border exchanges," in which men's market labor provided income for the family and families produced workers for the world of paid work. The entry of women (particularly White middle-class married women) into the paid labor force challenged prevailing mainstream definitions of the proper places of men and women and forced a reexamination of the value of home work, gender equity issues in the workplace, and division of labor and time use in families. These changes prompted scholarship focused on gender differences with an emphasis on gender inequality, which was seen as resulting from women's disadvantaged positions both at home and at work. However, this literature retained the concept of "separate spheres" of paid work and family.

At the beginning of the twentieth century the economy shifted from agriculture to industry. As we enter the twenty-first century we are on the threshold of another shift—this time to a global and technological economy. This change will reverberate through every aspect of U.S. culture and, as this introduction anticipates, will raise cutting-edge issues about how daily life becomes organized. We predict that women's experiences will once again be central to a rethinking of women's contribution to employment, to child raising and household labor, and to civic involvement and broader community participation. We suggest that to avoid the pitfalls of the dualism that places paid work and family in opposition to each other, a new model is needed that allows for more complex relationships between individuals' experiences in the workplace and in families and communities.

The chapters in this volume take a variety of approaches to this task. Some place the individual in the context of the family, viewing the couple as the locus of decision-making and thereby acknowledging the connections between the allegedly separate experiences of each partner in the workplace and the home. Other chapters build on the experiences of alternate family structures. Single parents and others embedded in extended kin or community networks challenge the old ideology that women were *either* mothers *or* paid workers; in the process, they revision work and family. When we understand women (and men) as both parents and paid workers, we are forced to weave a more complex conceptual tapestry of their accomplishment of everyday life. Still other chapters focus on the multiplicity of experiences and use this as the lens through which they formulate new understandings of work and family. In these chapters, the individual is a starting point for understanding the connections between individual experiences and broader social and political structures. Collectively as a volume, these chapters generate a new, more fluid vision of home work and paid work, and of the patterns of relationships between individuals, families, workplaces, and the larger social context.

REFERENCES

Ariès, Philippe. 1962. *Centuries of childhood.* New York: Vintage.

Baca Zinn, Maxine, and Bonnie Thorton Dill, eds. 1994. *Women of color in the U.S.* Philadelphia: Temple University Press.

Bianchi, Suzanne M., and Daphne Spain. 1983. Wives who earn more than their husbands. U.S. Bureau of the Census: *Special demographics analyses,* CDS-80-9. Washington, D.C.: U.S. Government Printing Office.

Casper, Lynne M., Mary Hawkins, and Martin O'Connell. 1994. Who's minding the kids? Child care arrangements: Fall 1991. U.S. Bureau of the Census: *Current population reports,* P70-36. Washington, D.C.: U.S. Government Printing Office.

Collins, Patricia Hill. 1990. *Black feminist thought.* Cambridge, Mass.: Unwin Hyman.

Coontz, Stephanie. 1992. *The way we never were: American families and the nostalgia trip.* New York: Basic Books.

Coontz, Stephanie, with Maya Parsons and Gabrielle Raley, eds. 1999. *American families: A multicultural reader.* New York: Routledge.

Gerstel, Naomi, and Judith Gerson. 1999. Feminisms and feminists: Intellectual agendas and political possibilities. Paper presented to the Eastern Sociology Society, Boston, 5 March.

Gerstel, Naomi, and Harriet Gross. 1984. *Commuter marriage.* New York: Guilford Press.

Glass, Jennifer L., and Sarah Beth Estes. 1997. The family responsive workplace. *Annual Review of Sociology* 23:289–313.

Hertz, Rosanna. 1986. *More equal than others: Women and men in dual-career marriages.* Berkeley: University of California Press.

Kanter, Rosabeth Moss. 1977. *Work and family in the United States: A critical review and agenda for research and policy.* New York: Russell Sage Foundation.

Lever, Janet. 1976. Sex differences in the games children play. *Social Problems* 23:478–87.

Lewis, Suzan, and Jeremy Lewis, eds. 1996. *The work-family challenge: Rethinking employment.* Thousand Oaks, Calif.: Sage Publications.

Papanek, Hanna. 1975. Men, women, and work: Reflections on the two-person career. *American Journal of Sociology* 78:852–72.

Pitt-Catsouphes, Marcie, and Bradley K. Googins, eds. 1999. The evolving world of work and family: New stakeholders, new voices. *Annals of the American Academy of Political and Social Science* 562.

Potuchek, Jean L. 1997. *Who supports the family? Gender and breadwinning in dual-earner marriages.* Stanford: Stanford University Press.

Raabe, Phyllis. 1990. The organizational effects of workplace family policies. *Journal of Family Issues* 11:477–91.

Rayman, Paula M., and Ann Bookman. 1999. Creating a research and public policy agenda for work, family, and community. *Annals of the American Academy of Political and Social Science* 562:191–211.

Starrels, Marjorie E. 1992. The evolution of workplace family policy research. *Journal of Family Issues* 13:259–78.

Taylor, Ronald L., ed. 1998. *Minority families in the United States.* 2d ed. Englewood Cliffs, N.J.: Prentice-Hall.

U.S. Bureau of the Census. 1997. *Statistics of U.S. business.* Washington, D.C.: U.S. Government Printing Office.

———. 1998. *Current population reports,* P23-194, *Population profile of the United States: 1997.* Washington, D.C.: U.S. Government Printing Office.

———. 1999. Table F19. Married-couple families with wives' earnings greater than husbands' earnings: 1981 to 1997 (selected years). www.census.gov/hhes/income/f19.html. (Last revised: 25 May 1999.)

Zelizer, Viviana A. 1985. *Pricing the priceless child: The changing social value of children.* New York: Basic Books.

PART ONE

CHANGING FAMILIES

CHAPTER I

The Rise of the Dual-Earner Family, 1963–1997

Linda J. Waite and Mark Nielsen

During the 1950s and early 1960s the traditional family was king. Young men and women married early and had rather large families relatively quickly. Divorce was rare and unmarried childbearing unheard of. Young women worked before they were married and some continued working until their first child was born, but almost all mothers of infants left the labor force for an extended period and many did not return. Women earned much less than men because they had less education and training, because they almost all worked in "women's jobs," and because they either had just started working or would soon leave (Blau, Ferber, and Winkler 1998; Cherlin 1992).

The world has changed since then. Most women, men, and children now live in constellations of adults and children that bear little resemblance to the male breadwinner/female homemaker families that symbolized the 1950s. Families today spend their time in ways our parents and grandparents never considered. They also often have resources available only to affluent families 35 years ago.

Changes in the structure of families, in the way they allocate the time of their members, and in their resources have dramatically altered the lives of women, men, and children (Waite and Gallagher 2000). Some types of families have seen enormous improvements in their fortunes,

This research was supported by a grant from the Alfred P. Sloan Foundation. We would like to thank Fay Booker for help on the files for the Current Population Survey.

while others have been left behind. Dual-earner families have been the big winners in this reshuffling of life chances—at least if we consider financial well-being our indicator of success.

FAMILY STRUCTURE

The many interrelated ways that society has changed have affected people's choices about marriage and family. Birth control, the sexual revolution, and more relaxed attitudes opened the door to sex outside marriage (Smith 1994). Divorce has become both a common and an acceptable solution to conflict between partners—or simply to boredom or the sight of greener pastures. Many couples live together without being married, either as a prelude to marriage or as a temporary convenience. The process of education, training, and becoming established in a career delays marriage much longer now than it did in our mothers' day (Oppenheimer, Kalmijn, and Lim 1997). And the rise in women's employment and earnings means that women are less economically dependent on marriage than they used to be (McLanahan and Casper 1995).

In the 1950s young women typically married at about age 20, young men at about age 22. No more. Today young women wait until about age 24 to tie the knot, their grooms until about age 26. But many young women begin their families earlier; about a third of children born in recent years had mothers who were not married (U.S. Bureau of the Census 1998). High rates of divorce and declining rates of remarriage have left more people without a spouse, although many of them have children (Cherlin 1992).

In all our discussions, figures about children's parents refer to the parent(s) with whom they are living. We are telling a story about changes in the work lives and family lives of women, men, and children, so we focus on those in the prime working ages (ages 25–55), after most have finished school and when few have retired. We calculated these figures from the March Current Population Survey (CPS) for each year. The Current Population Survey is a nationwide monthly sample survey of about 60,000 households conducted by the Bureau of the Census. The March CPS asks adults about their activities in the past week and over the past year, with a focus on employment and income. It also includes information about marital status and the structure of the household (U.S. Bureau of the Census 1998, 948). When discussing these figures, we always round to the nearest whole percentage point.

Changes in family structure come into focus clearly in table 1.1. This table shows the percentage of women, men, and children's parents aged 25 to 55 who are currently married, previously married, and never married. In the early years we see a clear picture of the traditional family. Table 1.1 shows that in 1963, the vast majority of adults were married (84% of women and 87% of men); only 6 percent of women and 9 percent of men had never married. Very few women or men had once been married but were not now—10 percent of women and 5 percent of men. But the picture for children is most striking: 91 percent of all children under 18 lived with two married parents (some of these were stepparents). Only 8 percent lived with a widowed or divorced parent, usually their mother. And only one child in a hundred lived with a never-married parent.

Over the next third of a century the picture changes. The share of adult women and men who are married falls steadily to two out of three by 1997, with growth in both the percent previously married and the percent never married. By 1997 one adult man in five had never been married, compared to one in ten when we first looked. The share of adult women who had never been married nearly tripled between 1963 and 1997, from 6 percent to 16 percent. As more men and women divorced, and as they entered new marriages more slowly, we can see an increase in the share who were previously married but not currently married. Men and women fare differently in the remarriage market or make different choices, because fewer men than women are in this state (19% of women vs. 13% of men were previously but not currently married in 1997).

In spite of all the movies and magazine articles about kids with divorced parents, table 1.1 shows that in 1997, as in 1963, a substantial majority of children lived with parents who were currently married (including, perhaps, a stepparent). In 1997, 73 percent of all children under 18 lived with married parents, a decrease from the 91 percent we saw in 1963, but still high. About one child in six lived with a divorced—or less commonly, widowed—parent, and one in ten with a parent who had never been married. Of course, many of the children in married-parent families spent some time in a single-parent family or will do so in the future. And some of the single-parent families included the mother's live-in boyfriend, who often becomes a stepfather

TABLE 1.1

MARITAL STATUS OF WOMEN, MEN, AND CHILDREN'S PARENTS, 1963–1997

Year	Women				Men				Children's Parents			
	Currently Married (%)	Previously Married (%)	Never Married (%)	N	Currently Married (%)	Previously Married (%)	Never Married (%)	N	Currently Married (%)	Previously Married (%)	Never Married (%)	Number of Children
1963	83.6	10.3	6.1	15,158	86.8	4.3	8.9	13,752	90.5	8.2	1.3	26,779
1965	82.8	11.6	5.6	14,836	87.4	4.5	8.1	13,500	90.3	8.3	1.4	25,854
1970	82.0	11.9	6.1	27,309	86.8	4.8	8.4	25,148	88.3	10.0	1.8	47,353
1975	78.0	15.0	7.1	25,152	83.7	7.0	9.3	22,993	83.7	14.1	2.2	38,165
1980	74.2	16.6	9.2	36,269	78.0	9.3	12.7	33,857	81.0	15.5	3.5	48,909
1985	70.4	18.3	11.4	34,316	73.9	10.6	15.5	31,810	78.2	16.8	5.0	41,354
1990	68.2	18.2	13.7	35,169	70.2	11.3	18.4	32,858	76.5	16.7	6.8	40,141
1995	66.9	18.3	14.8	34,055	68.5	11.9	19.6	31,641	74.3	17.3	8.4	38,369
1997	65.7	18.7	15.6	30,088	67.2	12.6	20.2	28,083	73.6	17.1	9.3	33,892

SOURCE: All tables in this chapter based on March Current Population Survey, 1963–1977, U.S. Bureau of the Census.

NOTE: All tables in this chapter refer to adults 25 to 55 years old.

(Bumpass and Raley 1995). So these figures mask some of the changes in the families of children that have occurred over the past 30-plus years.

WHO WORKS?

A second revolution—a revolution in women's employment—has altered the lives of women, men, and children. This revolution sent scores of young women into colleges and professional programs. It propelled them into traditionally male occupations and up career ladders. The change was dramatic and far-reaching, altering the character of the labor force and the lives of families (Blau, Ferber, and Winkler 1998). Men, on the other hand, responded to increased availability of generous pensions with a reduction in their ties to the labor force in their fifties and sixties (U.S. Bureau of the Census 1996).

The rise in women's time spent in paid employment shows up clearly in table 1.2. In 1963 only one woman in three was working full-time, compared to 86 percent of men. An additional 16 percent of women worked part-time. Half of the women did not hold a paid job at all.

But the revolution had already begun. Women moved from work in the home to work in the office or factory, slowly at first but then more quickly. Between 1963 and 1975 we see rises in both women's full-time and part-time work. The shift from work in the home into part-time paid employment pretty much stops by the mid-1970s, so that almost all the growth in the 1980s and the 1990s comes from a rapid increase in women's full-time work. By 1997, 57 percent of all women were working full-time, with another 23 percent working part-time. The share of women who did not work at all for pay shrank to just one in five in 1997—four out of five adult women held paying jobs, compared to one in two in 1963.

At the same time that women were pouring into the labor market, men were quietly withdrawing—at least a little. In 1963, 86 percent of men worked full-time. By 1997, this share had fallen to 83 percent as some men shifted to part-time work; very few men in either year did not work at all.

Married women—especially married mothers—were the shock troops in the revolution in women's employment, dramatically altering their allocation of time from working in the home to working for pay. Table 1.3 shows the percent of women working full-time, part-time, and

TABLE 1.2

PERCENTAGE OF WOMEN AND MEN WORKING
FULL-TIME, PART-TIME, OR NOT WORKING,
1963–1997

Year	Women Full-Time	Part-Time	Not Working	N	Men Full-Time	Part-Time	Not Working	N
1963	33.5	16.4	50.1	15,158	85.8	8.3	6.0	13,752
1965	37.6	18.0	44.4	14,836	88.3	7.2	4.5	13,500
1970	39.8	20.4	39.7	27,309	87.7	8.1	4.2	25,148
1975	41.9	22.1	36.1	25,152	84.6	9.6	5.9	22,993
1980	47.9	23.8	28.3	36,269	84.2	9.7	6.1	33,857
1985	51.6	23.2	25.3	34,316	83.4	9.5	7.1	31,810
1990	56.0	23.0	21.0	35,169	85.7	9.3	5.1	32,858
1995	54.9	24.4	20.8	34,055	81.8	11.3	7.0	31,641
1997	56.6	23.4	20.0	30,088	82.6	10.7	6.7	28,083

not working by marital status and presence of children. We see very modest changes in employment of single women without children. These women were about as likely to work full-time in 1997 as in 1963, a little more likely to be working part-time, and a little less likely to not be working. Single mothers changed their work behavior more but not dramatically—58 percent worked full-time in 1997 compared to half in 1963. One single mother in three did not work for pay in 1963, compared to one in five in 1997.

Changes in women's employment were driven by the choices made by married women, both because many more women are married than not *and* because the work choices of married women changed much more than the work choices of unmarried women. Both married mothers and married women without children were much more likely to work for pay and to work full-time in the late 1990s than in the early 1960s. In 1963, 42 percent of married women with no children at home worked full-time compared to 60 percent in 1997, and the share not working for pay fell from 43 percent to 19 percent. But married mothers were quite unlikely to work full-time in 1963, when fewer than one in four worked this much. By 1997 the proportion working full-time had *more than doubled* to 49 percent. Sixty percent of married mothers did not work outside the home in 1963; by 1997 less than one in four was not employed.

TABLE 1.3

PERCENTAGE OF WOMEN WORKING FULL-TIME, PART-TIME, OR NOT WORKING, BY MARITAL STATUS AND PRESENCE OF CHILDREN, 1963–1997

| | Single Women | | | | | | | | Married Women | | | | | | | |
| | No Children | | | | With Children | | | | No Children | | | | With Children | | | |
Year	Full-Time	Part-Time	Not Working	N	Full-Time	Part-Time	Not Working	N	Full-Time	Part-Time	Not Working	N	Full-Time	Part-Time	Not Working	N
1963	68.7	12.4	18.9	1,599	49.7	18.8	31.5	889	41.5	16.4	42.2	3,401	23.0	16.9	60.2	9,269
1965	70.4	12.6	17.1	1,695	50.8	17.6	31.5	856	45.1	17.6	37.3	3,497	27.0	19.3	53.7	8,788
1970	68.1	12.9	19.1	1,412	62.1	18.2	19.7	3,512	46.9	17.5	35.7	6,100	30.0	22.7	47.4	16,285
1975	63.9	14.8	21.3	1,345	59.2	18.6	22.2	4,197	48.5	19.2	32.3	5,734	31.7	25.1	43.2	13,876
1980	69.8	16.4	13.8	5,191	56.4	19.3	24.3	4,156	51.7	21.2	27.1	8,407	38.1	28.1	33.9	18,515
1985	71.5	15.3	13.2	5,874	52.9	19.2	28.0	4,300	56.2	20.2	23.6	8,292	41.5	28.7	29.8	15,850
1990	72.7	14.7	12.7	6,780	57.5	18.5	24.0	4,419	59.8	20.3	19.9	8,649	46.1	29.5	24.5	15,321
1995	68.3	17.5	14.1	6,800	53.5	20.8	25.7	4,476	59.0	22.3	18.7	8,474	46.5	30.0	23.6	14,305
1997	67.8	17.4	14.8	6,302	58.2	20.8	21.0	4,032	59.5	21.7	18.8	7,353	48.7	28.3	23.1	12,401

TRADITIONAL VERSUS DUAL-EARNER FAMILIES

Table 1.4 shows, for married couples, the number of earners in the family. In this and later tables, in couples with "two earners" both husband and wife are working full-time. Those with 1.5 earners have one spouse—usually the husband—working full-time and one—usually the wife—working part-time. In 1963 most married couples followed the male breadwinner/female homemaker model; 56 percent had only one earner. The dual-income family was uncommon—both spouses worked full-time in 21 percent of married couples. The contrast was even sharper for children's parents—six children in ten had one family breadwinner—almost always the father—with the other parent in the home full-time. Another 15 percent had one parent who worked full-time and one who worked part-time. Only 16 percent of couples with children chose the dual-worker model. By contrast, a minority of children of single parents—one in three—had a parent not working; seven out of ten had a parent who worked, most of them full-time.

Between 1963 and 1997 we see the rise of the dual-worker family. By 1970 the breadwinner/homemaker family was no longer a majority even among married couples, and more than one couple in four had two full-time earners. The transformation accelerated during the following decades, so that by the mid-1980s families with two full-time earners predominated. By 1990 out of every ten married couples, more than four had two full-time earners, more than two had one full-time and one part-time earner, and fewer than three followed the traditional breadwinner/homemaker model. The small remainder had either no earners or one part-time earner.

Couples with children—the most traditional in structure in 1963—changed the most. Among children in married-parent families, 60 percent lived in a breadwinner/homemaker family in 1963. By 1997 the situation had reversed so that 67 percent lived in families that had *more than one* earner, most often both working full-time. Families with a stay-at-home mom became a minority, and dual-worker families were the most popular choice. Families lost women's time in the home but gained the income they earned on the job.

FINANCIAL WELL-BEING

We can assess the financial impact on families of the shift to the dual-worker model by looking at their income. But an income of $50,000

TABLE 1.4

PERCENTAGE OF MARRIED COUPLES AND
CHILDREN'S PARENTS WITH ONE, ONE AND A
HALF, AND TWO EARNERS, 1963–1997

| | All Married Couples | | | Children's Parents | | | | |
| | | | | Married Couples | | | Single Parents | |
Year	1 Earner	1.5 Earners	2 Earners	1 Earner	1.5 Earners	2 Earners	Part-Time	Full-Time
1963	55.5	14.7	21.1	59.4	14.7	15.9	18.1	50.1
1965	50.8	16.9	25.4	55.4	17.7	19.1	17.3	50.2
1970	47.6	19.7	27.4	50.0	22.0	22.6	21.3	50.8
1975	42.9	21.4	29.2	45.0	23.4	25.0	18.4	48.7
1980	35.8	22.8	34.0	37.5	25.1	29.8	18.9	54.3
1985	31.8	23.9	37.6	34.0	27.3	31.7	17.9	51.1
1990	27.2	25.3	43.0	29.6	29.1	36.9	17.3	56.8
1995	25.8	25.9	42.2	28.0	29.2	36.8	19.8	52.7
1997	26.0	24.6	43.5	28.0	28.0	38.7	19.1	59.1

per year means something different to a family of two than a family of seven. So we adjust the income for the number of people it must support and for the number of adults and children (Citro and Michael 1995). We also adjust for inflation, so that any changes in income that we see reflect changes in *real* income. We look at the combined income of all people living in the household. For a single woman, household income would equal her own income. For a married couple, the combined income of the couple (and any other family members) would make up their household income.

Figure 1.1 shows income adjusted for needs for women in different family situations. We see clearly that unmarried women with children—single mothers—have the lowest level of financial well-being of any group and that they have made virtually *no* progress since 1963, while all other women have seen their financial situation improve. Married mothers had much lower needs-adjusted household incomes in 1963 than either single or married women without children at home. And although single women with no children gained financially over the period, married mothers gained *more,* closing the gap from almost $7,000 a year to just over $3,000.

But the biggest financial gainers clearly have been married women without children at home. In 1963 these women had needs-adjusted in-

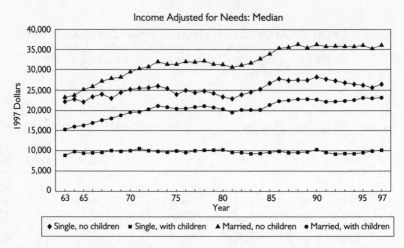

Figure 1.1.   Median household income adjusted for needs for women aged 25 to 55, by marital status and presence of children, 1963–1997

comes quite similar to those of single women without children. But these families pulled steadily ahead, so that by 1997 married women without children enjoyed incomes adjusted for needs that were about $13,000 higher than married mothers', $10,000 higher than single women's without children, and almost $26,000 higher than single mothers'.

Of course, the reason for the stunning improvements in family incomes of married women lies in their shift from unpaid work in the home to paid work in the market. Since 1963, lots of couples have decided that they would rather have the money that the wife can earn at a job than the goods and services that she would produce for the family if she worked only in the home. We saw the resulting transformation in the lives of couples and children in tables 1.2, 1.3, and 1.4.

We can see the financial consequences in figure 1.2. This figure shows financial well-being for one-earner and two-earner married couples with and without children. The one-earner breadwinner/homemaker families with children have the lowest income over the entire period. This is partly because these families share their income with children (note that breadwinner/homemaker families with no children at home are doing pretty well financially). Part of the reason is also that families with children at home are typically younger than those with no children—many of whom are empty-nesters at the peak of their earning power.

Here we see, again, the rise of the dual-earner family. Dual-earner

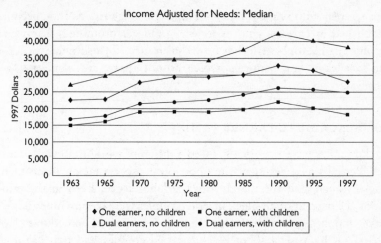

Figure 1.2.   Median household income adjusted for needs for married couples, by number of workers and presence of children, 1963–1997

families with kids have higher needs-adjusted incomes than one-earner families with kids—almost $7,000 a year higher in 1997. But dual-earner couples without children stand out for their very high levels of financial well-being compared to other families, even after we take into account the number of people that income supports. In 1997 dual-earner couples with no children at home—many of them empty-nesters—had over $10,000 a year more in income than breadwinner/homemaker couples in the same situation. The earnings of the wife in dual-earner families make a tremendous difference in financial well-being.

But this success comes at a price; one estimate suggests that dual-earner families need about 35 percent more income to have the same standard of living as families with one spouse—almost always the wife—working full-time in the home, to make up for all the things that person does at home and for clothes, transportation, and other costs of employment (Lazear and Michael 1988). So the rise in income of married-couple families has come partly from the choice to monetize the women's time; the family's money income goes up when the wife works and goes up more when she works full-time, but the family has to spend some of that income to buy child care, meals, and housecleaning for the family. And working itself brings added expenses—appropriate work clothes, meals out, transportation to work, costs of certification, dues for professional associations, and additional training. But in the long run, women who work for pay see their earnings rise as they become established in careers, gain experience, and get promoted. They also become eligible for benefits like health insurance, life insurance, vacation and sick leave, and pensions, which do not appear in calculations of earnings.

THE BLACK DUAL-EARNER FAMILY

Black families have historically faced a different world than white families. Perhaps as a result of the poor job prospects facing Black men, Black women lead the march into the labor force. Even in the mid-1960s, 45 percent of all Black married couples were breadwinner/homemaker families, compared to 57 percent of white married couples (see table 1.5). By 1997 half of Black married couples had two *full-time* earners, and both Black and white married couples were predominantly dual-earners, with only one in four a breadwinner/homemaker family. And among children with married parents, both Black and white children's parents made similar employment choices. But white married parents remained somewhat more likely to follow a traditional division of labor than Black married parents. White children with married parents were more likely than Black children with married parents to have one parent in the home full-time (29% vs. 24%) and less likely to have two parents who work full-time (38% vs. 47%).

More Black than white children lived with one parent (figures not shown), almost always their mother. And Black children living with a single parent were less likely to have a parent who worked and less likely to have a parent who worked full-time than white children of single parents (see table 1.5). In 1997, 54 percent of Black children in single-parent families lived with a parent who worked full-time, compared to 61 percent of white children of single parents. And more of the Black children in single-parent families had no working parent in the home (27% vs. 18%).

SOCIAL CLASS AND THE DUAL-EARNER FAMILY

Shifts in the economy over the last several decades altered returns to schooling so that men and women without a college degree found themselves doing worse financially, and those with at least a college education found themselves doing better financially. Of course, the family felt these changes keenly. In 1965 working-class couples (those in which neither spouse had a college degree) were less likely than middle-class couples (those with at least one spouse with a college degree) to be breadwinner/homemaker families (50% vs. 55%) and about as likely to have two earners (see table 1.6). But wives in middle-class couples surged into the labor force over the ensuing 30 years, so that by 1997, 48 percent of middle-class couples had two full-time earners compared to 41 percent of working-class couples. And working-class couples were *more likely* than middle-class couples to be breadwinner/homemaker families, although the differences were modest (29% vs. 22%).

We see the same transformation in families with children. In 1965 fewer working-class than middle-class children lived in breadwinner/homemaker families (54% vs. 62% among those living with married parents). But by 1997 more working-class than middle-class children living in married-couple families had one parent at home full-time, and middle-class children in two-parent families were more likely to have one parent who worked full-time and one who worked part-time. In 1997 nearly three out of four children in married-parent families—both working-class and middle-class—lived in families where both parents worked part-time or more.

Working- and middle-class single-parent families, almost all of which are headed by women, differ in important ways. In 1997, among working-class families, 57 percent of single parents worked full-time, compared to 77 percent in middle-class single-parent families. Another 19 percent of working-class single parents and 18 percent of middle-class single parents worked part-time. So in 1997, 95 percent of middle-class single parents worked for pay, compared to 76 percent of working-class single parents. Since women and men without college degrees earn much less than those who have completed college, the differences in parents' employment point to financial hardship for many more working-class than middle-class children.

CONCLUSIONS

If we had to pick the most dramatic, far-reaching change affecting women, men, and families during the 35 years surveyed here, the rise of the dual-worker family is a prime candidate. In the early 1960s, 56 percent of married couples had only one earner; in 1997, 44 percent had two full-time earners. In the early 1960s about a quarter of the children in two-parent families had a mother who worked full-time. By 1997 about half did.

TABLE 1.5

PERCENTAGE OF MARRIED COUPLES AND CHILDREN'S PARENTS WITH ONE, ONE AND A HALF, AND TWO EARNERS, BY RACE, 1963–1997

	All Married Couples								Children's Parents			
	Black				White				Married Couples			
									Black			
Year	1 Earner	1.5 Earners	2 Earners	N	1 Earner	1.5 Earners	2 Earners	N	1 Earner	1.5 Earners	2 Earners	Number of Children
1963	45.2	18.3	20.8	928	56.5	14.4	21.0	10,874	48.9	16.9	17.5	2,193
1965	40.0	20.5	30.8	980	51.9	16.6	24.9	10,671	40.3	23.0	25.5	2,231
1970	33.4	21.8	36.0	1,612	48.9	19.6	26.6	19,599	35.9	24.9	30.4	3,626
1975	34.5	17.1	37.8	1,302	43.5	21.8	28.5	17,173	34.3	18.1	35.2	2,447
1980	31.7	16.2	40.5	1,606	36.1	23.4	33.4	23,955	32.0	17.3	38.9	2,553
1985	27.5	15.8	45.6	1,463	32.2	24.7	36.9	21,056	26.6	16.9	43.8	2,068
1990	26.3	15.1	52.3	1,458	27.2	26.4	42.2	20,462	24.4	16.0	52.7	1,978
1995	25.8	18.6	47.4	1,343	25.3	27.1	42.0	18,737	22.4	21.0	48.7	1,672
1997	25.1	17.6	48.8	1,177	26.0	25.4	43.0	16,764	23.8	20.3	47.4	1,569

TABLE 1.5 — *Continued*

Children's Parents

Year	Married Couples				Single Parents					
	White				Black			White		
	1 Earner	1.5 Earners	2 Earners	Number of Children	Part-Time	Full-Time	Number of Children	Part-Time	Full-Time	Number of Children
1963	60.7	14.4	15.5	21,134	17.6	44.1	886	17.9	53.6	1,617
1965	57.1	17.2	18.4	20,580	24.2	39.9	762	14.5	54.2	1,719
1970	51.6	21.8	21.7	36,232	24.1	42.8	1,962	19.9	55.3	3,546
1975	46.0	24.1	23.9	27,279	19.8	40.7	2,066	17.7	52.6	4,116
1980	38.3	25.8	28.8	35,122	16.8	47.0	2,633	20.0	57.3	6,297
1985	34.7	28.3	30.6	28,207	16.2	42.7	2,481	18.6	54.7	6,171
1990	30.0	30.6	35.5	26,662	13.7	52.3	2,570	18.7	59.1	6,429
1995	27.9	30.7	36.1	23,970	17.7	46.8	2,450	20.8	55.6	6.577
1997	28.6	28.8	37.8	21,461	16.3	54.2	2,227	20.5	61.0	6,220

TABLE 1.6

PERCENTAGE OF MARRIED COUPLES AND CHILDREN'S PARENTS WITH ONE, ONE AND A HALF, AND TWO EARNERS, BY CLASS, 1965–1997

| | All Married Couples | | | | | | | | Children's Parents Married Couples | | | |
| | Working Class | | | | Middle Class | | | | Working Class | | | |
Year	1 Earner	1.5 Earners	2 Earners	N	1 Earner	1.5 Earners	2 Earners	N	1 Earner	1.5 Earners	2 Earners	Number of Children
1965	50.0	17.1	25.5	9,824	54.7	15.9	24.9	1,930	54.2	17.9	19.5	19,309
1970	46.6	19.8	27.9	17,416	51.8	19.6	25.3	3,962	48.2	22.2	23.6	32,811
1975	43.5	20.4	28.4	14,257	40.8	24.3	31.8	4,501	44.3	22.5	25.4	23,693
1980	37.7	21.5	32.4	18,909	30.7	26.3	38.3	7,369	38.2	23.5	29.7	28,700
1985	34.1	22.4	35.5	15,897	26.7	27.1	42.1	7,385	35.5	25.2	30.9	22,011
1990	29.6	24.2	40.5	15,000	22.2	27.3	47.9	7,823	30.6	27.4	36.2	20,045
1995	27.7	24.3	40.0	13,481	22.6	28.6	45.9	8,011	28.9	26.5	36.6	17,659
1997	28.6	22.9	40.9	11,676	21.7	27.4	47.8	7,055	29.6	25.3	38.1	15,551

TABLE 1.6—Continued

	Children's Parents									
	Married Couples				Single Parents					
	Middle Class				Working Class			Middle Class		
Year	1 Earner	1.5 Earners	2 Earners	Number of Children	Part-Time	Full-Time	Number of Children	Part-Time	Full-Time	Number of Children
1965	61.5	17.0	17.0	3,721	17.6	49.2	2,435	8.3	81.0	84
1970	57.9	21.0	18.0	7,381	21.5	49.9	5,339	16.6	71.9	235
1975	47.4	26.2	23.6	6,903	18.4	47.3	5,868	19.0	70.1	385
1980	35.6	29.4	30.1	10,245	18.9	52.6	8,580	18.8	73.7	725
1985	30.5	32.2	33.5	9,525	18.1	48.9	8,182	16.8	72.7	817
1990	27.5	32.4	38.2	9,931	17.2	54.7	8,488	18.0	75.6	932
1995	26.3	33.8	37.2	10,073	19.7	50.8	8,913	20.2	70.7	957
1997	25.2	32.9	39.6	8,522	19.2	57.2	8,076	18.0	77.3	859

As a result of the shift of married women out of the home and into paid employment, their families saw a substantial rise in financial well-being; the household incomes of married women rose faster during those 35 years than incomes of single women with or without children, even after taking into account the size and composition of the family. So women in dual-earner families gained ground compared to both un-married women and women in one-earner families.

The rise of the dual-earner family is part of a large set of social changes. As more women plan on careers, women invest more in their own education and training. Women earned 35 percent of all bachelor's degrees in 1960, compared to 55 percent in 1995. Eight percent of the M.D. degrees awarded in 1970 were earned by women; in 1995 women earned 39 percent. Women's share of law degrees went from 5 percent in 1970 to 43 percent in 1995, and their share of doctorates increased from 14 percent to 39 percent (U.S. Bureau of the Census 1998, 199–202). So today employed wives in dual-earner families hold professional jobs that are both demanding and rewarding much more often than employed wives did in the 1960s.

Women today are more likely than their mothers were at the same age to have "careers" rather than "jobs." A career follows an orderly progression of education and movement through a series of related jobs with increasing pay and responsibility. This shift toward the career model for women has meant that fewer leave the workforce for an extended period when they have young children. Changing family economics have also made the woman's earnings an essential component of the household budget. In 1960, 18 percent of married women with a child under six were in the labor force. In 1997, 64 percent of such women were in the labor force (U.S. Bureau of the Census 1998). Today, most employed women who give birth take a relatively short maternity leave and return to work (Desai and Waite 1991). Since work interruptions when children are young have a sizable negative effect on women's earnings, increased employment by mothers of young children has payoffs in higher family income over the long run (Waldfogel 1997).

The wives in dual-earner couples have more education, more training, and more experience than such wives did in the 1960s, and they enter different occupations and make more money as a result. So it isn't just the shift of wives into the labor force that has boosted the income of dual-worker families. These are different women, with a different outlook and different goals—for themselves and their families.

REFERENCES

Blau, Francine D., Marianne A. Ferber, and Anne E. Winkler. 1998. *The economics of women, men, and work.* Upper Saddle River, N.J.: Prentice-Hall.

Bumpass, Larry L., and R. Kelly Raley. 1995. Redefining single-parent families: Cohabitation and changing family reality. *Demography* 32:97–109.

Cherlin, Andrew J. 1992. *Marriage, divorce, and remarriage.* Cambridge, Mass.: Harvard University Press.

Citro, Constance F., and Robert T. Michael. 1995. *Measuring poverty: A new approach.* Washington, D.C.: National Academy Press.

Desai, Sonalde, and Linda J. Waite. 1991. Women's employment during pregnancy and after the first birth: Occupational characteristics and work commitment. *American Sociological Review* 56:551–66.

Lazear, Edward, and Robert T. Michael. 1988. *Allocation of income within the household.* Chicago: University of Chicago Press.

McLanahan, Sara, and Lynne Casper. 1995. Growing diversity and inequality in the American family. In *State of the union: America in the 1990s,* vol. 2, *Social trends,* ed. Reynolds Farley, 1–46. New York: Russell Sage.

Oppenheimer, Valerie K., Matthijs Kalmijn, and Nelson Lim. 1997. Men's career development and marriage timing during a period of rising inequality. *Demography* 34:311–30.

Smith, T. W. 1994. Attitudes toward sexual permissiveness: Trends, correlates, and behavioral connections. In *Sexuality across the life course,* ed. A. S. Rossi, 63–97. Chicago: University of Chicago Press.

U.S. Bureau of the Census. 1996. 65+ in the United States. *Current population reports, special studies,* P-23-190. Washington, D.C.: U.S. Government Printing Office.

———. 1998. *Statistical abstract of the United States.* Washington, D.C.: U.S. Government Printing Office.

Waite, Linda J., and Maggie Gallagher. 2000. *The case for marriage.* New York: Doubleday.

Waldfogel, Jane. 1997. The effect of children on women's wages. *American Sociological Review* 62:209–17.

CHAPTER 2

Gendered Careers

A Life-Course Perspective

Phyllis Moen and Shin-Kap Han

INTRODUCTION

One of the stories that surely defines the latter half of the twentieth century and the beginning of the twenty-first is the transformation of two fundamental societal institutions—work and family. As men's and women's biographies have intersected with the historical events of the past 50 years, workers' experiences and options have changed both at home and at work. In this chapter we apply a dynamic life-course approach (Elder, George, and Shanahan 1996) to the work/family interface. This perspective points to the need to recast conventional perspectives on occupational careers, taking into account their gendered nature and growing obsolescence.

STUDYING THE WORK/FAMILY INTERFACE

Since social scientists are embedded in the very social institutions they study, they typically use taken-for-granted classifications and definitions to frame their research. For example, most scholars study segmented

Support for the research reported here was provided by grants from the Alfred P. Sloan Foundation (Nos. 96-6-9 and 99-6-3) and from the National Institute on Aging (No. P50 AG11171). Particular thanks to Kathleen Christensen and the fellows at the Cornell Careers Institute, as well as to Sarah Demo.

domains of lives. Occupational and organizational sociologists and economists chart work careers (e.g., Breiger 1995; Doeringer and Piore 1971), and family sociologists concentrate on "family" careers (e.g., Aldous 1996; Hill 1970). Those looking at the work/family interface focus on the strains, conflicts, or well-being of workers, typically at one point in time, and still others consider changes in institutions (e.g., Brinton 1988).

The study of women's experiences has underscored the dynamic and intersecting nature of work and family roles, suggesting the need to broaden the concept of occupational career so that it reflects women's as well as men's life pathways.[1] The study of women's lives has revealed the value of a dynamic life-course approach to work and family. This perspective shifts the research question away from single-moment snapshots of *either* work *or* family *or* spillover/conflict between the two and reframes it in terms of work *and* family pathways.[2] A life-course approach puts the work/family interface in temporal motion. This necessitates synthesizing and integrating many lines of inquiry, incorporating time in order to capture the dynamic interplay between individual/family biographies, gender, institutions, and social change.

In our ongoing research program at Cornell we use the concept of "careers" to capture these dynamic connections across institutions, social relations, and lives. We aim to understand alternative life paths, moving beyond one-dimensional approaches to work and family experiences at one point in time. We also focus on the historical and cultural context of lives. For example, the work/family interface at the dawn of the twenty-first century looks very different from that of the 1950s or even the 1970s.

The Cornell Employment and Family Careers Institute and the Cornell Gerontology Research Institute draw on both quantitative and qualitative studies, spanning cohorts of women and men who were born from 1926 to 1974. In this chapter we use the life histories of the older cohorts (born 1926 to 1945) to construct typologies of alternative

1. Compare the way the following have charted women's distinctive experiences: Barnett and Rivers 1996; Clarkberg and Moen 2001; Forest, Moen, and Dempster-McClain 1995; Giele 1982; Han and Moen 1999a, 2001; Hochschild 1989, 1997; Moen 1989, 1992; Moen and Yu 2000; and Pavalko and Elder 1993.

2. The focus on conjoint work/family pathways is exemplified in Blossfeld and Huinink 1991; Clarkberg and Moen 2001; Conger and Elder 1994; Desai and Waite 1991; Gerson 1985; Han and Moen 1999a, b, 2001; Hareven 1984; Hogan 1981; Krueger 1996; Moen 1989, 1992, 1996; and Mortimer and Borman 1988.

occupational career and family paths in order to understand the nature of gendered careers. This can provide a baseline for insight into the experiences of more recent cohorts of workers.

CAREERS AND GENDER

A sociology of occupational careers is necessarily a sociology of *time*—referring to the processes of job development, mobility, and plateauing (Barley 1989). Moreover, the notion of "career" is itself a function of *historical* time—a modern invention that has emerged as a social fact only with the development of corporations, bureaucracies, and white-collar employment. As Mills (1951) pointed out, prior to the Industrial Revolution most people worked in either agriculture or a family business. Though individual farmers, craftspeople, and family entrepreneurs may have had life plans, they did not have careers.

Fundamental changes in the nature of work accompanied the Industrial Revolution. Moving from self- and family employment to a paid labor force led to the construction of career trajectories based on the (male) breadwinner model (see figure 2.1). As "career" was increasingly used to define occupational work history, unpaid work—whether participation in a family business, household labor, family caregiving, or (formal or informal) community service—was rendered marginal to the "business" of society, and consequently marginal to the business of mainstream social science. This bifurcation of productivity, distinguishing paid from unpaid work, also became heavily gendered, producing a "male as breadwinner/female as homemaker" template. Even though today both men and women work for pay and few workers—male or female—have the services of a full-time homemaker, both workplace policies and practices and cultural norms still lag behind contemporary reality, and the now-outdated breadwinner/homemaker template continues to shape men's and women's life choices and life chances (see figure 2.1).

Moreover, given the present-day trend toward an economy that is more global and more service-oriented, we are again witnessing profound changes in career progression and possibilities. Transformations in the structure of work, alterations in the economy and the labor force, and fundamental changes in gender roles, families, and the life course all mean that conventional views of careers are obsolete.

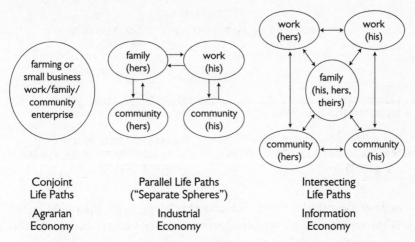

Figure 2.1.   The changing work/family/community interface

RESEARCH AND POLICY CHALLENGES

Governments and employers as well as scholars continue to define work, commitment, and career paths in ways that are increasingly out-of-date. The structural lag between the composition and time pressures of the contemporary workforce, along with the uncertainties of contemporary jobs on the one hand and the obsolete (male) breadwinner/(female) homemaker template on the other, is producing four key challenges to the traditional ways that researchers and policy makers frame career patterns and possibilities (see table 2.1). Those shaping research and policy agendas related to the organization of work need to (1) move from a linear to a multiplex view of career paths, (2) focus on relational rather than only individual careers, (3) consider career paths as personalized, not standardized, and (4) treat careers not as a separate domain but as part of a larger, life-course matrix.

FROM LINEAR TO MULTIPLEX MODELS OF CAREER PATHS

The old lock-step single-career path typical of middle-class male workers in the middle of the twentieth century (Kohli 1986; Spilerman 1977) characterizes the experiences of fewer and fewer contemporary workers. As increasing numbers of workers, both men and women, are juggling multiple obligations, the need for new typologies is becoming increas-

TABLE 2.1

FOUR CHALLENGES TO THE TRADITIONAL
VIEW OF OCCUPATIONAL CAREERS

Old	New
Linear (men)	Multiplex (men *and* women)
Individual (the autonomous worker)	Relational (linked lives)
Standardized (employ*er*-driven)	Personalized (employ*ee*-driven)
Separate domains (work *or* family *or* community)	Life-course matrix (work *and* family *and* community)

ingly evident (Hertz 1986; Kanter 1977; Moen 1998; Rosenfeld 1980). What are required are empirical accounts of the variety of contemporary career paths— men's *and* women's.

At Cornell we are analyzing data collected in the Cornell Retirement and Well-Being Study (CRWB) and comparing the experiences of this pre-baby-boom cohort with the younger cohorts in the Cornell Couples and Careers Study. We have identified five pathway types, based on sequence analysis of life history data: *delayed entry, orderly, high-geared, steady part-time,* and *intermittent* (see figure 2.2) (see also Han and Moen 1999a, b, 2001).

We find highly distinct and separate career pathways for men and women. Men in the CRWB cohort typically follow *orderly* or *high-geared* paths. There is, nevertheless, a sizable presence of women in these paths as well, suggesting that the discrepancy between men's and women's work experiences may be narrowing, at least for some groups of women. Men's career paths remain more standardized than women's. Women, however, follow all five types of career paths. This points to the need for the study of gendered careers, looking at variations within as well as across gender at various points in biographical and historical time.[3]

In our study what we call the *orderly* career reflects the ideal-typical male career path; it is stable, continuous, and upwardly mobile. About two-thirds of those in this traditional career path are in fact men (see table 2.2 and figure 2.2). Men who are highly educated and upwardly mobile are also found on the *high-geared* path. They start off high on

3. Compare Clarkberg and Moen 2001; Pixley and Wethington 1999; Quick and Moen 2000; and Still 1999. Race differences must be considered as well—see Rosenfeld 1980 and Tomaskovic-Devey 1993.

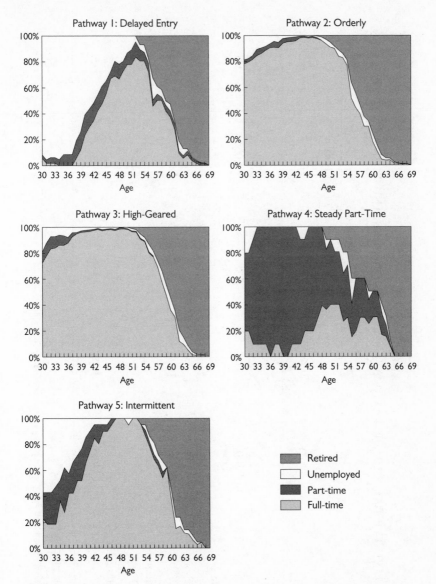

Figure 2.2.   Alternative career pathways from age 30 to retirement. *Source:* Cornell Retirement and Well-Being Study, Wave 1, 1994–95; see also Han and Moen 199a, b, 2001.

TABLE 2.2

FIVE TYPICAL CAREER PATHWAYS OF WORKING MEN AND WOMEN

	Career Pathway				
	1 Delayed Entry (N = 46)	2 Orderly (N = 154)	3 High-Geared (N = 160)	Steady Part-Time (N = 10)	Intermittent (N = 21)
Gender composition					
Men (%)	0	64.9	61.9	30.0	0
Women (%)	100	35.1	38.1	70.0	100
Educational level	Low	—	High	—	Low
Average number of organizations	Low	Low	High	Low	High
Proportion of adulthood (from age 30) working full-time	—	High	High	Low	High
Proportion of adulthood (from age 30) working part-time	—	Low	Low	High	—
Proportion of adulthood not employed or unemployed	High	Low	Low	Low	—

NOTE: Blanks indicate no significant difference.

SOURCE: Cornell Retirement and Well-Being Study, N = 391; see Han and Moen 1999b.

the occupational ladder and "ladder hop" across firms in order to advance their careers. The three other pathways would be "lost" if we focused only on men's occupational experiences.

FROM INDIVIDUAL TO RELATIONAL CAREERS

Most occupational research focuses on the individual as the unit of analysis. This reflects the fact that employers treat workers as if they had no family responsibilities and that Americans define careers in terms of individual workers' mobility patterns. But studying women's careers makes family factors immediately visible. It's impossible to view women's occupational experiences apart from their husbands' shifting family responsibilities and career paths. As two-earner couples become commonplace, men's and women's career paths must be viewed in tandem and in light of changing family circumstances (see also Hofmeister and Moen 1999; Moen, Kim, and Hofmeister 2001; Smith and Moen 1998).

Women's traditional career patterns—*delayed entry* (an extended period outside of the labor force early on), *intermittent* (frequent exits from and reentries into the workforce), and *steady part-time* (see figure 2.2)—reflect strategies of adaptation as women juggle multiple role obligations (Becker and Moen 1999; Moen and Wethington 1992).

Shifting the focus to couples and families illuminates how family adaptive strategies typically privilege men, providing them with comparative advantage (Becker 1981) and cumulative advantage (Elder and O'Rand 1995) in the occupational sphere. But today fewer workers have the support of a full-time homemaking spouse. Half the members of the U.S. workforce are married to other workers; another fourth are single (or single parents). This means that the domestic structure undergirding the traditional lock-step career path is no longer available to most workers, male or female.

PERSONALIZED RATHER THAN STANDARDIZED CAREERS

The occupational career has been a fundamental organizing force in shaping both individual biographies and institutions. Most life is arranged around paid work. The workweek and career trajectories have provided the organizational blueprint for daily rhythms and routines as well as for the entire life course (cf. Kohli 1986; Mayer and Mueller 1986; Moen 1994; Riley and Riley 1994). But old blueprints of the typical workweek and the typical career path are out of step with the realities of contemporary working families.

Today we see more discontinuities than continuities at work, in families, across generations, and in personal experience and development.[4] Women—and growing numbers of men as well—are moving in and out of roles in families, in the workplace, and in educational institutions at unprecedented rates. Divorce, single parenthood, job shifts, and geographic mobility are commonplace. Workers face the time squeeze and stress of combining work on the job with work at home, as well as coordinating both spouses' jobs.

In spite of these dramatic changes, family and career pathways remain caught in frequently outmoded rules and routines, producing strains as workers seek to synchronize the public and private aspects of their lives. At first it was women who experienced these tensions, and women continue to bear a disproportionate burden of meshing work and family obligations throughout their life courses. But the integration of work and family careers is a dilemma for growing numbers of workers (Moen 1994; Riley and Riley 1994). Today's workforce increasingly consists of (1) men whose partners are also in the labor force, (2) women whose partners are also in the labor force, and (3) men and women without partners but with family obligations (either children or infirm relatives).

At the beginning of the twenty-first century, the United States, like other advanced nations, still retains policies and practices supporting a lock-step path through the life course from education through employment in the prime adult years to the leisure of retirement in late midlife (Kohli 1986). This pattern reflects the outmoded (male) breadwinner template—a confluence of rules, roles, and routines that continue to affect both women's and men's choices and expectations. The challenge is to reinvent institutions that enable both working men and working women to have a "life" outside of work.

FROM CAREER AS A SEPARATE DOMAIN TO
A LIFE-COURSE MATRIX

The very notion of career is based on the breadwinner/homemaker cultural template. "When industrialization separated homes from work-

4. Compare Bradburn, Moen, and Dempster-McClain 1995; Elder and O'Rand 1995; Han and Moen 1999a; Rindfuss, Swicegood, and Rosenfeld 1987; Settersten and Mayer 1997.

places, the men's contacts with children were diminished. Childhood ended up in 'women's territory.' . . . Each parent developed a specialty: the one became a Mother, the other a Breadwinner" (Liljeström, Mellström, and Svensson 1978, 105).

This division between paid work and family work underscored the primacy of the breadwinner's job. Men lived to work; women were to support their husbands' careers by taking care of the domestic scene. Although many poor, immigrant, and minority women were in fact their families' breadwinners, this did not diminish the cultural legitimation of the breadwinner/homemaker template. This blueprint remains a theme shaping the lives of wives and mothers who are in the workforce, disadvantaging their career progression.[5] While men as breadwinners can be successful in both their jobs and their families, middle-class women have traditionally had to emphasize one or the other. In our studies (Han and Moen 1999a, 2001), we find that men following both the *orderly* and the *high-geared* career paths characteristically are married and remain married throughout the life course. By contrast, women on those paths are the ones experiencing discontinuity in their marital careers or else never marrying (see table 2.3).

In fact, the men and women in the Cornell Retirement and Well-Being sample have quite different marital histories (Han and Moen 1999a, 2001; Quick and Moen 1998, 2000). In terms of marital stability, men tend to be better off by a large margin. For the women in our sample (who have all spent a considerable period of time in the labor force), the likelihood of both getting married and staying married is far lower than for their male coworkers. Men in this late midlife sample are about 50 percent more likely to be currently married than women, whereas working women are more than 7 times more likely to have never married and 1.34 times more likely than men to have experienced a marital breakup at some point in their life course. This asymmetry between the sexes forces a zero-sum game—that is, a tradeoff between occupational careers and family careers—for women, but not for men.

CONCLUSION

Americans are experiencing a disconnection between the traditional career path as reflected in work policies and practices and their own

5. See Clarkberg and Moen 2001; Coser 1974; Curtis 1986; Goode 1960; Moen and Wethington 1992.

TABLE 2.3

MARITAL HISTORY IN RELATION TO CAREER PATHWAY AND GENDER

Marital History	Delayed Entry	Orderly	High-Geared	Steady Part-Time	Intermittent	Total	Percentage
MEN							
Never married	0	1	1	0	0	2	1.0
Married once, currently divorced/separated	0	3	5	0	0	8	4.0
Married twice, currently divorced/separated	0	3	3	0	0	6	3.0
Married once, currently widowed	0	1	5	0	0	6	3.0
Married twice, currently widowed	0	0	0	0	0	0	0.0
Married once, currently married	0	68	76	2	0	146	72.3
Married more than once, currently married	0	24	9	1	0	34	16.8
Subtotal	0	100	99	3	0	202	
Percentage	0.0	49.5	49.0	1.5	0.0		
WOMEN							
Never married	0	6	8	0	0	14	7.4
Married once, currently divorced/separated	3	5	9	1	5	23	12.2
Married twice, currently divorced/separated	0	0	2	0	3	5	2.7
Married once, currently widowed	12	6	6	1	1	26	13.8
Married twice, currently widowed	0	2	2	1	2	7	3.7
Married once, currently married	27	24	28	4	7	90	47.9
Married more than once, currently married	4	10	6	0	3	23	12.2
Subtotal	46	53	61	7	21	188	
Percentage	24.5	28.2	32.4	3.7	11.2		

SOURCE: Cornell Retirement and Well-Being Study, N = 390; see Han and Moen 1999b, c.

personal circumstances. This disconnection reflects in large part the changing nature of the labor force, with a shrinking minority of workers having the luxury of a full-time homemaker to lessen any demands that conflict with their career progression. Moreover, the occupational career itself is transforming as the links between seniority and job security are decoupled, and firms and employees move away from the contract implied by the notion of career jobs. Americans are in the midst of changes in the culture of occupational careers from a single, lock-step model to a multiplex of pathways.

As has been true for women historically, men are now becoming increasingly conscious of and self-reflective concerning their career biographies. This sense of shaping one's own life course is occurring in tandem with the absence of taken-for-granted pathways and the increasing tenuousness of jobs. The challenge for government and employers as well as social scientists is to understand the changing nature and perceptions of occupational careers and to link particular occupational patterns and paths with family, policy, and organizational change.

The growing heterogeneity of women's life courses throughout the twentieth century has been a precursor to the growing heterogeneity of life-course transitions for both men and women at the beginning of the twenty-first century. Individuals move into or out of cohabitation, marriage, school, parenthood, employment, and occupational careers at widely disparate ages and not always in any orderly sequence.[6] What is required is a thoughtful reappraisal of contemporary life patterns, leading to recognition of the complex and dynamic life-course matrix and reflecting the interplay between gender, work, community, and family.

REFERENCES

Aldous, Joan. 1996. *Family careers: Rethinking the developmental perspective.* Thousand Oaks, Calif.: Sage Publications.

Barley, Stephen R. 1989. Careers, identities, and institutions: The legacy of the Chicago School of Sociology. In *Handbook of career theory,* edited by M. B. Arthur, D. T. Hall, and B. S. Lawrence. New York: Cambridge University Press.

Barnett, Rosalind C., and Caryn Rivers. 1996. *She works/he works: How*

6. See, for example, Blair-Loy 1999; Bradburn, Moen, and Dempster-McClain 1995; Clarkberg 1999; Desai and Waite 1991; Esterberg, Moen, and Dempster-McClain 1994; Forest, Moen, and Dempster-McClain 1995; Henretta, O'Rand, and Chan 1993; Quick and Moen 1999; Rindfuss, Swicegood, and Rosenfeld 1987.

two-income families are happier, healthier, and better-off. New York: HarperCollins.

Becker, Gary S. 1981. *A treatise on the family.* Cambridge, Mass.: Harvard University Press.

Becker, Penny E., and Phyllis Moen. 1999. Scaling back: Dual-career couples' work-family strategies. *Journal of Marriage and the Family* 61:95–107.

Blair-Loy, Mary F. 1999. Career patterns of executive women in finance: An optimal matching analysis. *American Journal of Sociology* 104:1346–97.

Blossfeld, Hans-Peter, and Johannes Huinink. 1991. Human capital investments or norms of role transition? How women's schooling and career affect the process of family formation. *American Journal of Sociology* 97: 143–68.

Bradburn, Ellen M., Phyllis Moen, and Donna Dempster-McClain. 1995. An event history analysis of women's return to school. *Social Forces* 73:1517–51.

Breiger, Ronald. 1995. Social structure and the phenomenology of attainment. *Annual Review of Sociology* 21:115–36.

Brinton, Mary. 1988. The social-institutional bases of gender stratification: Japan as an illustrative case. *American Journal of Sociology* 94:300–334.

Clarkberg, Marin. 1999. The price of partnering: The role of economic well-being in young adults' first union experiences. *Social Forces* 77:945–68.

Clarkberg, Marin, and Phyllis Moen. 2001. Understanding the time-squeeze: Married couples' preferred and actual work-hour strategies. Paper presented at the annual meeting of the American Association for the Advancement of Science, January, Anaheim, Calif.

Conger, R. D., and Glen H. Elder, Jr. 1994. *Families in troubled times: Adapting to change in rural America.* New York: Aldine de Gruyter.

Coser, Lewis. 1974. *Greedy institutions: Patterns of undivided commitment.* New York: Free Press.

Curtis, Richard. 1986. Household and family theory on inequality. *American Sociological Review* 51:168–83.

Desai, Sonalde, and Linda J. Waite. 1991. Women's employment during pregnancy and after the first birth. *American Sociological Review* 56:551–66.

Doeringer, Peter B., and Michael J. Piore. 1971. *Internal labor markets and manpower analysis.* Lexington, Mass.: Heath, Lexington.

Elder, Glen H., Jr., Linda K. George, and Michael J. Shanahan. 1996. Psychosocial stress over the life course. In *Psychosocial stress: Perspectives on structure, theory, life course, and methods,* edited by H. B. Kaplan. Orlando: Academic Press.

Elder, Glen H., Jr., and Angela M. O'Rand. 1995. Adult lives in a changing society. In *Sociological perspectives on social psychology,* edited by K. S. Cook, G. A. Fine, and J. S. House. Needham Heights, Mass.: Allyn and Bacon.

Esterberg, Kristin G., Phyllis Moen, and Donna Dempster-McClain. 1994. Transition to divorce: A life-course approach to women's marital duration and dissolution. *Sociological Quarterly* 35:289–307.

Forest, Kay B., Phyllis Moen, and Donna Dempster-McClain. 1995. Cohort differences in the transition to motherhood: The variable effects of education and employment before marriage. *Sociological Quarterly* 36:315–36.

Gerson, Kathleen. 1985. *Hard choices: How women decide about work, career, and motherhood.* Berkeley: University of California Press.

Giele, Janet Z. 1982. *Women in the middle years: Current knowledge and directions for research and policy.* New York: John Wiley.

Goode, William I. 1960. A theory of role strain. *American Sociological Review* 25:483–96.

Han, Shin-Kap, and Phyllis Moen. 1999a. Clocking out: Temporal patterning of retirement. *American Journal of Sociology* 105:191–236.

———. 1999b. Work and family over time: A life course approach. *The Annals of the American Academy of Political and Social Sciences* 562:98–110.

———. 2001. Coupled careers: Men's and women's pathways through work and marriage in the United States. In *Careers of couples in contemporary societies: A cross-national comparison of the transition from male breadwinner to dual-earner families,* edited by H. P. Blossfeld and S. Drobnic. Oxford: Oxford University Press.

Hareven, Tamara K. 1984. *Family time and industrial time: The relationship between the family and work in a New England industrial community.* New York: Cambridge University Press.

Henretta, John C., Angela M. O'Rand, and Christopher G. Chan. 1993. Joint role investments and synchronization of retirement: A sequential approach to couples retirement timing. *Social Forces* 71:981–1000.

Hertz, Rosanna. 1986. *More equal than others: Women and men in dual-career marriages.* Berkeley: University of California Press.

Hill, Reuben. 1970. *Family development in three generations.* Cambridge, Mass.: Schenkman.

Hochschild, Arlie. 1997. *The time bind: When work becomes home and home becomes work.* New York: Metropolitan Books.

Hochschild, Arlie, with Anne Machung. 1989. *The second shift.* New York: Avon Books.

Hofmeister, Heather, and Phyllis Moen. 1999. Late midlife employment, gender roles, and marital quality: His and her perspectives. *Sociological Forces* 32: 315–33.

Hogan, Dennis P. 1981. *Transitions and social change: The early lives of American men.* New York: Academic Press.

Kanter, Rosabeth M. 1977. *Work and family in the United States: A critical review and agenda for research and policy.* New York: Russell Sage.

Kohli, Martin. 1986. Social organization and subjective construction of the life course. In *Human development and the life course: Multidisciplinary perspectives,* edited by A. B. Sorensen, F. E. Weinert, and L. R. Sherrod. Hillsdale, N.J.: Lawrence Erlbaum.

Krueger, H. 1996. Normative interpretations of biographical processes. In *Society and biography: Interrelationships between social structure, institutions and the life course,* edited by A. Weymann, and W. R. Heinz. Weinheim: Deutscher Studien Verlag.

Liljeström, Rita, Gunilla F. Mellström, and Gillan L. Svensson. 1978. *Roles in transition: Report of an investigation made for the advisory council on equality between men and women.* Stockholm: LiberFðorlag/Allmðanna fðorl.

Mayer, Karl U., and Walter Mueller. 1986. The state and the structure of the life course. In *Human development and the life course: Multidisciplinary perspectives,* edited by A. B. Sorensen, F. E. Weinert, and L. R. Sherrod. Hillsdale, N.J.: Lawrence Erlbaum.

Mills, C. Wright. 1951. *White collar.* New York: Oxford University Press.

Moen, Phyllis. 1989. *Working parents: Transformations in gender roles and public policies in Sweden.* Madison: University of Wisconsin Press.

———. 1992. *Women's two roles: A contemporary dilemma.* Westport, Conn.: Greenwood.

———. 1994. Women, work, and family: A sociological perspective on changing roles. In *Age and structural lag: The mismatch between people's lives and opportunities in work, family, and leisure,* edited by M. W. Riley, R. L. Kahn, and A. Foner. New York: John Wiley.

———. 1996. Gender, age, and the life course. In *Handbook of aging and the social sciences,* edited by R. H. Binstock and L. K. George. New York: Academic Press.

———. 1998. Recasting careers: Changing reference groups, risks, and realities. *Generations* 22:40–45.

Moen, Phyllis, Jungmeen E. Kim, and Heather Hofmeister. 2001. Couples' work/retirement transitions, gender, and marital quality. *Social Psychology Quarterly* (forthcoming).

Moen, Phyllis, and Elaine Wethington. 1992. The concept of family adaptive strategies. *Annual Review of Sociology* 18:233–51.

Moen, Phyllis, and Yan Yu. 1999. Having it all: Overall work/life success in two-earner families. In *Work and family: Research in the sociology of work,* vol. 7, edited by T. Parcel and R. Hodson. Greenwich, Conn.: JAI Press.

Mortimer, Jeylan T., and Kathryn B. Borman, eds. 1988. *Work experiences and psychological development throughout the life span.* Boulder: Westview Press.

Pavalko, Eliza K., and Glen H. Elder, Jr. 1993. Women behind the men: Variations in wives' support of husbands' careers. *Gender & Society* 7:548–67.

Pixley, Joy, and Elaine Wethington. 1999. Turning points in work careers: Gender and life course factors. Working paper from Bronfenbrenner Life Course Center, Cornell University, Ithaca.

Quick, Heather E., and Phyllis Moen. 1998. Gender, employment, and retirement quality: A life-course approach to the differential experiences of men and women. *Journal of Occupational Health Psychology* 3:44–64.

———. 2000. Careers in competition? An analysis of couples' employment trajectories. Unpublished draft.

Riley, Matilda White, and John W. Riley, Jr. 1994. Structural lag: Past and future. In *Age and structural lag: The mismatch between people's lives and opportunities in work, family, and leisure,* edited by M. W. Riley, R. L. Kahn, and A. Foner. New York: John Wiley.

Rindfuss, Ronald R., C. Gray Swicegood, and Rachel A. Rosenfeld. 1987. Disorder in the life course: How common and does it matter? *American Sociological Review* 52:785–801.

Rosenfeld, Rachel A. 1980. Race and sex differences in career dynamics. *American Sociological Review* 45:583–609.

Settersten, Richard A., and Karl U. Mayer. 1997. The measurement of age, age structuring, and the life course. *Annual Review of Sociology* 23:233–61.

Smith, Deborah B., and Phyllis Moen. 1998. Spouse's influence on the retirement decision: His, her, and their perceptions. *Journal of Marriage and the Family* 60:734–44.

Spilerman, Seymour. 1977. Careers, labor market structure, and socioeconomic achievement. *American Journal of Sociology* 83:661–93.

Still, Mary. 1999. The impact of gender and life course on family social capital: An examination of couples' social involvement. Working paper 99-09, Cornell Employment and Family Careers Institute, Cornell University, Ithaca.

Tomaskovic-Devey, D. 1993. *Gender and racial inequality at work: The sources and consequences of job segregation.* Ithaca: ILR Press.

CHAPTER 3

Getting Younger
While Getting Older

Family-Building at Midlife

Lillian B. Rubin

One would have to be living in a cave to miss the news that the generation that brought us the sexual revolution, the anti-war movement, the counterculture, feminism, and the gay rights movement—the one that thought it would be forever young when it coined the mantra "You can't trust anyone over 30"—is now turning 50. As this best-educated, most literate generation in history has brought middle age out of the closet, bookshelves bulge with volumes telling us that getting old isn't so bad, that women can still be "red hot mamas" and men great sexual studs.

Letty Cottin Pogrebin, looking svelte and gorgeous on the cover of her book *Getting Over Getting Older* (1996), assures us that distressing though they may be, the lumps, bumps, and thinning hair of aging don't really count. In *New Passages* (1995) Gail Sheehy offers up a vision of middle age that shows us leaping from what she calls the "flourishing forties" into the "flaming fifties" and flowing from there into the "serene sixties." Even Betty Friedan has gotten into the act with a book called *The Fountain of Age* (1993), in which she insists that age is a state of mind and that the seventies and eighties are a breeze so long as we find the secret to what she calls "vital aging." And in *The Superhormone Promise* (1997), Dr. William Regelson denies the aging process altogether, declaring that aging is "not a normal life event but a disease."

It's true, of course, that the two decades since I wrote about midlife women in *Women of a Certain Age* (1979) have brought revolutionary changes in when and how women and men make choices about the

58

various life transitions that confront them. But to talk about the "flaming fifties" and "serene sixties" so oversimplifies the modern midlife experience as to be nonsensical. There's nothing about the decade of the fifties that leads us inescapably to flaming, nor do the sixties assure serenity. Instead, much depends on how we're connected to the social and institutional world in which our lives are embedded. That, in very important ways, is what determines our experience at any age.

In my own life, for example, I was just three years out of graduate school when my fiftieth birthday came around, which meant that I had a very different experience as I lived that decade than did women who were living more traditional lives. It isn't a matter of good or bad, or better or worse; it was just different—and complicated with costs and benefits of its own.

In 1963—the year I turned 39 and decided it was time to get the college degree that my class and gender had denied me in my youth—such an experience was most unusual, since so few people, whether men or women, undertook that kind of life-changing adventure at midlife. In fact, throughout the eight years I spent on the Berkeley campus working my way through a B.A., M.A., and Ph.D., I hardly ever saw anyone over 25 in any of my classes. Now it's so common that most colleges have some kind of program to ease the way for what they call "returning students."

For me, there was enormous excitement about embarking on a career at a time when so many other women were depressed and anxious about what they would be doing with the rest of their lives. But it wasn't an unmixed blessing. On the positive side, being a student on a college campus during the turmoil of the mid-sixties and early seventies anchored me in generational issues that were very far from my own. Identifying with the students, sharing their struggles, kept me connected to them in powerful ways, allowing for brief moments the illusion that I was one with them.

But I was also 20-plus years their senior, which meant that I could never fully be one of them. Nor did I want to be. When I turned to people who were my age-mates, however—women who had been my friends before I became a student—I found that the bonds of common experience that formerly held those relationships together had frayed under the stress of lives that had taken such different roads.

By the time I got my Ph.D., I felt like a misfit in both places. Some parts of me and my life were connected to the students with whom I had gone through my graduate program, other parts to my 50-year-old peers. I was the quintessential marginal person—*of* each group but never fully *in* either. And I still am. The people I call my colleagues and friends today are almost universally many years younger than I am.

Now that age is no longer a predictor of the shape of a life, people commonly find themselves in a similar predicament to mine, as any older parent of a small child will testify. The particulars of the experience are different, as are some of the underlying conflicts. But many are also the same. I hear this repeatedly from both men and women whose lives are out of phase with their age.

Just recently, for example, a 47-year-old patient who's a highly successful professional woman came into my office saying that after having spent the morning registering her 3-year-old son in a preschool, she wasn't sure whether to laugh or cry. This strikingly attractive woman, who to me, at least, looks 10 years younger than her age, said:

> I felt ancient. When I walked into the room and looked around, I had this awful feeling. Most of the other mothers were probably around 30, and they looked even younger. It wasn't just how they looked; it was who they were. That kind of sense of myself seems like a lifetime ago, not now. Yet I know that in some ways I'm going to have more in common with them than with friends my age who never had kids or whose kids are in college. Their kids are the ones who will be David's playmates.

She paused for a moment of reflection, then continued with a pained laugh:

> There's not a lot more to say about it except that being there this morning was a humbling experience, especially when a couple of the other mothers came up and cooed over David and asked if I was his grandmother.

In 1979 when *Women of a Certain Age* was published, most people married young, had their children soon after marriage, and reached the stage we call midlife at roughly the same time that the nest was emptying. Therefore, I knew before I started that I'd be interviewing women whose children had either recently gone from the nest or were getting ready to fly away—a whole cohort of women who were roughly the same age and at the same stage of life. By 1999, when I embarked on another study of midlife, I had no idea what I'd find when I opened the door.[1]

---

1. The data for this paper are taken from a study of midlife families in which I compared families who delayed family-building at least until their forties with those whose lives followed a more traditional path. The research took me into the lives of 160 women and men, ages 40 to 65; 140 of them were married or partnered; 20 were single. Occa-

There were, of course, some class and cultural differences in the past, just as there are now. Working-class women, who married in their late teens and whose children did the same, were likely to be in their late thirties or early forties when their last child left home. College-educated middle-class women, who were older when they married, generally were in their mid- to late forties when they reached that stage. But the spread was relatively narrow, and the median clustered around 46.

These small variations aside, people of a similar age were almost universally at the same life stage and facing the same marker events. The transitions of adult life—the move from single to married, for example, or the passage to parenthood, or the end of its active phase—were behind them. A 50-year-old man could be pretty sure that the middle-aged guy at the next desk was worrying about college tuition and counting the years until he could call his life and his earnings his own. Now his neighbor could just as likely be thinking about changing diapers and having to pick up his 2-year-old at the child care center.

In that earlier work there were also some gender differences in how this transition was experienced, since the particular issues men and women faced were different. For men, this period brought them in a face-to-face confrontation with the fact that they had been at the same job or career for all or most of their adult lives; that perhaps they had not accomplished all they'd hoped; that their physical and sexual powers were waning; that what lay ahead was more of the same until retirement, which then was still mandatory at 65 in most institutions.

For women, most of whom had spent their lives in the traditional woman's role in the family, it meant a major shift. After years of family work, they were suddenly unemployed—or if not *un*employed, certainly *under*employed. The job-market skills of their youth were rusty; their confidence in their ability to make their way in the world outside the home shaky. After a lifetime of being busy and useful, they suddenly faced each day asking what they would do with the rest of their lives, how they would live the years ahead now that the children were gone.

What's more significant for this discussion, however, is that both were

---

sionally I interviewed only one partner, but generally I met with both—lengthy in-depth interviews in which I talked separately with each of them, sometimes more than once. Since I was particularly interested in those whose lives have not followed the traditional path, I focused most heavily on them. The sample, therefore, consists of 100 women and men who had their first child at 40 or later and 50 who followed the more traditional course. The respondents live in various places around the country, from Texas to Massachusetts and from New York to California.

brought into confrontation with the social and psychological realities of middle age at the same age and stage of the family life cycle. That's no longer true for either women or men.

The intervening years have brought with them revolutionary changes in when and how women and men make choices about the various life transitions that confront them. Perhaps for the first time in history, age is no longer a predictor of life stage for a very large number of Americans. Instead, the lock-step life course trajectory of earlier generations has given way before a complicated and dramatic series of changes in the culture, the economy, and the life span.

Forty-year-old women are just getting around to having their first child. The changing culture coupled with new reproductive technologies allows single women to have sperm-donor babies well into their forties. If aging eggs are the problem, no matter. Egg donors make it possible for a 50-year-old woman to carry a child. If that doesn't work, there are surrogates who, for a price, will carry the baby, then hand it over at birth. Clearly, the issues of living at middle age are not the same for these women as for those whose lives moved along a more traditional course.

The same is true for men, of course. Fifty-year-old men gaze adoringly at a new infant—sometimes a first child, sometimes the beginning of a second family. They may be chronologically middle-aged, but their place in the social world, the issues of living that engage them, the way they feel about themselves, their lives, and their aging are very far from those that preoccupy the man of the same age who has just sent his last child off to college. For the sociology and psychology of midlife, the sense of constraints and possibilities depends on the web of relationships and responsibilities within which a life is embedded.

Which brings us to the question: How and why have such changes come to pass? Obviously we have been witness in recent decades to a complicated and intertwined series of social, cultural, and demographic shifts that have profoundly changed our lives. But one thing is clear: Without the spectacular lengthening of the life span the past century has brought, none of this would be possible.

Just a hundred years ago the life expectancy at birth for the average American was 47; now it's nearly 80.[2] Then only half of all Americans who reached the age of 20 lived to see 65. When people died by 50, there was little between youth and old age to claim their attention. As

2. U.S. Bureau of the Census 1996, table 118.

we enter a new century, however, 65 seems young and people over 80 are the fastest-growing segment of our population. Even 100 no longer seems just a wistful dream. Measured in evolutionary time, this near-doubling of our life span is nothing less than a demographic miracle—an astonishing, exhilarating, frightening miracle.

When the life span was so much shorter than it is today, it made sense to marry and have children when people were young enough to be reasonably certain they'd live to launch them into adulthood. When, as is true now, what was once the whole of life is only about half of it, 50 can seem like a beginning, a chance at another adulthood with which to do what we will. And this time, one that comes when, we may be allowed to hope, we have learned from the mistakes of our first adulthood.

For all of us, then, no matter what our life situation may be, questions about how we'll live the years ahead are inescapable. One way of dealing with these questions is in the search for renewal, for ways to renew and revitalize ourselves and our lives. We change jobs; we go back to school to train for a new career; we refuse to retire or we quit and go off to climb a mountain, real or metaphorical; we move from city to country or the other way around; we have face-lifts, liposuction, and chemical peels to conceal from ourselves and the world the signs of our aging; we spend hours each week running along the city streets and lifting weights at the gym in an effort to defeat it altogether. Or most dramatic of all, we alter what has until now been the accepted path of the life course. We delay marriage and childbearing for 10, 15, 20 years beyond what was normal just a couple of decades ago and, presto, we have found a way to fill at least some of those years.[3]

I don't mean that people suddenly wake up one morning and say,

3. In 1980 women 30 to 34 produced just over 87,000 first births; by 1994 the number had tripled to more than 250,000. For women 35 to 39, the increase is even more dramatic: close to 14,000 in 1980 and over 80,000 in 1994, a nearly sixfold increase in just 14 years (Matthews and Ventura 1997). And although the *numbers* are still relatively small, the proportion of first-time mothers among the 40 to 44 age group jumped 5 percent between 1993 and 1994 alone (Matthews and Ventura 1996).

A couple of interesting footnotes to these statistics are the increasing number of baby boomers—20 percent of the 35- to 39-year-olds and 14 percent of those 40 to 44—who, for a variety of reasons, have never married, and the 13 percent of married women between 35 and 44 who remain childless, by choice or otherwise (U.S. Bureau of the Census 1996, tables 58 and 106).

Obviously, people who haven't taken the marital plunge, as well as those who remain childless, face a different set of issues at midlife than their age peers, some of whom are worrying about raising small children, others about how to parent children who have suddenly become adults.

"Hey, now that I know I'll probably live to be 80, I don't have to get married at 20 anymore." Or that they're conscious of what motivates their changed ideas about the timing and sequencing of these life events. It's more like an unconscious process whereby the changed social circumstances give birth to new options that seem to seep into consciousness when we're not looking.[4]

With the shape of the life course changed so radically, any discussion of the midlife transition becomes enormously complicated. It's true, of course, that most people turn 50. But what that event means in a life, how it is experienced, depends heavily upon the choices a person made— or didn't make—about marriage and family when he or she was 25.

Take age, for example. In my earlier study of midlife women, the lower end of the age range was 35, the upper end 54.[5] But with people marrying and bearing children so much later while they also live healthy, vigorous lives well beyond anything we might have imagined earlier, the definition of midlife has shifted upward dramatically.

Now 35 seems much too young to define the beginning of middle age, and 65 has barely seen the end of it. The same is true about old age. Yesterday 65 was old; today a 65-year-old is as likely to be seen jogging along the city streets in sweats and running shoes as to be rocking on the front porch and watching the world go by.

We can't define midlife by life stage anymore either. Not when one 45-year-old woman is inching toward grandmotherhood, while her next-door neighbor of the same age is clutching her pregnant belly as she chases after her 2-year-old. Or when one 55-year-old man is a new father, while the same-age guy who works at the next desk has just seen his last child leave home. For common ground, whether psychological or sociological, is vitiated where the life course has taken such different turns.

It isn't just that the lives of the pregnant 45-year-old and the grandmother are so at odds. It's that their very sense of themselves is different—the way they look at the world, the problems they see ahead, the way they deal with their own aging.

---

4. Twenty-five years ago, women were, on the average, under 21 when they married and less than 23 when they had their first child. By 1995, they weren't even married yet, since the median age of first marriage had climbed to nearly 25 years for women and 28 for men—an astonishing jump in such a short time (U.S. Bureau of the Census 1966, table 59).

5. In that study I defined midlife by the stage of family life. The sample, therefore, was comprised of women whose children had already flown the nest or were getting ready to do so.

Carolyn Kendall, a 48-year-old professional with two children, ages 3 and 5, talked about this issue:

> I have this next-door neighbor who's not much older than I am—maybe 50—but she got married right out of college and her kids are all grown. I like her; she's a very nice person, but I just don't have much in common with her. While she was raising her kids, I was still raising hell. Now she's free to do whatever she wants, and I'm working 30 hours a week while I try to be a good mom and a good wife, and I can hardly stay awake past nine o'clock. She's waiting for her kids to make her a grandmother, and I'm thinking about where we're going to get the money to send two kids to private school because the public schools in this city are so lousy.
>
> Don't get me wrong. I adore my kids, and I love being a mom. But talk to anyone my age who has little kids like this, and all you'll hear is how tired they are all the time. I sometimes think God or nature or whatever didn't mean for us to be having kids when we're so old.

Listening to Carolyn I couldn't help wondering whether she'd decide some things differently if she could rewrite the script of her life. So I asked. She looked at me thoughtfully, turning the question over in her mind, then shook her head.

> I don't think I'd do it differently. I know there are some advantages to having your children when you're younger, but I wasn't ready, and I would never have been the kind of mother I am now. I couldn't have done it. If I had put my career in low gear and done a mommy track kind of thing then, I would have resented it. Now that I've done the career thing and know the ups and downs of it, it's not that important to me anymore. I've done it, so I can slow it down now and it's fine. Also there's something about having little kids at this age that keeps you feeling young.

She stopped talking for a brief moment, then, with a rueful smile, said:

> Yeah, I know, I've been in the position where someone thought I was their grandmother, and I sure didn't like that. But I'm talking about how I feel inside myself. And there it's like I can't get with the idea that I'm not far from 50. I look at these two little creatures I just bore, and I think, *"Fifty just isn't me."*

It's not so simple, however. It's true that being the mother of young children allows the illusion of youth and vigor. But her body tells a different story, as the hot flashes of menopause thrust her willy-nilly into the realization of her aging. Repeatedly women in their forties talked of this anomaly—the disparity between the "young" lives they are living and their aging bodies. Shaking her head in wonder, 49-year-old Rebecca Morgan said:

When I think about the fact that I gave birth to a child four years ago and now I'm beginning menopause, it makes no sense at all. But that's what modern technology has done for me and a lot of other women. I'm grateful for it; I would never have been able to have a child without it. But I'm very much aware that there's something peculiar about being so close to childbirth *and* menopause. It's hard to get your mind around it, isn't it? I mean, *they're separated by only four years.*

But even menopause is a very different experience today. The biological changes are still with us, of course, but how they're defined culturally is light years away from what it was like for women of earlier generations. Even as late as 1970 menopause was still a quiet, if not shameful, secret—a biological event that couldn't be avoided but nobody talked much about, not even women among themselves. Consequently, the myths around menopause, none of them kind, were legion, while real knowledge was scarce. Now there are hundreds of articles about menopause in newspapers and magazines; books about it hit the best-seller list; seminars and conferences are devoted to the subject; and in a TV movie based on the old *Cagney and Lacey* series, Sharon Gless gets hot flashes while her partner Tyne Daley waves a little battery-operated fan in front of her face.

So although menopause is still with us, it's trendy now. Which makes a big difference in how the event itself is experienced. For while it's a distinctly biological phenomenon, the changed cultural norms surrounding it help to create a psychology of menopause that's very different from the old one. When it's no longer a shameful secret, when it's no longer defined as the end of womanhood—as if women were nothing but baby machines—when we no longer believe it's the end of sexuality, women come to this biological event with a sense of freedom and confidence few women of earlier generations knew. As one 48-year-old woman said, "No conversation with my friends ever goes by these days without at least one joke about menopause." Believe me, women of my generation didn't joke.

But what about the people who made more traditional decisions about how they'd live their first adulthood?

They're also dealing with the physical changes that aging brings, but because it fits the pattern of their lives, it doesn't seem so disjunctive to them. Marjorie Rathman, Carolyn Kendall's 50-year-old neighbor whose children are grown and no longer living at home, talks quite differently about turning 50. "I can't exactly explain it," she said as she struggled for words, "but it was like a door opened. I did everything I was supposed to do, and now I'm young enough to be able to do anything I want. When I look at Carolyn next door, I think, '*Whew, I wouldn't want to be there now.*' She's always pushed and rushed, never any time for herself or to enjoy life. I don't know how she does it."

"Did you ever feel cheated about not having a career in those earlier years?" I asked Marjorie.

Well, it's not like I gave up my work altogether. It's just that I didn't have the high-flying kind of career that women who didn't have children could have. So sure, sometimes I had a hard time when I'd begin to think their lives looked so glamorous while I was doing diapers and going to Little League and driving kids all over town. But all I can tell you is that I'm not sorry for the choices I made now. I'd rather be where I am than where people like Carolyn are. My life seems more in sync in every way than hers.

She paused a moment as if thinking over what she had been saying, then hastened to add:

Don't misunderstand me; I'm not criticizing how women like Carolyn live. It's a choice, and I think it's wonderful that people can make those kinds of choices now. But I think whatever way you go, it costs, and all I'm saying is I'd rather have paid my costs than hers. At least now when I'm 50, I feel like I have a whole life ahead of me. By the time Carolyn gets to this place, she'll be close to 70, and there won't be that much life left.

Marjorie's husband, Warren, echoed his wife's sentiments. Having watched other men who at his age are grappling with issues he long ago put away, he said with firm conviction:

I don't envy these 50- and 60-year-old guys who have little kids. Hell, they're going to be working to pay the bills right up to the day they die. Yeah, yeah, I hear all the talk about how great it is that people can have all these options, but you know, I never saw one of those guys who isn't feeling tremendous pressure. Who can blame them? They don't know whether they'll be able to work long enough to get their kids through school. How can you enjoy the kids when that's always there grating on you?

The other thing is, part of the fun of being a father is being able to play with your kids; I mean, really getting out there and roughing it up. I'd be out there batting balls around, shooting baskets, running around with them all the time. These guys can't do that; they get pooped right away.

An estimate that many older fathers of young children agree with.

When older mothers talked about being tired all the time, it usually meant that they didn't get enough sleep. For their husbands, whose definition of self is so often tied to physical prowess, it was more troubling to find themselves unable to keep up with a child. "I just don't have it anymore; my back won't take it," said 49-year-old Bruce Greenfield, his expression caught between sadness at the loss and anger at the realization of his limitations. "I can't do what I could do even ten years ago, but how do I tell my son I ran out of steam just when he came along? You know, it's the one thing you never think about when you keep saying later, later."

"Would you choose to do it differently if you could?" I asked.

Like so many others, he couldn't answer the question easily. After a long reflective pause, he sighed and said:

> In some ways, maybe. Yeah, I'd love to have the kind of stamina I had twenty years ago. But it wasn't in the cards then. I couldn't even imagine getting married and settling down when I was 29. So the answer is, I don't think so. I sure wouldn't want to give up all those years I had before Annie and the kids. The freedom to do what I wanted when I wanted, to work without being hassled all the time to be home and more "present." That's the word my wife uses all the time.

He stopped talking, turned inward for a moment or two, and then added:

> No, I wouldn't give up those years. So what do you think? I wanted it all, huh? I guess my generation thought we could have it all, too. But it never really works that way, does it?

In many ways the men I talked to seemed less comfortable with their choices than the women. It isn't that they love and value their children and family life less, but they tend to be more resentful of the work versus family conflicts that are inevitable for parents of young children. For women those conflicts are usually resolved on the side of family; men more often come down on the side of work. Which makes for conflicts with wives that men speak of angrily. Carolyn Kendall's husband, Joe Thurman, complained:

> I don't know what she wants. She wants to live this good life and wants me to cut back on work. But she's the one who wanted our second child. Don't get me wrong; I love that little guy. But somebody's got to be out there working to pay the bills now and make sure they have what they need later on, too. She says she doesn't want to work full-time anymore because she doesn't want to miss out on watching the kids grow up. That's great; I like that she's home more with them; she's a great mother and they need her. But then that means I'm it. I'm 52 years old; if I don't do it now, pretty soon there'll be no time left to make sure we've got those kids protected.

For those whose family life followed the traditional path, work-related problems and conflicts—from child care to maternal guilt to the division of family labor—are generally a thing of the past. With the children on their own, these families find themselves with a level of financial and social ease they could only dream about in their earlier years. For the late-starting families, however, all the problems of the early stages of family life are complicated by the issues that middle age thrusts upon them. True, at mid-career they have more resources to cope with problems such as child care and education than more traditional families had at the same stage of family life. Nevertheless, it's daunting when the aches, pains, and diminished energy of middle age combine with the fears of what the future will bring.

As I listened to these men and women, it was clear that despite all the talk about the changes in family roles and structure, some traditional gender expectations—even in such nontraditional families—often remain the rule. Repeatedly men talked about their fears for their financial future in ways that women did not. I don't mean that women don't also worry about providing financial security for their children and for their own old age, but the concerns they expressed about the future were generally relational ones: "I'm scared I won't live long enough to know my daughter as an adult." "It's such a shame that they didn't know my parents as they were years ago." "It saddens me to think that I'll probably never know my grandchildren." But the men still expect—and often are expected—to be the major family breadwinner. And most of the time they are. Which means that if a man has a new baby at 45 or 50 he's worried, not just whether he'll be around to see that child go off to college but how long he'll have to work to make sure she or he can get there.

A physician who was days away from his fifty-second birthday when we met mused about his feelings and worried about what lies ahead:

> I'm part of the generation that never thought about getting old. It's absurd. I don't know what I thought, but I never thought I'd be facing 52. So now it's like looking into the abyss. I have two little kids—my daughter just started first grade, my son's 4—and my new wife is pregnant. Fifty-two doesn't make sense in that life, but it's here, and I know it, and I'm not sure how I'll manage it. It feels crazy in a way. I'm living the life of a young man while I'm getting to be an old man. It doesn't compute in my head or my gut. I'm already tired and wondering how long I can go on. What's going to happen to these kids if I give out when they still need my financial support?

But many of these families would be grateful if this were all they had to worry about. For they are truly caught in the middle of the generational sandwich—women and men who, because they started so late, are raising small children at precisely the time when their parents are entering old age. So at the same time that their lives are consumed with work and family issues at home, a sick or failing parent makes a claim on their time, attention, energy, and perhaps money. For those whose parents live in distant cities, it means, as one man put it, "running back and forth across the country putting out fires." For those whose parents live nearby, there are the usual life needs—from taking them shopping to getting them to the doctor's office—that eat into time that isn't there. A set of complications for adult children that will become more and more frequent as their parents' lives are extended into their nineties and beyond.

It's true, of course, that families that followed a more traditional life trajectory also face the disruption that the needs of aging parents can set in motion. Men and women in these families talked often about the plans they had to set aside—long-awaited travel adventures, a move from city to country or from suburbs to city—because a parent needed care. But for the late-starting families, the problems of failing parents are immeasurably complicated by the fact that they're already greatly overstressed by the need to feed, house, clothe, and raise small children.

For all the problems of living that confront them, however, it's not all trouble for people whose lives are not patterned on the traditional timetable. Older parents generally have a better sense of themselves and what they want than younger parents. They've had years of freedom, plenty of good times, and careers that have been at least somewhat gratifying. Therefore, the constraints of parenthood don't weigh as heavily on them as on the 20-year-old. While there are no studies of child abuse among these older parents, I suspect that regardless of class and social circumstances, there are far fewer abused children in these families than among families with much younger parents, whose own unmet needs may make them less able to tolerate a small child's needs and demands.

Still, these are revolutionary social changes; and as with all revolutions, this one, too, has its costs and benefits. Some people celebrate these changes, believing that life is richer now. Some mourn the past, finding today's world more difficult to manage. In fact, comparing better or worse, harder or easier, makes little sense, partly because such comparisons nearly always rest on memories of the past that are better than the reality ever was. It's somewhat like the idealization of the dead, where even some pretty monstrous characters get whitewashed in the minds of those they left behind.

The fact is: Today women are tired because they have too much to do; yesterday they were depressed because they didn't have enough to keep them busy. In the past men worried about dying at 50; now they're concerned about what they'll do with their lives for 25 or 30 years beyond that marker event. We may think of our increased life span as a gift, a burden, or some combination of the two. But there's no doubt that it offers options for living that were impossible before—options that are driven by a set of social, cultural, and demographic shifts that won't go away because we wish they would.

As we reflect on these transformations, there's not much doubt that life has become more complicated—or at least differently so—as new possibilities have brought with them new ways of being along with a variety of new problems. For when you turn the sociology of aging on its head, as we have in these past two decades, there are inescapable social and psychological consequences. The task now, it seems to me, is not to waste time in nostalgia for a past that never was, but to figure out how we as a society will live with the possibilities that are open to us in the most fruitful way.

REFERENCES

Friedan, Betty. 1993. *The fountain of age.* New York: Simon and Schuster.

Matthews, T. J., and S. J. Ventura. 1997. Birth and fertility rates by educational attainment: United States, 1994. *Monthly Vital Statistics Report,* vol. 45, no. 10, supp. Hyattsville, Md.: National Center for Health Statistics.

Pogrebin, Letty Cottin. 1996. *Getting over getting older: An intimate journey.* Boston: Little, Brown.

Regelson, William. 1997. *The superhormone promise: Nature's antidote to aging.* New York: Pocket Books.

Rubin, Lillian B. 1979. *Women of a certain age: The midlife search for self.* New York: Harper and Row.

Sheehy, Gail. 1995. *New passages: Mapping your life course across time.* New York: Random House.

U.S. Bureau of the Census. 1996. *Statistical abstract of the United States.* Washington, D.C.: U.S. Government Printing Office.

Ventura, S. J., J. A. Martin, T. J. Matthews, and S. C. Clarke. 1996. Advance report of final natality statistics, 1994. *Monthly Vital Statistics Report,* vol. 44, no. 11, supp. Hyattsville, Md.: National Center for Health Statistics.

CHAPTER 4

Men's Family Work

Child-Centered Fathering and the
Sharing of Domestic Labor

Scott Coltrane and Michele Adams

As we move into the twenty-first century, work/family conflicts for mothers and fathers are becoming increasingly similar. At the same time, anxiety about marriage and the well-being of children has prompted some to call for a return to gender-segregated styles of parenting and family life. We are thus faced with troublesome questions about the proper roles of men and women both inside and outside of families. While most Americans now assume that mothers need to be employed to help support their families, we are less certain about how much family work men should do. Is it enough that fathers hold steady jobs, come home after work, and occasionally play with their children, or should they also be expected to assume responsibility for the more mundane tasks of parenting and housework?

In this chapter we contribute to debates about these issues by examining the behavior of fathers and mothers in a national sample of families with school-aged children. We are especially concerned with differentiating among different types of parenting behaviors, drawing a distinction between nurturing child-centered activities (e.g., having private talks, helping with homework, driving to school) and more adult-centered parent-child interactions (e.g., watching television together, playing a game, serving as a coach). Previous case studies of involved fathers suggest that men who perform more nurturant parenting tasks might be drawn into performing more of the routine cooking and cleaning tasks that are necessary to maintain homes and raise children (Coltrane 1996), but no studies have examined this possible relationship using a representative national sample and longitudinal data. In the following analysis, we not only document how parenting is associated with housework but also investigate the potential impact of a range of other variables, including occupational commitments, earnings, attitudes, and other life circumstances, on the domestic activities of mothers and fathers. In general, we find that more nurturant and child-centered fathering contributes to men's performance of routine household labor, whereas more conventional and adult-centered fathering is associated with men doing less domestic work.

Following assumptions about separate work and family spheres for men and women, most social science research on parenting has focused on mothers. Social theories from the 1950s and 1960s considered the potential significance of fathers, especially in terms of breadwinning, discipline, and modeling masculinity, but few studies paid attention to what fathers actually did around the house or with children (Parke 1995, 1996). In the late 1970s that pattern began to change. As a "new" fatherhood ideal surfaced in popular culture, family researchers began to report that fathers were indeed capable of participating in the routine aspects of parenting, like feeding infants and changing diapers, even though they typically remained in a helper role (Fein 1978; Lamb 1976; Parke 1981). During the 1980s more family researchers included men in their studies, and a few focused on nurturing fathers who shared in virtually all aspects of parenting (e.g., Coltrane 1989; Ehrensaft 1987; Pruett 1987; Russell 1983). Large-sample studies conducted about this time showed that as women entered the labor force in record numbers, they cut back on time spent in family work, even though the average husband increased his contributions to family work only slightly (Coltrane 1996; Pleck 1983).

Public debates about the future of marriage and the proper role of fathers became more heated in the 1990s (Blankenhorn 1995; Glenn 1997; Popenoe 1996; Stacey 1996), just as national time-use surveys began to document a significant shift toward more sharing of housework and child care between husbands and wives (Coltrane 1999; O'Connell 1994; Robinson and Godbey 1997). As described below, family researchers began to promote different ideals of what constitutes a good father, ranging from the sensitive egalitarian partner who changes diapers and cooks meals to the stern but kindly patriarch who exercises family leadership according to biblical teachings or biological imperatives. While a full review of competing perspectives on good fathering is beyond the scope of this chapter, we focus the following discussion on debates about how much family work men should do, which tasks they ought to perform, and what impact their various family involvements might have.

Many scholars who assume that fathers have a positive influence on children focus on family structure (e.g., married vs. unmarried, father-present vs. father-absent) and on "traditional" styles of paternal involvement (e.g., economic provision, maternal support, moral leadership) (Doherty, Kouneski, and Erickson 1998; Nock 1998; Popenoe 1996). Defenders of traditional fatherhood present a gender-segregated ideal of men's family roles: "Historically, the good father protects his family, provides for its material needs, devotes himself to the education of his children, and represents his family's interest in the larger world. This work is necessarily rooted in a repertoire of inherited male values. . . . These values are not limited to toughness, competition, instrumentalism, and aggression—but they certainly include them" (Blankenhorn 1995, 122). Although sometimes acknowledging historical and cultural variability in parenting practices, biological predispositions are routinely invoked to explain why mothering and fathering should be viewed as essentially and categorically different (Blankenhorn 1995; Mackey 1985; Popenoe 1996). Since distinct parenting styles and personality traits are assumed to derive from an underlying biological base, these authors argue that it would be a mistake for men and women to perform the same tasks around the house or with children. Similarly, some family researchers have recently begun to criticize fatherhood studies for using a "deficit model," suggesting that a direct comparison of fathers' parenting behaviors with mothers' makes men look bad and ignores what is unique and most important about fatherhood (Doherty 1991; Hawkins and Dollahite 1997; LaRossa 1988). Even some proponents of greater father involvement, like the author of The Nurturing Father (Pruett 1987), warn men against trying to act too much like mothers: "Obviously, fathers are not mothers—they never will be and shouldn't try. . . . Fathering is not mothering any more than mothering is ever fathering" (Pruett 1993, 46).

Belief in unique and non-overlapping roles for mothers and fathers resonates with the late-nineteenth-century ideology of separate gender spheres, but historical studies show that mothers and fathers have actually shared a fairly wide range of parenting activities (Coltrane and Parke 1998; Griswold 1993; Mintz 1998). Nevertheless, some recent attempts to measure fathering have called for a return to a gender-segregated model of parenting. For example, a 1998 study called *Nurturing Fatherhood* published by the Federal Interagency Forum on Child and Family Statistics suggested that fathers' direct care or nurturing of children was the *least* important of the four major ways they might influence their children (Marsiglio et al. 1998, 109). According to this view, a father's economic provisioning (breadwinning) is his primary contribution, followed by emotional and physical support of his wife, and by moral and ethical guidance. Similarly, Coleman (1994) suggests that fathers contribute three things to children: human capital (achievement skills), financial capital (money, goods, and purchased experiences), and social capital (family and community relations benefiting children) (see Marsiglio et al. 1998, 146). These positional or structural approaches to fatherhood privilege conventional notions of breadwinning and public authority as men's most important contributions to their children. Implicitly following such reasoning, social scientists have typically assumed that men's employment is sufficient to encourage positive child development, whereas mothers' employment, in contrast, has often been assumed to harm children. As Pleck (1997) and others have noted, in order to understand how breadwinning influences children and families, we ought to abandon gender-segregated models and allow for assessment of positive as well as negative impacts of both men's and women's jobs.

We agree with Hawkins and Dollahite (1997, 20–21) that father*hood* describes cultural or normative expectations, whereas father*work*—including activities like housework and other labor that involves men in sustained effort—describes the actual conduct of fathering. While acknowledging that more positional or structural aspects of father*hood* can influence children, we are more concerned with direct and indirect father*work*—those father-child interactions and child maintenance activities that have substantial influence on both children and wives. In adopting this approach we follow Lamb, Pleck, Charnov, and Levine (1985), who suggested that fathers' involvement with children includes three components: (1) engagement or interaction with the child, (2) accessibility or availability to the child, and (3) responsibility for the care of the child. Most child development researchers have measured father involvement in terms of engagement or one-on-one interaction, exemplified by holding, talking to, and especially playing with one's child (McBride 1989; Parke 1999). In a review of several large-scale studies, Pleck (1997) found that fathers recently increased the amount of time they spend interacting with their children to about half (44%) that of women, and Levine and Pittinsky (1997, 25–26) found that between 1977 and 1997, employed fathers increased their time interacting with children (in both care and play) by one half hour per workday, from 1.8 to 2.3 hours (versus 3 hours per workday for employed mothers in both 1977 and 1997). When compared to mothers, fathers are likely to spend a much greater proportion of their interaction time with children in play or leisure, leading to calls for specifying the type and context of father-child interaction. In general, studies find that children fare better when fathers interact more frequently with them: for example, preschool children of engaged fathers show more cognitive competence, more internal locus of control, more empathy, and less gender stereotyping (Lamb 1987; Pleck 1997; Radin 1994), and older children of engaged fathers show a cluster of positive outcomes including higher self-control, greater self-esteem, better life skills, more social competence, and less gender stereotyping (Amato 1987; Pleck 1997).

Several researchers have also stressed the importance of the responsibility dimension of father involvement, which includes the more hidden managerial aspects of child care (Parke 1999). As Pleck (1997) notes, mothers remain child care managers in the vast majority of households, though some evidence indicates that at least some fathers are taking a more active role in this domain (Coltrane 1996; Risman and Johnson-Sumerford 1998). Most developmental psychologists now distinguish between parenting activities on the basis of the functional context in which the interaction occurs (e.g., play, leisure, caretaking, instruction) but rarely include measures of maintenance activities like housework in their studies. In contrast, sociologists and economists who study housework rarely include direct measures of child interaction in their domestic labor studies.

According to several large-scale surveys, the five most time-consuming of the major household tasks (apart from child care) are (1) meal preparation or cooking, (2) housecleaning, (3) shopping for groceries and household goods, (4) washing dishes or cleaning up after meals, and (5) laundry (including washing, drying, folding, ironing, and mending clothes) (Blair and Lichter 1991; Robinson and Godbey 1997). These routine household tasks are not only the most time-consuming of the domestic tasks, but are also less optional and less able to be postponed than other tasks. Studies consistently show that this routine housework is even more segregated by gender than child care, with married women reporting that they spend at least three times as much time on these tasks as their husbands (Coltrane 1999; Demo and Acock 1993;

Hersch and Stratton 1997; Presser 1994; Shelton 1992). Men's share of housework has several consistent predictors, including women's employment patterns, ideology, and relative earnings, followed by men's employment hours and ideology. Other predictors of men's relative share of housework, including age, marital status, and presence of children, are sometimes correlated with the relative share of housework performed by men. Studies consistently show that when couples have children, they move toward less sharing of family work between men and women. In most cases, mothers become the child care and housework experts, even though both parents tend to increase the amount of time they devote to family work (Cowan and Cowan 1992; Johnson and Huston 1998; MacDermid, Huston, and McHale 1990; Shelton 1992). Because it is typically assumed that women should be responsible for managing both housework and child care, it is not surprising that employed mothers enjoy less leisure and experience more stress than employed fathers (Barnett and Shen 1997; Hochschild 1989; Robinson and Godbey 1997). Only a few studies have suggested that as men get more involved in child care they might also begin to assume more responsibility for housework (Coltrane 1996; Fish, New, and Van Cleave 1996; Presser 1994). In the following analysis, we assess both child care and housework as well as track couples over time to see which types of father involvement might be associated with greater sharing of family work.

ANALYSIS OF NATIONAL SURVEY DATA

This research examines data taken from the first and second waves of the National Survey of Families and Households (NSFH), conducted in 1987–88 and 1992–93, respectively, by the Center for Demography and Ecology at the University of Wisconsin, Madison. NSFH1 used a national probability sample of 13,017 individuals interviewed between March 1987 and May 1988. Cohabiting couples were oversampled, as were African American and Hispanic households, single-parent families, families with stepchildren, and recently married couples (Bumpass and Sweet 1989). For each household, a randomly selected adult was chosen as the main respondent, who was interviewed and asked to complete a self-administered questionnaire dealing with attitudes, values, and behaviors. A reduced version of the self-administered questionnaire was also given to present spouses and partners. Interviews with main respondents lasted approximately 100 minutes, with interview lengths varying depending on the complexity of respondents' answers (see Bumpass and Sweet 1989). For the current research, we rely on information from main respondents and their spouses or cohabiting partners.

NSFH2 consisted of a follow-up interview and survey that included many of the measures incorporated earlier (see Zill and Daly 1993, 296–97). NSFH2 included responses from original (NSFH1) primary respondents as well as their current partners; for NSFH2, the spouse/partner interview and questionnaire was nearly identical to that provided to the main respondent. Response rates for the second wave were 82 percent for primary respondents and 86 percent for current partners/spouses (Smock and Manning 1997); a total of 10,007 respondents were interviewed for the second wave of the survey.

Our study draws on a sample that includes couples (main respondents and their spouses or partners) having at least one child (biological, step-, or adopted) between the ages of 5 and 18 living in the household at each of time 1 and time 2. We did not include those who divorced or separated during the period between the two waves of the survey. The total number of couples in our data subset is 1,357.

In order to assess the impact of men's involvement in child-centered family work on their participation in routine household labor, we present five statistical models. Ordinary Least Squares (OLS) regression procedures are used for the first four models, and panel regression for the fifth. Much existing research examining housework participation relies on cross-sectional data, which hampers investigation of the causes of domestic labor inequity while also precluding analysis of change over time. The present research is an advance over previous cross-sectional designs in that it relies on longitudinal data and can therefore accommodate both time and change dynamics. For example, our panel regression model takes advantage of the longitudinal nature of the data by including the lagged dependent variable, men's proportion of housework at time 1, as a predictor of men's proportion of housework participation at time 2. The panel model also includes various time 2 measures of attitudes and fathering activities, as well as time 1 to time 2 "change scores" for key employment and earnings variables. This technique allows us to control for baseline rates of housework sharing and isolate how change occurring in one area may generalize to other areas, thus mitigating against simultaneity bias or reciprocal causation (Kposowa 1993). Demographic characteristics of the studied respondents by gender (table 4.1) precede the regression analyses described above.

MEASUREMENT

The outcome variable for this study is the percentage of the routine housework performed by men, measured at both time 1 and time 2. We included the five most time-consuming routine chores in this measure: meal preparation, washing dishes/meal cleanup, shopping, washing/ironing clothes, and cleaning house. Each main respondent and spouse/partner was asked to estimate the time per week that he or she devoted to each task, as well as the amount of time spent by their spouse/partner on each chore. Because of possible reporting biases (see Press and Townsley 1998), we averaged the responses of the main respondents and their spouse/partners to obtain each partner's time invested in housework. Since we are interested in gender-equity issues, we separated women's from men's household labor performance hours. The gendered tasks were then summed to create a routine housework participation index for men. Finally, the number of hours invested by men was divided by the number of hours spent by the couple as a whole, in order to obtain men's percentage of total routine housework.

Time Availability　　Time availability is measured by the number of hours each spouse worked for pay outside of the home, under the assumption that for each spouse the more time spent in the paid workforce, the less time available to perform household chores. This measure includes time spent in primary and secondary employment. To control for overreporting and to avoid problems associated with outlying values, we truncated the total amount of weekly paid employment to 80 hours for each respondent.

Relative Resources　　We examined partners' relative resources in order to assess the material power in the relationship. We assume, in effect, that the greater a spouse's available material resources, the more substantial will be her or his bargaining position when negotiating a division of household labor. We calculated the percentage of couple earnings contributed by the wife (or female partner), since historically she has been the one to be relatively disadvantaged in terms of remuneration for her paid labor. We expect therefore that the greater her percentage of the total couple income, the greater will be her advantage in eliciting housework from her spouse or male partner; that is, the greater will be his proportional participation in routine housework.

Ideology   We included three measures of ideology for each partner—attitudes toward (1) sexual practices, (2) separate spheres, and (3) sharing of housework. For each index or item, higher scores indicate a more liberal orientation and lower scores a more conservative orientation. Attitudes toward sexual practices are included because individuals harboring more liberal sexual attitudes are assumed to hold concomitantly liberal attitudes about other practices relating to marriage, gender equality, and civil liberties. The additive index includes questions regarding the respondent's views on the propriety of unmarried couples (particularly 18-year-olds) living together and/or having sexual relations; it also includes a question regarding the suitability of women having children outside of marriage. Individual measures were recoded, where necessary, to relate higher scores with more liberal sexual behavior ideology; the measures were summed for time 1 (Cronbach's alpha = .780 and .759 for men and women, respectively) and for time 2 (Cronbach's alpha = .789 and .778 for men and women, respectively). We measured separate-spheres ideology with questions about the respondent's belief that men should be the primary family breadwinner, as well as worries about young children if mothers work full-time or if children are placed in day care. Responses were summed for time 1 (Cronbach's alpha = .775 and .787 for men and women, respectively) and for time 2 (Cronbach's alpha = .730 and .743 for men and women). This three-item separate-spheres index is intended to tap a "global" sense of the propriety of distinct work/family spheres for mothers and fathers. The third ideology measure uses a single question to ascertain "localized" attitudes toward sharing household labor, simply asking if men and women should share housework when both are employed full-time.

Interaction with Children   Ten separate measures of men's involvement with their school-aged children are analyzed. Some measures asked how frequently certain activities occurred, including (1) leisure activities away from home, (2) playing together or working on a project at home, (3) private talks, (4) helping with homework, and (5) watching television (time 2 only). The six possible responses for these questions were (1) never or rarely, (2) once a month or less, (3) several times a month, (4) about once a week, (5) several times a week, or (6) almost every day. Other measures assessed the average number of hours spent per week (6) driving children (and other family members), and being involved in organized youth activities as a participant, advisor, coach, or leader for (7) parent-teacher association or other school activities, (8) religious youth groups, (9) community youth groups, and (10) sports or youth athletic clubs.[1] We use the label "child-centered" to describe the variables representing parent-child interaction or engagement focused on meeting the children's routine needs (e.g., helping with homework, driving to activities, having private talks). In contrast, we use the label "adult-centered" to describe parent-child activities that focus as much on the adults' enjoyment or self-fulfillment as the children's (e.g., playing together, watching television together, spending leisure time away from home). We label a third set of activities "community-centered" because the adults' participation signals maintenance of public family status as well as potential service to children (e.g., attending school activities, attending community youth groups, serving as a religious youth group leader, coaching a child's sports team). Gender-segregated models of parenting assume that adult-centered and community-centered activities are more appropriate for fathers, whereas child-centered activities are more appropriate for mothers. Nevertheless, men can and do perform child-centered activities, with positive outcomes for children. In the following analysis, we hypothesize that when men perform more child-centered activities, they will share more housework with wives as well.

Controls   We incorporated a number of demographic controls previously found to impact relative housework participation (see Coltrane 1999), including men's age measured in years and men's education level.[2] We also included the number of children in the household age 4 or younger, as well as the number of children in the household age 5 to 18, assuming that more children, and more preschool children, would increase the overall demand for family work in the household.[3]

---

1. While both respondent and spouse/partner made self-reports of invested time for activities (1) through (6), questions regarding activities (7) through (10) were answered at time 1 by respondent only for both self and spouse/partner. At time 2, both respondent and spouse/partner answered the questions for their own time use. In order to maintain consistency, we used respondent's report of both self and spouse time investments for activities (6) through (9) for both time 1 and time 2.

2. At time 1, although the main respondent was asked her/his years of completed education, the respondent's spouse/partner was not. The latter was asked the *level* of education completed. In order to include men's education level (whether the responding male was the main respondent or not), the education of both main respondent and spouse/partner was recoded to reflect education level, rather than years of education, completed. This methodological issue was resolved by time 2, where both main respondent and spouse/partner answered the same educational question; thus, when time 2 measures of education are used, they reflect years, and not level, of education completed.

3. In other regression models not shown here, we included additional control variables sometimes included in studies of household labor, such as marital satisfaction and total

As noted, we use OLS regression to assess the cross-sectional relationships among variables, as well as panel regression techniques to evaluate change over time. Table 4.2 displays the cross-sectional results of OLS regression models predicting men's relative participation in routine housework first at time 1 and then at time 2. Baseline models include economic factors, attitudes, and the demographic controls outlined above. The full models extend the baseline by including all measures of father's involvement with children.

Table 4.3 gives the results of the panel regression model using indicators from both the time 1 and time 2 surveys. This model uses men's proportional contribution to housework at time 2 as the outcome variable—predicted both by time 2 scores on attitudes (expected to be relatively static over time) and controls, as well as by *changes* between time 1 and time 2 in women's and men's employment hours and in women's relative resources. Measures of men's involvement with their children at time 2 are also included as predictors, as is the lagged dependent variable, men's percentage of housework at time 1. The use of a combination of change scores and time 2 measures to predict the dependent variable allows us to assess the impact of men's involvement with their children, while controlling for *changes* in time availability and resources.

FINDINGS

As table 4.1 shows, although women continue to do the bulk of the routine housework, men increased their proportionate participation over the five-year period, from 19 percent to 22 percent. Men's absolute hours increased slightly only in the areas of laundry and grocery shopping, but because women's total hourly contributions declined even more, men ended up doing a greater percentage of the total housework by the time of the latter survey. Paid employment hours for both men and women increased significantly over the five-year period (5.5 hours for the men and 6.4 hours for the women), though the women, on average, continued to work many fewer hours than the men (26.7 vs. 44 hours at time 2). Even so, the mean percentage of the couple's income contributed by the woman increased from 25 percent to 31 percent. At

---

household income (see Coltrane 1999). Adding these variables did not significantly alter the results for any other variables in the equations, and coefficients for the introduced control variables did not approach statistical significance. To avoid problems associated with missing data, we do not include these additional controls in the regression models.

both time periods, men are significantly more conservative on work/ family issues than women: they endorse separate-spheres ideology and are less likely to endorse the sharing of housework. Nevertheless, they are more likely than women to embrace liberal attitudes toward sexual practices. In terms of age, the men in our sample average 42.4 years old at time 2, while the women are slightly younger (average 40.1 years); not unexpectedly, therefore, these couples have fewer children in the 0 to 4-year-old age bracket and more children 5 to 18 years of age. Finally, the men in our sample appear to be slightly better educated than the women.

Both men and women reported spending slightly less time with their children in all measured activities (except attending sports for women and driving for both men and women) at time 2 as compared to time 1. As shown in table 4.1, however, patterns of parent-child interaction at both time periods varied considerably by gender. In nine out of ten activities, mothers spent more time with children than fathers. Differences between mothers and fathers were largest for child-centered activities. For example, the average father helped a child with homework less than once per week, whereas the average mother helped a child with homework about twice per week. Mothers also had more frequent private talks with their children and spent an hour more each week driving children than did fathers. Similarly, mothers tended to spend about an hour more per week than fathers attending school activities. Only for attending or coaching youth sports activities did men's contributions exceed women's. In fact, the coaching variable represented the leading youth group activity for fathers, constituting just over half of the time spent by fathers at time 2 in such public pursuits (2.22 hours/week for coaching vs. 2.18 hours/week for attending a combination of school activities, religious groups, or community youth groups). In summary, though both fathers and mothers spend time in nurturing and child-centered activities, such parenting practices are the most gender-segregated. Adult-centered activities of leisure, play, and watching television are more equally divided between mothers and fathers. Finally, relative participation of mothers and fathers in community-centered activities varies by specific group or setting, with fathers most likely to be involved with sports, and mothers most likely to be involved with school.

Table 4.2 allows us to isolate the cross-sectional predictors of men's relative participation in routine housework at each of the two survey dates. If the mother is employed more hours and if she earns a greater

TABLE 4.1

PARTICIPATION IN ROUTINE HOUSEHOLD TASKS BY GENDER

Variables	Time 1				Time 2			
	Men		Women		Men		Women	
	Mean	S.D	Mean	S.D.	Mean	S.D.	Mean	S.D.
Routine housework								
Percent of couple hours	19%	0.16	81%	0.16	22%	0.16	78%	0.16
Cooking (hours per week)	2.72	3.90	11.07	6.09	2.70	3.31	9.82	5.53
Meal cleanup (hours per week)	2.09	3.27	7.05	5.05	1.92	2.47	6.33	4.38
Housecleaning (hours per week)	2.11	3.28	9.68	6.57	2.0	2.76	8.61	5.74
Laundry (hours per week)	0.88	1.97	5.56	4.27	1.0	1.82	5.41	3.80
Grocery shopping (hours per week)	1.51	2.04	3.49	2.99	1.56	1.93	3.67	2.57
Economics								
Paid employment hours (hours per week)	38.54	21.88	20.33	20.27	44.0	19.06	26.71	20.69
Percent of couple income	75%	0.26	25%	.25	67.1%	0.289	31.2%	0.278
Attitudes								
Liberal dual-spheres ideology (range = 4 to 24)	11.34	4.57	12.11	4.80	10.44	3.21	11.27	3.38
Liberal sexual attitudes (range = 4 to 24)	10.67	3.97	10.25	3.88	10.33	3.61	10.03	3.58
Belief in sharing housework (range = 1 to 5)	4.03	0.77	4.25	0.75	3.60	0.98	3.75	0.92
Demographics								
Age	36.58	6.42	34.28	5.70	42.4	6.49	40.08	5.65
Level of education[a]	3.69	1.89	3.45	1.86	13.08	2.89	12.83	2.65
No. of children in household age 0 to 4	0.49	0.71	—	—	0.15	0.44	—	—
No. of children in household age 5 to 18	1.99	1.02	—	—	2.02	1.01	—	—

Activities with children

Frequency leisure outings (range = 1 to 6)	3.53	1.29	3.79	1.34	3.23	1.33	3.33	1.27
Frequency at-home play (range = 1 to 6)	4.34	1.31	4.66	1.32	3.67	1.35	3.99	1.39
Frequency private talks (range = 1 to 6)	3.64	1.46	4.45	1.34	3.27	1.34	4.19	1.29
Frequency helping with homework (range = 1 to 6)	3.90	1.57	4.96	1.31	3.41	1.61	4.41	1.57
Frequency watching TV (range = 1 to 6)[b]	—	—	—	—	4.50	1.28	4.82	1.16
Driving household members (avg./wk.)	1.97	3.08	2.99	2.64	2.05	2.64	3.04	3.14
Attending school activities (avg./wk.)	1.16	7.25	2.01	7.68	0.81	3.12	1.78	4.15
Attending religious youth groups (avg./wk.)	1.19	7.16	1.58	7.76	0.84	3.63	1.40	4.30
Attending community youth groups (avg./wk.)	0.92	7.47	0.97	6.58	0.53	2.58	0.76	3.18
Attending sports youth groups (avg./wk.)	2.52	10.15	1.35	5.36	2.22	6.08	1.83	5.37

[a] Due to inconsistencies in the coding for education at time 1 between main respondent and spouse/partner, time 1 education completed has been recoded categorically, such that, educational level 3 is roughly equivalent to an Associate Degree (i.e., some college education completed). For time 2, education is measured in years completed.
[b] Measured at time 2 only.

TABLE 4.2

OLS REGRESSION COEFFICIENTS PREDICTING MEN'S PERCENTAGE OF HOUSEWORK

	Regression Models			
	Time 1		Time 2	
Independent Variables	Baseline[a]	Full Model[a]	Baseline[a]	Full Model[a]
Economics				
Woman's employment hours	0.218***	0.230***	0.202***	0.192***
Man's employment hours	-0.144***	-0.199***	-0.173***	-0.170***
Woman's proportion of couple income	0.183***	0.176***	0.113***	0.106**
Attitudes				
Man's liberal dual-spheres ideology	-0.024	-0.010	0.113**	0.133***
Woman's liberal dual-spheres ideology	0.046	0.016	0.049	0.035
Man's liberal sexual attitudes	0.145***	0.104*	-0.014	0.007
Woman's liberal sexual attitudes	0.014	0.073	0.042	0.040
Man's attitude toward sharing housework	0.266***	0.237***	0.124***	0.110***
Woman's attitude toward sharing housework	0.110**	0.120**	0.034	0.057
Demographics				
Man's age	0.049	0.043	0.022	0.038
Man's educational level	0.045	0.073	0.120***	0.087**
No. of children in household age 0 to 4 years	0.010	0.035	0.005	0.001
No. of children in household age 5 to 18 years	0.010	-0.008	0.022	0.014

Men's activities with children

	(1)	(2)	(3)	(4)
Leisure outings	—[a]	−0.006	—	−0.015
Playing at home	—	−0.032	—	−0.017
Private talks	—	−0.110*	—	0.028
Helping with homework	—	0.170***	—	0.124***
Watching television[b]	—	—	—	−0.047
Driving household members	—	0.099**	—	0.144***
Attending school activities	—	0.049	—	0.009
Attending religious youth groups	—	−0.013	—	−0.022
Attending community youth groups	—	0.015	—	0.085*
Attending sports youth groups	—	−0.056	—	−0.021
R^2	0.277	0.395	0.190	0.258
Adjusted R^2	0.261	0.363	0.179	0.235
F-score	17.226***	12.652***	17.397***	11.357***
N	598	450	981	777

*$p < .05$ **$p < .01$ ***$p < .001$

[a] Standard coefficient.

[b] Measured at time 2

share of the couple income, then her partner does a larger share of the housework. Similarly, if the father is employed fewer hours, then he does a larger share of the housework. Ideology as a predictor is less consistent, though results are provocative. His liberal sexual attitudes predict his greater participation at time 1, and his liberal separate-spheres ideology predicts more participation at time 2 (but neither her sexual attitudes nor her separate-spheres ideology are significant predictors of his housework at either time 1 or time 2). In terms of more "localized" housework-sharing attitudes, while the man's attitude toward sharing is strongly and positively associated with his doing more housework at both time 1 and time 2 (and for both the baseline and full models), the woman's attitude toward sharing is only associated significantly with the man contributing to household labor at time 1 (at $p < .01$), and her attitude proves to be a less powerful predictor than his. Contrary to findings from some earlier studies suggesting that men only respond to women's attitudes and beliefs about family work, in this sample, men's participation in housework is more clearly aligned with their own attitudes and beliefs than with those of their female spouse/partner. Following earlier research, we also find that more highly educated men report doing a larger percentage of the housework, although this finding is stronger and more consistent at time 2.[4]

In terms of men's involvement with their children, time spent in private talks, time spent helping children with homework, and time spent in driving (chauffeuring) are all significant predictors of men's proportional participation in routine housework at time 1, with homework help predicting the most variance of the three. At time 2, both homework help and driving continue to be strong and significant predictors, although driving overtakes homework as the leading indicator. Also at time 2, men's time participating as a leader or advisor in a community youth group (such as Cub Scouts, Brownies, or Campfire Boys and Girls) becomes significant, somewhat below the level of helping with homework and driving. Though not reaching statistical significance, signs are negative for coefficients associated with fathers playing with children, watching television with them, attending religious youth groups, or participating with sports teams. Looking at the R^2 for each of the models,

4. As mentioned (see footnote 1), there was a methodological discrepancy with measurement of education at time 1. This could account for the lack of significant finding regarding men's education in the baseline model for time 1; the strong and consistent finding of significance at time 2 suggests that when measured as "years of education completed," men's education is related to their greater participation in routine housework.

we note that by including variables for men's involvement with their children, the amount of explained variance in men's level of housework increases substantially, with R^2 rising from .277 to .395 at time 1 (baseline to full model) and from .190 to .258 at time 2. As noted above, this substantial increase in explained variance is attributable to the inclusion of variables measuring child-centered fathering activities.

Table 4.3 shows the results of changes over time. As expected, men's percentage of housework at time 1 (the lagged dependent variable) is the best predictor of how much of the housework they do at time 2. Moreover, the *change* in both women's and men's paid employment hours from time 1 to time 2 affects men's proportion of housework at time 2: the more men's employment hours decrease and the more women's employment hours increase, the more housework men will do at time 2. Interestingly, the change in women's employment hours has about twice the impact on men's relative contribution than does the change in his employment hours (beta [standardized regression coefficient] = 0.152 for women and beta = −0.075 for men). Unlike some previous studies, we find that change in women's proportion of couple earnings significantly predicts a change in men's share of routine housework (beta =.110, $p < .01$). Net of these employment effects, men's liberal separate-spheres ideology and women's liberal attitudes toward sharing housework predict greater sharing ($p < .05$). Of the demographic controls, only men's age is significant, with relatively older men contributing more to routine housework. In terms of variables measuring men's involvement with children, driving and spending time in religious group activities are the only variables to reach statistical significance. Driving performs well, accounting for almost as much of the explained variance (beta = .134, $p < .001$) as the change in women's employment hours. Even after controlling for the amount of housework sharing at time 1 and other variables, men who spend more time driving their children are significantly more likely than other men to share housework at time 2. In contrast, men who spend more time attending religious youth groups with their children are significantly *less* likely to share the housework (beta = −.089, $p < .05$). As in the cross-sectional models, the signs for variables measuring men's time playing with children, watching television with them, and coaching their sports teams are all negative. The longitudinal analysis thus confirms the cross-sectional finding that child-centered fathering is associated with more sharing of domestic work, whereas adult-centered fathering is associated with less sharing of domestic work.

TABLE 4.3

PANEL REGRESSION COEFFICIENTS PREDICTING MEN'S PERCENTAGE OF HOUSEWORK

Independent Variables	Panel Regression Model		
	Regression Coefficient	Standardized Regression Coefficient	Standard Error
Lagged dependent variable men's percentage of housework at time 1	0.485***	0.473	0.039
Economics			
Change in woman's employment hours	0.001***	0.152	0.0003
Change in man's employment hours	−0.001*	−0.075	0.0003
Change in woman's proportion of couple income	0.067**	0.110	0.022
Attitudes (measured at time 2)			
Man's liberal dual-spheres ideology	0.005*	0.100	0.002
Woman's liberal dual-spheres ideology	0.003	0.069	0.002
Man's liberal sexual attitudes	0.001	0.019	0.002
Woman's liberal sexual attitudes	0.001	0.020	0.002
Man's attitude toward sharing housework	0.007	0.042	0.006
Woman's attitude toward sharing housework	0.014*	0.083	0.006
Demographics (measured at time 2)			
Man's age	0.002*	0.078	0.001
Man's educational level	0.002	0.036	0.002
No. of children in household between 0 and 4 years old	0.011	0.029	0.015
No. of children in household between 5 and 18 years old	0.007	0.040	0.007

Men's activities with children (measured at time 2)

Leisure outings	0.002	0.017	0.005
Playing at home	−0.004	−0.031	0.006
Private talks	0.003	0.024	0.005
Helping with homework	0.005	0.053	0.004
Watcing television	−0.007	−0.057	0.005
Driving household members	0.009***	0.134	0.002
Attending children's school activities	0.001	0.009	0.002
Attending religious youth groups	−0.005*	−0.089	0.002
Attending community youth groups	0.004	0.045	0.003
Attending sports youth groups	−0.000	−0.012	0.001
R^2	0.396		
Adjusted R^2	0.367		
F-score	13.665***		
N	526		

*$p < .05$ **$p < .01$ ***$p < .001$

DISCUSSION

We began this chapter by highlighting the increasing similarity between men's and women's work/family conflicts. We also cited some rhetoric from family values advocates who warn men against trying to act like mothers. We are now in a position to evaluate the merits of these opposing views.

Our analysis of national survey data shows that while mothers continue to shoulder most of the burdens of housework and child care, things are slowly changing. As men's relative contributions to family work inch up, it is useful to explore the conditions under which more sharing of the most mundane and burdensome tasks might occur. As women increase their employment hours and earnings, they cut back on the number of hours they spend in domestic work. We thus find that the hidden aspects of economic power in the marriage play a major role in the allocation of the most routine and mundane parenting and housekeeping tasks. It does matter what jobs people hold, how many hours they work, and how much money they make. Though people like to think that market forces and power politics do not operate within marriages and families, our analysis shows that they are ever-present. This does not mean that most men and women fight openly about who should do the housework; quite the opposite. These underlying economic imbalances undergird domestic divisions of labor and help set the stage for subtle negotiations about who should do what in families. One of the most important implications of our findings is that as women's occupational resources come to resemble those of men, we will see more sharing of housework. Our study is also about how parenting might draw men into doing more housework. In particular, we find that when men get involved in specific types of parenting activities, they are more likely to share housework and child maintenance with their wives and partners. This has important implications for the future of gender equality within marriages and for the future well-being of children.

Our analysis of national survey data shows that men's child-centered parenting, including driving, helping with homework, and having private talks, is associated with more sharing of the cooking, meal cleanup, shopping, housecleaning, and laundry.[5] In other words, when men par-

---

5. When we substitute means for missing values, we obtain substantially similar results in all regression models (results not shown). In the final panel regression model, however,

ticipate in the more nurturing and supportive activities that serve children, they are also more likely to share in child and home maintenance activities. In contrast, when men participate in adult-centered parenting, they are somewhat less likely to share domestic work with their wives. If fathers' time with children revolves around play, leisure activities, and watching television, they are no more likely than other fathers to take responsibility for the routine work of child maintenance and household upkeep. And in general, if men are involved with children as leaders or members of religious or sports groups, they are less likely to participate in the housework.

Among the different parenting variables in the final panel regression model, only change in men's time with religious youth groups is negatively and significantly associated with men's other family work. This calls into question the assertion by Promise Keepers and other religious-based organizations that making men moral leaders will make them "submissive" to their wives' hopes of getting help around the house. Fathers' participation with children in these community activities, though hypothesized to increase children's social capital, may not relieve any of the responsibility women carry for domestic work. Though fathers' involvement in community youth groups such as Cub Scouts and Brownies, or perhaps the PTA, is associated with men sharing more housework, their participation in other youth groups tends to have the opposite effect. Although men are most likely to participate in their children's sports activities, there is some indication that this type of father involvement lessens the likelihood that a man will participate in the more routine child and home maintenance tasks.[6]

RAISING EXPECTATIONS FOR FATHERS

In this analysis, we have shown that child-centered forms of father engagement are associated with men doing more domestic work. Our analysis suggests that when men take responsibility for the care and nurturing of children, they also begin to assume more responsibility for routine household tasks like cooking, cleaning, and laundry. The aver-

---

helping children with homework becomes a significant predictor of men doing more of the housework.

6. When change scores for father involvement are used in the panel regression, men's participation as a coach or sports activity attendant replaces religious youth group participation as a significant predictor of men doing less of the housework.

age mother still does over three-fourths of this work, but there are indications that the gender-segregated division of labor is no longer taken
for granted in many American households. The conditions promoting
the sharing of family work—including more equal earnings, more similar employment schedules, and gender egalitarian ideologies—are all
more likely to occur than they were just a decade ago. In addition, child-
centered fathering appears to pull men into doing more of the housework. Since men's child-centered parenting has been found to promote
positive outcomes for both children and fathers, and because men's partial assumption of responsibility for housework reduces wives' stress,
why don't we ask men to do more?

According to some recent advocates of "responsible" fatherhood,
most academics have focused too much on how men interact with children and placed too much emphasis on the things that men do not do.
In place of this "deficit model" they propose a nostalgic vision of fatherhood, one that focuses on the breadwinning and moral leadership
that males are supposedly biologically equipped to provide. Instead of
focusing on men's emotional or domestic shortcomings and their lack
of direct participation in child care and housework, researchers and
practitioners are encouraged to make men feel better about themselves
so that they will stay involved in family life.

LaRossa (1988) suggests that marital conflict may be on the rise because the "culture" of involved fatherhood far outstrips the actual "conduct" of fathers, leading American men to become increasingly ambivalent about their participation in family life. To address these "very real
negative consequences," LaRossa contends that "scholars and representatives of the media must commit themselves to presenting a balanced
picture of 'new fatherhood'" (1988, 454, 456). Presumably, the pro-
moters of gender-segregated responsible fatherhood are attempting this
when they call for a focus on men's economic provisioning and moral
leadership (rather than on their actual contributions to housework and
child care). But promoting a categorical distinction between mothering
and fathering and lowering our expectations for direct participation
from fathers carries a risk. Most mothers and fathers *do* act differently,
and many *are* happy with that arrangement. But even apparently benign
assumptions about inherent parenting differences resonate with claims
made by those who advocate a return to patriarchal family arrangements
(Coltrane and Hickman 1992). Critical theories show that an emphasis
on essential gender difference helps men maintain power over women
and other, less privileged men (Connell 1987; Lorber 1994). Men's do-

mestic incompetence and emotional inexpressiveness (both feigned and real) also act as resources that men use to protect their privileged status (Goode 1992; Sattel 1998). Accepting parental gender differences as natural thus serves to maintain hierarchical structures both inside families and in the larger society. Whether absent or physically present and doing little, the ability of fathers to stay aloof from day-to-day family life is fundamentally linked to the reproduction of systemic male dominance (e.g., Coltrane 1996; Hochschild 1989; Thompson and Walker 1989).

Because categorical beliefs in parenting and gender differences mask relations of power and inequality, asking fathers to do more family work is both discomforting and necessary. It may be overly optimistic to assume that men will do half the parenting and housework in most families, but we should not automatically set significantly lower standards for fathers than for mothers. We need to stop assuming that men are incapable of nurturing children, folding the laundry, or cleaning the toilets. Direct comparisons between fathers and mothers can lead to discomfort and marital conflict, but these direct comparisons can also open productive dialogues about women's reluctance to share family work and men's inattentiveness to home and children. As men share more of the burdens of child care and housework, their stress levels go up, but Hawkins and Belsky (1989, 383) warn against simplistic interpretation of such "negative" findings: "Changes in which some men become a little more caring of others and a little less happy with themselves could hardly be described as negative." Instead of seeing an increase in men's discomfort as justification for lowering expectations and returning to patriarchal definitions of fatherhood, we ought to view men's and women's struggles to share more family work as an opportunity for promoting three worthy goals: (1) emotional growth of men through nurturing father work, (2) optimum development of children through child-centered parenting, and (3) equal rights for women through equitable marriages.

REFERENCES

Amato, Paul. 1987. *Children in Australian families: The growth of competence.* New York: Prentice-Hall.
Barnett, Rosalind C., and Yu-Chu Shen. 1997. Gender, high- and low-schedule-control housework tasks, and psychological distress: A study of dual-earner couples. *Journal of Family Issues* 18:403–28.
Blair, Sampson Lee, and Daniel T. Lichter. 1991. Measuring the division of

household labor: Gender segregation of housework among American couples. *Journal of Family Issues* 12:91–113.

Blankenhorn, David. 1995. *Fatherless America: Confronting our most urgent social problem.* New York: Basic Books.

Bumpass, Larry L., and James A. Sweet. 1989. National estimates of cohabitation. *Demography* 26:615–25.

Coleman, James S. 1994. *Foundations of social theory.* Cambridge, Mass.: Harvard University Press.

Coltrane, Scott. 1989. Household labor and the routine production of gender. *Social Problems* 36:473–90.

———. 1996. *Family man: Fatherhood, housework, and gender equity.* New York: Oxford University Press.

———. 2000. Research on household labor: Modeling and measuring the social embeddedness of routine family work. *Journal of Marriage and the Family* 62:363–89.

Coltrane, Scott, and Neal Hickman. 1992. The rhetoric of rights and needs: Moral discourse in the reform of child custody and child support laws. *Social Problems* 39:400–420.

Coltrane, Scott, and Ross D. Parke. 1998. Reinventing fatherhood: Toward an historical understanding of continuity and change in men's family lives. Philadelphia: National Center on Fathers and Families, WP 98-12A.

Connell, R. W. 1987. *Gender and power: Society, the person, and sexual politics.* Stanford: Stanford University Press.

Cowan, Carolyn P., and Philip A. Cowan. 1992. *When partners become parents.* New York: Basic Books.

Demo, David H., and Alan C. Acock. 1993. Family diversity and the division of domestic labor: How much have things really changed? *Family Relations* 42:323–31.

Doherty, William J. 1991. Beyond reactivity and the deficit model of manhood: A commentary on articles by Napier, Pittman, and Gottman. *Journal of Marital and Family Therapy* 17:29–32.

Doherty, William J., Edward F. Kouneski, and Martha F. Erickson. 1998. Responsible fathering: An overview and conceptual framework. *Journal of Marriage and the Family* 60:277–92.

Ehrensaft, Diane. 1987. *Parenting together.* New York: Free Press.

Fein, Robert A. 1978. Research on fathering: Social policy and an emergent perspective. *Journal of Social Issues* 34:122–35.

Fish, Linda Stone, Rebecca S. New, and Nancy J. Van Cleave. 1996. Shared parenting in dual-income families. *American Journal of Orthopsychiatry* 62: 83–92.

Glenn, Norval. 1997. *Closed hearts, closed minds: The textbook story of marriage.* New York: Institute for American Values.

Goode, William J. 1992. Why men resist. In *Rethinking the family,* edited by B. Thorne, with M. Yalom. Boston: Northeastern University Press.

Griswold, Robert L. 1993. *Fatherhood in America: A history.* New York: Basic Books.

Hawkins, Alan J., and Jay Belsky. 1989. The role of father involvement in personality change in men across the transition to parenthood. *Family Relations* 38:378–84.

Hawkins, Alan J., and David C. Dollahite. 1997. Beyond the role-inadequacy perspective of fathering. In *Generative fathering: Beyond deficit perspectives,* edited by A. J. Hawkins and D. C. Dollahite. Thousand Oaks, Calif.: Sage Publications.

Hersch, Joni, and Leslie S. Stratton, 1997. Housework, fixed effects, and wages of married workers. *Journal of Human Resources* 32:285–307.

Hochschild, Arlie, with Anne Machung. 1989. *The second shift: Working parents and the revolution at home.* New York: Viking.

Johnson, Elizabeth M., and Ted L. Huston. 1998. The perils of love, or why wives adapt to husbands during the transition to parenthood. *Journal of Marriage and the Family* 60:195–204.

Kposowa, Augustine J. 1993. The impact of immigration on native earnings in the United States, 1940 to 1980. *Applied Behavioral Science Review* 1(1):1–25.

Lamb, Michael E. 1976. *The role of the father in child development.* New York: John Wiley.

———. 1987. *The father's role: Cross-cultural perspectives.* Hillsdale, N.J.: Lawrence Erlbaum.

Lamb, Michael E., Joseph H. Pleck, Eric L. Charnov, and James A. Levine. 1987. A biosocial perspective on paternal behavior and involvement. In *Parenting across the lifespan: Biosocial dimensions,* edited by J. B. Lancaster, J. Altmann, A. S. Rossi, and L. R. Sherrod. New York: Aldine de Gruyter.

LaRossa, Ralph. 1988. Fatherhood and social change. *Family Relations* 37:451–57.

Levine, James A., and Todd L. Pittinsky. 1997. *Working fathers: New strategies for balancing work and family.* New York: Harcourt Brace.

Lorber, Judith. 1994. *Paradoxes of gender.* New Haven: Yale University Press.

MacDermid, Shelley M., Ted L. Huston, and Susan M. McHale. 1990. Changes in marriage associated with the transition to parenthood: Individual differences as a function of sex-role attitudes and changes in the division of household labor. *Journal of Marriage and the Family* 52:475–86.

Mackey, Wade C. 1985. *Fathering behaviors: The dynamics of the man-child bond.* New York: Plenum Press.

Marsiglio, William, Randal D. Day, V. Jeffery Evans, Michael Lamb, Sanford Braver, and Elizabeth Peters. 1998. Report of the Working Group on Conceptualizing Male Parenting. In *Nurturing fatherhood: Improving data and research on male fertility, family formation, and fatherhood.* Washington, D.C.: Federal Interagency Forum on Child and Family Statistics.

McBride, Brent A. 1989. Stress and fathers' parental competence: Implications for family life and parent educators. *Family Relations* 38:385–89.

Mintz, Steven. 1998. From patriarchy to androgyny and other myths: Placing men's family roles in historical perspective. In *Men in families: When do they get involved? What difference does it make?,* edited by A. Booth and A. C. Crouter. Mahwah, N.J.: Lawrence Erlbaum.

Nock, Steven L. 1998. *Marriage in men's lives.* New York: Oxford University Press.

O'Connell, Martin. 1994. *Where's papa?: Fathers' role in child care.* Washington, D.C.: Population Reference Bureau.

Palkovitz, Rob. 1984. Parental attitudes and fathers' interactions with their 5-month-old infants. *Developmental Psychology* 20:1054–60.

Parke, Ross D. 1981. *Fathers.* Cambridge, Mass.: Harvard University Press.

———. 1995. Fathers and families. In *Handbook of parenting,* vol. 3, edited by M. H. Bornstein. Hillsdale, N.J.: Lawrence Erlbaum.

———. 1996. *Fatherhood.* Cambridge, Mass.: Harvard University Press.

———. 1999. Father involvement: A developmental psychological perspective. *Marriage and Family Review* 29:43–58.

Pleck, Joseph H. 1983. Husbands' paid work and family roles: Current research issues. In *Research in the interweave of social roles,* vol. 3: *Families and jobs,* edited by H. Lopata and J. Pleck. Greenwich, Conn.: JAI.

———. 1997. Paternal involvement: Levels, sources, and consequences. In *The role of the father in child development,* 3d ed., edited by M. E. Lamb. New York: John Wiley.

Popenoe, David. 1996. *Life without father: Compelling new evidence that fatherhood and marriage are indispensable for the good of children and society.* New York: Martin Kessler/Free Press.

Press, Julie E., and Eleanor Townsley. 1998. Wives' and husbands' housework reporting: Gender, class, and social desirability. *Gender & Society* 12:188–218.

Presser, Harriet B. 1994. Employment schedules among dual-earner spouses and the division of household labor by gender. *American Sociological Review* 59:348–64.

Pruett, Kyle D. 1987. *The nurturing father.* New York: Warner Books.

———. 1993. The paternal presence. *Families in Society* 74:46–50.

Radin, Norma. 1994. Primary-caregiving fathers in intact families. In *Redefining families: Implications for children's development,* edited by A. E. Gottfried and A. W. Gottfried. New York: Plenum Press.

Risman, Barbara J., and Danette Johnson-Sumerford. 1998. Doing it fairly: A study of postgender marriages. *Journal of Marriage and the Family* 60:23–40.

Robinson, John P., and Geoffrey Godbey. 1997. *Time for life: The surprising ways that Americans use time.* University Park: Pennsylvania State University Press.

Russell, Graeme. 1983. *The changing role of fathers.* St. Lucia, Queensland: University of Queensland Press.

Sattel, Jack W. 1998. The inexpressive male. In *Men's lives,* 4th ed., edited by M. S. Kimmel and M. A. Messner. New York: Macmillan.

Shelton, Beth A. 1992. *Women, men, time.* New York: Greenwood.

Smock, Pamela J., and Wendy D. Manning. 1997. Cohabiting partners' economic circumstances and marriage. *Demography* 34:331–41.

Stacey, Judith. 1996. *In the name of the family: Rethinking family values in the postmodern age.* Boston: Beacon.

Thompson, Linda, and Alexis J. Walker. 1989. Gender in families: Women and
    men in marriage, work, and parenthood. *Journal of Marriage and the Family*
    51:845–71.
Zill, Nicholas, and Margaret Daly. 1993. National survey of families and house-
    holds. In *Researching the family: A guide to survey and statistical data on
    U.S. families*. Washington, D.C.: Child Trends.

PART TWO

CHANGING WORKPLACES

CHAPTER 5

Family-Responsive Benefits and the Two-Tiered Labor Market

Cynthia H. Deitch and Matt L. Huffman

INTRODUCTION

The literature on gender and the welfare state makes frequent reference to the history of a two-tiered benefit structure in public policy whereby women, especially mothers with dependent children, do not receive the same benefits, entitlements, or treatment as wage-earning men (e.g., Mink 1990; Pearce 1990). Unlike most Western industrialized nations, where more extensive provision of "family-responsive" benefits such as paid parental leave is provided or mandated by public policy as an extension of the welfare state (Kamerman and Kahn 1996), in the United States paid leave and other family benefits are mostly a matter of private employer provision. We ask: As more women and men become both wage earners and family caregivers, are private corporate and organizational policies creating yet another two-tiered family benefits structure in the United States?

A number of sources indicate that the burden of the conflict between work and family is greater for low-income than for more affluent women workers (Lambert 1999). Women in high-paying or upper-level professional and managerial jobs have more access to family-responsive benefits than do women in lower-paying jobs (Gerstel and McGonagle

The data used in this analysis were made available by the Interuniversity Consortium for Political and Social Research (ICPSR). Neither the collectors of the data nor the ICPSR are responsible for the analyses, interpretations, or conclusions presented here.

1999; Glass and Camarigg 1992; Raabe 1990; Starrels 1992). Individuals from upper-income households also tend to have more financial resources for resolving conflicts between work and family and consequently have more options available to them than do low-income working parents. As recent changes in U.S. welfare policy increase the pressure on single mothers living in poverty to take low-wage jobs with few benefits, lack of access to family-responsive benefits for the working poor may become a more urgent public policy problem.

One explanation for the unequal distribution of employer-provided family benefits for low-income versus more affluent workers is that professional and managerial workers have more leverage to individually negotiate with an employer for better leave arrangements and other benefits. Additionally, they are often in a position to be more selective about choosing jobs with superior benefits. Such explanations focus on the human capital and bargaining power of individuals. Another line of explanation, not incompatible with the first, focuses on employer practices, the structure of labor markets and work organizations, and other demand-side factors. Employers who invest meagerly in their workforce and hire primarily low-wage, less-skilled workers (which often means a large proportion of women and non-white employees) are unlikely to provide family benefits. In contrast, employers who have made a greater investment in their employees by offering opportunities for advancement and training and who rely primarily on a highly skilled, high-paid workforce are more likely to be concerned with issues such as employee turnover. Consequently, such employers are more likely to provide desirable benefit packages as a way to reap the greatest returns on their investment by reducing turnover, absenteeism, and training costs. Following the second line of explanation, in this chapter we examine the relationship between organizational characteristics and employer provision of family-responsive employment benefits in work organizations.

We also ask: Are family-responsive benefits simply an extension of more traditional fringe benefits—such as health, life, and disability insurance, and retirement pensions—such that organizations that already offer a wide range of benefits are most likely to expand their offerings to include family-responsive policies? Or are there different or additional factors that determine the provision of family-responsive benefits? There are a number of reasons to expect some differences. The expansion of conventional (or standard) fringe benefits took place in an earlier historical period; the development of newer, family-responsive benefits is occurring under markedly different social and economic conditions. As

Glass and Fujimoto (1995) suggest, standard fringe benefits developed at a time when the normative assumption was that the typical worker was a male breadwinner with a wife at home. Today that assumption no longer holds. Labor unions played a role in the spread of standard fringe benefits, and many of those benefits were institutionalized in a period of greater union strength (Freeman 1986) than today. The interest in and need for family-responsive benefits have spread in a period when employment instability due to downsizing, outsourcing, and use of contingent workers (such as part-time, temporary, and contract workers) is growing in many occupations, industries, and workplaces (Smith 1997). Contingent workers rarely receive fringe benefits. Finally, employer provision of conventional benefits is also changing as many employers shift more of the costs and provision of health insurance and retirement accounts to the individual employee. Given these changes, we cannot assume that the same factors associated with the development of conventional fringe benefits will necessarily explain the growth of family-responsive benefits.

WHAT PREVIOUS RESEARCH SUGGESTS

Previous research clearly establishes that there is a great deal of variation in the provision of family-responsive benefits by employers, both in the extent and type of benefits provided (Glass and Estes 1997). While several previous studies have attempted to determine how employer characteristics contribute to or constrain the development of family-supportive policies (Glass and Fujimoto 1995; Goodstein 1994; Guthrie and Roth 1999; Ingram and Simons 1995; Knoke 1996; Osterman 1995), the empirical results have been somewhat inconclusive. Inconsistent results may be due to differences across studies in the types of organizations sampled, the specific benefits studied, the specific organizational characteristics considered, or the explanatory frameworks used. Even when the results are similar, the theoretical explanations may differ, as discussed in this chapter (see Glass and Estes 1997 for a more complete review of this literature).

Organizational size, gender composition of the workforce, and unionization are among the most frequently considered explanatory variables in previous research. The most consistent finding is that larger organizations are more likely to offer family leave and child care benefits (Glass and Fujimoto 1995; Goodstein 1994; Knoke 1996; Osterman 1995). However, smaller organizations may be more likely to allow flexible work schedules (Glass and Fujimoto 1995). On the question of gender composition, Auerbach (1990), Goodstein (1994), and Seyler, Monroe, and Garan (1995) all found a higher percentage of women employees to be predictive of various family-supportive benefits. However, Osterman (1995) noted that the relationship was not significant when he controlled for a professional-technical core occupation, and Knoke (1996) found no significant effect of gender composition on the provision of family benefits. For unionization, Auerbach (1990) found a negative association between unionization and child care benefits, whereas Glass and Fujimoto (1995) reported no effect of unions on child care benefits and a negative effect on flexible scheduling. Both Osterman (1995) and Knoke (1996) found no significant effect for unionization on measures combining family leave and child care benefits.

Several studies contrast an economic rationality model with an institutionalist framework on organizations to explain the provision of family benefits (Glass and Fujimoto 1995; Goodstein 1994; Ingram and Simons 1995; Osterman 1995). Economic rationality models emphasize cost effectiveness and efficiency in the form of reduced turnover and absenteeism, increased productivity, and economic returns to investments in employee human capital as motivating the provision of family-responsive benefits. It would be more cost effective to provide family-responsive benefits in a large organization than a small one, and where the costs of turnover are high, considering the employer's investment and the need for experienced workers. If the external labor market is tight, employers may offer additional benefits to compete for workers, and family-responsive benefits may increase the likelihood of a parent, especially a mother of young children, to enter the workforce. On the other hand, increased competition for a share of market profits is likely to lead to a concern for the bottom line and to exert a negative impact on potential expansion of benefits.

Researchers using institutional theory argue that organizations respond to social pressures and constraints, not simply to cost effectiveness. Organizational environments, government regulatory policies, and the rise of professionalized human resource departments have helped shape employment policies in organizations (Glass and Fujimoto 1995; Goodstein 1994; Guthrie and Roth 1999; Ingram and Simons 1995; Osterman 1995). Institutionalists hypothesize that large organizations are more sensitive both to public image and to the policies and practices of other organizations in their environment; as such, the existence of a parent organization and location in the public sector may increase external pressure to conform to noneconomic pressures toward innovation (Scott 1992). Likewise, human resource professionals tend to advocate family-responsive benefits. Curiously, those drawing from institutional theory seem to assume that external pressure from professional associations, government agencies, and public opinion all support the expansion of family-responsive benefits despite the lack of clear public policy mandates. The institutional framework suggests that a greater concentration of women workers represents a larger constituency and therefore may increase the pressure for family benefits.

Glass and Fujimoto (1995) suggest that in contrast to the institutional framework, theories of workplace conflict and bureaucratic control would predict that because women workers and workers in predominantly female occupations and industries are less organized and have fewer employment alternatives, they have less power to secure benefits. Tight labor markets and unionization may ameliorate this disadvantage. As noted earlier, unions and collective bargaining agreements represent one form of employee power and have played an important role historically in the expansion of conventional employment fringe benefits such as health insurance and pensions. Professional associations may also help employees. Professional and managerial workers often use their skills and marketability as leverage in bargaining individually for benefits.

A LABOR MARKET STRATIFICATION PERSPECTIVE

The idea of a two-tiered or segmented labor market suggests a distinction between good and bad jobs, with limited opportunity for mobility across strata (see Beck, Horan, and Tolbert 1978). Well-paying jobs, career ladders, opportunity for further training, union strength, and regular employment (full-time, nontemporary) are structural features of organizations often associated with "good" jobs, though not all workers within an organization necessarily benefit equally from these features. We use the phrase "two-tiered labor market" as an abstract metaphor to represent a diverse range of bifurcation processes described by contemporary organization and labor market analyses (Smith 1997), not literally limited to only two mutually exclusive strata. Stratification processes, such as hiring contingent versus "regular" employees, occur within organizations, occupations, and industries, as well as between them.

Focusing on the stratification dimensions of the provision of family-responsive benefits, we investigate how the gender, race, and class composition of an establishment's workforce is related to employer policies in providing family-responsive benefits. We consider unionization an indicator of the level of collective organization and bargaining strength of rank-and-file workers. We also examine how the use of contingent workers affects the structuring of benefits offered by organizations. We view well-developed internal labor markets and availability of job training as stratification measures (and not just benchmarks of bureaucratization) because they indicate career ladders and opportunities for advancement—key features distinguishing upper-tier or "good" jobs from dead-end jobs.

Regarding the gender composition of an organization's workforce, previous studies have only considered a linear relationship whereby an increase in the proportion of women is predicted to result in a simple additive change in the availability of benefits. After reviewing the divergent hypotheses and inconclusive results from previous studies, we predict a curvilinear relationship between women as a percentage of the workforce and provision of family-responsive benefits, with either a very high concentration or relative exclusion of women associated with less family-responsive policy. When the representation of women is very low, women as a group tend to have little power and employers are unlikely to perceive economic or institutional incentives to initiate family-responsive benefits. Predominantly female workplaces, industries, and occupations are often associated with lower wages, fewer benefits, and less bargaining power for workers than settings with a more gender-balanced or predominantly male workforce.

In our analysis we also explore the effects of organizational size, bureaucratic structure, and organizational environment by examining a number of variables suggested in the literature by both the economic rationality and the institutional perspectives. We note that the competing explanatory frameworks outlined earlier sometimes predict similar results and that their competing interpretations are not always incompatible. All else equal, we expect that larger size, the existence of a parent organization, the presence of a separate human resources (or personnel) department, operation in the public sector, and a tight labor market will be positively associated with the level of family-responsive benefits. In contrast, we expect a competitive product environment to have a negative effect on benefits.

Following Raabe (1990), we view all work organizations as having a work/family structure, with the total absence of any family-responsive benefits representing a specific (but not uncommon) structural condition of employment. We conceptualize the distribution of family-responsive benefits as not simply a question of how individuals fare in the labor market, but also as an outcome of how work organizations are structured. Accordingly, we use the work establishment as the unit of analysis for this study. We use the term "family-responsive" to refer to a range of benefits and options that potentially help workers reduce conflict between the demands of holding a job and taking care of dependent family members. We focus primarily on fringe-benefit policies such as family leave and child care assistance, and treat flexible scheduling separately.

DATA, MEASURES, AND MODELS

To explore the link between organizational characteristics and the provision of family-responsive benefits, we analyze data from the 1991 National Organizations Survey (NOS) (Kalleberg et al. 1991). The NOS is a nationally representative sample of organizations that provides detailed information on the workforce composition, employment policies and practices, benefits, and other organizational features of 727 U.S. work establishments. While a number of other studies of employer provision of family-responsive benefits are limited to data on only medium or large organizations (Guthrie and Roth 1999; Osterman 1995), private-sector companies (Osterman 1995), or specific geographic areas (Auerbach 1990; Glass and Fujimoto 1995; Goodstein 1994), the NOS data do not have these limitations.[1] As with previous studies cited earlier,

---

1. The NOS is a follow-up to the 1991 General Social Survey (GSS), a representative sample of U.S. adults. The 1991 GSS contained a section on work attitudes and employment that included questions about job circumstances, supervisory duties, and other work-related issues. Employed GSS respondents and their spouses identified their places of employment, which resulted in the identification of approximately 1,100 establishments. Of these, 727 establishments agreed to a request for an interview with a knowledgeable personnel official. These "NOS informants" were typically personnel directors, owners, or chief managers (Kalleberg and Van Buren 1994). They were asked about job- and establishment-level attributes of the employing organization. The result is a statistically representative national sample of 688 unique work establishments (39 of the original 727 were duplicates), with organizational-level information provided by the NOS informant. Because of the sampling design, the NOS observations can be weighted inversely proportional to the number of employees in an establishment if one wants to describe the population of work establishments as if each has an equal chance of inclusion in the sample (Marsden, Cook, and Knoke 1994). In contrast, the unweighted data represent the typical work settings encountered by workers in the United States. Because we are interested in the kinds of workplaces experienced by individuals, our analyses are based on the unweighted NOS sample.

the NOS data tell us about the existence of formal policies, but not how extensively a policy is actually implemented or who is eligible for benefits.

MEASURES

Family-Responsive Benefits   We constructed an additive index of family-responsive benefits by summing seven individual items, each coded 1 for the presence of the policy and 0 for no policy. The seven items are: (1) maternity or paternity leave with full reemployment rights, (2) paid parental leave for employees who have just had children, (3) other unpaid parental leave, (4) assistance in caring for elderly family members (not further defined), (5) sick leave with full pay, (6) either employer-provided child care (a day care program for employees' children either on site or off site) or child care subsidy (help for employees in covering any of the costs of child care, including "flexible spending"), and (7) provision of information to employees on child care services in the community. An establishment's score on this index is equal to the number of policies present out of the possible seven. The reliability coefficient for the index (Cronbach's alpha of 0.70) indicates that statistically the seven family benefits are appropriately intercorrelated to combine in a single index.

We include sick leave with pay in this index for two reasons. First, Knoke (1996) showed that this item fits with other family benefits in his factor analysis of the NOS data. Second, paid sick leave is an important source of unofficial family leave. In the index we combine provision of child care services and child care subsidy as either/or (as did Knoke 1996) because it is extremely rare for any of the organizations in the sample to do both. We do not include flexible scheduling in the family benefits index because flextime does not correlate strongly enough with other family benefit items (Knoke 1996), and because flexible scheduling may mean flexible in terms of the employer's convenience in some cases and in terms of the employee's choice in others. In portions of the analysis we examine, separate from the additive index, selected individual policy items, including paid parental leave, child care services, child care cost subsidy, and flextime.

We also use an additive index of conventional or standard fringe benefits. Following Knoke's (1996) factor analysis of the NOS benefits measures, the index includes six items: medical or hospital insurance, dental care benefits, life insurance, pension or retirement programs, long-term disability insurance, and drug or alcohol abuse programs. As before, the score on this index equals the number of policies provided out of the six possible. The conventional benefits index has a reliability coefficient (Cronbach's alpha) of 0.87, again indicating that the items are appropriately intercorrelated.

Organizational Characteristics   We examine the relationship between the prevalence of family-responsive and conventional benefits described above and several organizational characteristics suggested in the literature. One group of variables we consider relates to organizational size and bureaucratic structure. These include organizational size (log of the number of full-time employees) plus dichotomous (two-category) variables indicating whether the organization is affiliated with a parent company (1 = yes, 0 = no), whether it operates in the public sector (1 = yes, 0 = no), and whether it has a separate personnel department (1 = yes, 0 = no). Another set of variables reflects the external environment in which the organization operates, including a tight labor market index (range of 0–8), which indicates difficulty in hiring and retaining qualified workers, and a competitive product environment (range of 1–4).

Many NOS questions targeted the "core" occupation, which is the job title that the respondent gave as most directly associated with the organization's main product or service (Kalleberg and Van Buren 1994). Our labor market stratification variables include a dichotomous variable coded 1 for a professional or managerial core occupation (as defined by the U.S. Bureau of the Census) and 0 for any other core occupation, as well as the log of annual earnings of most core employees. Core income, as reported by the NOS informant, is the response to a question about what most core employees earn. Women as a proportion of full-time employees is measured on a 0 to 100 percent scale. A dichotomous variable for race is coded 1 for establishments whose total workforce is at least 10 percent non-white (0 otherwise) because approximately 10 percent non-white is the average for the NOS sample. We use full-time workers for gender and race composition because a large number of establishments did not provide information on the gender composition of their part-time workforce, and the NOS survey did not ask about the racial composition of part-time employees. Along with percentage of women, we include a variable for percentage of women squared in the regression equations; this enables us to test for a curvilinear effect of gender composition. Other variables of substantive interest related to the bifurcated labor market concept are: proportion of unionized workers in each establishment's industry, opportunity for advancement and training measured by an internal labor market index (range of 0–5), annual training dollars spent per full-time employee, and use of contingent (defined here as part-time and temporary) workers (index range is 0–4). All variables are described in more detail in the appendix to this chapter.

MODELS

After presenting descriptive statistics (means and percentages) for selected variables (table 5.1), we move to multivariate analyses, where we estimate two kinds of models. First, we model the number of conventional and family benefits found across the NOS establishments to be a function of organizational and job-level characteristics. In this first set of models (table 5.2), we use a statistical technique called Poisson regression to examine the number of specific benefits provided to employees.[2] The first model examines the relationship between organizational characteristics and the number of conventional benefits offered. The second model examines the relationship between these same organizational characteristics and the number of family benefits provided. The third model adds the conventional benefits index to the second model.

Our second set of models (table 5.3) investigates the presence of specific individual benefits rather than the total number of benefits. In this portion of the analysis, we estimate four logistic regression models, each predicting the presence of one of the following benefits: paid family leave, employer-provided day care, child care subsidies, or flexible scheduling. These models are estimated using logistic regression because in each case the dependent variable is dichotomous (a yes or no response). For technical details regarding logistic regression models, see Agresti (1996), Fox (1997), and Gardner, Mulvey, and Shaw (1995).

RESULTS

THE DISTRIBUTION OF FAMILY-RESPONSIVE BENEFITS

As table 5.1 indicates, 31 percent of organizations in the NOS sample reported having paid parental leave policies and 21 percent provide child care subsidies or services. The average (mean) number of conventional

---

2. For the models in table 5.2 the outcomes of interest are the number of specific benefits; as such, the dependent variables in these models have discrete counts as possible outcomes. Because of this, the appropriate analytical technique is Poisson regression.

benefits is 4.2 out of a possible 6; for family-responsive benefits, the average score is lower, only 2.4 of a possible 7.

Table 5.1 also displays the associations between family-responsive policies and selected organizational characteristics. Core occupation, core income, gender, and race composition of the workforce are related to the bifurcated labor market concept. If the core occupation of an establishment is professional or managerial, the organization is significantly more likely to provide paid parental leave (40% vs. 26%, $p <$ .001), and either partially subsidize child care costs or directly provide child care (35% vs. 14%, $p < .01$). Additionally, these establishments offer, on average, significantly more conventional benefits (4.7 vs. 4.0, $p < .001$), and more family benefits (3.8 versus 2.9, $p < .001$), than establishments with nonprofessional core occupations. Similarly, we find that low income (lowest third of the sample) for the core occupation is associated with both reduced likelihood of paid parental leave or child care subsidy as organizational policy and fewer conventional and family benefits. Tests for the differences between means on both benefits indexes demonstrate that the largest difference exists between establishments with a relatively low-income core occupation and the other two income categories. In other words, the gap in benefits is larger between low- and middle-income establishments than it is between middle- and high-income establishments. In fact, no significant difference in benefits offered exists between middle- and high-income establishments for either index.

Defining organizations as predominantly male (less than 35% women), gender-mixed (35%–75% women), or predominantly female (greater than 75% women), we find that as the gender composition shifts from predominantly men to gender-mixed, the provision of paid leave, child care, number of family-responsive benefits as well as number of conventional benefits tend to increase (although not all the increases are statistically significant). The gender composition of the workforce is strongly related to the overall level of family benefits. Number of family benefits increases from 2.8 for organizations with less than 35 percent women to 3.6 for mixed-gender organizations, but then decreases to 3.1 for organizations with a predominantly female workforce. A similar pattern holds for child care and conventional benefits, with gender-mixed establishments offering the most benefits on average. Thus, the means and percentages in table 5.1 suggest the possibility of a curvilinear relationship between workforce gender composition.

Half of the organizations in the sample had a full-time workforce that

TABLE 5.1

PROVISION OF EMPLOYEE BENEFITS BY SELECTED ORGANIZATIONAL CHARACTERISTICS

Organizational Characteristics	Organizations in Each Category (%)	Organizations Providing Specific Benefit		Average Number of Benefits	
		Paid Parental Leave (% Yes)	Child Care: Provide or Help Subsidize (% Yes)	Conventional Benefits (Range: 0–6) (Mean)	Family Benefits (Range: 0–7) (Mean)
All organizations (N = 688)	100	31	21	4.2	2.4
Core occupation					
Professional or managerial	34	40***	35**	4.7***	3.8***
Other	66	26	14	4.0	2.9
Modal income of core occupation					
1. Lowest one-third	34	21***	12***	3.6	2.0
2. Middle one-third	31	40	30	5.1	3.0
3. Highest one-third	35	39	29	5.2	3.0
Mean contrasts (ANOVA)				1–2, p < .05 1–3, p < .05 2–3, n.s.	1–2, p < .05 1–3, p < .05 2–3, n.s.
Percentage women					
1. Less than 35%	35	31	11***	4.1	2.8
2. 35%–75%	35	35	29	5.2	3.6
3. Greater than 75%	30	26	23	3.8	3.1
Mean contrasts (ANOVA)				1–2, n.s. 1–3, n.s. 2–3, p < .05	1–2, p < .05 1–3, n.s. 2–3, p < .05

Percentage non-white					
1. Zero	35	19***	10***	2.8***	2.2***
2. Less than 20%	34	41	29	5.1	4.0
3. 20% or more	31	35	23	4.9	3.6
Mean contrasts (ANOVA)				$1\text{–}2, p < .05$	$1\text{–}2, p < .05$
				$1\text{–}3, p < .05$	$1\text{–}3, p < .05$
				$2\text{–}3,$ *n.s.*	$2\text{–}3,$ *n.s.*
Sector					
Private	86	19**	28***	4.0***	3.1***
Public	14	33	50	5.2	4.1
Personnel department					
Separate department exists	35	37***	42	5.6***	4.3***
No specific department	65	12	25	3.5	2.6

**p < .o1 ***p < .oo1. Significance tests are t-tests for mean differences and chi-squared for percentage differences.

was less than 10 percent non-white, and a full 35 percent had no full-time non-white employees at all. This distribution affects the findings for race composition. Those organizations with an all-white workforce were, on average, the lowest on all the benefits measures in table 5.1. We suspect this is at least partially explained by the smaller-than-average size and disproportionately private-sector location of the all-white organizations. Among establishments with any non-white workers, the provision of benefits appears to decrease somewhat when the percentage of non-whites is above 20 percent; however, the differences are not statistically significant.

The results discussed thus far support a stratification analysis, finding that a low-income, non-professional-managerial core occupation, and a highly sex-segregated workforce (less than 35% women or more than 75% women) is associated with a less family-responsive policy as well as less generous provision of conventional fringe benefits. Two other variables in table 5.1 provide support for selected hypotheses suggested by the institutionalist perspective discussed earlier. Public-sector establishments are significantly more likely to offer both paid parental leave and child care ($p < .01$) and to offer more conventional and family benefits ($p < .001$) than private-sector establishments. Similarly, establishments with a separate personnel department tend to have more generous benefit structures, except for the provision of child care. Next, we turn to the multivariate models, which enable us to assess the impact of organizational characteristics of interest when a number of other relevant factors are controlled.

MULTIVARIATE RESULTS: PREDICTING THE LEVEL OF CONVENTIONAL AND FAMILY-RESPONSIVE BENEFITS

In table 5.2 we report the results of our Poisson regression models.[3] These models allow us to explore the relationships observed in table 5.1

---

3. The results in table 5.2 are adjusted for underdispersion in the response counts. When count data show less variability than one would expect if the distribution of the response variable were truly Poisson, the data are said to be underdispersed. Poisson distributions have identical mean and variance. However, if the response variance is not equal to the mean, then a scaling factor is used to adjust the standard errors of the estimated coefficients. This scaling factor is multiplied by the standard error of the estimates, which are inflated in the case of underdispersion and understated in the case of overdispersion. The adjustment by this scaling factor does not affect the point estimates, but affects only the standard errors (and therefore the significance tests). We estimated

TABLE 5.2
ORGANIZATIONAL VARIABLES PREDICTING NUMBER OF BENEFITS PROVIDED TO EMPLOYEES: POISSON REGRESSION RESULTS

Independent Variable	Model 1 Conventional Benefits (Coefficient)	Model 2 Family Benefits (Coefficient)	Model 3 Family Benefits (Coefficient)
Labor market stratification variables			
Professional-managerial core occupation	−0.020	0.017	0.016
Modal earnings of core occupation	0.206***	0.177***	0.111*
Women as proportion full-time employees	0.561†	0.996**	0.816**
Women as proportion full-time squared	−0.543†	−0.923**	−0.739**
10% or more non-white employees	−0.039	−0.062	−0.051
Internal labor market index	0.070***	0.059**	0.034†
Log of training dollar per employee	0.037***	0.045***	0.033***
Proportion union in industry	0.556*	0.170	−0.002
Contingent workers index	−0.010	0.071**	0.072**
Size and bureaucratic structure			
Organization size (log of full-time employees)	0.046**	0.049**	0.030†
Part of a larger organization	0.197***	0.149**	0.079†
Public sector	0.080	−0.013	−0.029
Separate personnel department	0.032	0.009	−0.001
External environment			
Tight labor market index	0.014	0.023*	0.018
Competitive product environment	−0.009	−0.041†	−0.038†
Other benefits			
Conventional benefits index			0.413***
Intercept	−1.492**	−1.435**	−1.137**
Log likelihood	1038.6	532.3	608.6
N	396	385	382

† $p < .10$; * $p < .05$; ** $p < .01$; *** $p < .001$.

NOTE: Understandized coefficients reported. Standard errors not shown, but available upon request.

in a multivariate context, thereby highlighting the net effects of establishment characteristics on the provision of benefits. The number of conventional benefits is the dependent variable in the first model, and the number of family-responsive benefits is the dependent variable in the other two models. In model 1, modal earnings of the core occupation, internal labor market index, proportion of unionized workers in the industry, establishment size, investment in job training, and being part of a larger organization all have significant positive net effects on the provision of conventional benefits.

The effects in model 2, which predicts the number of family benefits, are similar to those in model 1 for core earnings, size, parent organization, internal labor market, and investment in job training. However, the effect of a tight labor market becomes significant in model 2, and our measure of a competitive market environment becomes marginally significant ($p < .10$). Additionally, in model 2 the provision of family benefits is strongly predicted by the use of contingent workers—establishments that rely heavily on contingent workers tend to provide a larger number of family benefits, independent of the other variables. Greater use of contingent workers is associated with increased levels of family benefits (model 2) but has no effect on conventional benefits (model 1). The effect of contingent workers in model 2 is quite large—a one-unit increase in the contingent worker index (the index range is 0 to 4) increases the mean number of family benefits by approximately 7 percent.[4]

Another important finding in model 2 is that the effect of gender composition of an organization's workforce is strongly nonlinear, suggested by the statistically significant coefficients for proportion of women and its square. The form of the association is an inverted-U shape, with calculations based on this model indicating that the relationship between family benefits and female representation is positive until percentage female reaches approximately 54 percent, at which

---

our Poisson regression models using PROC GENMOD in SAS (v6.12) and used the DSCALE option to account for underdispersion (see Agresti 1996; Gardner, Mulvey, and Shaw 1995; Le 1998; SAS Institute Inc. 1993).

4. Because of the Poisson specification, a one-unit increase in an independent variable has a multiplicative effect of exp(b) on the dependent variable. So, for the case of contingent workers, the coefficient of 0.071 suggests that a one-unit increase in the contingent worker index predicts a multiplicative effect of exp(0.071) = 1.07 on the predicted number of family benefits offered. This translates to a 7 percent increase per unit increase in the use of contingent workers.

point the relationship becomes negative.[5] Establishments increase their provision of family benefits as the number of women in the workforce increases, but only until the workforce becomes predominantly female. After the gender composition "tips" toward becoming female-dominated, however, the availability of benefits decreases as the proportion female approaches 100 percent. Moreover, this effect is not attributable to firm size, unionization, the use of contingent workers, or other variables that have been controlled in the model.

Model 3 is nearly identical to model 2, but includes conventional benefits as a predictor of family benefits. Organizations with a greater number of conventional benefits were more likely to offer more family benefits. Importantly, we find that family benefits are not simply an extension of conventional benefits, since the number of conventional benefits alone is not enough to predict which organizations will offer family benefits. Rather, core earnings, training dollars, and contingent workers remain important in the model over and above the level of conventional benefits. We also see that similar to model 2, the relationship between gender composition of the workforce and family benefits is complex. When female representation is no more than 51 percent of the workforce, the greater the representation of women, the more family benefits are offered. However, when more than 51 percent of the workforce is female, the greater the representation of women, the *lower* the number of family benefits provided.

Consistent with the economic rationality or cost-effectiveness framework, we find that level of family-responsive benefits increases with organizational size, connection to a larger organization, a tight labor market, a more competitive product market ($p < .10$ in model 2), and greater investment in job training. The findings for size and parent organization are also consistent with the institutionalist framework. However, the institutionalists also suggest that public-sector organizations and establishments with a separate personnel department should provide more family-responsive benefits, which we found at the bivariate level (relationship between just two variables) in table 5.1, but not when we include other factors in the multivariate models in table 5.2.

5. For a quadratic relationship, the inflection point (minimum or maximum) is given by $-b_1$ divided by $2b_2$ where b_1 is the estimated coefficient for the linear (non-squared) variable, and b_2 is the coefficient for the squared term (see Agresti 1997).

PREDICTING SPECIFIC FAMILY-RESPONSIVE BENEFITS

Table 5.3 presents results from logistic regression analysis of four individual family-responsive benefits. Here the dependent variable in each equation is a dichotomous (yes or no) response, coded 1 for organizations that offer the particular benefit. The independent variables are the same as in table 5.2, but fewer of the organizational characteristics considered are statistically significant in predicting individual benefits than for the benefits index in table 5.2. Model 4 shows predictors of paid parental leave. Modal core earnings, employee training expenditures, and the presence of an internal labor market ($p < .10$) are all positively related to the likelihood that an organization offers paid family leave. In contrast, competition in an establishment's product environment significantly decreases the likelihood of offering family leave ($p < .01$). Expressed in a different metric, each unit increase in the four-point competitive product environment index decreases the odds of an establishment offering paid family leave by approximately 30 percent.[6]

The next two equations in table 5.3 predict whether the employer provides child care (model 5) and whether the employer helps cover child care costs in any way (model 6). Results indicate that provision of child care services, which is quite rare, is most likely found in the public sector and in large establishments affiliated with a parent organization. Subsidy of child care costs (model 6) is related to a professional-managerial core occupation and to greater investment in employee training. The effect of investment in employee training is quite large (odds ratio = 1.42). Use of contingent workers is not associated with help covering child care costs (model 5) but is positively related to the provision of child care services (see model 6), with each unit increase in the use of contingent workers associated with a 51 percent increase in the odds of an establishment offering this benefit (odds ratio = 1.51).

The final equation in table 5.3 is for flexible scheduling (model 7),

---

6. Because logistic coefficients express effects in a log odds metric, they are not easily interpretable. However, exponentiating the logistic coefficient expresses the effect in an odds-ratio metric. This is the effect of an independent variable in terms of the multiplicative impact on the odds (rather than the log odds) that the dependent variable takes a value of 1. The odds ratio takes values greater than 1 when the effect of X is positive, and less than 1 when the effect of X is negative. Thus, for the coefficient of -0.339 (for competitive product environment in model 4), the odds ratio is equal to $\exp(-0.339) = 0.71$. This suggests that each one-unit increase in the competitive product environment has a multiplicative effect on the odds that $Y = 1$ of 0.71 (or, decreases the odds by about 29%). See Agresti (1997), Demaris (1992), and Le (1998) for further discussion.

TABLE 5.3

ORGANIZATIONAL VARIABLES PREDICTING SPECIFIC BENEFITS PROVIDED TO EMPLOYEES: LOGISTIC REGRESSION RESULTS

Independent Variable	Model 4 Paid Family Leave Coefficient	Model 5 Employer-Provided Child Care Coefficient	Model 6 Child Care Subsidy Coefficient	Model 7 Flexible Schedule Coefficient
Labor market stratification variables				
Professional/managerial core occupation	0.165	1.002	0.959*	0.246
Modal earnings of core occupation	0.634*	0.049	0.030	-0.217
Women as proportion full-time	2.093	-5.008	3.415	4.271**
Women as proportion full-time squared	-2.583	4.591	-2.661	-4.230**
10% or more non-white employees	0.052	0.442	-0.550	0.042
Internal labor market index	0.191†	-0.045	0.186	-0.158
Log of training $ per employee	0.121*	0.142	0.351***	0.076
Proportion union in industry	1.419	-4.577	2.053	-0.736
Contingent workers index	0.091	0.218	0.416*	0.310**
Size and bureaucratic structure				
Organization size (log of full-time)	-0.035	0.339†	0.082	-0.024
Part of a larger organization	0.058	0.808†	0.245	-0.140
Public sector	0.369	1.389*	-0.440	-0.665†
Separate personnel department	0.048	0.077	0.500	0.265
External environment				
Tight labor market index	0.022	0.165	0.095	0.159**
Competitive product environment	-0.339**	-0.035	0.020	-0.014
Intercept	-7.821**	-5.975	-7.010*	1.765
-2 log likelihood[a]	65.7***	54.8***	81.8***	40.7***
N	392	399	397	399

† $p < .10$; * $p < .05$; ** $p < .01$; *** $p < .001$.

NOTE: Unstandardized coefficients reported. Standard errors not shown but available upon request.
[a]Test of improvement in model fit over the intercept-only model. DF = 15 for all models.

which we do not include in previous analyses. The use of contingent
workers is a positive and statistically significant predictor of flextime as
an option, as is a tight labor market. The effect of contingent workers
remains large (odds ratio = 1.36). Public sector is negative and marginally significant, suggesting that all else being equal, public-sector organizations are less likely to allow flextime. The effect of proportion
women and its square are both significant ($p < .01$), again showing a
strong nonlinear (inverted-U-shaped) relationship between flextime benefits. Calculations based on model 7 once again suggest a "tipping
point" of approximately 50 percent female; the association is positive
until the proportion of women exceeds the proportion of men. Once this
switch occurs, the likelihood of an establishment offering flexible scheduling decreases as female representation increases.

FINDINGS RELATED TO RACE AND CLASS COMPOSITION OF AN ORGANIZATION'S WORKFORCE

Racial composition was not significantly related to benefits in any of the
equations in tables 5.2 or 5.3. This was true whether it was measured
dichotomously (as 10% or more non-white) or on a percentage
(0–100%) metric (not shown). Additionally, the inclusion of a squared
racial composition variable did not alter these results. Thus, it appears
that the racial composition of the workforce effects observed at the bivariate level in table 5.1 were explained by size and other variables in
the multivariate models. Similarly, the status of the core occupation
(whether it is professional-managerial or not) was largely unrelated to
the provision of benefits in many of the models because modal core
earnings, which is highly correlated with core occupation, was also included. Additional analysis (not reported) indicates that if the core earnings variable is excluded, then the core occupation variable would be
highly significant in models 1 to 3 and model 6. Thus class composition
is significant, whether measured by core occupation or core earnings.

DISCUSSION AND POLICY IMPLICATIONS

In summary, we found that all else being equal, organizations with
higher-salaried core employees, more opportunity for advancement
within the organization, and greater employer investment in employee
training were more generous in providing family-responsive as well as
conventional fringe benefits. Increased sex segregation, either in the ex-

clusion of women or a strong preference for hiring women, was associated with decreased provision of family benefits. A higher rate of unionization in the industry was associated with a more generous provision of conventional fringe benefits but had no effect on family-responsive benefits. Increased use of contingent workers had no effect on conventional benefits but was associated with more generous family benefits in a number of different models. The findings for unionization, gender composition of the workforce, and use of contingent workers in determining the provision of benefits by employers merit further discussion.

UNIONIZATION

A positive effect of unionization on benefit levels reflects class-based gains won through collective bargaining. A heavily unionized industry tends to raise compensation levels in non-union establishments as well. Our finding that unionization affected conventional fringe benefits but not family-responsive benefits is consistent with our suggestions that family-friendly benefits tend to be available to a professional elite and to be distributed on a more class-stratified basis than conventional benefits, and are often won by individual leverage or negotiating strength rather than collective bargaining. This is the case even though some unions and the national AFL-CIO leadership have paid increased attention to work and family issues in recent years. Organized labor was a key player in the coalition that passed the Family and Medical Leave Act (FMLA) and is active in the lobbying coalition for child care legislation (Marks 1997). In the current climate, unions may be more effective lobbying for family benefits as public policy than winning them for members through collective bargaining. The effect of unionization on conventional but not family benefits is one of the main differences we found between the two types of benefits.

WOMEN AS A PROPORTION OF THE WORKFORCE

As discussed, previous researchers have hypothesized that family benefits should increase with a greater percentage of women in an organization's workforce because the demand is greater and the potential cost in turnover and sick leave would be a greater consideration. Previous research on how the percentage of women in an organization affects family benefits has been inconclusive. There are a number of reasons to suspect that employers do not respond to demand in providing family benefits. Employers may fear that potential costs will be too great when there are large numbers of women employees. More importantly, in predominantly female "ghettoized" workplaces, employers often expect high turnover and perceive women workers as easily replaceable. Women's individual leverage may be lower in highly sex-segregated, predominantly female occupations and organizations.

Our finding of a curvilinear relationship between the gender composition of the workforce and the level of benefits shows that the gender structure of the workforce is important. Benefit levels are lowest when percentages of women are either very high or very low. This fits a power explanation whereby the more gender imbalance, the less power (Kanter 1977) and negotiating strength women hold. This describes both instances of gender imbalance (predominantly female contexts and predominantly male contexts). It also fits a cost-effectiveness explanation whereby it does not pay for an employer to have a formal policy if there are very few women and it becomes too costly (or that is the perception) when a large majority of workers are women. In both the power and the cost-logic explanations, the relative number of women makes a difference. Although work/family benefits are often gender neutral in principle, our results show that relative numbers of women do make a difference. Finally, we note that the gender composition effect was also evident for flextime, which was not part of our family benefits index.

USE OF CONTINGENT WORKERS

Recent research on alternative work arrangements (Kalleberg et al. 1997; Spalter-Roth et al. 1997) finds that contingent workers are less likely than those in standard work arrangements to have health insurance or pension fringe benefits and that this is also true for contingent workers in professional and managerial jobs. On one hand we might have expected organizations that report more extensive use of contingent workers to have *less* generous family-responsive as well as conventional benefit policies because these are employers who are not willing to invest in a long-term stable workforce. However, in the current economy, increased use of contingent workers—largely without benefits— can also provide a means of financing good benefits for a smaller force of "real" employees (Smith 1997). This effectively creates a two-tiered workforce within organizations as well as in the economy as a whole.

Our results show that greater use of contingent workers is associated with an increased number of family-responsive benefits and a strongly increased likelihood that an employer will provide some child care costs and offer flextime. Use of contingent workers was the only variable showing consistently significant effects (or close to significant) in predicting family benefits but not at all significant in predicting provision of conventional benefits. As already explained, there is no reason to believe that the contingent workers are the ones receiving the family-responsive benefits, with the possible exception of flexible scheduling, which part-time and temporary workers may have.

Besides the likelihood that contingent workers help employers afford better benefits for their "real" employees, organizations that regularly use part-time and temporary workers may find it easier to accommodate various forms of family leave and flexible scheduling for their noncontingent employees. Allowing workers to go part-time is, for some, a family-friendly policy. Thus, the interpretation of the positive association between use of contingent workers and family-responsive benefits is not necessarily one of employer malevolence. Despite friendly intentions, however, the effect is a two-tiered workforce where some workers have full-time employment with relatively generous family benefits and others try to balance work and family through nonstandard work arrangements with few or no family benefits.

POLICY IMPLICATIONS

Although the data we analyzed were collected in 1991, thus predating the passage of the Family and Medical Leave Act (FMLA) of 1993, it is doubtful that the legislation would have had much affect on our results. The FMLA mandated only unpaid leave (with reinstatement) and only covered workplaces with 50 or more employees (within a 75-mile radius), also excluding those with limited hours or very short tenure (less than 1,250 hours in the previous year). It has been estimated that workers most likely to be covered by the FMLA were already participating in private leave plans, and these workers were in higher-paid, higher-status jobs than those excluded (Marks 1997). Research by Gerstel and McGonagle (1999) on the impact of the FMLA, using data collected by the Congressional Commission on the FMLA, strongly suggests that low-income women are less likely to use family or medical leave, despite greater need, compared to those with higher income. Thus the FMLA, as the major expansion of public policy mandating a family-responsive benefit, did not alter the two-tiered benefit structure of private provision apparent in the research we have presented.

One major limitation of the FMLA is the exemption of establishments of fewer than 50 employees. Our results as well as previous research on the effect of organizational size strongly suggests that without public policy intervention, smaller organizations will continue to offer fewer family-responsive benefits. Efforts to extend FMLA coverage to at least a substantial subset of smaller organizations could make a real difference. Another major limitation of the FMLA is that it does not mandate any paid leave—a policy much more difficult to change than expanding the number of employers covered. Previous research on family-responsive benefits has paid little attention to paid leave (Guthrie and Roth 1999). Our own attention to the question showed that few of the factors we considered were especially helpful in understanding which organizations provide paid family leave. Additional research is needed in this area. We did find, consistent with predictions in the literature, that all else being equal, the more competitive the market for the organization's main product or service, the less likely that paid family leave was provided. In contrast, a tight labor market had no notable effect. This finding strongly suggests that simply leaving the question of paid family leave to market forces, as conservatives advocate, is unlikely to produce a substantial increase in voluntary provision of paid family leave by employers.

Gerstel and McGonagle (1999) note that despite its substantial limitations, the FMLA "is de jure recognition that work and family are profoundly intertwined." It has increased the visibility of work/family issues in popular discourse and among researchers. However, as Lambert (1999) laments, the problems of low-wage working parents are largely absent from both the public discourse and much of the research on employer work/family policies. We have attempted to begin to fill this gap by focusing on how the provision of family-responsive benefits simultaneously reflects and reinforces existing structures of inequality in a two-tiered labor market, especially for those at the bottom.

APPENDIX: MEASURES USED IN THE DATA ANALYSIS

SINGLE-ITEM MEASURES

Variable	Description or coding
Size of organization	Natural log of number of full-time employees
Part of a larger organization	Yes (part of larger organization) / No (independent)

Public sector	Yes (public) / No (private)
Separate personnel department	Yes (has separate personnel department) / No
Professional-managerial core occupation	Three-digit census code for main occupation fits census categories of professionals or managers
Modal earnings of core occupation	Natural log of what most core employees earn
Proportion women	Women as proportion of full-time employees
10% or more non-white	Non-white > 10% full-time employees / Non-white < 10%
Proportion unionized in industry	Proportion of industry sector that is unionized
Dollars spent on training per employee	Natural log of dollars spent on training per full-time employee
Competitive product environment	Amount of competition in organization's main product or service area; range = 1–4 (none to great deal)

MULTI-ITEM MEASURES

Index	Range	Component items	Alpha
Family benefits (7 items)	0–7	Maternity/paternity leave with reemployment; paid parental leave after birth of child; other unpaid family leave; assistance for elderly family members; sick leave with pay; child care program or help with child care costs; information on child care services provided	.70
Conventional benefits (6 items)	0–6	Medical or hospital insurance; dental care benefits; life insurance; pension or retirement program; long-term disability insurance; drug or alcohol abuse program	.87
Tight labor market (4 items)	0–8	Shortage of qualified people important in determining	.70

Index	Range	Component items	Alpha
		earnings for core employees; the same important for other employees; difficulty hiring qualified workers; difficulty retaining qualified workers	
Internal labor market (5 items)	0–5	Core employee vacancies ever filled by hiring within; different levels exist for core employees; frequency of promotion of core employees; managerial vacancies ever filled from within; different levels exist for managers	.74
Contingent workers (2 items)	0–4	Part-time as percentage of all workers (0 = 0, 1–20 = 1, 21–100 = 2); temporary as percentage of core employees or managers (0 = 0, 1–20 = 1, 21–100 = 2).	N/A

REFERENCES

Agresti, Alan. 1996. *An introduction to categorical data analysis.* New York: John Wiley.

————. 1997. *Statistical methods for the social sciences.* Upper Saddle River, N.J.: Prentice-Hall.

Auerbach, Judith. 1990. Employer-supported child care as a woman-responsive policy. *Journal of Family Issues* 11:384–400.

Beck, E. M., Patrick M. Horan, and Charles M. Tolbert II. 1978. Stratification in a dual economy: A sectoral model of earnings determination. *American Sociological Review* 43:704–20.

Demaris, Alfred. 1992. *Logit modeling: Practical applications.* Newbury Park, Calif.: Sage Publications.

Fox, John. 1997. *Applied regression analysis, linear models, and related methods.* Thousand Oaks, Calif.: Sage Publications.

Freeman, Richard B. 1986. Effects of unions on the economy. In *Unions in transition,* edited by S. M. Lipset. San Francisco: ICS Press.

Galinsky, Ellen, James T. Bond, and Dana E. Friedman. 1996. The role of employers in addressing the needs of employed parents. *Journal of Social Issues* 52:111–36.

Gardner, William, Edward P. Mulvey, and Esther C. Shaw. 1995. Regression analyses of counts and rates: Poisson, overdispersed Poisson, and negative binomial models. *Psychological Bulletin* 118:392–404.

Gerstel, Naomi, and Katherine McGonagle. 1999. Job leaves and the limits of the Family and Medical Leave Act: The effects of gender, race, and family. *Work and Occupations* 26:510–34.

Glass, Jennifer, and Valerie Camarigg. 1992. Gender, parenthood, and job-family compatibility. *American Journal of Sociology* 98:131–51.

Glass, Jennifer, and Sarah Beth Estes. 1997. The family responsive workplace. *Annual Review of Sociology* 23:289–313.

Glass, Jennifer, and Tetsushi Fujimoto. 1995. Employer characteristics and the provision of family responsive policies. *Work and Occupations* 22:380–411.

Goodstein, Jerry. 1994. Institutional pressures and strategic responsiveness: Employer involvement in work-family issues. *Academy of Management Journal* 37:350–82.

Guthrie, Doug, and Louise Marie Roth. 1999. The state, courts, and maternity policies in U.S. organizations: Specifying institutional mechanisms. *American Sociological Review* 64:41–63.

Ingram, Paul, and Tal Simons. 1995. Institutional and resource dependence determinants of responsiveness to work-family issues. *Academy of Management Journal* 38:1466–82.

Kalleberg, Arne L., David Knoke, Peter Marsden, and Joe Spaeth. 1991. *National organizations survey*. Machine Readable Data File and Codebook, ICPSR Study no. 6240. Ann Arbor: Interuniversity Consortium for Political and Social Research.

Kalleberg, Arne L., Edith Rasell, Ken Hudson, David Webster, Barbara F. Reskin, Naomi Cassirer, and Eileen Appelbaum. 1997. *Nonstandard work, substandard jobs: Flexible work arrangements in the U.S.* Washington, D.C.: Economic Policy Institute and Women's Research and Education Institute.

Kalleberg, Arne L., and Mark E. Van Buren. 1994. The structure of organizational earnings inequality. *American Behavioral Scientist* 37:930–47.

Kamerman, Sheila, and Alfred Kahn. 1996. *Starting right: How America neglects its youngest children and what we can do about it.* New York: Oxford University Press.

Kanter, Rosabeth M. 1977. *Men and women of the corporation.* New York: Basic Books.

Knoke, David. 1996. Cui bono? Employee benefit packages. In *Organizations in America,* edited by A. L. Kalleberg, D. Knoke, P. V. Marsden, and J. L. Spaeth. Thousand Oaks, Calif.: Sage Publications.

Lambert, Susan J. 1999. Lower-wage workers and the new realities of work and family. *Annals of the American Academy of Political and Social Science* 562:174–90.

Le, Chap T. 1998. *Applied categorical data analysis.* New York: John Wiley.

Marks, Michelle R. 1997. Party politics and family policy: The case of the Family and Medical Leave Act. *Journal of Family Issues* 18:55–70.

Marsden, Peter V., Cynthia V. Cook, and David Knoke. 1994. Measuring organizational structures and environments. *American Behavioral Scientist* 37:891–910.

Mink, Gwendolyn. 1990. The lady and the tramp: Gender, race, and the origins of the American welfare state. In *Women, the state, and welfare,* edited by L. Gordon. Madison: University of Wisconsin Press.

Osterman, Paul. 1995. Work/family programs and the employment relationship. *Administrative Science Quarterly* 40:681–700.

Pearce, Diana. 1990. Welfare is not *for* women. In *Women, the state, and welfare,* edited by L. Gordon. Madison: University of Wisconsin Press.

Raabe, Phyllis Hutton. 1990. The organization effect of workplace family policies: Past weaknesses and recent progress toward improved research. *Journal of Family Issues* 11:477–91.

SAS Institute. 1993. *SAS/STAT software: The GENMOD procedure, release 6.09* (SAS Technical Report P-243). Cary, N.C.: SAS Institute.

Scott, W. Richard. 1992. *Organizations: Natural, rational, and open systems.* Englewood Cliff, N.J.: Prentice-Hall.

Seyler, Diane L., Pamela A. Monroe, and James C. Garan. 1995. Balancing work and family: The role of employer-supported child care benefits. *Journal of Family Issues* 16:170–93.

Smith, Vicki. 1997. New forms of work organizations. *Annual Review of Sociology* 23:315–39.

Spalter-Roth, Roberta M., Arne L. Kalleberg, Edith Rasell, Naomi Cassirer, Barbara F. Reskin, Ken Hudson, David Webster, Eileen Appelbaum, and Betty L. Dooley. 1997. *Managing work and family: Nonstandard work arrangements among managers and professionals.* Washington, D.C.: Economic Policy Institute and Women's Research and Education Institute.

Starrels, Marjorie E. 1992. The evolution of workplace family policy research. *Journal of Family Issues* 13:259–78.

CHAPTER 6

How Are Small Businesses Responding to Work and Family Issues?

Marcie Pitt-Catsouphes and Leon Litchfield

INTRODUCTION

During recent decades the public, as well as the research community, has focused a great deal of attention on the profound changes in two fundamental social institutions: family and work. One major change has been a steady increase in the percentage of women in the workforce. According to the Bureau of Labor Statistics, 63.7 percent of all married mothers with children under the age of six were working outside the home in 1998. This increase in labor force participation has been especially notable among mothers of very young children. For example, in 1985, 49.4 percent of mothers with children under one year of age were employed or were looking for work. This rate increased to 61.8 percent by 1998 (cited in U.S. Bureau of the Census 1999).

In response to the changes in the lives of working families that have occurred during the past two decades, employers across the country have begun to establish programs designed to help employees fulfill their responsibilities at home and work (Eichman and Reisman 1991; Kalleberg et al. 1996). A survey conducted by Hewitt Associates (1996) found a significant increase in the number of workplaces offering various work/family supports (e.g., dependent care assistance, flexible work options) during the 1990s.

Many studies have examined this work/family phenomenon.[1] However, most of these investigations have focused on the experiences of employees in large corporations. As a consequence, there has been little documentation of the responses of small businesses to their employees' work/family situations. This oversight has significantly limited our understanding of work and family issues, since the majority of U.S. businesses have fewer than 20 employees, and a high percentage of workers are employed by these smaller companies.

THE GROWTH AND CONTRIBUTION OF SMALL BUSINESSES

Despite some earlier predictions that small businesses would become increasingly peripheral to the national economy, there is evidence that the number of small businesses has increased, along with their contributions to the national economy. For example:

1.   The U.S. Bureau of the Census has reported that over 2.3 million of the 5.8 million business establishments included in its *Enterprise Statistics* have only 1 to 4 employees. Nearly three-fourths (72.3%) have fewer than 20 employees (U.S. Bureau of the Census 1992).

2.   In recent years small businesses have provided substantial numbers of new jobs. Nearly 60 percent of the 3.3 million new jobs created during 1994 were established in "industries dominated by small businesses" (*The State of Small Business* 1996). Small businesses are striking in this regard compared with medium and large businesses. For example, between 1988 and 1990, businesses with fewer than 20 employees *created* 4 million new jobs, whereas firms with more than 20 workers *lost* approximately 1 million jobs (Oppenheimer 1994).

3.   Small businesses account for 44 percent of all sales and 38 percent of the United States gross national product (Eichman and Reisman 1991).

---

1. As noted by Barnett (1999), the language pertaining to the study of work and family issues has reflected the evolution of several fundamental concepts in this field. Even today, some researchers continue to use the words "work/family" or "work and family." Many practitioners have adopted the words "work/life" to refer to the interactions between people's experiences at work and outside of work (including personal, home, and family experiences). We have decided to use the terms "work/family" and "work and family" in this chapter because they seem to be the most relevant to the owners of small businesses.

FIRM CHARACTERISTICS AND WORKPLACE RESPONSIVENESS TO WORK/FAMILY ISSUES

In previous studies researchers have identified several organizational factors that appear to influence the work/family responsiveness of businesses:

- decentralization and formalization of policy and business decisions
- human resource benefits
- structural and workforce characteristics

DECENTRALIZATION AND FORMALIZATION

The results of several studies have confirmed that in comparison to medium and large firms, small companies are more likely to centralize decision making and adopt informal procedures (Aldrich 1979; Daft 1986, cited in Arthur and Hendry 1990; Jackson et al. 1989, cited in Arthur and Hendry 1990; Kalleberg et al. 1996). These tendencies are manifested with regard to human resource issues as well as other business practices. Information gathered by the 1996 National Organizations Study (Kalleberg et al. 1996) confirmed that small firms are less apt to establish formal human resource policies and procedures. For instance, they are much less likely to create documents such as job descriptions or written personnel procedures (e.g., performance evaluation processes).

The findings of some organizational studies suggest that small businesses tend to respond to their employees' work/family priorities on a case-by-case basis. This informality may lead to inconsistent human resource decisions on the part of some small business owners (Kats de Vries 1977, cited in Curran 1984). Thus the response of small businesses to work and family issues may depend more on the characteristics and needs of employees than on a formal set of policies and practices.

HUMAN RESOURCE BENEFITS

Among large corporations there are indications that a progressive orientation toward human resources is correlated with organizational support for work/family issues (Pitt-Catsouphes, Mirvis, and Litchfield

1995). If this is true, one might expect small businesses to offer fewer human resource benefits that would help employees to balance their work and nonwork responsibilities; this is confirmed by at least one research study (Knoke 1996). This finding is to be expected, given the ability of larger companies to achieve an economy of scale in providing fringe benefits and other human resource programs to their employees.

It is apparent that there could be negative consequences for employees if small businesses offer only a limited range of policies and benefits. As MacDermid and Targ (1995) have observed, "Poorly paid work or work with inadequate benefits may interfere with workers' abilities to provide necessities of life for their families, and thus increase feelings of tension." These authors found that mothers who worked at smaller banks reported more demanding work schedules and lower wages than those at larger banks. However, these mothers were also more apt than those at larger banks to use close coworker relationships to mitigate negative spillover from work into marital relationships.

Workplaces, regardless of size, can use either formal or informal strategies to respond to their employees' work/family concerns. In a study of formal child care supports and flexible work options, Goodstein (1994) found that small businesses (fewer than 50 employees) were less likely to establish work/family benefits than either medium or large companies. A 1990 study conducted by Nelson and Couch concluded that small business owners were the most likely to offer personal leave for child and family responsibilities—a finding supported by another study, which found that small businesses were more apt to offer flexible scheduling than other types of work/family benefits (Kingston 1990).

In the 1997 National Study of the Changing Workforce, researchers found that employees at smaller companies had the option of telecommuting (i.e., working at home for part or all of their workweek) more often than those at larger companies. While this was an option for 30 percent of those with less than 25 workers, it was only a possibility for 25 percent of those in companies with 25 to 249 employees and 22 percent of employees in firms with more than 249 workers (Bond, Galinsky, and Swanberg 1997).

STRUCTURAL AND WORKFORCE CHARACTERISTICS

Previous research has revealed structural and workforce characteristics that appear related to the responsiveness of companies to employees' work/family balance issues. While some of these areas have not been researched specifically for small businesses, they are important to discuss with respect to their potential impact on company responsiveness.

Public versus Private Firms Osterman's research suggests that certain structural factors are predictive of responsiveness to issues concerning work and family. For example, publicly traded firms are more likely than privately held companies to establish work/family policies and programs (Osterman 1994, cited in Knoke 1996). This finding indicates that small businesses, which are less likely to be publicly traded than larger firms, may also be less likely to establish these types of supports.

Presence of a Human Resource Department Several studies have discovered a relationship between having a human resource department and establishing work/family policies and programs (Kalleberg et al. 1996; Osterman, cited in Knoke 1996). Since a separate human resource department is less viable for smaller businesses, fewer benefits may be available to help employees balance work and nonwork responsibilities. However, it is unclear whether assigning human resource responsibilities to one or more employees (perhaps more common at small companies than establishing a separate human resource department) also results in greater responsiveness to the work and family needs of employees.

Perception of Supportive Organizational Culture It has been widely noted that workplace culture can affect the development and utilization of work/family policies and programs. The 1997 National Study of the Changing Workforce gathered information from nearly 3,000 employees and found that a greater percentage of workers at smaller businesses reported supportive workplace cultures than those at larger firms. For example, employees were asked to agree or disagree with the statement: "At my place of employment, employees have to choose between advancing in their jobs or devoting attention to their family or personal lives." While 73 percent of those at smaller companies (fewer than 25 employees) *disagreed* with this statement, this was true for only 67 percent of employees at medium-sized businesses (50–249 employees) and only 59 percent at large companies (250 or more employees) (Bond, Galinsky, and Swanberg 1998).

Proportion of Women in the Workforce A number of researchers have discovered that businesses with a higher percentage of women in the workforce tend to be more responsive to the work/family needs of their employees (Galinsky and Bond 1998; Galinsky, Friedman, and Hernandez 1991). Goodstein (1994) also found that companies in industries with low female unemployment rates were more likely to have established work/family benefits. However, since these studies did not specifically focus on organizational size, it is unclear whether these relationships would be found in small businesses.

Return on Investment and Family-Friendly Policies   A recent study by the Families and Work Institute asked companies to assess their returns on investments in work/family policies and programs. Among the 475 companies that participated in the research, 46 percent felt that the benefits of flexible work options outweighed the investments, while only 18 percent reported the opposite (i.e., that their investments exceeded the benefits). Similarly, while 31 percent felt that the benefits of child care supports outweighed the investments, a smaller percentage (27%) reported a negative return on investment (Galinsky and Bond 1998).

A second research study, conducted by the Child Care Action Campaign, focused specifically on smaller businesses. This qualitative study examined the benefits of company support for employee child care responsibilities in 29 companies. The authors concluded that small businesses have experienced some of the same organizational benefits as medium and large companies, including improved productivity, increased capacity to attract and retain workers, and enhanced company image (Eichman and Reisman 1991).

THE NATIONAL STUDY OF SMALL BUSINESSES

In response to the need for studies examining work and family issues in small businesses, the Center for Work and Family at Boston College conducted the National Study of Small Businesses. This study collected information from 188 small companies and a comparison group of 88 medium and large businesses drawn from a national sample. The remainder of this chapter will examine the following three areas of inquiry:

What do small businesses identify as their most important human resource priorities?

How often do work and family issues arise among the employees of small businesses?

What types of policies and programs have been established by small businesses to assist employees in fulfilling their work and family responsibilities?

In each of these areas, issues faced by small businesses are compared with those faced by medium and large companies.

METHODOLOGY

Written questionnaires were developed to measure the following areas related to the work and family needs of employees in small companies: organizational characteristics of participant firms, characteristics of their workforces, human resource management priorities, manifestation of work/family issues at the workplace, and policies and programs established to help employees with work and family issues.

Respondents were given the choice of completing the survey themselves or providing the information via telephone interviews. It should be noted that the unit of analysis for the study was the company, not the individual employee. Thus, representatives provided information about the company they worked for, not about their own experiences with work and family.

Noting that previous researchers have not reached a consensus regarding what constitutes a "small business,"[2] for purposes of this study a small business was defined as a company that employs between 1 and 49 employees. A random sample of 500 small businesses was drawn, and a total of 188 small businesses participated in the study (a response rate of 37.6%). Two-fifths (41.9%) of the small business respondents who participated in the study were either managers or general managers, while an additional one-quarter (28.0%) were the owners or presidents of their firms.

In order to compare the responses of these participants with those of medium and large companies, information was also collected from respondents at 77 medium (50–499 employees) companies and 11 large (500+ employees) businesses. Human resource managers were most of-

2. There is even discussion about the variables that should be used to represent size, with number of employees the most common (in addition to net worth/annual sales). The U.S. Small Business Administration has gone one step further by developing a multidimensional definition that includes patterns of ownership along with number of employees and annual sales and considers size within the context of specific industry sectors/business groups.

ten represented among the participants at the medium and large companies (comprising more than one-third of the respondents in these companies).

SELECTED FINDINGS

Organizational Characteristics   The "typical" small business that participated in the study was an incorporated, privately held, for-profit service organization that had been in business for over 19 years. It had 13 employees, three-quarters of whom were employed as permanent full-time workers, and annual sales were about two and a half million dollars. At this "average" small business, responsibilities for human resources were assumed by either the owner/president or the manager/general manager, who spent approximately one-fourth of his/her time on human-resource-related tasks.

Respondents in the study were asked to identify their ownership structure. Whereas nearly one-half of the small businesses were either sole proprietorships or partnerships, only one-fifth of the medium and large businesses reported similar ownership structures.[3] In comparison to the medium and large companies in the study, the small businesses were more than twice as likely to be characterized as sole proprietorships.

Respondents were asked to indicate the title of the person(s) who assumed responsibility for personnel/human resource issues in their businesses. In comparison to the medium and large companies, the owners/managers of small businesses were *more* likely to assume responsibilities for human resource issues and *less* likely to have a human resource manager or other specialist. Individuals who assume responsibilities for the management of personnel-related issues in small companies tend to devote much less time (on average, 26.5% of their work hours) to these duties than their counterparts in either medium (60.9%) or large (78.6%) businesses.

Workforce Characteristics   On average, the small businesses had higher percentages of managers but smaller percentages of either professional/technical or production employees than the medium and large

---

3. According to the Internal Revenue Service, there were 21,280,000 active enterprises in 1993. Of these, 18.6 percent were corporations, 7.0 percent were partnerships, and 74.5 percent were nonfarm proprietorships (U.S. Department of Commerce 1997).

businesses. In comparison to the companies with 500 or more employees, the small and medium businesses reported *higher* percentages of permanent full-time positions and *lower* percentages of temporary full-time positions.[4] There were no significant differences between companies of different sizes with respect to either the percentage of employees who were male and female or the percentage of minority and non-minority employees.

Interestingly, the data from this study suggest that there is a relationship between firm size and the percentage of employees with responsibilities for dependent children and elders. In comparison to the medium and large companies, the small businesses in this study reported the lowest percentage of workers with responsibilities for either dependent children (39.3%, compared to 48.3% in medium and 45.7% in large companies; $F = 4.29$; $p < .015$) or elders (4.1%, 7.9%, and 14.3%, respectively; $F = 6.43$; $p < .002$). It is unclear why workers in small firms would be less likely to have responsibilities for children or elders.

Human Resource Management Priorities   Respondents were asked to assess the extent to which 15 issues related to human resource management were considered to be priorities for their businesses. The percentages of respondents who reported that each human resource priority was "very important" are listed in table 6.1.

Small businesses were *more* likely to perceive the issues listed on the survey as human resource priorities for their businesses. While the differences between the three groups were not statistically significant for all of the priorities (with one exception—providing training and development opportunities), a greater percentage of small companies indicated that these priorities were "very important" (see table 6.1). These differences were supported by the creation of a Human Resource Management Priorities Index that ranged from 15 to 75, with mean scores of 61.1 for small companies and 56.6 for medium and large firms ($t = 2.79$; $p < .006$).

Interestingly, when the top two ratings ("important" and "very important") were combined, four of the top five priorities were identical

4. The U.S. Bureau of Labor Statistics reports that approximately one-fifth of the U.S. workforce is comprised of part-time employees (Tilly 1991). In addition, approximately 10 percent of the workforce in 1996 was involved in "alternative" work arrangements, including independent contractors (8.3 million), "on-call" workers (2 million), workers for temporary agencies (1.2 million), and contract company employees (650,000) (Cohany 1996).

TABLE 6.1
HUMAN RESOURCE PRIORITIES REPORTED
AS "VERY IMPORTANT"

Human Resource Priority	Small Businesses (1–49 Employees)	Medium/Large Businesses (50 + Employees)	χ^2
Being sure that employees understand business goals	57.6	35.2	13.2**
Caring for employees as people	77.4	63.2	11.1*
Developing employees' skills	61.8	39.8	13.9**
Developing skills of employees with health or medical conditions	35.9	13.8	25.8***
Developing skills of employees with physical/mental disabilities	35.4	8.2	30.3***
Encouraging employee involvement in work decisions	48.1	25.0	13.8**
Encouraging employees to take initiative for quality work	72.7	59.1	9.4*
Encouraging two-way communication with employees	71.1	55.7	8.9
Establishing flexible policies to respond to individual needs	48.7	23.9	18.0***
Helping employees with work/family balance	36.8	13.6	20.3***
Offering innovative human resource policies	35.5	21.8	12.6**
Promoting teamwork	69.7	53.5	8.1
Promoting workforce diversity	46.2	25.0	13.4**
Providing information to employees about policies	59.9	48.9	5.2
Providing training and development opportunities	57.1	44.3	4.6

* $p < .05$; ** $p < .01$; *** $p < .001$
N = 268–275

regardless of company size, though there was some variation in the rank order among the groups. One of these top priorities was "caring for employees as people." The others were more directly related to business issues: promoting teamwork, encouraging employees to produce high-quality work, and the importance of two-way communication with employees.

Two priority areas included in the questionnaire were directly related to work/family concerns: helping employees balance their work and family responsibilities and establishing flexible policies and programs. Neither of these areas was among the top five identified by businesses of all sizes. In fact, the percentage of companies that rated helping employees balance work and family as "very important" was among the lowest for all companies, regardless of size. Notably, small businesses (36.8%) were significantly more likely than the medium (14.3%) and large (9.1%) businesses to indicate that employees' work/family balance was a "very important" priority for their businesses ($\chi^2 = 21.4$; $p <$ .006). Establishing flexible policies and practices that respond to employees' individual circumstances was not quite as far down the list as helping employees achieve a balance of work and family needs. However, small businesses (48.7%) were also significantly more likely to list this priority as "very important" than either the medium (24.7%) or large (18.2%) companies ($\chi^2 = 21.7$; $p < .006$).

Manifestation of Work/Family Issues at the Workplace   Workplace awareness of work/family issues may reflect their visibility for decision makers. Companies often begin their establishment of work/family programs by distributing employee-needs assessments to determine the extent of unresolved conflicts between work and family at the workplace. The results of these assessments may be used to create programs, policies, and benefits that respond to the greatest work/family needs of the employee population.

To accommodate the differing management information capacities of different-sized businesses identified during pilot testing, a decision was made to adopt two approaches to measuring the manifestation of work/family issues at the workplace:

small businesses: the number of times each issue had occurred during the past week (regardless of the number of people who had experienced them)

medium/large businesses: the percentage of employees who had experienced each issue (regardless of the number of times each one had occurred)

Respondents were asked to estimate the extent to which 16 different personal and family issues were manifested at the workplace. Eight of these were considered to be indicators of work/family issues that had "spilled over" into the workplace:

- employees were late or absent in order to take care of family members
- employees' personal or family problems interfered with work performance
- employees' family responsibilities interfered with work performance
- employees asked for time off to take care of family responsibilities
- employees asked for time off to care for sick family members
- employees asked for schedule adjustments due to personal or family problems
- employees asked for schedule adjustments to accommodate school holidays/vacations
- employees asked for schedule adjustments to care for family members

Table 6.2 lists the average number of times that each of these eight work/family issues arose at small businesses during the preceding week. According to the respondents, two of these issues had occurred at least once: (1) employees were late or absent in order to care for family members, and (2) employees' personal or family problems interfered with work performance.

The eight indicators of work/family situations were combined to create a subindex, Manifestation of Work/Family Situations at Small Businesses. The range of this composite index was from 0 to 56 times per week, with a mean of 5.29 times per week. However, since the number of occurrences is relative to firm size (even within this category of "small businesses," the number of employees could vary from 1 to 49), a ratio score was created for each business, taking into account the number of employees. The mean ratio for the small businesses was .532 times per week/employee, with a median of .333 times per week/employee.

Using the mean number of employees per small business (13.2), it is possible to estimate the number of times that work/family issues might arise during an average month. According to this estimation, at the "typical" small business in this study such issues would become visible (e.g., manifested by one or more employees) between 14 and 27 times each month. It is unclear how accurately this reflects the actual number of times these situations occur, since respondents were only reporting on their occurrence during the previous week. However, while some of the

TABLE 6.2
MANIFESTATION OF WORK/FAMILY ISSUES AT SMALL BUSINESSES: NUMBER OF OCCURRENCES DURING PAST WEEK

Work/Family Issue	Mean	S.D.
Late or absent in order to take care of family members	1.40	2.32
Personal or family problems interfered with work performance	1.07	1.83
Family responsibilities interfered with work performance	0.77	1.48
Employees asked for time off to take care of family responsibilities	0.69	1.00
Employees asked for time off to care for sick family members	0.32	0.64
Employees asked for schedule adjustments due to a personal/family problem	0.54	0.90
Employees asked for schedule adjustments for school holidays/vacation	0.29	0.89
Employees asked for schedule adjustments to care for family members	0.27	0.70

N = 185–188

issues reported may not occur every week, others may arise that had not occurred during the past week.

Thus, while this calculation may not result in an exact count of work/family issues in small companies, it does begin to give us a sense of how often small businesses are dealing with these issues. Although we are not able to compare these numbers directly with those for medium and large businesses due to differences in data collection efforts, it would appear that work/family situations are occurring in small businesses at a rate that warrants serious attention by small business owners or managers.

Workplace Responsiveness The degree of workplace "family-friendliness" is often measured by the scope of policies, programs, and practices that promote the quality of family life and/or help employees to meet some of their family/home management responsibilities. Respondents were asked to provide information about the availability of 27 different policies, benefits, supports, and practices that could help employees and/or their family members. Respondents could indicate that the different policies and programs were (1) not available, (2) available only on a case-by-case basis, (3) available to some (but not all) groups of employees (e.g., to full-time employees only), or (4) available to all employees. The second option—available only on a case-by-case basis—was considered a measure of work/family supports that are offered on a more informal basis.

As reported in table 6.3, approximately two-fifths (44.9%) of the small business respondents stated that all of their employees had access to health insurance through the workplace. Although fewer than one-fifth (18.3%) offered paid time off to take care of family responsibilities to all their employees, nearly half (46.5%) gave all their employees *unpaid* family leave.

For the most part, small businesses were *less* likely to offer work/family benefits to their employees than medium and large businesses (with a few exceptions—see table 6.3). In order to compare the different-sized companies with respect to all of the policies and programs presented in table 6.3, three summary indices were created to measure overall responsiveness, benefits offered on a formal basis, and benefits offered on an informal basis. In creating the overall responsiveness index, companies received increasing amounts of credit for benefits offered using the three different options (case by case, to certain groups, and to all employees).[5] While the formal index was created by calculating those benefits offered to some groups or to all employees, the informal index only summed the number of policies offered on a case-by-case basis. Table 6.4 compares the scores for the small and medium/large companies on each of the indices.

As expected, when considering policies or programs that were offered in any of the ways specified on the survey, small companies reported fewer available benefits than either medium or large companies (as reflected by scores on the Total Work/Family Index). A similar pattern was discovered in examining policies and practices offered in a more formal way (as indicated by the Formal Work/Family Index). Finally, while we anticipated that small companies might be more likely than larger companies to offer benefits informally (i.e., on a case-by-case basis), there were no significant differences between the different-sized companies with respect to the Informal Work/Family Index. In fact, for

5. The Total Personal/Family Policies and Practices Index was created using a weighting system that assigned the following values: 0 = not offered at all, 1 = offered on a "case by case" basis, 2 = offered to certain groups of employees, and 4 = available to all employees. Scores were calculated by adding the scores for the 27 items, with a potential range of 0 to 108.

many of the individual policies and programs, medium and large companies were actually *more* likely than small companies to offer these benefits on an informal basis (see table 6.3).

CONCLUSIONS AND IMPLICATIONS

The National Study of Small Businesses was intended to collect information about human resource management priorities, manifestation of work/family issues at the workplace, and responsiveness to these issues. In order to compare these issues at small businesses with those at medium and large companies (where such issues have been more commonly studied), information was also collected from a comparison group of larger businesses.

In contrast to medium and large firms, small companies in the study were more likely to perceive the importance of specific human resource management priorities. Since the data collection techniques used to measure the manifestation of work/family issues were different for small and larger businesses, it was not possible to compare their respective occurrences. However, small businesses reported the occurrence of work/family issues at a rate of 14 to 27 times each month (nearly every day, or at least every other day). If these rates of occurrence are similar for other small businesses, it is certainly an area that these businesses cannot afford to ignore.

The last section of the survey asked businesses about a variety of responses to the work and family issues of their employees. These included both formal (available to certain groups or to all employees) and informal (available on a case-by-case basis) responses. Not surprisingly, larger companies offered a greater number of formal policies and programs than smaller businesses. In addition to greater financial resources, large businesses have the advantage of being able to purchase services and benefits at an economy of scale (i.e., they can guarantee a greater number of employees than smaller companies).

Interestingly, however, small businesses in the study were also *less* apt to offer policies and programs on an informal basis. While we had speculated that smaller companies might be able to benefit from the informality of having fewer workers, at least for the benefits that we asked about and the phrasing that we used ("on a case-by-case basis"), this did not appear to be the case. In addition to the possibility that respondents may have interpreted the phrase "case by case" in different ways, it may be that informal responses are more common in medium

TABLE 6.3

INDIVIDUAL WORKPLACE POLICIES AND BENEFITS

Policy or Program	Small Businesses (1–49 Employees) Available				Medium/Large Businesses (50+ Employees) Available				χ^2
	To No One	Case by Case	To Some Groups	To All	To No One	Case by Case	To Some Groups	To All	
Adoption assistance	96.8	2.1	0.0	1.1	94.3	0.0	0.0	5.7	7.0*
After-school care	96.3	2.1	0.0	1.6	98.9	1.1	0.0	0.0	1.8
Backup child care for sick kids	94.7	3.7	0.5	1.1	95.5	2.3	0.0	2.3	1.5
Breaks: used for personal/home	27.8	24.6	2.7	44.9	13.6	27.3	8.0	51.1	9.6*
Career counseling	87.8	8.5	1.1	2.7	67.0	12.5	3.4	17.0	23.1***
Dental insurance	54.8	2.7	14.9	27.7	18.2	1.1	27.3	53.4	35.2***
Disability insurance	40.5	4.9	13.5	41.1	19.8	0.0	25.6	54.7	19.0***
EAP/counseling	66.8	14.1	2.7	16.3	48.9	12.5	2.3	36.4	13.8**
Employee support groups	83.9	7.0	1.6	7.5	85.2	6.8	2.3	5.7	0.5
Financial assistance for child care	92.5	3.8	0.5	3.2	92.0	3.4	1.1	3.4	0.3
Health insurance	24.1	5.9	25.1	44.9	2.3	2.3	28.7	66.7	23.7***
Help finding child/elder care	93.0	2.7	0.5	3.7	84.1	10.2	0.0	5.7	8.2*
Info. re: community programs	66.5	15.1	0.5	17.8	47.1	19.5	0.0	33.3	11.1**
Long-term-care insurance	74.7	2.7	8.8	13.7	50.0	2.3	18.2	29.5	17.8***
Mentoring	73.4	12.2	2.1	12.2	58.0	17.0	5.7	19.3	7.5
On-the-job training	6.9	7.4	4.8	80.9	5.7	10.2	15.9	68.2	10.8**

Paid sick days	35.8	7.0	25.1	32.1	19.3	3.4	29.5	47.7	11.0**
Paid time off: care for chronic medical problems or disabilities	53.8	21.2	7.6	17.4	26.4	28.7	10.3	34.5	19.3***
Paid time off: family care	58.6	18.3	4.8	18.3	33.3	26.4	10.3	29.9	15.7***
Periodic adjustment of work hours	19.9	39.2	7.0	33.9	17.0	43.2	18.2	21.6	10.6**
Pre-tax dependent care accounts	89.1	3.8	1.6	5.5	60.2	0.0	11.4	28.4	45.5***
School vacation care	95.7	2.7	0.0	1.6	97.7	1.1	0.0	1.1	.75
Tuition assistance: employees	70.6	11.2	6.4	11.8	29.5	15.9	14.8	39.8	45.8***
Tuition assistance: family	97.9	1.1	0.5	0.5	96.6	3.4	0.0	0.0	2.8
Unpaid leave: sick family care	27.0	22.7	3.8	46.5	6.8	15.9	4.5	72.7	20.8***
Work from home	81.8	13.9	3.7	0.5	60.2	29.5	9.1	1.1	14.9***
Work part-time	12.3	41.2	15.5	31.0	8.0	45.5	31.8	14.8	15.1**

* $p < .05$; ** $p < .01$; *** $p < .001$

NOTE: The responses of the medium and large businesses have been combined to facilitate comparisons with the small businesses.

TABLE 6.4

INDICES OF WORKPLACE POLICIES
AND BENEFITS

Work/Family Index	Small Businesses (1–49 Employees)	Medium/Large Businesses (50+ Employees)	t
Total work/family policies and practices index	26.6	38.7	−6.8***
Formal work/family policies and practices index	6.7	10.2	−7.5***
Informal work/family policies and practices index	3.0	3.4	−1.1

*** $p < .001$

and large companies than anticipated. In fact, units or departments in a larger company may act more like small businesses, especially in more decentralized environments. Representatives in larger companies may consider this in determining whether benefits are offered on a case-by-case basis or in a more formal way (i.e., available either to groups of employees or to all workers).

FUTURE STUDIES OF SMALL BUSINESSES

As indicated earlier, very few studies have focused specifically on the work and family issues of employees in small businesses. Therefore, this study was an attempt to begin the development of a database to explore this topic. Due to the difficulties inherent in collecting data from employees in small companies, future studies should employ innovative methodologies such as case studies using participant observation techniques to gather data. The viewpoints of different stakeholders (e.g., owners, managers, supervisors, employees, families, and customers) should also be considered in conducting future research. A more comprehensive study with multiple respondents would allow for a variety of opinions and would present a more complete picture of these complex issues.

Finally, the issue of cooperation between small businesses in providing work/family supports is largely unexplored. A special survey asking about instances in which small businesses cooperate with each other regarding work/family issues could be part of a future research study. This survey could also measure attitudes toward possible collaboration in the future and thus might encourage companies who already do business with one another to consider possible collaborations to better meet the work and family needs of their employees.

WHAT CAN SMALL BUSINESSES DO FOR THEIR EMPLOYEES?

Despite the fact that small businesses are less likely to provide work/family supports (both formally and informally), it may be possible to apply some of what researchers have learned about these issues in large companies to smaller businesses. It seems likely that some of these would help employees in companies of all sizes. Thus, the types of benefits that make sense for smaller companies and ways that smaller companies can afford to offer them need to be considered.

Along these lines, and related to the recommendation that research studies examine cooperation between small businesses, it is possible that these companies could work together to create the same economy of scale that naturally exists in larger companies. In this way, some of the formal benefits currently available only in larger companies might also be offered to employees in smaller businesses. Cooperative efforts could occur between companies that (1) are geographically located near one another, (2) belong to the same industry group (i.e., companies that have something in common), or (3) work together to provide certain goods or services.

As a first step, "best practice" case studies could be developed to document instances where small companies are already cooperating. Further, data could be collected on the extent to which and ways in which small businesses might be *interested* in collaborating in the future. Other ideas for developing more work/family supports in smaller companies include:

- focusing on lower-cost benefits when small companies can't work together to offer benefits
- developing training sessions for small business owners to highlight other initiatives they might pursue
- creating a web site for small business owners about work and family issues. This may be the most economical way to disseminate information, since more and more businesses have access to the Internet. Furthermore, it would allow those companies who are interested to seek out information without wasting resources on companies that might not use the materials.

This study demonstrates that the small businesses surveyed are aware of work/family issues and are facing on almost a daily basis many of the same issues as larger firms. However, they are doing much less for their employees in terms of providing supports to balance the needs of work and family. The recommendations here are provided as a beginning for development of additional work/family supports for the majority of American workers who are employed by smaller companies.

REFERENCES

Aldrich, H. E. 1979. *Organizations and environments*. Englewood Cliffs, N.J.: Prentice-Hall.

Arthur, M. B., and C. Hendry. 1990. Human resource management and the emergent strategy of small to medium sized business units. *International Journal of Human Resource Management* 1(3): 223–50.

Barnett, R. 1999. A new work-life model for the twenty-first century. *The Annals of the American Academy of Political and Social Science* 562: 143–58.

Bond, J. T., E. Galinsky, and J. E. Swanberg. 1997. *The 1997 national study of the changing workforce*. New York: Families and Work Institute.

Cohany, S. R. 1996. Workers in alternative employment arrangements. *Monthly Labor Review* 119(10): 31–45.

Curran, J. 1984. The sociology of the small enterprise. *Reviewing Sociology* 3(2):3–14.

Eichman, C., and B. Reisman. 1991. *Not too small to care: Small businesses and child care*. New York: Child Care Action Campaign.

Galinsky, E., and J. T. Bond. 1998. *The 1998 business work-life study: A sourcebook*. New York: Families and Work Institute.

Galinsky, E., D. Friedman, and C. Hernandez. 1991. *The corporate reference guide to work-family programs*. New York: Families and Work Institute.

Goodstein, J. 1994. Institutional pressures and strategic responsiveness: Employer involvement in work-family issues. *Academy of Management Journal* 37(2):350–82.

Hewitt Associates. 1996. *Salaried employee benefits provided by major U.S. employers in 1990 and 1995: A comparison study*. Lincolnshire, Ill.: Hewitt Associates.

Kalleberg, A., D. Knoke, P. Marsden, and J. Spaeth. 1996. *Organizations in America: Analyzing their structures and human resource practices*. Thousand Oaks, Calif.: Sage Publications.

Kingston, P. 1990. Illusions and ignorance about the family-responsive workplace. *Journal of Family Issues* 11(4):438–54.

Knoke, D. 1996. Cui bono? Employee packages. In *Organizations in America: Analyzing their structures and human resource practices*, edited by A. Kalleberg, D. Knoke, P. Marsden, and J. Spaeth, 232–49. Thousand Oaks, Calif.: Sage Publications.

MacDermid, S., and D. Targ. 1995. A call for greater attention to the role of employers in developing, transforming, and implementing family policies. *Journal of Family and Economic Issues* 16(1):145–70.

Nelson, P., and S. Couch. 1990. The corporate perspective on family responsive policy. *Marriage and Family Review* 15(3/4):95–107.

Oppenheimer, M. 1994. Small-minded: Despite the hype, smaller isn't better in the business world. *Dollars and Sense* 196:20–21, 39–40.

Pitt-Catsouphes, M., P. Mirvis, and L. Litchfield. 1995. *Behind the scenes: Corporate environments and work-family initiatives.* Boston: Center on Work and Family, Boston University.

The state of small business: A report of the president. 1996. Washington, D.C.: U.S. Government Printing Office.

Tilly, C. 1991. Reasons for the continuing growth of part-time employment. Excerpt from *Monthly Labor Review* 114(3).

U.S. Bureau of the Census. 1992. *Enterprise statistics.* Washington, D.C.: U.S. Government Printing Office. www.census/gov/epcd/www/smallbus.html.

———. 1997. *Statistics of U.S. business.* Washington, D.C.: U.S. Government Printing Office.

———. 1999. *Statistical abstract of the United States.* Washington, D.C.: U.S. Government Printing Office.

U.S. Department of Commerce. 1997. *Statistical abstract of the United States: 1997.* Washington, D.C.: U.S. Government Printing Office.

CHAPTER 7

Part-Time Work Arrangements and the Corporation

A Dynamic Interaction

Marcia Brumit Kropf

One of the major challenges for employees trying to combine work and family responsibilities is flexibility at work—the ability to adjust their work schedules and/or work location in order to manage family obligations. There are increasing pressures on corporations, both from employees and from the changing nature of work, to provide a more flexible work environment. However, the need for and use of these alternative arrangements collide with the traditional structures and cultures of today's corporations.

Catalyst, a not-for-profit research and advisory organization working with business to advance women, undertook its study, published as *A New Approach to Flexibility: Managing the Work/Time Equation,* in order to develop an understanding of successful implementation and management of voluntary part-time arrangements, and by extension, flexible work arrangements in general, in a range of work environments (Catalyst 1997).[1] We wanted to examine the impact of these arrangements on professionals and managers who used them, employees who worked with them, and the organization itself.

The study, funded by the Alfred P. Sloan Foundation, began in January of 1995. We studied the use and effectiveness of these arrangements over a two-year period in two corporations (a pharmaceutical company and a technology company) and two professional firms (a law firm and

1. The author wishes to thank Julia Resnick for her work on this research.

a consulting firm). Because these four organizations were large, encompassing a wide variety of work activities and geographic locations, we focused our study on specific work sites or work groups within each company and firm.

The study examined part-time arrangements primarily from the perspective of three key groups: professionals using part-time arrangements, their supervisors, and their full-time colleagues. However, we also included a wide range of perspectives, from senior management, human resources staff members, new hires, alumni, clients, and internal experts on relevant issues. We collected information from all these constituents, relying on both qualitative and quantitative methods. In all, the study involved a number of activities. We reviewed each company's policies, procedures, and communication related to flexible arrangements. We conducted 28 focus groups with 214 participants, 17 in-person interviews, and 80 telephone interviews. We distributed a Work Schedule Questionnaire to assess work arrangements to all 6,134 employees in the targeted segments of the workforce (2,124 responded—a 35% response rate). And we distributed to 1,695 volunteers from that questionnaire (1,105 responded—a 65% response rate) an In-Depth Survey designed to allow for comparison of responses between the part-time employees, their full-time colleagues, and supervisors of participating part-time employees.

The information collected for this study helped us to understand the use of voluntary part-time arrangements within the context of the organizational culture, the ways the need for part-time options affects the organization, and the ways organizational structures and systems affect use of these arrangements.

PRESSURE TO INCREASE FLEXIBILITY

In focus groups and interviews in all four organizations, participants described the changing nature of work and the workplace—changes that have increased the demand for flexible schedules on the part of both employers and employees.

EVOLVING BUSINESS NEEDS

In all four organizations, participants described the expansion of work schedules beyond the traditional Monday to Friday, 9 A.M. to 5 P.M., 40-hour workweek as motivation for businesses to offer a variety of flexible arrangements. Nearly 50 percent of full-time and part-time professionals reported that they are "usually" expected to change their schedules to accommodate work demands. Fifty-five percent reported that they "usually" do just that.

One reason for this expansion beyond the traditional workday/week is the increasing focus on the client/customer-service nature of work. Sixty-eight percent of participants provide service to external clients and 46 percent to internal clients. In all four organizations, customers and clients were often located in different time zones. In both firms and in the technology company, professionals reported an emphasis on responding to customers or clients whenever help is needed, regardless of the hour.

In fact, the group studied at the technology company provided 24-hour, 365-day service for customers. Work teams often included members in different geographic regions and time zones. This did not necessarily lengthen schedules, but it did require that professionals work a wide range of shifts and schedules. The need to provide round-the-clock service to customers motivated experimentation with flexible arrangements, including part-time and full-time telecommuting and compressed week arrangements. Staff groups at the pharmaceutical company worked with internal clients located all over the world, requiring travel in some cases and telephone contact at irregular hours.

LONG WORK HOURS

In our survey, full-time professionals reported that they worked, on average, 9.6 hours per day and 50 hours per week. At the consulting firm, professionals worked long hours to meet client demands, and because the work often took place at the client's offices, considerable travel was a normal part of the workweek. At the law firm, professionals described long hours as part of the work culture. They, too, had clients in many parts of the world, and although they might travel less, they found that working with people in different time zones lengthened the workday.

In addition, in all four organizations employees perceived long hours as an important cultural value; 44 percent of participants rated this factor as high or very high in being viewed as a good performer.

OUTSIDE FORCES

Outside forces increasingly compel organizations to make work arrangements more flexible. The federal Family and Medical Leave Act's mandated 12-week leave can be used intermittently, creating a part-time arrangement. The federal Clean Air Act has forced companies to create a wide range of daily schedules, compressed week arrangements, and options to work at home. Participants also described lengthy commutes and difficult weather conditions as personal motivations for working at home. One employee noted that a blizzard had helped her organization learn that people can work away from the office and still be productive.

ADVANCES IN TECHNOLOGY

Technological advances have made it easier to reach employees outside of the office, thereby creating more opportunities and interest in working off-site. Almost all of the professionals responding to our survey had technological support that made it possible to work away from the office. The most common were internal e-mail and voice mail, both available to 92 percent of respondents. Besides making work away from the office both more practical and more acceptable, technology also supports the use of part-time schedules. Part-time professionals can catch up on work activities that occurred during their time off when information is shared through e-mail and voice mail.

CHANGING DEMOGRAPHICS

The changing demographics of the labor force require different work structures and responses from employers. Women with children are a growing proportion of the labor force: 40 percent of employed women are mothers of children under 18, and fully seven in ten mothers with children under 18 are employed (U.S. Bureau of Labor Statistics 1996). In addition, the composition of families is changing: in 1996 only 17 percent of all families conformed to the tradition of a wage-earning dad, a stay-at-home mom, and one or more children (U.S. Bureau of Labor Statistics 1998). Further, more and more Americans are responsible for the care of adults. The number of households providing elder care for relatives or friends 50 or older has risen from 7 million in 1987 to 22.4 million in 1997 (National Alliance for Caregiving/AARP 1997).

RETENTION AND RECRUITMENT OF VALUABLE TALENT

A majority of the survey participants recognized that flexible work options benefit more than the individual employee. Through the focus groups and interviews we learned about the benefits that part-time work arrangements offer the employer.

Retention   Retention of valued employees was the critical business reason for offering part-time work arrangements in all four organizations. In the two companies, we heard several examples of situations where a professional resigned because a part-time request was denied, but when the employers relented, the employee agreed to remain. We also heard directly from many employees that their flexible work arrangements were why they stayed with their employers. Retention was recognized as a major benefit. Seventy-eight percent of full-time professionals and 98 percent of part-time professionals agreed that offering flexible work arrangements helps their employer retain valuable employees. Thirty-seven percent of part-time professionals said that the arrangement was essential for them to continue with their employers.

Recruitment   Recruitment of valuable talent was also described as an important reason for offering flexible work arrangements of various kinds. We heard this especially at the technology company and the law firm.

PRODUCTIVITY AND MORALE

Increases in productivity, consistency of productivity, morale, work quality, and proactive management were business benefits observed after the part-time arrangements were in place. These benefits were not the primary reasons for approving an arrangement, but they were observed by managers, professionals with part-time arrangements, and colleagues after arrangements were implemented. Responses to the survey questions confirmed these perceptions. Eighty percent reported increases in morale for individuals working part-time or telecommuting. Forty-six percent agreed that individuals working part-time realize productivity gains. Nearly half (48%) reported increases in commitment to the company or firm on the part of part-time employees.

RESISTANCE TO FLEXIBILITY

Along with the increase in the demand for flexible schedules just described, Catalyst also found systems, structures, and attitudes that work against the implementation of a more flexible work environment within each of the four organizations studied.

APPARENT CONFLICT WITH PROFITABILITY

Catalyst found a conflict between an organization's support of work/life balance in theory and a competitive, economically driven practice. Concern about the conflict between flexibility and profitability was present in all four organizations; however, the conflict was most apparent in the professional firms, where the number of hours worked is equated with profitability rather than with work produced. Participants indicated that the value placed on long hours and demanding workloads often inhibits opportunities for flexibility. Many commented that certain positions could not accommodate any form of flexibility, let alone reduced-hour arrangements.

SYSTEMS AND STRUCTURES

The assumption that part-time arrangements conflict with profitability results from the use of traditional systems and structures for managing productivity, performance, payroll, and compensation. Organizations have tended not to address the problem of clarifying and adjusting systems that were designed to support employees who work standard and typical schedules.

Employee Tracking Systems   Employee tracking systems often exclude part-time employees. In three of the four organizations, computer systems did not handle professional part-time employees effectively. Conversions to and from part-time were extremely complicated. In one company, for example, part-time employees were not included in the computer-generated listing of those eligible for raises. A part-time professional explained her situation: "I show up on the charts as being 60 percent available and 40 percent on maternity leave, which isn't quite appropriate since my oldest is two and a half years old." The human resources department is often unaware of specific arrangements because of the lack of effective tracking systems and because of arrangements made by supervisors without involving that department. This makes it difficult for the human resources department to provide support to managers or employees.

Performance Rating Systems   Performance rating systems can put part-time employees at a disadvantage. The two companies both used a forced distribution performance rating system, which limits the number of people who receive excellent ratings. When given the choice between two high performers, one full-time and one part-time, managers reported giving the higher rating to the full-time professional. As a compensation specialist explained: "We are a pay-for-performance company, and maybe we don't give part-time employees as high a rating as our full-time employees because we can only have so many high ratings and we don't want to waste them on part-time employees. I'd much rather give my high rating to someone I have to look at eight hours a day versus four hours a day."

Productivity Measurements   Productivity measurement systems need to be examined. The two companies used head count rather than full-time equivalency as a way of allocating human resources. Under this practice, one person is counted as one employee regardless of the time worked, and managers are limited to a specific number of employees. For this reason, managers were reluctant to approve part-time arrangements, because while head count would remain constant, actual work hours would decrease. In addition, participants were concerned that the head count allotted to departments did not reflect work to be done, resulting in too much work even for full-time employees and therefore making it difficult for managers to approve reduced schedules. Within the firm environments, hours billed were a primary measure of performance and individual value. Those who billed the most hours were seen as the most valuable. Some law firm participants explained that part-time professionals were in some sense less valuable to the firm because of this structure. Sixty-five percent of full-time law firm respondents indicated that "long hours" were a highly important part of performing well, compared with only 43 percent of other full-time respondents.

Lean Infrastructure   Participants commented that operating with a very lean infrastructure creates heavy individual workloads. They questioned the practicality of and the organization's commitment to workplace flexibility, given other organizational decisions that reinforced lean staffing and heavy workloads. Participants shared concerns about downsizing and about organizations being "too skinny" to support part-time work options. A full-time professional in the technology company noted: "The number of accounts I have keeps increasing. I find that I just live for doing the job here and going home and being a daddy. It is increasingly difficult." Only 16 percent of participants who work full-time reported that they "always have sufficient clerical/secretarial support"; 28 percent said they rarely or never do. Participants believed strongly that without additional resources to support infrastructure flexibility, flexible arrangements are difficult to accommodate.

Lack of Career Alternatives   There is a lack of career alternatives. In the firms with a tradition of "up-or-out," professionals were concerned about the impact of a part-time arrangement on their advancement to eventual partnership. Participants in one firm supported recent efforts to establish a legitimate alternative to the up-or-out system. Nonetheless, traditional values persist. One male associate explained how perceived lack of interest in becoming a partner can hurt one's career: "I think the up-or-out structure of the partnership is changing now. There are going to be more positions where people who do not want to be a partner will be satisfied with less money. But if people perceive you as not being serious about the partnership track, that is detrimental to your career. You won't get the good deals, you won't get the premium work."

STEREOTYPES AND ATTITUDES REGARDING
FLEXIBLE ARRANGEMENTS

Throughout the study we found examples of how stereotypical thinking about flexible arrangements limited their use.

Part-Time as an Accommodation   Part-time arrangements are commonly viewed as an accommodation for a specific employee, rather than an integrated strategy for managing work and people. Many focus group participants viewed part-time alternatives as available only for highly valued individuals who threaten to leave.

Only for Women with Children   Part-time arrangements are considered an option available for women with young children, rather than for anyone who might need them. Eighty-two percent of the part-time professionals responding to the survey were women; 75 percent were motivated by a need to address child care responsibilities. Twenty-two percent of full-time survey respondents agreed that it was not acceptable for a man to use a part-time arrangement.

Incompatible with Client Service   There is a common view that professionals working in part-time arrangements cannot serve clients well.
Participants who are employed full-time described working with clients
and their demands as prohibitive to part-time arrangements. Twenty-
nine percent agreed that the ability to provide outstanding external client
service declined when part-time professionals did the work. Thirty-six
percent agreed that the ability to provide outstanding internal client
service declined.

Interestingly, most part-time professionals reported either no change
or an increase in their ability to provide outstanding client service (91%
for external clients, 90% for internal clients). Their direct supervisors
agreed (86% for external clients, 84% for internal clients). In addition,
the few clients interviewed indicated that they were very comfortable
with and had confidence in the part-time professional's responsibility
and availability. In fact, they believed that there was no noticeable impact on projects.

Representing a Lack of Commitment   In previous research, Catalyst
reported that part-time professionals were viewed as less committed to
their jobs and careers than full-time professionals (Catalyst 1993). These
views also surfaced in the present study. An alumna of one company
noted: "I knew this wouldn't help my career. I decided that in order to
prevent anyone from thinking of me as not serious about my job, I would
stop working for a while and return at a later date." However, most
full-time-employed respondents to the survey agreed that the commitment of part-time professionals to the employer and the job stayed the
same or increased (to the employer, 77%; to the job, 77%).

THE IMPORTANCE OF A CORPORATE RESPONSE

Corporations must respond to business pressures to provide more flexible work arrangements as described above. At the same time, they must
address the systemic, structural, and cultural forces that inhibit effective
use of these arrangements. In all four corporations studied we found
that the impact of flexible work arrangements was felt throughout the
organization.

EXPECTATIONS FOR FULL-TIME FLEXIBILITY

We found that in response to the evolving business pressures to work
beyond the traditional time boundaries, traditional full-time arrange-

ments were no longer standard. Employees are looking for ways to adjust their schedules as they struggle to respond to increasing work demands. Less than half of the Work Schedule Questionnaire respondents reported that they have a "traditional full-time work arrangement," such as working 9 A.M. to 5 P.M. Monday through Friday. Fifty-two percent of men and 56 percent of women described their work arrangements as "nontraditional," which means any variation of the standard workweek. These statistics were reinforced by our observations in the four organizations. In focus groups, when we expected traditional schedules, we continually found professionals with some sort of full-time flexible arrangement.

EXPECTATIONS FOR LONG-TERM FLEXIBILITY

Part-time arrangements have often been introduced in organizations as a transitional arrangement for women returning to full-time work from maternity leave or for people phasing into retirement. However, in many instances individuals have ongoing interests and responsibilities requiring that they curtail the lengthy hours typically required of full-time employees. In Catalyst's 1993 study, for example, we learned that mothers do not view part-time arrangements as transitional, but rather see them as necessary to address ongoing child care responsibilities (Catalyst 1993).

Findings from the present study confirm that part-time arrangements are not short-term and temporary. Among the 91 part-time professionals interviewed:

- 32 percent reported that they never expect to return to full-time work
- 46 percent answered that they didn't know if they would return to full-time work
- only 3 percent expected to return to full-time work in less than a year

WIDE IMPACT ON EMPLOYEES

Although the actual number of professionals working part-time at any time may be relatively low, a high percentage of employees are directly affected by part-time arrangements. Over half (57%) of respondents have direct exposure to some kind of part-time work arrangements. They use or have used these arrangements themselves, or they supervise a part-time professional, or they have a part-time professional colleague. When telecommuting arrangements are considered (meaning that the employee is working off-site full- or part-time), even more professionals—almost seven of every ten (67%)—have been directly exposed in some way.

The extensive use and impact of flexible arrangements, as revealed in this study, underlines how urgent it is that organizations learn how to handle such arrangements effectively. Considering the number of individuals affected, the cost of poor management of part-time arrangements could be considerable:

- A small but meaningful percentage of professionals are actually working in part-time arrangements at any given time. The Work Schedule Questionnaire listed a variety of types of full-time and part-time work arrangements and asked employees to check the type that applied to them. An average of 7 percent reported currently using a reduced work schedule: 11 percent of the women and 4 percent of the men. The In-Depth Survey was sent to full-time and part-time employee volunteers (representing 28% of the questionnaire population). Because of the nature of the In-Depth Survey, part-time professionals were more likely to be interested in responding. Nearly one in four (23%) of the women and 5 percent of the men who responded were currently using a part-time arrangement or had used one in the past.

- A substantial group of employees expect to use a part-time arrangement at a later date. Ten percent of the full-time employees—17 percent of the women and 7 percent of the men—reported that they anticipate working part-time in the future. More surprisingly, 29 percent of the full-time employees—41 percent of the women and 22 percent of the men—responded "don't know" to that question. In other words, they did not reject the idea out of hand. Nearly one in five of the survey participants will work part-time at some point in their career (they had used, were using, or anticipated using a part-time arrangement)—36 percent of the women and 11 percent of the men.

- Many of the full-time professionals in our study either supervise part-time professionals (14%) or work with them as colleagues

(51%). What's more, one in five managers supervise professionals using some type of a flexible arrangement. We can presume, then, that they have discussed these arrangements with employees, negotiated alternatives, and experienced the effects of these arrangements on their own work.

IMPACT OF UNSUCCESSFUL ARRANGEMENTS

Employees learn about policies and programs from organizational communications, but they also learn from observing the experiences of those around them and hearing the stories disseminated informally within organizations. Unsuccessful experiences create a view of part-time arrangements as "costing" those involved and, in turn, create barriers to implementing part-time arrangements. This leads to the conflict employees see between the promises of their "family-friendly" employers and the reality of the workplace. One participant explained: "Certain people will tell you the company has wonderful flexible policies and show anecdotal situations where flexible situations work. The reality is that 99 percent of managers hate flexibility, ignore the policy, and frown upon employees who dare to even approach the subject."

AN EFFECTIVE APPROACH

The wide range of information collected in this study, including a variety of perspectives and examples, allows for the development of a recommended approach to implementing flexible work arrangements. Catalyst identified a number of actions that are critical to implementing successful flexible arrangements.

STRENGTHEN AND COMMUNICATE LEADERSHIP
COMMITMENT AND VISION

A clear, articulated commitment regarding flexibility must be made to the organization by senior management. Throughout the focus groups and interviews Catalyst asked participants to discuss their organization's vision for a flexible work environment. Few had answers. Many responded that not many senior managers use flexible arrangements of any type, either formally or informally, so there are few role models. It is the responsibility of senior management to define the workplace they envision and share that vision in words and actions. A senior manager noted: "Division heads have to make it clear in their staff meetings with employees and the management of their division that managers are to take these requests seriously. They've got to enter into discussions on flexible arrangements in good faith with the idea, 'Let's make this work. Let's figure out what are the tests to make sure an arrangement is working right and let's start doing some of these things.' "

ARTICULATE A BUSINESS RATIONALE

Each of the four organizations studied has learned the benefits of providing part-time options to professional employees, including retention of experienced employees, recruitment of valuable talent, improved employee morale and commitment, expanded client service, realization of "best-in-industry" standards, and increases in work productivity and quality. However, supervisors and full-time colleagues often do not understand these benefits, and understanding is critical to acceptance and support. The importance of alternative work arrangements to the business and to the bottom line must be clearly communicated.

FOCUS ON CONTINUOUS LEARNING AND IMPROVEMENT

Participants speaking from varying perspectives and from all four organizations explained that flexible work arrangements are in effect still new and are viewed as special cases. In interviews and focus groups participants talked at length about the ways in which current arrangements are learning opportunities. They want to learn from each other. Managers expressed interest in learning from other managers. Professionals with flexible arrangements wanted to be connected with others with similar arrangements. Suggestions included using technology, such as websites and intranets, to create networks and employee groups and provide greater access to information about these options.

PROVIDE GUIDANCE AND SUPPORT FOR FLEXIBLE ARRANGEMENTS

Over and over again, participants described the lack of clarity about the following:

· the policy regarding eligibility for a flexible work arrangement

- the process for proposing a flexible work arrangement
- guidelines regarding benefits, compensation, and advancement when using a flexible option
- the technology to support the flexible work arrangement and how to acquire it
- skills and activities the professional with the flexible arrangement has
- the supervisor's need for the option to succeed

In addition, participants asked for centralized and easily accessible information to reduce the amount of research required for setting up a single arrangement. They also wanted a centralized source of support. One part-time professional explained: "It's a fishing expedition to find out who the current person is who knows the most about it." Many managers and part-time professionals also suggested that they be included in discussions for designing policy and guidelines about flexible arrangements so that their experience can inform decisions.

ESTABLISH EXPLICIT EXPECTATIONS
REGARDING PERFORMANCE

Many participants described the lack of clarity that surrounds performance expectations. All understood the importance of competent, skilled performance, and in all four organizations participants identified beyond-competence criteria as critical to good performance as well as to compensation and advancement. These beyond-competence criteria were clearly and consistently identified, but not clearly defined. The lack of definition can result in full-time employees connecting part-time work with poor performance. The lack of discussion about important performance criteria between part-time professionals and their supervisors leads to unsuccessful arrangements.

For example, participants consistently understood the need to be responsive. In our focus groups and interviews, however, participants did not share an understanding of expectations about how and within what time frame to be responsive. They did not consistently understand their ability to manage that responsiveness proactively.

Clear expectations help to resolve the key dilemmas faced by part-time professionals. Part-time employees need to be responsive and flexible, adjusting and expanding their work schedules to accommodate work peaks and client requests. Yet they must be wary of being overly flexible, especially to the inflexible or unplanned requests of others, as this can result in a part-time arrangement with a full-time workload. Arrangements should be seamless and integral, avoiding adverse impact on coworkers, supervisors, and clients. At the same time, the focus on invisibility is another reason for an inequitable workload and can obscure success stories and models.

PROVIDE SYSTEMS AND STRUCTURES
THAT SUPPORT FLEXIBILITY

As described earlier, current systems and structures continue to limit the success of these arrangements. These internal systems are one of the reasons supervisors find flexible options so difficult to manage and a major reason they view part-time arrangements as problems. No matter how great the philosophical commitment to the issue and to the employee, these organization-wide systems perpetuate the perception that these arrangements are in opposition to the way work is handled and evaluated at the organization. These systems and structures must be reevaluated and restructured so that they support successful flexible arrangements.

Several participants noted how much work in their organizations is changing. These changes are already requiring shifts in systems and structures. The trend toward teamwork, for example, is altering the ways performance is evaluated, and these changes provide substantial opportunities for flexibility. A manager described an approach to evaluation: "I don't look at individual performances day to day. I look at the team's performance day to day. If we're successful, I know it. And I can use the team as a feedback mechanism for individual performance."

FOCUS ON WORK PRODUCTIVITY

In response to our question about a vision for the organization, many participants described a workplace with a focus on productivity instead of on face-time, one where professionals were trusted to have some discretion and control over their schedules. In the words of one participant, "The ideal is that you are expected to put in a certain number of hours and complete a certain number of tasks. As long as you do this, your work is fine. This gives employees flexibility on a day-to-day basis to respond both to the needs of their job and their needs at home. This requires a high degree of trust, but one which would be invaluable to both partners, the employer and the employee."

REFERENCES

Catalyst. 1993. Flexible work arrangements 2: Succeeding with part-time arrangements. New York: Catalyst.

———. 1997. A new approach to flexibility: Managing the work/time equation. New York: Catalyst.

National Alliance for Caregiving/AARP. 1997. *National caregiving survey.* Washington, D.C.: AARP, June.

U.S. Bureau of Labor Statistics. 1996. *Employment and earnings.* Washington, D.C.: U.S. Government Printing Office.

———. 1998. *Labor news* (USDL 98-217). Washington, D.C.: U.S. Government Printing Office, 21 May.

CHAPTER 8

Toward a New View of Work and Family Life

Ellen Galinsky

Much of the early research on work and family life was predicated on the notion that the intersection of the two is characterized by competing demands, interference, and conflict. During the past decade, however, both researchers (Barnett 1999; Galinsky and Johnson 1998) and business leaders have begun to shift toward a new view that also includes the ways that work and family life can enhance each other. This chapter outlines the history and rationale for this change in approach, describes the current prevalence of work-life programs and policies that reflect this new thinking, and examines the predictors of companies' being family-friendly.

EVOLVING VIEWS OF WORK AND FAMILY LIFE

A Focus on Conflict between Work and Family   Over the past 30 years there has been an evolution in the business response to the work and family needs of employees. This evolution is one of an ever-widening view; like a zoom lens that opens wider and wider to capture more and more terrain, the views of the past are not lost but become incorporated into the new picture.

As with attempts to map any social transformation, neat, distinct lines cannot be drawn between these views. They overlap, blur, and blend one into another. Yet despite such ambiguities, there has been a historical progression that can be described, and likewise, there has been research during each of these phases on the impact of employer support on employee well-being and on the bottom line.

Women and Child Care   As record numbers of women streamed into the workforce in the 1970s and 1980s, researchers and business leaders focused on the conflict that dual roles—especially among women—engendered. Voydanoff (1988) defined work-family conflict as inter-role friction, in which the demands of one role interfere with fulfilling the demands of the other. Piotrkowski (1979) identified two types of work-family conflict: structural and psychological. Structural conflict occurs when the demands of one role create practical difficulty in managing the demands of the other, while psychological conflict occurs when moods or levels of energy transfer from one domain to the other.

A goal of many studies in the 1970s and 1980s was to identify the workplace antecedents of work-family conflict, stress, anxiety, and poor well-being. Among the most frequently recurring antecedents were amount of time worked, lack of control over work schedule, low job autonomy, unsupportive supervisors, unsupportive coworkers, and high job demands or pressures (Greenberger et al. 1989; Hoffman 1989; Karasek 1979; Repetti and Cosmas 1991; Staines and Pleck 1983; Voydanoff 1988).

Similarly, studies looked at the family antecedents of work-family conflict. A number of these studies examined the cost of not responding to employees'—particularly women's—child care needs. They found that employees were more likely to miss work or to experience stress when they spent long hours trying to locate child care or when they dealt with the often tenuous or poor-quality arrangements they had made, especially when these child care arrangements broke down (Fernandez 1986; Galinsky, Bond, and Friedman 1993; Galinsky and Hughes 1987; Shinn et al. 1990).

During this time the focus of employers was on addressing work-family conflict, particularly by helping women with child care. A frequent rationale for providing assistance was that if employers could reduce the conflict experienced by employees, the employees could concentrate on their work and therefore be more productive (Galinsky and Johnson 1998).

Dependent Care and Flexibility for All Employees   In the late 1980s employers began to recognize that all employees can experience conflict between their work and home life at all stages of their life cycle. In response, leading companies began to widen their view to include all employees (women and men, young and old), to broaden the range of family and personal life issues addressed to include elder care and flexibility, and to expand their definition of family.

Research on family-supportive workplaces during this period began to extend beyond the costs of not responding to employees' work-family needs to include the benefits to employers of such solutions. Overall, these studies found some positive results. For example, when Aetna extended its parental leave to six months, allowed a part-time return, and trained supervisors in managing leaves, turnover among leave-takers was reduced by 50 percent—to between 9 and 12 percent—saving approximately $1 million per year (Aetna 1988, 1990). Another study at AT&T found that leaves that are managed by supervisors with the least family-supportive attitudes are the most costly (Marra and Lindner 1992; Staines and Galinsky 1992). A study at Johnson & Johnson (Families and Work Institute 1993) found that the average number of days absent among all Johnson & Johnson workers declined over the two-year period following the introduction of much more generous flexible time and leave policies. Furthermore, users of the company's flexible time program were more likely to recommend Johnson & Johnson as an employer to prospective employees and to want to remain at the company than nonusers. Likewise, a study of an integrated array of work-life programs and policies at the auto gasket company Fel-Pro (Lambert and Hopkins 1993) found that the most frequent users of work-family benefits had the best performance evaluations, the lowest intention of leaving the company, and fewer disciplinary actions taken against them. Similarly, IBM found that among their top performers, the second most important reason given for staying at the company was IBM's work-family program and policies (IBM 1991).

Shifting the Focus to Include Work and Family Synergy   In the early 1990s a substantive shift in how a number of employers thought about work-life issues began to take place. Instead of dwelling only on the conflict between work and family—instead of seeing family life primarily as a "problem" to be addressed—these employers also began to look at the synergy between these domains of life. Moving beyond the question of how to reduce the negative impact of family life on productivity (such as absenteeism, inability to concentrate on work), they began to consider how to increase discretionary effort and improve organizational effectiveness by promoting a better integration of work and family life.

The most important trend affecting this new vision was widespread downsizing, with some estimates concluding that as many as 43 million jobs were lost to downsizing between 1979 and 1996. The survivors of downsizing—those who remained—became somewhat dispirited, committed to doing their own jobs well, but less so to helping their organizations succeed (Bond 1999). Thus, the relationship between employer and employee needed rekindling at every level of the organization to ensure that employees would go that extra mile for their employers.

Supervisors and Family-Friendly Workplace Cultures   Employers interested in work and family synergy first focused on how supervisors implemented the companies' programs and policies and how family-friendly the organization really was. There was a growing sense among employers that company programs would only be able to achieve their intended effects if supervisors implemented them well and if they were within a supportive workplace culture.

Several studies, including the Families and Work Institute's 1997 National Study of the Changing Workforce (NSCW), supported the attention to supervisors and culture change. For example, the NSCW found that workers with supportive supervisors and working in a family-friendly culture were more willing than workers without this support to go that extra mile to help their companies succeed (Bond, Galinsky, and Swanberg 1998).

Work Structure and Work Processes   The late 1990s witnessed yet another shift in the thinking of a few leading-edge employers. This change was triggered by mounting pressure on the job caused by fewer employees in downsized organizations doing more work; by the increased use of technology, creating for some workers the "everytime, everyplace" office; and by the rush to market in a fast-paced, global economy. In addition, the tight labor market of the late 1990s led employers to consider how to attract and retain employees and how to prevent job burnout in an era when "overwork" had become standard fare. These employers began to turn their attention to work structure and work processes in an attempt to improve organizational effectiveness and worker health and well-being.

This emerging concern with the quality of jobs and the supportiveness of the workplace environment is echoed in new research. For example, the 1997 National Study of the Changing Workforce found that employees with more supportive workplaces as well as better-quality jobs are more likely than other workers to have higher levels of job satisfaction, more commitment to their companies' success, greater loyalty, and a stronger intention to remain with their companies. The 1997 NSCW also found that employees with more demanding jobs and less supportive workplaces experience more stress and have poorer coping skills, worse moods, and less energy off the job—all of which jeopardize their personal and family well-being. Additionally, when employees' personal and family well-being is compromised by work, they experience more negative spillover from home to work, which diminishes their job performance (Bond, Galinsky, and Swanberg 1998).

THE PREVALENCE OF WORK-LIFE SUPPORT

The Families and Work Institute's 1998 Business Work-Life Study (BWLS) is one of the first and most comprehensive studies of how U.S. companies are responding to the work-life needs of the nation's changing workforce (Galinsky and Bond 1998).[1] The 1998 BWLS enables us to assess the extent to which businesses are addressing this ever-widening view of what it means to be a family-supportive workplace. Specifically, we asked:

To what extent do companies provide benefits, programs, and policies and create supportive workplace environments that address the work-life needs of their employees?

What are the characteristics of companies most likely to provide this assistance and support?

The 1998 BWLS surveyed a representative sample of 1,057 for-profit (84% of the sample) and not-for-profit companies (16% of the sample) with 100 or more employees.[2] Interviews were conducted with human resources directors whenever possible.

1. The 1998 Business Work-Life Study was funded by Allstate Insurance Company, The Chase Manhattan Bank, The Commonwealth Fund, Freddie Mac Foundation, Kaiser Permanente, and Travelers Foundation.
2. Companies were drawn from lists maintained by Dun & Bradstreet using a stratified random sampling procedure in which selection was proportional to company size. In analyses for this chapter, the sample was weighted to the proportions of companies of different sizes in the universe of companies with 100 or more employees.

Flexible Work Arrangements   Of the eight flexible work arrangements considered (see table 8.1), companies with 100 or more employees are most likely to allow workers to take time off to attend school and child care functions (88%) and to return to work on a gradual basis following childbirth and adoption (81%). Two-thirds of employers allow traditional flextime and more than half allow employees to move back and forth from full-time to part-time and to work at home occasionally. Less common are job sharing, regular work at home, and daily flextime. However, job sharing and regular work at home are the flexibility options most likely to be under consideration by companies not currently offering them.

Only 18 percent of companies offering one or more flexible work arrangements perceive the costs of their investments in these policies as outweighing the benefits, while 36 percent perceive these programs as cost-neutral, and 46 percent perceive a positive return on their investments.

Leaves   Except for those companies meeting the legal exemption of having fewer than 50 employees within a 75-mile radius of one of their work sites, companies interviewed for the 1998 BWLS are mandated to comply with the federal Family and Medical Leave Act (FMLA) of 1993. This law requires that 12 weeks of unpaid, job-guaranteed leave for childbirth, adoption, foster care placement, a serious personal medical condition, or care of a child or spouse with a serious medical condition be granted to employees who have worked at least 1,250 hours over the preceding year.

Between 7 and 10 percent of companies with 100 or more employees nationwide provide fewer than 12 weeks of leave of different types, while 15 through 33 percent provide 13 weeks or more (table 8.2). Among companies offering fewer than 12 weeks, we estimate that 2 percent or fewer are clearly out of compliance with the law, based on having only one site *and* 100 or more employees at that site. Although additional companies may be out of compliance, survey data do not permit accurate estimates of this number. On the other hand, a large number of the 37 percent of companies in this sample with an average of fewer than 50 employees per site are undoubtedly complying with the law, even though they may not be required to. Again, we are unable to estimate the actual percentages.

Although paid time off to care for mildly ill children is not required by law, 49 percent of companies with 100 or more employees allow

TABLE 8.1
FLEXIBLE WORK ARRANGEMENTS

Does your company allow employees:	Yes (%)	No, But Considering (%)
To periodically change starting and quitting times?	68	9
To change starting and quitting times on a daily basis?	24	7
To return to work gradually after childbirth or adoption?	81	7
To move from full-time to part-time and back again while remaining in the same position or level?	57	5
To share jobs?	38	17
To work at home *occasionally*?	55	6
To work at home or off-site on a *regular basis*?	33	14
To take time off for school/child care functions?	88	N/A

N = 1,057
N/A = not asked

TABLE 8.2
SUMMARY OF LEAVE POLICIES

Leave Policy	Less Than 12 Weeks (%)	12 Weeks (%)	13–26 Weeks (%)	More Than 26 Weeks (%)	Median and Mean Number of Weeks
Maternity leave	9	58	25	8	Median: 12 Mean: 17
Paternity leave	10	74	13	3	Median:12 Mean: 14
Adoption/ foster-care leave	10	74.5	13	3	Median: 12 Mean: 14
Leave to care for seriously ill children	7	78	11	4	Median: 12 Mean: 14

N = 1,057

employees to take some time for this purpose without having to use vacation days or losing pay.

Women on maternity leave are the most likely of all workers to receive some pay during leave (table 8.3). Most companies (81%) fund this pay by a general temporary disability insurance plan.

Only 17 percent of companies think the costs of leave programs exceed the benefits, while 42 percent think leave programs are cost-neutral and another 42 percent perceive a positive return on investments in these programs.

Use of Flexible Time and Leave Policies without Jeopardizing Advancement   Only 10 percent of company representatives responding to the 1998 BWLS survey felt that the use of flexible time and leave policies jeopardizes employees' opportunities for advancement. In contrast, the Institute's 1997 NSCW found that among employees of private-sector companies with 100 or more employees nationally, 40 percent felt somewhat or strongly that using flexible schedules and taking time off for family reasons impedes job advancement. Although the questions in the two surveys were not identical, the difference between employers' and employees' views is large enough to suggest that there is significant disagreement between them regarding the extent to which use of flexible time and leave policies jeopardizes advancement.

Child Care Assistance   Not unexpectedly, companies are more likely to provide low- or no-cost child care options (such as Dependent Care Assistance Plans [DCAPs]) than options that are more costly (table 8.4). The number of companies considering new options, such as resource and referral (12%) and on- or near-site child care centers (12%), suggests that there could be growth in employer-supported child care in the coming years.

Among companies offering any child care benefit, 24 percent perceive negative returns on their investments—seven to eight percentage points higher than the percentages reported for flexible work arrangements and family leave policies. Another 40 percent perceive child care assistance programs to be cost-neutral, and 36 percent think the benefits of these programs outweigh their costs.

Elder Care Assistance   While 23 percent of companies with 100 or more employees currently offer elder care resource and referral services, only 9 percent offer long-term care insurance for family members and

TABLE 8.3
REPLACEMENT PAY DURING LEAVE

Leave Policy	At Least Some Replacement Pay (%)
Maternity leave	53
Paternity leave	13
Adoption/foster-care leave	13

N = 1,057

TABLE 8.4
CHILD CARE ASSISTANCE

Does your company provide:	Yes (%)	No, But Considering (%)
Access to information to help locate child care in the community?	36	12
Child care at or near the work site?	9	12
Payment for child care with vouchers or other subsidies that have direct costs to the company?	5	5
Dependent care assistance plans (DCAPs) that help employees pay for child care with pretax dollars?	50	N/A
Reimbursements of child care costs when employees work late?	4	N/A
Reimbursements of child care costs when employees travel for business?	6	N/A
Child care for school-age children on vacation?	6	2
Backup or emergency care for employees when their regular child care arrangements fall apart?	4	4.5
Sick care for the children of employees?	5	3
Financial support of local child care through a fund or corporate contributions beyond United Way?	11	N/A
Public/private partnership in child care	5	N/A

N = 1,057
N/A = not asked

only 5 percent make direct financial contributions to elder care programs in the communities where they operate. Another 5 percent are considering resource and referral services, while 2 percent are considering direct financial support for local programs. Most notably, 12 percent of companies are considering long-term care insurance for family members—a benefit of growing interest to the aging workforce and the aging population at large (table 8.5).

TABLE 8.5
ELDER CARE ASSISTANCE

Does your company provide:	Yes (%)	No, But Considering (%)
Elder care resource and referral services?	23	5
Long-term-care insurance for family members?	9	12
Direct financial support for local elder care programs?	5	2

N = 1,057

Among companies offering any form of elder care assistance, 19 percent perceive the costs for these programs as outweighing benefits—somewhat lower than the 24 percent who perceive a negative return on investments in child care assistance and in line with the 17 and 18 percent who perceive a negative return on investments in flexible work arrangements and family leave policies. In addition, 60 percent view investments in elder care programs as cost-neutral, while 21 percent perceive positive returns on their investments.

Helping Employees Resolve Family Problems   More than one-half of companies (56%) provide Employee Assistance Programs (EAPs) that address work-life issues. In addition, one-quarter (25%) provide work-life seminars or workshops at the workplace (table 8.6).

Programs for Teenage Children of Employees   Twelve percent of companies with 100 or more employees offer some type of program for the teenage children of employees (table 8.7). Most frequently offered are EAPs (5%) and counseling (3%), suggesting that some companies have expanded the scope of their EAP/counseling programs to specifically address the problems and needs of teenagers and their families.

Supportive Supervisors, Workplace Culture, and Business Decision Making   Company representatives were asked to assess the supportiveness of their workplaces (table 8.8). More than half responded "very true" to statements assessing whether men and women who must attend to family matters are equally supported by the organization (66%) and whether supervisors are encouraged to be supportive of employees with family problems (55%). Far fewer responded "very true" when asked

TABLE 8.6
RESOLVING FAMILY PROBLEMS

Does your company provide:	Yes (%)	No (%)
An Employee Assistance Program designed to help employees deal with problems that may affect their work or personal life?	56	44
Workshops or seminars on parenting, child development, care of the elderly, or work-family problems?	25	75

N = 1,057

TABLE 8.7
PROGRAMS FOR TEENAGERS

Program Options	Provide (%)	Do Not Provide (%)
Any program	12	88
After-school programs	0.5	99.5
Financial support for community programs	1	99
Seminars/workshops	2	98
Summer programs	0.3	99.7
Employee Assistance Programs	5	95
Referral information servicess	1	99
Scholarships/educational assistance	1	99
Counseling	3	97
Other	1	99

N = 1,057

whether the company makes a genuine effort to inform employees of the availability of work-life assistance (19%).

One aspect of paying attention to work structure and work processes with the employees' personal and family life in mind is whether management takes employees' personal needs into account when making business decisions. The fact that 31 percent endorse this statement indicates that some companies may have shifted toward seeing work-life issues as a part of their organizational change strategy.

Company Efforts to Develop Supportive Supervisors   Companies with 100 or more employees are most likely to train supervisors in managing diversity and least likely to have a career counseling or manage-

TABLE 8.8
SUPPORTIVENESS OF SUPERVISORS AND WORKPLACE CULTURE

Statements about Supportiveness	Very True (%)	Somewhat True (%)	Not Very True/Not True at All (%)
Supervisors are encouraged to be supportive of employees with family problems and to find solutions that work for both employees and the organization	55	41	4
Men and women who must attend to family matters are equally supported by supervisors and the organization	66	30	5
The organization makes a real and ongoing effort to inform employees of available assistance for managing work and family responsibilities	19	44	37
Management takes employees' personal needs into account when making business decisions	31	51	22

N = 1,057

ment/leadership program for women—62 versus 22 percent, a striking difference of 40 percentage points (table 8.9). Falling between these extremes are training for supervisors to respond to the work-family needs of employees and consideration of how well supervisors manage work-family issues when making job performance appraisals.

Company Involvement in Community Life   Eleven percent of companies with 100 or more employees are engaged in some type of partnership with local or state government to assist employed people in the community to meet their family and personal responsibilities (table 8.10). In addition, 73 percent of companies with 100 or more employees allow their workers to volunteer in community activities—to an unknown extent—during work hours.

PREDICTORS OF FAMILY SUPPORT AT THE WORKPLACE

Industry   The type of industry is the most frequent predictor of work-life benefits, programs, and policies, with the finance/insurance/real

TABLE 8.9

PROGRAMS FOR SUPERVISORS AND CAREER
DEVELOPMENT

Program	Provide (%)	Do Not Provide (%)
Trains supervisors in responding to work-family needs of employees	43	57
Trains supervisors in managing diversity	62	38
Considers how well supervisors manage the work-family issues of employees in making job performance appraisals	44	56
Includes career counseling program or a management/leadership program for women	22	78

N = 1,057

TABLE 8.10

PUBLIC-PRIVATE PARTNERSHIPS

Type of Initiative	Involved (%)	Not Involved (%)
All types	11	89
Child care programs	5	95
Parent education and support programs	7	93
Health care programs	6	94
Welfare to work programs	7	93
Education programs	9	91

N = 1,057

estate services standing out as the most generous of industries in most areas, while the wholesale and retail trades emerge as least generous time and again. The 1998 BWLS also reveals that professional and "other" services, and in some cases manufacturers, are more likely to provide certain types of work-life assistance.

Company Size The next most frequent predictor of work-life assistance and a supportive work environment is company size. Overall, 25 percent of companies in the 1998 BWLS have 1,000 or more employees. These larger companies are more likely than their smaller counterparts to provide flexible work options and longer maternity leaves, paternity leaves, and leaves for adoptive parents, as well as wage replacement during maternity leave. However, smaller companies are more likely to provide wage replacement for paternity leave. Of the eleven child care options we examined, larger companies are more likely to provide seven. Likewise, larger companies are more likely to provide elder care programs, employee assistance programs, programs for the teenage children of employees, work-life seminars, and work-life training for supervisors.

Proportion of Top Executive Positions Filled by Women   One of the most provocative findings of the 1998 BWLS is the broad extent to which a larger proportion of top executive positions filled by women is associated with the provision of work-life assistance. It is the third most frequent predictor and quite close to company size in importance. Interestingly, 30 percent of companies have no women in top executive positions (either the CEO or those who report directly to the CEO), while 70 percent have one or more women in such leadership positions, and 20 percent have women in half or more of their top positions. Some of the findings are quite dramatic:

· Eighty-two percent of companies with women in half or more of their top executive positions provide traditional flextime, compared with 56 percent of companies with no women in top positions.

· Six times as many companies (19%) with women in half or more of their top executive positions provide on- or near-site child care as those with no women in top management (3%).

· Sixty percent of companies with women in half or more of their top executive positions provide Dependent Care Assistance Plans, compared with 37 percent who have no women in these senior positions.

· Thirty-three percent of companies with women in half or more of their top executive positions offer elder care resource and referral programs, compared with 14 percent of companies with no women in key positions.

Proportion of Top Executive Positions Filled by Minorities   A similar and equally provocative pattern of findings emerges when we examine the relationship between the proportion of top executive positions filled by minorities and the prevalence of work-life supports. The proportions of top executive positions filled by minorities and women are equally important predictors. Since the majority of companies in the sample

(63%) have no top positions filled by minorities, minority employees in even one, if not more, top position can have an impact. For example:

- More than 80 percent of companies with minorities in 25 percent or more of top executive positions offer traditional flextime, versus 64 percent of companies with no minorities in key positions.
- About twice as many companies with at least one top executive position filled by a minority employee offer pay during leaves for adoption and foster care placement, compared with companies with no top positions filled by minorities.
- Four times as many companies (26%) with minorities in 50 percent or more of top executive positions offer on- or near-site child care, compared with companies with no minorities in key positions (6%).

Women as a Percentage of the Workforce   The percentage of women in a company's workforce is also predictive of work-life assistance in many areas we examined, albeit in both negative and positive ways. When women constitute a *larger* proportion of the workforce, companies are more likely to provide a number of options, some of which could be considered costly, some not—such as job sharing, part-time work, time off for parents to attend school and child care functions, longer maternity leaves, care for children during school vacations, direct subsidies for child care, and so forth. Conversely, we found that companies are more likely to invest in certain more costly options when women constitute a *smaller* percentage of the workforce—such as wage replacement during maternity leave. Overall, in 31 percent of companies, women represent 60 percent or more of the workforce, while in 32 percent, they represent less than 40 percent.

Hourly Employees as a Percentage of the Workforce   While it could be argued that hourly workers have greater needs for work-life assistance because they tend to be concentrated in lower-paid jobs, the 1998 BWLS reveals that companies with *larger* proportions of hourly workers are less likely than other companies to provide many forms of assistance. For example, they are less likely to provide replacement pay during maternity leave and during leave for adoption or foster care placement. They are also less likely to offer employee assistance programs, work-life seminars, and leave to care for mildly ill children without loss of pay. On the other hand, companies with larger proportions of hourly employees are more likely to report that they take employees' personal needs into account when making business decisions.

Part-Time Employees as a Percentage of Workforce   Companies with larger proportions of part-time workers are more likely than companies with smaller proportions of part-timers to offer the following flexible work arrangements: gradual return to work after childbirth, movement from full- to part-time work and back again, and job sharing. As is the case for companies with larger proportions of hourly workers, companies with larger proportions of part-time workers report that they are more likely to take employees' personal needs into account when making business decisions.

Union Members as a Percentage of Workforce   Seventy-eight percent of companies with 100 or more employees have no unionized workers, while 12 percent have 30 percent or more unionized workers. Companies with larger proportions of unionized workers are less likely to provide part-time options, a gradual return to work after childbirth, and flexibility in moving from full-time to part-time and back again. However, they are more likely to provide longer leaves for paternity and adoption, paid maternity leave, and leave for mildly ill children. Some of the findings are very impressive. For example:

· Sixty-five percent of companies with 30 percent or more unionized workers provide time off to care for mildly ill children without lost pay, compared with 46 percent of companies with no unionized workers.

· Eighty-seven percent of companies with 30 percent or more unionized workers provide temporary disability insurance, versus 66 percent of companies with no unionized workers.

On the other hand, the proportion of unionized workers is not predictive of any of the child care options examined in the 1998 BWLS.

Number of Sites   Having a larger number of company sites is associated with rather diverse work-life benefits and policies. Companies with more locations are more likely to provide traditional flextime, flexibility in moving from full-time to part-time work and back again, occasional work at home, Dependent Care Assistance Plans, training to manage diversity, temporary disability insurance, scholarships for children of employees, and partnerships with state and local government.

Downsizing, Difficulty in Filling Skilled and Entry-Level or Hourly Positions, and Financial Performance   In the late 1990s business climate, we expected that downsizing, recruitment, and financial performance would be related to the presence or absence of work-life assistance programs. However, business conditions did not emerge frequently as predictors in the 1998 BWLS.

Companies reporting difficulty in filling skilled positions (68% of the sample) are more likely than other companies to provide traditional flextime and to offer career counseling or management/leadership training for women. On the other hand, companies that find it easy to fill skilled positions are more likely to reimburse child care costs for employees who work late.

Companies finding it difficult to fill entry level or hourly positions (40% of the sample) are more likely to allow flexibility in moving from full-time to part-time work and to allow time off to care for mildly ill children. On the other hand, companies that find it easier to fill entry-level or hourly positions are more likely to reimburse child care costs for working late and overnight business travel.

Companies that have downsized in the past year (29% of the sample) are more likely to allow employees to work at home occasionally. They are also more likely to provide backup care and sick child care. Since companies that downsize often rely on fewer people to do the same amount of work as before, work-life options that minimize absenteeism make sense. Companies that have downsized are also more likely to offer EAPs, presumably for the survivors and the "pink-slipped."

Finally, companies that are underperforming their competitors are more likely to allow employees time off to attend school or child care functions. Companies that are outperforming their competitors are more likely to make direct contributions to elder care programs in the community, keep employees well informed of the work-life assistance available to them, and offer career counseling and management/leadership programs for women.

CONCLUSION

The mere fact that so many companies provide programmatic assistance and supportive work environments indicates that many company executives are aware that meeting the needs of employees not only helps these employees and their families but also can benefit the bottom line.

However, the findings of this study also suggest that a number of executives still do not share this belief, as evidenced by the small proportions of companies providing many of the benefits, programs, and policies we examined. To the extent that company leadership itself reflects the growing diversity of the workforce—particularly by promoting more women and minorities into top executive positions—one might expect to see an increase in work-life support, as our findings suggest.

Finally, the fact that some companies are focusing on increasing supervisor support, improving the family-friendliness of the culture, and even making business decisions with the employees' personal and family life in mind suggests that some business leaders are moving away from the notion of family life as merely presenting "problems" to be solved and toward a broader view of the synergies that are possible when work life and home life fit together in more positive ways.

REFERENCES

Aetna. 1988. Internal research conducted by the Work/Life Strategies Department of Aetna, Hartford, Conn.

————. 1990. Internal research conducted by the Work/Life Strategies Department of Aetna, Hartford, Conn.

Barnett, R. 1999. A new work-life model for the twenty-first century. *The Annals of the American Academy of Political and Social Science* 562: 143–58.

Bond, J. T. 1999. *The impact of downsizing on employees.* New York: Families and Work Institute.

Bond, J. T., E. Galinsky, and J. E. Swanberg. 1998. *The 1997 national study of the changing workforce.* New York: Families and Work Institute.

Families and Work Institute. 1993. *An evaluation of Johnson & Johnson's work-family initiative.* New York: Families and Work Institute.

Fernandez, J. 1986. *Child care and corporate productivity: Resolving family/work conflicts.* Lexington, Mass.: Lexington Books, D. C. Heath.

Galinsky, E., and J. T. Bond. 1998. *The 1998 business work-life study.* New York: Families and Work Institute.

Galinsky, E., J. T. Bond, and D. E. Friedman. 1993. *The national study of the changing workforce.* New York: Families and Work Institute.

Galinsky, E., and D. Hughes. 1987. The *Fortune* magazine child care study. Paper presented at the annual convention of the American Psychological Association, New York.

Galinsky, E., and A. A. Johnson. 1998. *The new business case for addressing work-life issues.* New York: Families and Work Institute.

Greenberger, E., W. A. Goldberg, S. Hamill, R. O'Neil, and C. K. Payne. 1989.

Contributions of a supportive work environment to parents' well-being and orientation to work. *American Journal of Community Psychology* 17:755–83.

Hoffman, L W. 1989. Effects of maternal employment in the two-parent family. *American Psychologist* 44:283–92.

IBM. 1991. Internal work-life survey conducted by IBM, Armonk, N.Y.

Karasek, R. A. 1979. Job demands, job decision latitude, and mental strain: Implications for job redesign. *Administrative Science Quarterly* 24:285–314.

Lambert, S. J., and K. Hopkins. 1993. *Added benefits: The link between family-responsive policies and work performance at Fel-Pro, Inc.* Chicago: University of Chicago.

Marra, R., and J. Lindner. 1992. The true cost of parental leave: The parental leave cost model. In *Parental leave and productivity: Current research,* edited by D. E. Friedman, E. Galinsky, and V. Plowden. New York: Families and Work Institute.

Piotrkowski, C. S. 1979. *Work and the family system.* New York: Macmillan.

Repetti, R. L., and K. A. Cosmas. 1991. The quality of the social environment at work and job satisfaction. *Journal of Applied Psychology* 21:840–54.

Shinn, M., D. Phillips, C. Howes, E. Galinsky, and M. Whitebook. 1990. *Correspondence between mothers' perceptions and observer ratings of quality in child care centers.* New York: Families and Work Institute.

Staines, G. L., and E. Galinsky. 1992. Parental leave and productivity: The supervisor's view. In *Parental leave and productivity: Current research,* edited by D. E. Friedman, E. Galinsky, and V. Plowden. New York: Families and Work Institute.

Staines, G. L., and J. H. Pleck. 1983. *The impact of work schedules in the family.* Ann Arbor: Institute for Social Research, University of Michigan.

Voydanoff, P. 1988. Work role characteristics, family structure demands, and work/family conflict. *Journal of Marriage and the Family* 50:749–61.

CHAPTER 9

Work, Family, and Globalization

Broadening the Scope of Policy Analysis

Harriet E. Gross

From a disconnect to a celebrated reconnect—that's the story of work and family as told for the last decade or so. Broadcast and print media regale us so often with the difficulties of "balancing" work and family that yesterday's myth of their separation has become today's cliché about their connection. More than a decade ago Gerstel and Gross (1987) called attention to the now generally acknowledged ways in which nineteenth-century events and ideologies—particularly the notion of work and family as gender-segregated spheres—clouded understanding of an enduring, though historically varied, relationship between work and family. The changes attendant upon the continuing growth of industrial capitalism, commercialization, and urbanization brought with them the physical as well as ideological separation of work site from family site and home site. These ideologically separated "spheres" designated "work" as what drew wages outside the home (normatively associated with men's "breadwinning") and "family" as the privatized care of spouses, children, and households (normatively associated with women's "homemaking"). Along with others, we have argued that the legacy of this historical construction of work and family as separate spheres no longer fits contemporary realities, which, among other changes, usually require the waged and family work of both parents (assuming there are two), and often that of their teen-aged children as well.[1]

---

1. To avoid the clarifying but redundant phrasing, I will hereafter forgo the modifier

Today, what constitute normatively defined "work" and "family" are once again undergoing redefinition; for example, home-based waged work and workplace sensitivity to family responsibilities are further dislodging acceptance of these spheres as truly separate. This ongoing reconstitution of work and family prompts the metaphor of a kaleidoscope—where what we think of as "work" and "family" shape and morph into each other, revealing their mutual contingency. Just as in the past, today there is a relationship between the two that is protean, reciprocal, and mutually constitutive. However interdependent this relationship may be, it is not always well understood, as current discomfiture with boundaries delineating the "where" and the "who" of "caring" (associated with the home) and "production" (associated with the workplace) make clear. The thesis of this chapter is that although research and analysis have demystified the myth of separate spheres, new problems now result from the acknowledged, but narrowly circumscribed, *connection* between work and family.

My purpose here is fourfold: (1) to critique this circumscribed relationship, (2) to argue that the narrowed version of the link between work and family diverts attention away from the social and economic structural underpinnings of the most significant work and family consequences, (3) to analyze how this diversion misdirects policy, and (4) to suggest that this restricted and privatized focus also eclipses an important resource for addressing work/family issues—community-based support systems.

THE ENCAPSULATION OF THE CONNECTION
BETWEEN WORK AND FAMILY

A distinct myopia attends the current conceptualization of the work/family connection. An acknowledged work/family loop has become encapsulated, viewed as a subset of social problems, cut away and isolated from its larger economic and political moorings. As a result, solutions have come to inhere in the manipulation of one or the other parts of this subset. Maintaining the connection between work and family in such a self-contained loop results in piecemeal solutions—attempts to fix one (at home) or another (at work) specific tension that family members (mostly women) and workers deal with in their day-to-day lives.

"waged" to distinguish this labor from that of family or other kinds of "work," e.g., volunteering.

A burgeoning industry of consultants available to corporations, as well as the increasingly available in-house "coordinator of work and family" (see, for example, Johnson and Rose 1992), has emerged to urge implementation of policies said to promote work/family "balance." The list is growing, making available one or more of the following: maternity (usually) and/or paternity (rarely) leave and benefits; child care referral or availability, which usually amounts to subsidies to parents for external care or provision of on-site care or, less frequently, sitter services for sick children and/or travel obligations; similar referrals and/or assistance for elder care for parents both far and nearby; and finally, efforts to assist workers with day-to-day obligations such as time off for children's school functions, for dentist and doctor appointments, and even for getting clothes to the cleaners or having someone at home to meet repair personnel.[2] Here, too, must be listed the increasing attention paid to part-time employment, job sharing, and flextime (Connor, Hooks, and McGuire 1997) as accommodations to family needs.

At home, families develop individualized strategies to cover child care and family care demands. Employed parents resort to alternating shifts, reliance on available family members, or home-based work (Riley and McCloskey 1997). Working parents struggle over gender-defined responsibilities to urge greater father involvement in home care, child care, and elder care—assuming he's there (Hochschild 1989, 1997).

It is not, of course, that these responses are insignificant. Redress for the tensions they identify is necessary as families struggle with day-to-day urgencies. But all such proverbial band-aids—necessary, stopgap accommodations to real tensions between work and family—should not overshadow or indeed obscure the need for more fundamental and wholesale change. Understandably, such programs that accommodate families' and workers' immediate needs earn praise for the "enlightened" corporate leaders who make them available, especially since even this degree of enlightenment is by no means widespread. Yet from my perspective, limiting solutions to such measures under the rubric "work/family programs" is a problem in itself for at least two reasons.

2. Even these programs are not routinely available, nor are they often offered together. If they are offered, subtle messages may convince employees that full utilization may be frowned upon. Or, it may be impractical for an employee to make use of a work/family program (Kaitin 1994, 92; Bond, Galinsky, and Swanberg 1998). Or, if there is acknowledgment of the need to broaden the focus of work/family constraints, such "broadening" strategies may be restricted to increasing flexibility of work-site conditions—a still highly restricted view in terms of the critique argued here (see, for example, Kropf 1997).

First, typically only large corporations recognize the need for and are even able to offer these programs.[3] This defining characteristic—the corporations' willingness and ability to make use of such consultants—promises to exacerbate existing social inequalities. The piecemeal "fix-its" the consultants devise are least likely to serve the already disadvantaged and most vulnerable—women and minorities—who typically do not work in the settings where such benefits exist (see Danaher 1996, 111–12; Greider 1998, 98–100).

Second and even more important, the present casting of work/family "programs," while undoubtedly better than no response at all, has a major drawback. Limiting work/family programs to these "solutions" sidetracks critical scrutiny of underlying economic and political forces that are changing the very availability, structure, and security of work. It is these changes that are a most fundamental source of work/family tensions, viewed not only from the perspective of U.S. workers and families but from that of our global counterparts as well.

AVOIDING THE ECONOMIC AND POLITICAL
BACKDROP OF WORK AND FAMILY

Scholars who work within the present casting of research variables and available remedies help legitimate the encapsulation of work and family. Research attention to determinants and consequences is heavily oriented to topics such as "stress," "balance," or "integration," for example, with respect to relationship quality between working parents and their children (e.g., Eckenrode and Gore 1990).[4] This nearly exclusive focus on determinants and consequences for individuals and within individual families (see also Benjamin and Sullivan 1996; Parcel and Menaghan 1994; Walzer 1996; for a cross-national perspective, see Chafetz and Hagan 1996) has the unhappy consequence of narrowing possible policy considerations.[5] The focus on individualized factors artificially

---

3. For example, a consultant service in Evanston, Illinois, that addresses this corporate recognition only serves firms with at least 500 employees.

4. See the whole April 1994 issue of *Family Relations,* titled "Work, Stress, and Families." In this vein, too, are studies about work's effect on parental and gender identities (e.g., Aaltion-Marjosola and Lehtinen [1998]; Greenstein [1996]; Hojgaard [1997]).

5. See, for example, Burstein, Bricher, and Einwohner (1995); Galinsky, Bond, and Friedman (1996); and Idhii-Kuntz (1994). The Alfred P. Sloan Centers set up at several universities around the country (Berkeley, Chicago, Michigan, Cornell) appear to focus mainly on problems typically associated with middle-class families and internal family issues. The implication is that specific work-site and home-site factors dictate and encompass what is relevant. There is no consideration of the relationship to work/family issues

limits the research to discussion that fails to challenge institutions—most importantly the national and transnational corporations, which, not incidentally, are among the primary providers of funds for research in this area.

Yet how can we ignore the fact that having a job and being able to afford a family in the first place is a fundamental work/family issue? How can we watch income disparity grow, see wage stagnation and job insecurity persist, and acknowledge the erosions of worker protection attendant upon undermined unionization without connecting these events to work/family policy? Why isn't the common fate of American workers and foreign workers—usually cast only as competitors—addressed? Or the health care system, which leaves 43 million people uninsured? Or the dilemma for Medicare recipients who must choose between needed medications and food? Why do even those work/family programs that exist legitimize and reinforce cultural acceptance of the notion that family options should serve the imperatives of work? Why is an ethic that has made work ascendant and family derivative not "on the table"? We can understand why this ethic is not questioned inside corporate boardrooms, but why not in the academy? Why have we tolerated a definition of relevant policy options dictated by corporate beneficence? In short, how can we justify the circumscription of contributing factors and possible avenues of redress so as to limit critique of those social institutions that are root sources of work/family tensions?

I suggest that attending to the larger economic and political forces shaping the relationship between work and family from the late twentieth century on should be the business of work-and-family scholars. Of course, this is not to deny the useful services of those corporate responses to work/family problems already in place, and we should recognize these. But we should also examine the way sociopolitical forces constrain what comes to be recognized as relevant to work and family. We should be teaching how the current work/family incarnation responds to contemporary forces of immense import to our concerns.

---

of economic globalization, multinational corporate dominance, wage stagnation, and/or growing income disparity. This same individual/couple and business/professional concentration of work/family "topics" is evident in the "Selected New Additions to the Work-Family Researchers' Literature Database" posted on the new web site of the Center for Work and Family of Boston College (3/26/99), where topics such as "psychological distress," "time norms," and "marital quality" predominate.

CONTENDING WITH THE ECONOMIC AND
POLITICAL CONTEXT OF WORK AND FAMILY:
POLICY ISSUES

One need not be an expert on international economics or social policy
to make a plausible argument that scholars of work and family should,
in particular, relate the effect of market globalization and capital flight
to their subject matter.[6] We should consider how these buzzwords of the
nineties have contributed to unprecedented transnational corporate
power that has far-reaching consequences for work and family. The
growing power of transnational corporations to impose their socially
disrupting, profit-seeking excesses on vulnerable employees as well as
on whole communities far outpaces national governments' abilities or
willingness to regulate and control them (see especially Danaher 1996;
Grieder 1998; Mander and Goldsmith 1996).

Economists have shown how corporate dominance over labor and
trade markets (1) eliminates jobs even in profitable corporations, (2)
leads to wage stagnation and job insecurity for those still working, and
(3) contributes to a politically destabilizing growth in income disparity.
Among those who have endured the worst of globalization's negative
effects are women and girls, especially in Third World but also in First
World nations (typically minority women). They bear the brunt of low
wages, unsafe working conditions, nonexistent benefits, and job insecurity (Greider 1997, 98). Greider (1998, 342) explains this persistent
pattern as a corollary of the likelihood that the harshest conditions will
be assigned to the weakest members of society and to those already
habituated to patriarchal domination in the household. Whatever the
source, these women are the "enablers" of the corporate growth in profits and the rising executive salaries that have allowed managers and
administrators to reap unprecedented levels of financial rewards. As
"maids to the world economy," the relationship of Third World women
in Latin America and Asia to First World workers parallels the relationship in Western societies of the housekeeper/child care worker to the

6. In this section I rely on the following analyses and suggestions for dealing with the
problems outlined: Bluestone, Harrison, and Baker (1981); Brenner (1998); Danaher
(1996); Galbraith (1998); Greider (1997); Henwood (1997); Korten (1995); Longworth
(1998); Mander and Goldsmith (1996); Moberg (1998); Scott, Lee, and Schmitt (1998);
Wade and Veneroso (1998).

dual-career couple whose employment and family work she sustains (see Wrigley 1995).[7]

Investors reward corporations that freely seek out low-waged and minimally regulated production sites employing the seemingly endless streams of women and girls—whose abundance as a "reserve army" undercuts the security of all. In the process, not only jobs but also the economic underpinnings of whole communities in the United States disappear. Why, then, is it not the responsibility of work/family specialists to address these job security issues with the same attention we give to the provision of child care, for example? On-site child care, after all, presumes the existence of a job site.

Or take the issue of wages stagnating under the downward pressure of competition from lower-waged foreign workers. Freely moving capital withdraws from one country's currency when more favorable exchange rates elsewhere make it profitable to do so. Withdrawing capital destabilizes local economies. Destabilization contributes to loan defaults. Loan defaults dry up credit for the very capital investment that would raise productivity so that wages could rise. Rising wages in newly developing countries would lessen the depressant effect of their wages on our workers—thereby eliminating the basis for an "us" versus "them" logic.

Threats to job stability are burdensome in their own right. But work/family scholars should also examine how such vulnerability compromises the likelihood that employers will address non-wage-related work/family concerns—e.g., expendable "frills" such as time to care for children and aging parents. If your job is on the line, you're not likely to ask for time to take your turn in your child's carpool or to drive your mother-in-law to the doctor. In short, work/family specialists should understand how machinations of markets and capital undermine even modest requests that have been sought to address one or another unmet need on the job or in the family. As job security becomes more and more anachronistic, the issue of "work/family benefits" becomes an oxymoron for all but a thin slice of the labor force's privileged elite.

So what is to be done?

7. Except that some maids and nannies in the United States are now demanding and getting higher wages and better working conditions. See "Demands for Nannies Increases Perks and Pay in Field," *Milwaukee Journal and Sentinel*, 9 December 1998; "Parents Are Willing to Pay More for Quality Child Care," *Greensboro [N.C.] News and Record*, 5 January 1999.

FROM BAND-AID TO MAJOR SURGERY

This is not the place to undertake a wholesale critique of the effects of the economic and political underpinnings of these corporate machinations on working families.[8] But a sampling of proposals as topics appropriate for work/family policy consideration is instructive. Consider, for example, the issues of capital flight and income disparity. With respect to the former, constraints on the level of profit from financial manipulation have been suggested. Economist James Tobin has proposed a tax (called a "Tobin Tax") on foreign exchange transactions that would limit the rewards of short-term speculations over long-term investment (Longworth 1998, 256–57).[9] This proposal attests that mainstream economists, like Tobin, have recognized the consequences to workers of financial manipulation and wage stagnation. But since most economists have not specifically addressed the work/family implications of these issues, whether the policy proposals they design are family-friendly is still an open question. To consider this question, the value of examining such effects must first be recognized. While apparently far removed from work/family problems, in fact financial manipulation that threatens wage levels of foreign workers and therefore U.S. workers' wages is at least as much related to work and family as is the more acknowledged absence of suitable child care options.[10]

While seemingly remote from what are currently identified as work/family concerns (by work/family scholars if not by working families), growing inequalities of income and wealth—unparalleled in other industrialized nations—seriously threaten the financial security of American middle-class families, who find it ever harder to maintain their parents' aspirations and lifestyle. Capital flight and corporate power operate in the United States too, as corporations overcompensate top

8. Such a critique would take notice of the recent argument made by Nicholas Kristoff and Edward Wyatt in a four-part series titled "Global Contagion" in the *New York Times* (Kristoff and Wyatt 1999). The series suggests that far from being an inevitable outgrowth of anonymous and "natural" economic forces, recent upheavals attributed to globalization (for example, in Indonesia, Thailand, and Russia) were a response to policies promoted by the U.S. financial community and taken up by the U.S. government (see also Pfaff 1999).

9. This is just one possible mechanism. As an example of another, Greider (1997, 257) suggests that the Federal Reserve could not allow U.S. banks to accept transfers from offshore banking centers, which would, then, eliminate "the leakage" from such centers. See also Freidman (1999) for the view that such capital controls do not serve the goal of more equitable gloalization effects in the long term.

10. See Wade and Veneroso (1998) for the wage-lowering impact of efforts to deal with the recent Asian financial crisis.

executives whose decisions close plants and businesses, leaving few income-producing prospects for the employees left behind. Those who make these decisions in deference to bottom-line demands of capital investors raise their own incomes as they eliminate those of employees. Yet not just assembly line workers but managers and executives, too, face seriously eroded opportunities to recoup the gains of years of dedicated service to corporations no longer identified with the countries of their national headquarters, let alone their former local communities (see Scott, Lee, and Schmitt 1997 on U.S. loss of jobs).

Understanding the structural forces threatening job security, on which requests for all other measures directed at work and family depend, moves policy considerations away from piecemeal requests—this or that corporation "fix-it." Recognizing growing corporate control as the source of the weakening of working people's leverage underscores the need for comprehensive means to strengthen working people's organizing efforts—worldwide. Such organizing would press for trade regulations to get all trading partners (wherever the flagship bases of the transnational corporations involved) to adhere, for example, to wage-floors, health and safety conditions, and pollution standards for workers everywhere to undercut the overall decline in working conditions and wages that has been dubbed the "race to the bottom."[11]

As such organizing goes forward, effort should also be directed to challenging presumptions about how work is organized, particularly the eight-hour day, the forty-hour week, and the on-site job. The technology that enables global markets, allowing production to go wherever labor is cheapest, also eliminates the basis for previous presumptions about work site and work time. The increasing (but still relatively meager) use of—for example—home-based and part-time work with full benefits and adequate health care, extended unemployment benefits, and subsidized retraining opportunities attests to the fact that responses to work/family issues affect all working people, from blue-collar service to white-collar management.

Perhaps the most far-reaching and fundamental mechanism aimed at reducing the growing income and wealth disparity in the United States is Employee Stock Option Programs (ESOPs), which give working people an opportunity to participate in the profit-taking of the organizations

---

11. For a different perspective on the possible impact of making adherence to American human rights and labor standards a condition of trade with foreign countries, see Amsdenm and Kikino (1999).

for whom they work. ESOPs not only allow individual workers to accumulate a measure of wealth;[12] they are, as Greider (1997) points out, a means by which the leveraging power of jointly accumulated assets can be used for the benefit of working families and their communities. These assets could be used to underwrite large-scale projects that workers as individuals could never achieve. As such, ESOPs and similar redistributive mechanisms consistent with democratic capitalism should be recognized for their profound work/family policy implications. Some policy analysts have already acknowledged the enabling potential of combined assets from ESOPS for working families and the communities in which they live, work, and educate their children (see discussion of the New Birth Transformation Corporation in Greider 1997, 433–35). By investing their combined assets and using their joint borrowing power for projects to benefit their own and their communities' futures, working families would be taking advantage of the credit basis and leveraging potential of wealth accumulation (Greider 1997, 431–39). In so doing they would be erecting the basis for the economic independence and political power that underlies real accomplishment of the kind of capitalism, i.e., democratic capitalism, that working people in a democratic society must realize is their right.[13]

Finally, the scope of the workplace's family-relevant policy should be broadened further still to directly engage with its global implications. Transnational corporate hegemony points to the need at the global level for regulatory counterparts to our national institutions (e.g., the Federal Trade Commission, the Securities and Exchange Commission, the Internal Revenue Service) to level sanctions for violations of mandatory codes of corporate conduct (Moberg 1998). Work-and-family scholars should join efforts to promote such global regulatory institutions to penalize predatory practices such as production by child labor, use of hazardous materials, and violations of fair trade practices.

The possibilities identified here just scratch the surface of suggestions

12. ESOPs are not the only mechanism to enable employee ownership. See Morris (1996, 440).

13. Efforts to use the power of working families within common work associations have a long history, going at least as far back as in the guilds of the Middle Ages in Europe. More recently, at the end of the nineteenth century Emile Durkheim (1964, 5), a founding father of modern sociology, called for work-based associations to accomplish the organic social organization he saw as the basis of a healthy society. Durkheim was from France, where syndicalism, a movement to allow workers to share control and participate in the profits of their industries, had developed.

to rein in growing corporate control and shore up the leverage of working families in response to it.[14] Included, too, should be other related social and political objectives, e.g., instituting a "living wage," organizing contingent workers, promoting campaign finance reform, and making tax laws more progressive. Whatever the mechanisms, work/family scholars need to relinquish a narrow (i.e., privatized) view of relevant "family policies" to address a broad range of political issues and possibilities for redress. It is our responsibility to clarify the impact of everything that affects working lives and families' initiatives in the face of forces that have such fateful effects. It is our obligation, too, to foster the political alliances upon which effective social action depends.

BROADENING COMMUNITY-BASED SUPPORT FOR WORK/FAMILY CONCERNS

A second major policy focus largely eclipsed by encapsulating work and family—that is, by not acknowledging their broader social context—involves the use of local, extrafamilial resources. Some work/family activists have connected work/family concerns to community resources (e.g., Southwick et al. 1998).[15] However, for the most part we have not considered how reorganization of community/family boundaries could have the far-reaching consequence of deprivatizing the work/family connection. In not making the case for such reorganization, we as scholars contribute to and are complicit (however inadvertently) in the continuation of the legacy of the privatized " family." Neglect of work/family/community relations echoes the wider cultural penchant for denying the viability of shared responses to shared problems, just as it also individualizes and privatizes both causes and consequences of work/family concerns (Currie and Skolnick 1988, chapter 1; see also Morris 1996).

Notable exceptions to the underdevelopment of community-based responses to work/family concerns are four projects managed by Work Family Directions on behalf of a consortium of corporate sponsors known as the American Business Collaboration (ABC) for Quality Dependent Care. The projects undertaken are aimed at increasing the supply and quality of early child care, programs for school-age children,

14. See also growing interest in employee-initiated programs in Firestein and Grundy (1998).
15. Publication of a new journal, *Community, Work, and Family* (especially Roddick 1998), suggests commitment to this topic.

and elder care services. Such efforts are valuable not only for the services they seek, but also for their expressed intent to enhance new partnerships among community members and organizations (Southwick et al. 1998).

There are several strategic reasons for activating such community networks beyond the obvious efficiencies of meeting the needs of many families simultaneously, rather than attempting to respond to each family's concerns one at a time. Enlisting community-based networks engenders and reinforces the very social cohesion on which community response depends. While building such an enabling community infrastructure is an expressed goal of these programs, there is even more radicalizing potential to such programs than published reports about them suggest (Southwick et al. 1998, 8). Such locally based structures could become the apparatus not only for meeting existing work/family concerns but also for anticipating them. Such a community-based infrastructure could also be the seedbed for further challenging existing institutions and for involving more community members in institution-building projects. Arguably, it is the decline today (relative to earlier decades) of just such institutions, which undergird social cohesion, that both contributes to and is an expression of the constraints facing working families (e.g., Hochschild 1997, 243–44).

Several possibilities beyond those being attempted come to mind: more widespread coordination between schools, park districts, and community health facilities to help working families use these existing physical plants for pre- and after-school care as well as for elder care programs (which could also enlist elders in child care along the lines of existing grandparent/children efforts). Such extension of the uses of these publicly supported structures and facilities could open up possibilities for all kinds of people-centered programs. Older schoolchildren in the upper grades could hone care-taking skills as aides in these before- and after-school programs. Given widespread concern about children needing to cultivate caring skills, not to mention rules of basic civility and ethical behavior, such school programs could serve multiple goals. Then, instead of being only remedial, such efforts to deploy the skills of community members of all ages would become the threads of the very social fabric that would enable creative, not just reactive, response.

Corporate and government financing for such programs is not unrealistic. Corporations purportedly concerned with work/family issues could encourage employee implementation of such community facilities via monetary and service credits—a mechanism already used by many corporations to promote a beneficial corporate image. Local business, too, could support the implementation (if not the execution) of such community projects. Employees working within their own communities to coordinate work/family support systems would be serving their personal as well their company's interests—goals that are, of course, not necessarily incompatible. Both corporations and businesses, in turn, could receive tax relief and other subsidies for underwriting their employees' involvement. Most important, with such an infrastructure in place, community members would develop many more such services specifically tailored to *local* work/family problems. In sum, programs to integrate work/family/community relations around common concerns would enable the unleashing of a potentially powerful but as yet untapped resource.

CONCLUSIONS

The argument of this chapter is that it is not enough to acknowledge the relationship between work and family by setting up a child care center or having a work/family consultant recommend options to beleaguered employees. These meager responses are, in any case, too narrowly focused. Piecemeal "fix-its" do little to empower working families—to enable them to erect institutions able to counter the influence of concentrated capitalist corporate dominance over their lives. Analysis of the work/family relationship must be grounded in today's socioeconomic reality—a globalizing economy with profound implications for working families—if substantive protections for those families are to materialize. Analysis of the impact of the forces set in motion with globalization must direct policy response. Major encompassing efforts are needed to shore up working people's security and stability vis-à-vis the hegemony of transnational corporations.

This power has weakened a social contract that existed for much of the past century between corporate and business America, government, and working people. This contract, as many have observed, assured protection from the vicissitudes of an unbridled market-driven economy for the most economically vulnerable. It also allowed a large middle class to achieve satisfying incomes and lifestyles. This contract is eroding just when the work/family relationship needs more, not less, support in the face of the consequences of the brand of capitalism practiced in the United States. The case is well documented for the claim that the United States is less responsive to the social welfare needs of its population than any other industrialized capitalist country (e.g., Greider 1997, chapter

16). Americans who scoff at the likelihood that profitable businesses could exist alongside such supports do not realize that many such programs to protect working families in other countries have been in place for decades and that these countries have prospered. To the argument that it is just these social programs in Western Europe and Japan that are currently under siege because of their "excesses" comes counterevidence: it is the imperatives of the current global market at work that are undermining the viability of these programs too (e.g., Brenner 1998,138–80; Greider 1997, 363). Moreover, working people recognize this, and (for instance, in France, Germany, and Japan) they are resisting attempts to dislodge the supports that were previously consistent with prosperous economies.

Our recognition that the relationship between work and families reflects the social and economic pressures in which it is embedded could be the catalyst for rethinking the logic of the social contract. We could use the threats to working families not just to call for protection of what was won in the past, but to reconsider the contract's very scope. Changing realities of our daily lives make clear that the two connected engines, work and family, are fatefully enmeshed in a changing global economy. We should make awareness of this fact open to the terms of the new social contract. The weakening of working people's power to maintain necessary supports, along with heightened sensitivity to other work/family needs, could be the impetus for this reconstitution. The old social contract attempted to soften the harsher consequences of capitalism. A new one could catapult work/family concerns to center stage.

Today we know that family needs cannot remain neglected under the misbegotten privacy shield of a purported personal realm. We know that empowering working people means strengthening their ability to protect their families. Using the knowledge gained from European social welfare economies, we too could build support for families into the economic calculus through the efforts suggested here. Families should not always succumb to work requirements. The relationship between work and family should not be considered derivative—as something that needs shoring up *after* consideration of the effects of the economy. A new social contract would recognize the connection; how people earn a living and how they protect their families must take their rightful place among the economic and political factors routinely given a hearing in the business and financial decision-making of corporations and governments.

REFERENCES

Aaltion-Marjosola, Iiris, and Jyri Lehtinen. 1998. Male managers as fathers? Contrasting management, fatherhood, and masculinity (Peter Banning in the movie *Hook*). *Human Relations* 51(February):121–36.

Amsdenm, Alice H., and Takashi Kikino. 1999. The left and globalization. *Dissent,* Spring, 7–9.

Benjamin, Orly, and Oriel Sullivan. 1996. The importance of difference: Conceptualizing increased flexibility in gender relations at home. *Sociological Review* 44(May):225–51.

Bluestone, Barry, Bennett Harrison, and Lawrence Baker. 1981. *Corporate flight: The causes and consequences of economic dislocation.* New York: Progressive Alliance.

Bond, J. T., E. Galinsky, and J. E. Swanberg. 1998. *The 1997 national study of the changing workforce.* New York: Families and Work Institute.

Boyd, Monica. 1997. Feminizing paid work. *Current Sociology* 45(April):49–73.

Brenner, Robert. 1998. The economics of global turbulence. *New Left Review* 229(May/June):1–264.

Burstein, Paul, Marie R. Bricher, and Rachel L. Einwohner. 1995. Policy alternatives and political change: Work, family, and gender on the congressional agenda. *American Sociological Review* 60(1):67–83.

Chafetz, Janet Saltzman, and Jacqueline Hagan. 1996. The gender division of labor and family change in industrial societies: A theoretical accounting. *Journal of Comparative Family Studies* 27(Summer):187–219.

Connor, Monique, Karen Hooks, and Terry McGuire. 1997. Gaining legitimacy for flexible work arrangements and career paths: The business case for public accounting and professional services firms. In *Integrating work and family: Challenges and choices for a changing world,* edited by S. Parasuraman and J. H. Greenhaus, 154–66. Westport, Conn.: Quorum Books.

Currie, Elliot, and Jerome H. Skolnick. 1988. *America's problems: Social issues and social policy.* 2d ed. Glenview, Ill.: Scott, Foresman.

Danaher, Kevin, ed. 1996. *Corporations are gonna get your mama.* Monroe, Maine: Common Courage Press.

Durkheim, Emile. [1893] 1964. *The division of labor in society.* New York: Free Press.

Eckenrode, John, and Susan Gore, eds. 1990. *Stress between work and family.* New York: Plenum.

Firestein, Netsy, and Lea Grundy. 1998. *Work, family and the labor movement.* Cambridge, Mass.: Radcliffe Public Policy Institute.

Friedman, Thomas. 1999. A manifesto for the fast world. *New York Times Magazine,* 28 March, 40ff.

Galbraith, James K. 1998. With economic inequality for all. *The Nation* 268(7): 24–26.

Galinsky, Ellen, James Bond, and Dana E. Friedman. 1996. The role of employers in addressing the needs of employed parents. *Journal of Social Issues* 52(Fall):111–36.

Gerstel, Naomi, and Harriet Gross, eds. 1987. *Families and work.* Philadelphia: Temple University Press.

Googins, Bradley K. 1997. Shared responsibility for managing work and family relationships: A community perspective. In *Integrating work and family: Challenges and choices for a changing world,* edited by S. Parasuraman and J. H. Greenhaus, 220–31. Westport, Conn.: Quorum Books.

Greenstein, Theodore N. 1996. Husbands' participation in domestic labor: Interactive effects of wives' and husbands' gender ideologies. *Journal of Marriage and the Family* 58(August):585–95.

Greider, William. 1997. *One world ready or not: The manic logic of global capitalism.* New York: Touchstone.

———. 1998. The global crisis deepens. Now what? *The Nation* 267(12): 11–16.

Henwood, Doug. 1997. *Wall Street: How it works and for whom.* London: Verso.

Hochschild, Arlie. 1997. *The time bind: When work becomes home and home becomes work.* New York: Henry Holt.

Hochschild, Arlie, with Anne Machung. 1989. *The second shift.* New York: Avon.

Hojgaard, Lis. 1997. Working fathers—caught in the web of the symbolic order of gender. *Acta Sociologica* 40(3):245–61.

Idhii-Kunta, Masako. 1994. Work and family life: Findings from international research and suggestions for future study. *Journal of Family Issues* 15(September): 490–506.

Johnson, Arlene A., and Karol L. Rose. 1992. *The emerging role of the work-family manager.* New York: Conference Board.

Kaitin, Katherine Karr. 1994. Congressional responses to families in the workplace: The Family and Medical Leave Act of 1987–1988. In *More than kissing babies? Current child and family policy in the United States,* edited by F. H. Jacobs, and M. W. Davies, 91–120. Westport, Conn.: Auburn House.

Korten, David C. 1995. *When corporations rule the world.* West Hartford, Conn.: Kumarian.

Kristof, Nicholas D., and Edward Wyatt. 1999. Global contagion: A narrative. *New York Times,* 15–18 February.

Kropf, Marcia Brumit. 1997. A research perspective on work-family issues. In *Integrating work and family: Challenges and choices for a changing world,* edited by S. Parasuraman and J. H. Greenhaus, 69–76. Westport, Conn.: Quorum Books.

Longworth, Richard C. 1998. *Global squeeze: The coming crisis for first-world nations.* Chicago: Contemporary Books.

Mander, Jerry, and Edward Goldsmith, eds. 1996. *The case against the global economy and for a turn toward the local.* San Francisco: Sierra Club Books.

Miller, John H., ed. 1994. *Curing world poverty: The new world of property.* Washington, D.C.: Center for Economic and Social Justice.

Moberg, David. 1998. The challenge of globalization. Paper presented at the Back to Basics Conference, Chicago, 7–9 October.

Morris, David. 1996. Communities: Building authority, responsibility and capacity. In *The case against the global economy and for a turn toward the local,* edited by J. Mander and E. Goldsmith, 434–45. San Francisco: Sierra Club Books.

Parcel, Toby L., and Elizabeth G. Menaghan. 1994. *Parents' jobs and children's lives.* New York: Aldine de Gruyter.

Pfaff, William. 1999. International bookkeeping: The inside story on the globalization policy of the U.S. *Chicago Tribune,* Op-Ed, 2 March.

Riley, Francine, and Donna Weaver McCloskey. 1997. Telecommuting as a response to helping people balance work and family. In *Integrating work and family: Challenges and choices for a changing world,* edited by S. Parasuraman and J. H. Greenhaus, 133–42. Westport, Conn.: Quorum Books.

Roddick, Anita. 1998. Reflections on community, work, and family linkages. *Community, Work, and Family* 1(April):11–12.

Rodrik, Dana. 1997. *Has globalization gone too far?* Washington, D.C. : Institute for International Economics.

Scott, Robert E., Thea Lee, and John Schmitt. 1988. *Trading away good jobs: An examination of employment and wages in the U.S., 1979–94.* Washington, D.C.: Economic Policy Institute.

Southwick, Betty, Sharon Myrick, Leanne Barrett, Celeste Reid Lee, and Jill Landauer. 1998. *Building community infrastructure in response to changing work and family roles.* Boston: Work Family Directives.

Vannoy, Dana, and Paula J. Dubeck. 1998. *Challenges for work and family in the twenty-first century.* Hawthorne, N.Y.: Aldine de Gruyter.

Wade, Robert, and Frank Veneroso. 1998. The Asian crises: The high debt model versus the Wall Street treasury–IMF complex. *New Left Review* 228(March/April):3–23.

Walzer, Susan. 1996. Thinking about the baby: Gender and divisions of infant care. *Social Problems* 43(May):219–34.

Wohl, Faith. 1998. A panoramic view of work and family. In *Integrating work and family: Challenges and choices for a changing world,* edited by S. Parasuraman and J. H. Greenhaus, 15–24. Westport, Conn.: Quorum Books.

Wrigley, Julia. 1995. *Other people's children: An intimate account of the dilemmas facing middle-class parents and the women they hire to raise their children.* New York: Basic Books.

Zvonkovic, Anisa M., Cynthia J. Schmiege, and Leslie D. Hall. 1994. Influence strategies used when couples make work-family decisions and their importance for marital satisfaction. *Family Relations* 43(April):182–88.

PART THREE

HEARTSTRINGS AND PURSESTRINGS

Gendered Views from Within

CHAPTER 10

Changing the Structure and Culture of Work

Work and Family Conflict,
Work Flexibility, and Gender Equity
in the Modern Workplace

Kathleen Gerson and Jerry A. Jacobs

Once considered "separate spheres," the domains of work and family can no longer be so easily divided. As women, and especially mothers, have joined the workplace, the notion of distinct but complementary spheres has been replaced by a growing concern that the demands of work are increasingly at odds with the needs of families. Most families now depend on either two earners or one (female) parent. Yet the organization of work remains based on the principle that commitment means uninterrupted, full-time, and even overtime attention for a span of decades. This clash between family needs and workplace demands has produced a new dominant image based not on separate spheres, but on "work-family conflict."

Debate about the rise of work-family conflict has centered on the issue of working time.[1] Analysts such as Schor (1991) argue that Americans today are putting in more time at work than did earlier generations. Hochschild adds that increasing working time reflects basic cultural shifts in which home has become work and work has become home (1997, 38). Others, however, have disputed these claims, pointing to time-use studies that suggest leisure time has actually increased in recent decades (Robinson and Godbey 1997).

---

1. To distinguish clearly between public and private responsibilities, this chapter will use the terms "work" and "worker" to refer to paid work and paid workers only, even though unpaid domestic tasks surely qualify as "work" broadly conceived.

We offer a more complicated picture. Our analysis suggests that while average time at work has not increased substantially in the last several decades, this average masks a new dispersion among workers (Jacobs and Gerson 1998, 1999; see also Bluestone and Rose 1997; Rones, Ilg, and Gardner 1997). The labor force appears to be increasingly divided, with a growing group of workers putting in very long workweeks (well beyond the 40-hour standard) and another sizable group unable to find enough work to meet their needs. When the focus shifts from individuals to households, moreover, long workweeks appear to be concentrated among families with two earners (or one parent). These families are experiencing the greatest time crunch, not because they are working more as individuals but rather because their joint working time has become so large.

Working hours are fundamental, but taken alone they cannot tell the whole story of how workers' lives are changing. We also need to understand how in the context of growing work commitments people are coping with new conflicts between family and work. How are workers balancing their multiple obligations, what kinds of balance would they prefer, and what conflicts do they experience? Given the time that most must devote to work, what kind of workplace arrangements make a difference in workers' abilities to resolve the conflicts they face? And, finally, do workers perceive that serious costs and risks are associated with options that are ostensibly designed to ease their plight?

To answer these questions, we draw on the National Study of the Changing Workforce, a survey of the American labor force conducted in 1992.[2] Unique in the range of questions asked about workers' values and preferences and in its focus on the links, conflicts, and tensions between work and family, this survey also asked unusually detailed questions about workplace policies, organization, and culture. For these reasons, the Changing Workforce study makes it possible to untangle how work structures and processes—crucial factors that are usually hidden or overlooked in census and economic surveys—shape and constrain worker outlooks and strategies.

We use this rich material to examine the links between work and

---

2. Conducted by the Families and Work Institute, this study involved hour-long telephone interviews with a national probability sample of 3,381 employed men and women aged 18 through 64. For a general report on the findings, see Galinsky, Bond, and Friedman (1993).

family life, paying special attention to the role of workplace structure and culture in mediating conflicts between the home and the workplace. First, we examine workers' views about how they would like to balance family, work, and personal commitments. Who experiences conflict, and how and why does the perception of conflict vary across different groups of workers? Then we turn our attention to the kinds of work arrangements that might help alleviate such difficulties. Indeed, we argue that the current focus on hours spent working neglects an equally important aspect of work-family conflict—the actual conditions of work. Especially for workers who must put in long hours, aspects of the job such as flexibility, autonomy, and control over when one works are as likely to matter as working time. We thus investigate how the structure and culture of the workplace can either exacerbate or alleviate the conflicts workers face.

Finally, we consider a central but typically overlooked aspect of work-family conflict: Even when family-friendly policies are formally available, workers may conclude that taking advantage of them entails unspoken but very real costs. We thus complete our analysis by examining worker perceptions about potential conflicts between family-friendly and high-opportunity work environments. Do workers perceive that having and using policies that provide for family support are at odds with long-term career prospects?

In a social and economic context in which most workers simply cannot choose to work the amount of time they prefer, it is critical to discover if other circumstances at work can alleviate work-family conflicts. For workers in high-demand jobs, flexibility and autonomy are likely to be as or more important than working hours. Although we cannot investigate the innumerable and subtle ways that job conditions influence workers' options, we are able to explore one important aspect of job structure: the degree of flexibility and control a worker possesses in scheduling her or his work hours. Not only is control over scheduling important in its own right, especially for those who put in long hours, but it is also likely to be linked to other workplace circumstances, such as having a sense of personal autonomy and support.

If work arrangements that offer flexibility, autonomy, and control help workers resolve conflicts between family and work, we need to understand how such arrangements can be implemented fairly. The challenge is to develop social and economic policies that alleviate current dilemmas without sacrificing the principles of gender equity and responsible parenthood. Otherwise, new policies run the risk of reinstituting old inequalities in a new form. First, however, we need to know who is experiencing conflict and why.

BALANCING WORK AND FAMILY: PERCEPTIONS OF ACTUAL AND IDEAL ALLOCATIONS

Although most workers do not experience extreme levels of work-family conflict, the Changing Workforce survey suggests that close to half experience some.[3] These figures, however, may underestimate the scope of the problem because, taken alone, they do not tell us how workers would prefer to allocate their time. Do workers wish to spend more time with their families, more time working, or more time pursuing personal avocations beyond the bounds of either family or work?

The answer to this question is not obvious. If workers now perceive that work offers the pleasures once sought at home while home now poses the problems once posed by work, then most would prefer allocating more time to the job. Yet there is good reason to expect that those experiencing conflicts would, if given an opportunity, devote more time to family and personal pursuits. To understand how work-family conflict is experienced by workers, we need to know not only how they are currently balancing the various aspects of their lives but also how they would do so if they had more choice.

Table 10.1, which compares the actual and desired balance between family, self, and work for women and men, offers some insight.[4] It shows that both women and men would prefer, on average, to devote a larger percentage of their time to family and personal pursuits than they currently do. Similarly, each group would prefer to spend a smaller percentage of time at work. In considering their ideal balance between family, work, and self, women say they wish to spend 13 percent less time at work and 4 percent more time with their families. Men display a similar outlook, wishing for 14 percent less time on the job and 7 percent more time on family activities. Both groups, on average, would also like to have considerably more time available for pursuing individual and

3. We discuss the data on the extent of work-family conflict elsewhere (Jacobs and Gerson 1997).
4. Unfortunately, the Changing Workforce survey asked only a third of respondents about their ideal balance between family, self, and work or career. Thus, the percentages for actual and ideal time allocations are not strictly comparable. Since the smaller group is a random subset of the entire sample, there is good reason to have confidence in the comparisons.

TABLE 10.1
IDEAL VERSUS ACTUAL BALANCE BETWEEN
WORK AND FAMILY

	Women		Men	
	Actual	*Desired*	*Actual*	*Desired*
Total				
Percentage time for:				
Family	44.9	49.2	40.9	47.5
Self	19.5	39.8	21.0	37.5
Work	35.9	22.9	38.5	24.8
Like division	60.2		64.8	
Workweek of 1–34 hours				
Percentage time for:				
Family	50.3	49.3	41.0	47.0
Self	20.5	42.4	26.1	37.1
Work	29.6	23.8	32.8	26.8
Like division	65.8		70.2	
Workweek of 35–49 hours				
Percentage time for:				
Family	44.0	49.1	42.7	48.5
Self	19.5	40.1	21.6	38.9
Work	36.7	22.6	36.3	24.4
Like division	60.1		69.2	
Workweek of 50+ hours				
Percentage time for:				
Family	39.6	49.4	37.1	46.2
Self	17.9	32.8	18.4	34.7
Work	43.5	22.5	44.5	24.8
Like division	50.9		54.4	

SOURCE: National Study of the Changing Workforce.

personal activities, with women wishing for 20 percent more time and men hoping for 15 percent more.

The gap between the actual and desired balance grows as workers' hours increase. Those who work 50 hours per week or more are most likely to report that their actual distribution of time to work is too high and to family is too low. For both men and women, these are the workers most likely to report that their ideal balance is far from their actual balance. These preferences, moreover, are consistent with other findings, which also show that those men and women who put in the longest hours on the job are most likely to report a preference for working less (Jacobs and Gerson 1999).

It thus appears that if workers could act on their fondest wishes, they would create a new balance in which work would occupy less time and family life would get more attention. While there are surely exceptions, most workers are not working long hours in order to escape their homes and families. Rather, in the competition among work, family, and self, the self appears to be losing. The costs of work-family conflicts appear to have settled on the employed women and men themselves, who in their desire to meet work demands and family needs have less personal time.

FLEXIBILITY AT THE WORKPLACE

Are there social conditions and factors that can help alleviate work-family conflicts? For many workers, flexibility in scheduling work hours and increased control in work conditions may matter as much as actual time spent working. For full-time workers in particular, 45 flexible hours may seem less onerous than 35 rigidly scheduled ones. Indeed, many workers may be willing to work more hours in exchange for greater flexibility.

Flexibility gives workers some sense of control over when (and in some cases, where) they work. It also provides workers with greater discretion over how they meet their family responsibilities and balance the public and private aspects of their lives. Despite the often-criticized notion of "quality time," there are good reasons to believe that workers with flexibility and control over their working conditions will derive greater pleasure from work and also be happier, more supportive family members. Indeed, decades of research have consistently shown that satisfaction with work and good child care arrangements are the critical factors affecting the welfare of employed parents and their children.[5]

It is thus important to know who has flexible schedules and whether flexibility makes a difference. To find out, we examine answers to the question "Overall, how much control would you say you have in scheduling your work hours—none, very little, some, a lot, or complete flexibility?" Surprisingly, the overall perception of personal control is remarkably similar for women and men. Forty-four percent of women and 42 percent of men respond that they have "none" or "very little,"

5. The voluminous literature on comparisons between employed mothers and mothers who do not have a paid job has shown that working, taken alone, has no effect on the well-being of children. What matters are the mother's level of satisfaction with her choices, the involvement of the father, and the degree of satisfaction with child care arrangements. See, for example, Harvey (1999), Hoffman (1987), and Nye (1988).

while another 26 percent of women and 27 percent of men say they have "some." At the other end of the spectrum, 30 percent of women and men report having "a lot" or "complete flexibility." At this general level, gender does not appear to be linked to job flexibility, as some have suggested (e.g., Glass and Camarigg 1992).

Despite the commonsense expectation that flexible schedules might represent an adaptation or accommodation to long work hours, there appears to be no strong or significant link between working time and flexibility. Among men, no relationship emerges between control over scheduling and hours worked.[6] Women who work long hours do report less flexibility than those with less demanding jobs, but the relationship is not strong ($r = -.13$). Work flexibility is thus not simply a reflection of overall hours worked; it deserves attention in its own right.

A closer look reveals some hidden effects of gender beneath the apparently similar and generally weak link between working time and control over scheduling. Figure 10.1 shows a curvilinear relationship between workers' perceptions of flexibility and the number of hours they usually work in their main job, but the extent of the curve differs by gender. It is not surprising that a high percentage of both women and men with relatively short workweeks report more flexibility. Nor is it surprising that the percentage who enjoy a sense of control declines steadily for both women and men until they reach a level of 40 to 49 working hours. Part-time work, almost by definition, is more flexible. While flexibility may be an unintended by-product of shorter working hours, many may opt for shorter hours as a strategy for obtaining flexibility.

Among workers who work very long hours, however, men and women diverge in unanticipated ways. While men who work 50 or more hours per week report substantial increases in flexibility, women in this situation experience this rebound to a much smaller degree. For men, working relatively short or long hours bestows flexibility, leaving those in the middle relatively squeezed. For women, however, there is no such counterbalancing reward for working longer hours. Women at the high end of the spectrum lack the autonomy and control that similarly situated men enjoy.

6. For men, the correlation between working hours at one's main job and control over scheduling is .05, and the correlation between total hours worked and control over one's schedule is .04. Neither correlation is significant. For women, the respective correlations are −.13 and .10.

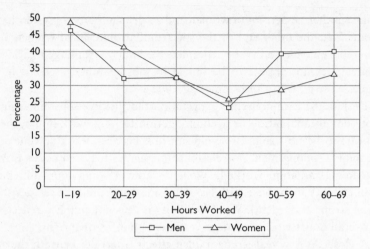

Figure 10.1. Scheduling flexibility, by sex and hours, 1993: Percentage reporting jobs with "a lot of" or "complete" flexibility. *Source:* National Survey of the Changing Workforce.

The lack of flexibility available to highly committed women workers signals difficulties for women (and their families) on several fronts. Most obviously, it implies that those workers most likely to be shouldering heavy burdens at work and at home are the least likely to have the flexibility they need. Equally problematic, the lack of control at work is also likely to reflect a hidden consequence of the "glass ceiling," which limits women's upward mobility despite their strong work commitment. While men who put in long hours at work may enjoy the rewards of achieving positions of authority, women who do the same are less likely to attain sufficient status to control their schedules.[7]

Since supportive job and workplace conditions appear as consequential as amount of working time in shaping workers' experiences, it is important to ascertain what structural and personal factors either enhance or diminish perceptions of control over work scheduling. Most important, do work conditions remain consequential even when personal attributes, such as family situation, are taken into account? Economists, especially those who emphasize the role of "human capital" in labor market processes, argue that men and women make contrasting

7. Although the Changing Workforce survey lacks specific information on men's and women's structural positions at work, it is clear from other studies that male managers and professionals are more likely than their female counterparts to occupy high-level positions in organizational and occupational hierarchies.

work choices because they prefer a different balance between family and work (e.g., Becker 1981). This perspective contends that men prefer to maximize earnings and job success to support their families, while women are willing to sacrifice economic reward and upward mobility in order to invest more time in family pursuits. This argument implies that women, especially married mothers, are more likely to choose more flexible jobs, while men, especially married fathers, are more likely to make work choices based on other criteria.

GENDER AND FAMILY SITUATION

Is work flexibility linked to gender and family situation? The answer appears to be no. For women, flexibility at work is not related to family responsibilities, such as being married and having children in the household.[8] For men, this family situation is actually linked to having less flexibility at work. Men with family obligations may feel an increased pressure to work at inflexible jobs, but there is no evidence that women are trading off other job benefits for flexible work. Moreover, having an employed spouse has no influence on either women's or men's own work flexibility, and neither do the work hours of a spouse. For women, there is also no connection between placing a higher importance on a husband's job and choosing flexible work. And men who place more importance on a wife's job are more rather than less likely to experience less flexibility in their own jobs.

There is thus no support for the contention that women choose and men eschew flexible work in order to reproduce a gendered division of labor in the home. Family obligations may increase the pressures on working parents, but neither mothers nor fathers enjoy more flexibility to meet these demands.

THE RELATIVE IMPORTANCE OF INDIVIDUAL, FAMILY, AND WORKPLACE CONDITIONS

Since few have the power to choose the conditions of their work based on their private needs, it should come as no surprise that family situation is not linked to flexible work. Despite the rise of dual-earner and

---

8. Due to space constraints, the results for the bivariate relationships between workplace flexibility and all the variables included in table 10.2 are not shown. They may be found in Jacobs and Gerson (1997).

single-parent homes, employers, far more than workers, set the conditions under which parents balance work and family obligations.

The crucial importance of work conditions becomes especially clear in table 10.2, which presents the multivariate relationships between workplace flexibility and a range of individual, family, and workplace factors. Even after such personal attributes as age, education, job experience, and family situation are taken into account, work structure and culture remain the most consistently important factors linked to job flexibility.

Among men, education enhances flexibility, while children in the household, a long commute, and feeling insecure in a job dampens it. For women, white-collar positions enhance flexibility, while public sector and union jobs dampen it. Most important, work conditions remain influential for men and women alike. Those who have supportive supervisors and workplace cultures are more likely to have flexibility as well. Moreover, autonomy provides the most powerful link with workplace flexibility. Job autonomy increases the explained variance from 13 to 18 percent for men and from 11 to 18 percent for women. When autonomy is taken into account, the relative importance of such factors as workplace culture and supervisor support appears to diminish. However, all of these contextual factors are highly intertwined and tend to occur together. They are actually different aspects of the overall work environment, and they have similar consequences for men and women in similar situations.

Workplace structure and culture make an important difference in workers' lives. Employers' support for flexible work arrangements, especially in the form of understanding supervisors and a supportive work culture, give both women and men more control over how to balance work and family. While similar work conditions affect female and male workers in similar ways, it remains clear that men are more likely than women to obtain privileges that give them more felicitous work circumstances.

THE AVAILABILITY, USE, AND DESIRABILITY
OF FLEXIBILITY AT WORK

There can be little doubt that workers, especially parents with young children and employed partners, benefit from family-supportive arrangements such as work flexibility, autonomy, and control over scheduling. Yet how widely available are such arrangements? Are workers with

TABLE 10.2

MULTIVARIATE ASSOCIATIONS WITH
WORKPLACE FLEXIBILITY

Demographic Variables	Men		Women	
	Beta	S.E.	Beta	S.E.
Intercept	0.55	(.49)	0.31	(.44)
Age groups:				
Age 25 or under (reference)	—	—	—	—
Age 26–35	−0.27*	(.14)	−0.37*	(.13)
Age 36–45	−0.07	(.16)	−0.32*	(.14)
Age 46–55	−0.22	(.17)	−0.43*	(.15)
Age 56–65	−0.08	(.21)	−0.39*	(.18)
Tenure:				
Firm	−0.003	(.007)	−0.002	(.008)
Job	−0.006	(.009)	0.003	(.010)
Education:				
College graduate	0.42*	(.16)	0.05	(.18)
Some college	0.29*	(.15)	0.12	(.17)
High school graduate	0.17	(.14)	0.08	(.16)
High school dropout	—	—	—	—
Family situation:				
Kids in home under age 18	−0.16	(.12)	−0.12	(.17)
Kids in home under age 6	−0.04	(.13)	0.08	(.12)
Married	0.04	(.12)	0.25	(.14)
Spouse works	−0.58*	(.23)	−0.37	(.26)
Spouse's hours	0.01*	(.005)	0.001	(.004)
Spouse's job importance	−0.01	(.06)	0.02	(.05)
Workplace culture:				
Demands	−0.06	(.08)	−0.06	(.08)
Autonomy	0.53*	(.07)	0.62*	(.06)
Initiate	0.05	(.04)	0.05	(.04)
Culture	0.18*	(.08)	0.18*	(.07)
Insecure	−0.04	(.05)	−0.02	(.04)
Supervisor support	0.08	(.08)	0.06	(.07)
Job attributes:				
Supervisor	0.13	(.09)	0.22	(.09)
Eligible for overtime	−0.23*	(.10)	0.16	(.08)
Union	−0.25	(.10)	−0.42	(.10)
Commute	−0.03*	(.01)	0.01	(.01)
Annual earnings (in thousands)	−0.002	(.002)	0.004	(.002)
Total hours worked	0.002	(.004)	−0.01	(.003)
Occupation:				
Professional/technical worker	0.13	(.12)	0.45	(.16)
Manager	0.08	(.14)	0.70	(.19)
Clerical	0.30	(.20)	0.62	(.15)
Sales/service	0.08	(.12)	0.59	(.16)
Blue-collar (reference)	—	—	—	—
Industry:				
Manufacturing (reference)	—	—	—	—
Retail trade	0.18	(.12)	0.09	(.14)
Business services	0.25	(.13)	−0.05	(.13)
Social services	−0.24	(.13)	−0.07	(.12)
Personal services	0.28	(.16)	0.20	(.18)
Public sector	−0.33*	(.16)	−0.40	(.20)
R^2	0.18		0.18	

SOURCE: National Study of the Changing Workforce.

*$p < .05$

access to them willing to use them? Among those without access to such options, how strong is the desire to obtain them? The answers to these questions shed additional light on the larger question of whether the growing time squeezes between work and family reflect workplace constraints or worker preferences. To answer these questions we briefly consider to what extent family-friendly options that provide more flexibility and control at work are available, used, or desired in modern workplaces.[9]

AVAILABILITY AND USE OF FLEXIBLE SCHEDULING

While a large proportion of the workforce (almost 86%) has the discretion to change their working hours "as needed," far fewer can set their own hours (29%) or change them daily (40%). Professional men, including those with preschool-age children, are the most likely to be able to set their own working hours (about 40%), but professional men with young children are the least likely to be able to change their hours daily (23%) or to change their hours as needed (74%). Among women, professionals with preschool-age children are the least likely (26%) to be able to set their hours and are also less likely than other employed women to be able to change their hours daily (38%). Again we find that, at least among professional and managerial workers, those most likely to need flexible scheduling face greater obstacles in obtaining it.

There is some good news for some employed parents. Professionals with young children have comparatively more access to such benefits as extended breaks, working at home, and working more one day in order to work less the next. It appears, however, that these benefits accrue to professional status and, to a lesser extent, to gender rather than to family status. In general, professional men fare better than either professional women or nonprofessional workers. Among professional men, 63 percent can take extended breaks at work (compared to 41% for nonprofessional workers), 50 percent can vary the length of the workday (compared to 41% for nonprofessionals), 39 percent can work at home regularly (compared to 13% for nonprofessionals), and 25 percent can do so occasionally (compared to 8% for nonprofessionals). Women professionals fare better than nonprofessionals, but not as well as their male

---

9. A more detailed analysis of the availability, use, and desire for a wide range of family-supportive workplace options and benefits can be found in Gerson and Jacobs (1999).

counterparts, who are more likely to be able to take extended breaks and work at home occasionally.

Among those who have the option to shift their work hours and location, a very high proportion of workers choose to do so. When, for example, the option to work more one day and less the next is available, 75 percent of workers take advantage of it (including 81% of professional women and 74% of professional men with preschool-age children). Similarly, among those who are allowed to work at home occasionally, 79 percent choose to do so (including 88% of professional women and 84% of professional men with preschool-age children). It is instructive that women professionals with young children are much less likely to take extended breaks (63%) than to work at home. When given a choice, both women and men with young children seem to prefer more time at home and less time socializing at the office. While this may not seem surprising, it casts additional doubt on the argument that parents are trading time at home to socialize at work. Indeed, the high proportion of workers who take advantage of the options to work at home and to vary the length of their working day suggests a large demand for work arrangements that allow people to integrate work and family life more thoroughly and flexibly.

THE DEMAND FOR FLEXIBILITY AMONG THOSE WHO LACK IT

The majority of workers do not enjoy options such as flexible scheduling or working at home. Among these workers we find that many not only desire these benefits but would be willing to trade other benefits and even change their jobs to get them.

Among workers who do not have flexible schedules, about 28 percent would be willing to trade other benefits and 26 percent would be willing to change jobs to get such control. The desire among professional women with young children is especially high, with 49 percent of those with preschool-age children stating that they would trade other benefits for flexibility at work and 32 percent saying they would even change jobs. Professional men with young children agree, albeit to a lesser extent. While only 12 percent would be willing to change jobs, 29 percent would trade other benefits for flexibility in scheduling.

The chance to work at home is also in high demand. Among all workers, 21 percent would trade other benefits to obtain such an option, and 22 percent would change jobs. For professional mothers, the percentages rise to 48 percent and 32 percent. For fathers, 18 percent would trade another benefit, and 24 percent would change jobs.

AVAILABILITY AND DESIRABILITY OF PART-TIME WORK

The option to work part-time is substantially less popular than flexible scheduling or working at home. While about 55 percent of workers claim the option, among those without it only 16 percent would be willing to trade other benefits and only 11 percent would be willing to change jobs to obtain it. Among professionals with young children, the part-time option remains equally unattractive. Professional women, especially those with young children, are the most likely to have this option (59%), but only 45 percent of professional men with young children can choose to work part-time. More noteworthy, however, is the lack of desire to obtain the part-time option when it is not available. While 32 percent of professional women with young children would be willing to give up another benefit, only 15 percent would be willing to change jobs. Among professional fathers, only 9 percent would trade away other benefits and only 5 percent would be willing to change jobs. Women may be more able and willing than men to cut back on their careers, but this difference does not bode well for gender equality in professional careers. As important, the general reluctance to cut back from work, even temporarily when the children are young, suggests that women and men alike perceive that such a choice might exact a high price in the long run.

THE HIDDEN COSTS OF FAMILY-SUPPORTIVE POLICIES: ARE FAMILY-FRIENDLY POLICIES ALSO WOMAN-FRIENDLY?

If given a genuine choice, both women and men, especially those with young children, appear to prefer more flexibility at work and more time at home. When available, a high proportion of workers take advantage of the chances to work at home and to vary the length of their working day. Similarly, when flexible scheduling is not available, a remarkable number of women and men appear willing to make other work sacrifices to obtain it. In contrast to the growing concern that workers are pursuing personal gratification at work over the needs of their families and children, this picture suggests instead that they are striving for more flexible and fluid options for integrating these once separate spheres.

Yet despite the large and often unmet desire for family-supportive work arrangements, many workers may be fearful that choosing to use family-friendly policies can be costly to their long-term prospects at work. The relatively low desire for part-time work, for example, suggests that workers are reluctant to take advantage of options that might threaten economic and career opportunities. It is thus crucial to understand whether workers perceive that hidden penalties are attached to making use of family-friendly policies that may be formally available but informally stigmatized. Only by understanding how workers perceive these trade-offs can we gain a clearer picture of not only what workers need but also what obstacles prevent them from meeting these needs or even expressing their concerns to those in a position to help them.

In theory, family-friendly policies are built on the principles of family support and gender equity. Many workers, moreover, appear prepared to make substantial sacrifices in order to obtain them. Yet if such policies target only women and penalize those who use them, they threaten to re-create earlier forms of gender inequality in a new form. "Mommy tracks," for example, ask mothers to forgo upward mobility and thus confront women with an unfair choice between motherhood and a work career (Schwartz 1989). They also exclude men from the responsibilities and opportunities of parental involvement. Although "gender-neutral" family policies may appear less pernicious, stigmatizing parental involvement in general simply shifts the penalties to both involved mothers *and* involved fathers. It is a dubious social policy that rewards parents of either sex for subordinating family needs to work and career.

In the best of all possible worlds, neither mothers nor fathers would be penalized at work for taking care of their children. And such a world would clearly not exact a higher price from women than from men. Yet in today's world there are good reasons to be concerned that "family-friendly" does not necessarily mean either woman-friendly or parent-friendly. Despite the heralding of policies to ease the plight of employed mothers, options that provide family support at the expense of work advancement exact significant costs to anyone who might choose them. In contrast, policies that not only provide for a fluid balance between family and work but also safeguard the work opportunities of the person who uses them would be more than just family-friendly. By protecting the rights of employed women and acknowledging the needs of work-committed parents of either sex, such policies would be genuinely woman-friendly and parent-friendly. Family-supportive policies, however, have more often been conceived and enacted in ways that reinforce and reproduce both public and private gender inequality by penalizing employed mothers and excluding fathers altogether.

Since employers are reluctant to admit that their policies come with costs attached for those who choose them, it is difficult to ascertain the exact nature of the risks workers take when they seek or use family-supportive options. It is possible, however, to ascertain whether workers perceive that formally available policies contain informal but heavy sanctions. Moreover, the perception of risk, regardless of its objective validity, is crucial to how workers weigh their options and make their choices. We thus examine the relationship between workers' perceptions of whether their workplace culture is family-supportive and their perceptions about whether their work environments offer advancement opportunities.

As table 10.3 reveals, workers with supportive workplace cultures typically report having supportive supervisors as well, and for women, the link is especially strong ($r = .44$). Yet family-friendly workplaces do not appear to provide the best opportunities to advance. Cultural support is thus negatively related to women's perceptions of women's chances for advancement, whether they are white or minority. Equally noteworthy, these women also report that such workplaces do not necessarily provide good opportunities for white or minority men either. Perhaps most significant, women's perceptions of their *own* chances for advancement are negatively related to their perceptions that their workplaces are family-supportive.

When the focus is supervisor support for family-friendly arrangements rather than the level of supportiveness at the workplace as a whole, the same pattern emerges and the relationships are even stronger. The negative link between supervisor support for family-friendly arrangements and women's perceptions of their own chances for advancement is the strongest ($r = -.31$). Moreover, these patterns are virtually identical for men. Men also perceive that family-supportive supervisors and workplace cultures are less likely to provide chances to advance for *any* group. They agree with women that having a supervisor who is supportive of family needs is also less likely to enhance their *own* chances for advancement ($r = -.32$).

Do these perceptions persist when other factors are taken into account? While a family-supportive workplace culture remains negatively associated with chances for advancement, the effects become attenuated

TABLE 10.3

RELATIONSHIP BETWEEN FAMILY-FRIENDLY
WORKPLACE CULTURE AND SELF-REPORTED
CHANCES FOR ADVANCEMENT

	Workplace Culture[a] (r)	Supervisor Support[b] (r)
Women		
Workplace culture	1.00	.44
Supervisor support scale	.44	1.00
Chances to advance:		
White women	−.12	−.21
Minority women	−.17	−.28
White men	−.07	−.07
Minority men	−.15	−.22
Respondent's chances to advance	−.18	−.31
Men		
Workplace culture	1.00	.46
Supervisor support scale	.46	1.00
Chance to advance:		
White women	−.12	−.17
Minority women	−.15	−.18
White men	−.09	−.19
Minority men	−.14	−.21
Respondent's chances to advance	−.18	−.32

SOURCE: National Study of the Changing Workforce.
NOTE: All correlations statistically significant, $p < .05$.
[a]Workplace Culture is a composite of four items designed to tap whether the respondent's working environment is sensitive to work-family issues.
[b]Supervisor Support is a composite of nine items designed to tap whether the respondent's supervisor is attentive to workers' needs and concerns.

as other factors, such as personal autonomy at work, are added.[10] When supervisor support is included, the effect of workplace culture disappears altogether, but the effect of supervisor support remains. This pattern occurs whether the measure of advancement opportunities refers to the woman herself or to other women, and it holds for men as well.

Women and men alike thus tend to perceive that family-friendly workplace policies come with costly strings attached. If workers feel confronted with a choice between family involvement and career building, their perceptions are probably well founded. The *New York Times* (1996) has reported, for example, that there is no overlap between the

10. The detailed results of this analysis are presented in Jacobs and Gerson (1997).

companies with the best record for promoting women and those with the most supportive family policies. Genuine family support, however, must move beyond mere tinkering at the edges of organizations to restructure the basic assumptions on which they are built. To be woman-friendly and parent-friendly as well as family-friendly, workplaces must be committed to supporting the careers of those who wish time to care for their families even as they strive at work.

BEYOND WORKING TIME: CREATING FLEXIBLE, EGALITARIAN WORKPLACES

While the debate over changes in work and family in America has focused largely on the issue of overwork, we have found that working time is only one of several important ingredients contributing to the problems of work-family conflict and gender inequality. Workplace structure and culture matter, and workers who enjoy job flexibility and employer support are better off than those who do not. Rather than preferring work over family, most full-time workers desire family-supportive workplace options that offer them ways to better integrate and balance their lives. Unfortunately, they also perceive that these benefits can only be gained at considerable cost.

Gender inequality persists in institutional arrangements, yet women and men find their personal dilemmas converging. As women build ever-stronger ties to the workplace and families confront the time squeezes posed by dual-earning arrangements, mothers and fathers must cope with conflicts that are structured not simply by family demands but more fundamentally by intransigent job constraints. When women and men face similar situations, their responses are also similar. In the struggle to resolve work-family conflicts, however, persisting gender inequality continues to place women at a disadvantage. Women not only shoulder more of the burden of domestic work; they also face larger obstacles at the workplace, including less autonomy and flexibility on the job and more pressure to make career sacrifices by cutting back when children are young.

While the problems workers face take different forms, most workers hold the same desire—to balance gratifying work with family involvement. Beyond economic security and opportunity, women and men alike wish some measure of flexibility in how they choose to integrate the many obligations they shoulder. In a world where both mothers and fathers must work, no group should have to sacrifice opportunity and economic welfare in order to make time for their families.

Since the problem of work-family conflict has institutional roots, the resolutions depend on institutional transformations. To understand the circumstances that can genuinely provide opportunities for committed workers to be involved parents, analysis needs to extend beyond worker preferences or choices to focus on workplace organization and the structure of opportunities that parents (and those who would like to become parents) face. If we fail to acknowledge the social sources of personal dilemmas, we are left blaming ordinary women and men for conditions they did not create and cannot control. A social and institutional focus makes it clear that social policy needs to uphold two important and inextricable principles: equal opportunity for women and unencumbered support for involved parents, regardless of sex.

We cannot afford to build work-family policies on outdated stereotypes that cast women as less committed to work than men. Yet we also cannot afford to create new stereotypes that cast employed mothers, and to a lesser extent fathers, as shortchanging their children. These images place all who would endeavor to balance family and work in an impossible bind in which work commitment is defined as family neglect and family involvement is defined as a lack of work commitment. If our findings are a guide, these are inaccurate images that offer untenable choices. What workers need and want is flexible work in a supportive setting that offers them a way to resolve the double binds they face.

REFERENCES

Becker, Gary. 1981. *A treatise on the family*. Cambridge, Mass.: Harvard University Press.

Bluestone, Barry, and Stephen Rose. 1997. Overworked and underemployed: Unraveling an economic enigma. *American Prospect* 31(March/April):58–69.

Bond, James T., Ellen Galinsky, and Jennifer E. Swanberg. 1998. *The 1997 national study of the changing workforce*. New York: Families and Work Institute.

Galinsky, Ellen, James T. Bond, and Dana E. Friedman. 1993. *The changing workforce: Highlights of the national study*. New York: Families and Work Institute.

Gerson, Kathleen, and Jerry A. Jacobs. 1999. The availability and use of family-friendly workplace policies. Unpublished manuscript.

Glass, Jennifer, and Valerie Camarigg. 1992. Gender, parenthood, and job-family compatability. *American Journal of Sociology* 98(July):131–51.

Harvey, Lisa. 1999. Short-term and long-term effects of early parental employment on children of the national longitudinal survey of youth. *Developmental Psychology* 35(March):445–59.

Hochschild, Arlie R. 1997. *The time bind: When work becomes home and home becomes work.* New York: Metropolitan Books.

Hoffman, Lois. 1987. The effects on children of maternal and paternal employment. In *Families and work,* edited by N. Gerstel and H. Gross, 362–95. Philadelphia: Temple University Press.

Jacobs, Jerry A., and Kathleen Gerson. 1997. The endless day or the flexible office? Working hours, work-family conflict, and gender equity in the modern workplace. Report to the Alfred P. Sloan Foundation.

———. 1998. Who are the overworked Americans? *Review of Social Economy* 56(4):442–59.

———. 1999. The overworked American debate: New evidence comparing ideal and actual working hours. In *Work and family: Research informing policy,* edited by T. Parcel and D. B. Cornfield. Thousand Oaks, Calif.: Sage Publications.

New York Times. 1996. Somber news for women on corporate ladder. 6 November, D1, D19.

Nye, F. Ivan. 1988. Fifty years of family research, 1937–1987. *Journal of Marriage and the Family* 50(May):305–16.

Robinson, John P., and Geoffrey Godbey. 1997. *Time for life. The surprising ways Americans use their time.* University Park: Pennsylvania State University Press.

Rones, Philip L., Randy E. Ilg, and Jennifer M. Gardner. 1997. Trends in the hours of work since the mid-1970s. *Monthly Labor Review* 120(4):3–14.

Schor, Juliet. 1991. *The overworked American.* New York: Basic Books.

Schwartz, Felice N. 1989. Management women and the new facts of life. *Harvard Business Review,* January–February, 65–76.

CHAPTER 11

Workplace Policies and the Psychological Well-Being of First-Time Parents

The Case of Working-Class Families

Heather-Lyn Haley, Maureen Perry-Jenkins, and Amy Armenia

INTRODUCTION

According to U.S. Department of Labor statistics, mothers with children under one year of age have become an increasingly large subgroup of working mothers, with approximately 53 percent of women returning to the labor force within six months following the birth of their first child (U.S. Bureau of Labor Statistics 1994). Couples with infants face the most difficult challenges in managing the demands of work and family life for a number of reasons: (1) infant care is especially costly and difficult to find, (2) the daily demands of caring for an infant are high, and (3) employed mothers are still recovering both physically and emotionally from pregnancy and childbirth (Piotrkowski et al. 1993). When

The research for this chapter was supported by a grant from the National Institute of Mental Health R29-MH56777-03 to the second author. The authors would like to acknowledge the contributions made by the research team: Senior staff: Kelly Mason, Bill Miller, Heyda Martinez, Michael Meade, Andrea Chakour, Laura O'Sullivan, Jessica Payne, Liz Hendricks, Diane Manning. Undergraduate staff: Cindy Hubbard, Laura Arbour, Leigh Hacker, Angela Childs, Toni Farrell, Delma Rivera, Amy Taylor, Sari Turan, Tara Wolfson, Jenna Kalis, Jennifer Flaherty, Christina Stafford, Megan Fogarty, Jennifer Ladouceur, Steve Simolari, Kelly Keveany, Karen Zaidberg, Amelia Heddens, Elizabeth Hoey, Sherri Cohen, Liam Gillen, Sarah Kleinman, Marni Thompson, Lucienne Robinson, Catherine Freund, Kimberly Milberg, Julie Christopher, Sarah Wanczyk, Magdalana Reis, Allison Kahn, Jamie Rodrigues, Erica Cohen, Diane Wolf, Stephanie Albert, Maureen McKinney. Administrative support: Susan Stern, Laura Wiles, Department of Consumer Studies, University of Massachusetts, Amherst. Statistical consultant: Stanley Wasserman, University of Illinois.

we couple these striking demographic shifts and the stresses of infant care with the fact that approximately 38 percent of families in the United States are working class (i.e., high school or associate's degree, employed in semiskilled or unskilled low-paying jobs [U.S. Bureau of the Census 1988]), important questions arise as to how couples with fewer resources cope as they care for their new infants and hold down jobs.

In recent years there has been growing recognition among business professionals, managers, and family scholars that workplace policies and conditions are related to employee morale and commitment and to the quality of family life (Bowen 1995; Friedman 1983). Bowen documents a number of family-oriented policies that have gained popularity in recent years, such as flexible scheduling, extended parental leave provisions, paid personal days for family responsibilities, information and referral services, and on-site day care. A number of scholars point out, however, that corporate responses to promoting the integration of work and family life lag far behind the need. Moreover, policies and programs that have been highlighted in journals or the popular press cater to middle- to upper-middle-class employees—high-investment employees that companies do not want to lose. Little data describes the availability of policies and supports for working-class and working-poor families.

In one of the first studies to address the case of new mothers in the workplace, Piotrkowski et al. (1993) examined the relationship of family-friendly workplace policies to women's prenatal and postnatal labor force participation, work/family stress, and overall well-being. The women in the study were "relatively affluent, educated, and predominantly white . . . with women in blue collar and service jobs underrepresented" (iii). Findings revealed that flexible time policies and practices mediated the connections between social support at work, work/family stress, and job satisfaction. Moreover, supportive supervisors enabled new mothers to more effectively manage their work and family responsibilities.

A less positive theme also emerged from these data. Results indicated that family-friendly workplace policies were not uniformly distributed to all employees. Barriers that limited women's access to these policies included working in low-paying, nonprofessional jobs; working for a smaller organization; working part-time; and having a shorter length of service. These barriers were shown to have a cumulative effect such that women facing more of these constraints had access to fewer workplace supports.

While the issues facing employed new mothers are in obvious need of attention, a critical gap in much of the research on workplace policy has been the virtual exclusion of issues concerning fathers. As Levine and Pittinsky (1997) point out, our focus on the real needs of working mothers, and mothers alone, reinforces the notion that men experience no work/family conflict. Some research has suggested that men are simply less likely to use family-friendly workplace policies because whatever the policies, the work culture does not really endorse their use (Levine and Pittinsky 1997). Other research, however, points to the ways that conditions of fathers' employment hold implications for children's well-being (Menaghan and Parcel 1995) and for marriage (Perry-Jenkins and Crouter 1990). Thus, especially in the case of dual-earner families, it is important to understand how *both* spouses' work conditions affect the nature of their family life.

Bowen's (1995) conceptual model of work and family linkages elaborates on the basic tenets of the "spillover" hypothesis (Kanter 1977) and provides the theoretical underpinnings for the current study. Bowen's model hypothesizes a set of relationships whereby "corporate culture and philosophy shape the work environment, both its structural and its dynamic components, and that the work environment, in turn, influences outcomes both at work and at home" (426). This chapter focuses on one aspect of Bowen's model, namely, the relationship between the structural and the dynamic aspects of work and worker well-being. The *structural components* of the work environment include the benefits and policies offered by a company, such as paid parental leave or flextime. The *dynamic components* of the workplace include social-environmental characteristics of the job, such as job challenge, autonomy, organizational commitment, opportunity for growth, and coworker and supervisor relations. This chapter furthers our understanding of how workplace policies and supports affect workers' lives by examining the understudied population of working-class families and by including both fathers and mothers in its models.

The goal of this chapter is twofold. At a descriptive level, our first aim is to document the frequency and type of benefits and policies available to expectant parents employed in working-class occupations. Second, we examine how workplace benefits and policies (what Bowen refers to as structural dimensions of work) as well as workers' perceptions of informal organizational supports and commitment (referred to as the dynamic dimensions of work) relate to new mothers' and fathers' psychological well-being. These relationships are examined at two distinct time points, one prenatally and one postnatally. In addition, longitudinal analyses will explore relationships between work conditions prior to the baby's birth and parents' well-being once their baby has arrived and they have returned to work.

SAMPLE AND METHODS

Data were obtained in face-to-face interviews conducted with 70 couples from western Massachusetts. Couples in the third trimester of pregnancy were recruited through prenatal education classes. Several criteria were employed to screen interested couples in order to obtain a working-class sample of dual-earner families: (1) both husband and wife must be working 30 or more hours prior to the baby's birth, (2) both husband and wife must be planning to work full-time within six months after the baby's birth, (3) both husband and wife must have less than a bachelor's degree of education, and (4) the baby must be a first child for both husband and wife. While marriage was not a necessary criterion, couples must be cohabiting at the time of inclusion.

Data for this study are taken from a larger longitudinal project examining the transition to parenthood over a year's time, with five points of data collection for 150 couples (Perry-Jenkins 1993). Data used for this chapter include measurement at two points in time—the first interview (time 1), during the third trimester of the couple's first pregnancy, and the third interview (referred to here as time 2), which occurred one month after the wife had returned to work full-time following the baby's birth. At each time point a team of interviewers visited the couple's home. Following a brief introduction, men and women were separated and interviewed simultaneously in different rooms. Interviews lasted between 1.5 to 3.5 hours. During this time, respondents completed a series of standardized questionnaires that tapped workplace conditions, psychological well-being, and demographic information. In addition, respondents answered a number of open-ended questions regarding their feelings about the supportiveness of their work environment. Responses to the open-ended questions were tape-recorded and later transcribed.

The age of respondents ranged from 19 to 41. The mean age of men during pregnancy was 29.9, while women's average age was 27.8. Nearly 80 percent (79.7%) of the couples were married. The average length of relationship was 3.3 years, with a range from less than 1 year to 16 years. A high percentage of those in the study were white (92.2 % of women, 90.6% of men), a fact we feel may have been influenced by our use of prenatal classes as a primary recruiting site.

While all participants had less than a bachelor's degree, there was still some range in educational attainment among our sample. Approximately 16 percent of the women and 22.5 percent of the men ended their education directly after high school graduation or attainment of a General Educational Development (GED) degree. The majority (44.8% of women and 63.4% of men) had some formal schooling or vocational training after high school, but less than an associate's degree. Thirty-nine percent of the women and 14.1 percent of the men had an associate's degree or higher.

Individually reported income ranged from $2,000[1] to $54,000 annually for the men and from $6,000 to $70,000 for the women. Median salaries were $27,000 for men and $22,000 for women, while the median family income was $53,000. Thirty-five percent of the women and 18 percent of the men earned less than $20,000 per year. The majority of respondents—57.2 percent of the women and 68.9 percent of the men—claimed to earn within the $20,000 to $40,000 per year category. Only 7.9 percent of the women and 13.1 percent of men had earned $40,000 or more in the past year.

Questions arise as to what role education and income play in defining a family as working class (Hughes and Perry-Jenkins 1996). Although the issue is open to debate, this study places greater emphasis on educational level than income for two reasons. First, educational level is an indicator of one's potential career trajectory. Since all respondents in this study had ended their education with either high school or associate's degrees, their ability to move up the "career ladder" was limited. Second, reports of income must be examined with caution. Two examples explain the need for such caution. One woman in our sample had a one-year, post-high-school degree that licensed her as a practical nurse. She worked on commission approximately 60 hours a week, which allowed her to earn over $60,000, although she had no benefits or health insurance. Despite her high income, the conditions of her work and educational level squarely place her in the working-class category. Moreover, in our sample we have uncovered problems with the reliability of reported salaries in cases where men report high gross incomes while calculations based on weekly paycheck stubs indicate substantially lower annual salaries. Our strategy, therefore, has been to allow income

1. The man reporting a $2,000 salary had only worked for a portion of the previous year. The minimum annual salary for a man with a full year's employment the previous year was $6,000.

to vary but to limit educational attainment to an associate's degree at the highest.

Length of time working for the same employer ranged widely, from 1 month to 25 years for men and from 3 months to 21 years for women. Median length of employment was 36 months for men and 39 months for women. More of the men (90.7%) felt secure in their jobs than did the women, of whom 83.8 percent felt that they were unlikely to lose their jobs in the next few years.

MEASURES

STRUCTURAL COMPONENTS

The availability and use of formal workplace policies were assessed using a scale developed by Greenberger et al. (1989). The scale listed 20 benefits that may be offered by employers, such as the option to work from home, various types of parental leave, and on-site child care. Respondents were asked first whether their employer formally offered them the listed benefit. If the listed benefit was available, the respondents were asked whether they had ever used that particular benefit. The benefits listed fell into four categories: (1) scheduling of work, (2) parental leave policies, (3) assistance with child care, and (4) other benefits, such as the right to refuse a relocation or transfer. Those items classified as "other" have been dropped from analysis, since they appeared with low frequency in this working-class sample.

During the course of interviewing couples, it became clear that the work-policies measure was biased toward a more professional, middle-class occupational stratum. Many of the benefits listed were rarely offered to our working-class sample of employees. For example, less than 10 percent of either men or women reported access to benefits such as paternity leave with pay, the presence of an employer-subsidized child care center, a child care center at the workplace, or employer reimbursement for child care expenses. Following the example of Greenberger et al. (1989), we collapsed each of the three subscales (i.e., scheduling, child care, and leave benefits) and scored them dichotomously before statistical analysis, separating the sample into those with any benefit in the category under consideration and those with no available benefits of that type. When examining data from time 1, we focus only on what benefits are offered to employees, since many of the policies could only be used following the birth. When examining data from time 2, we focus more on what benefits have actually been used by respondents. Although both men and women were asked about the presence of both maternity and paternity leave benefits, results focus on the parental leave options that would be available to the respondent, that is, maternity leave for women and paternity leave for men.

DYNAMIC COMPONENTS

Several different instruments have been employed to highlight dynamic components of informal workplace support. This study relies upon separate measures of (1) organizational commitment and support (OCS), (2) supervisor support, and (3) coworker support.

Organizational Commitment and Support (OCS)   Each respondent completed a 16-item questionnaire designed to measure organizational commitment and perceived organizational support (Eisenberger et al. 1986; Lambert et al. 1993). Using a 4-point Likert scale with options "strongly disagree," "disagree," "agree," and "strongly agree," respondents gave their opinions regarding statements such as "I am proud to tell others that I work for my organization" and "My organization would ignore any complaint from me." The coefficient alpha for this scale was .95 for men and .94 for women at time 1. At time 2, the alpha coefficients were .92 for men and .93 for women.

Supervisor Support and Coworker Support   A 9-item scale was devised based upon the work of Caplan et al. (1975) and Briggs, Freeman, and Yaffe (1987). Respondents were asked to rate their level of agreement, using a 5-point Likert scale, regarding statements such as "My supervisor can be relied upon when things get tough" and "My coworkers are easy to talk to." These items divide into two subscales; the first (5 items) measures supervisor support, and the second (4 items) focuses on coworker support. The coefficient alphas for supervisor support at time 1 were .90 for men and .88 for women. At time 2, alphas were .93 for men and .84 for women. Coefficient alphas for coworker support at time 1 were .80 for men and .85 for women; at time 2, these alphas were .85 and .90 for men and women respectively.

WELL-BEING MEASURES

The psychological well-being of each respondent was measured in terms of depression, anxiety, and role overload.

Depression   This study utilized the 20-item scale devised by the Center for Epidemiological Studies of the National Institute for Mental Health (Radloff 1975). Respondents were asked to consider the previous seven days and indicate how often during that time they had experienced several different moods or thoughts. Using a 4-point scale ranging from "none of the time (less than 1 day)" to "most or all of the time (5–7 days)," respondents noted the frequency of feelings corresponding with such items as "I was happy," "I felt that people dislike me," and "My sleep was restless." Scale reliability alpha for the 20 items was .86 for men and .87 for women at time 1. At time 2, the alpha coefficient was .90 for men and .92 for women.

Anxiety   Levels of anxiety were measured using a 20-item scale adapted from Spielberger (1972). Items such as "I feel rested," "I feel secure," and "Some unimportant thought runs through my mind and distracts me" were rated by respondents using a 4-point scale ranging from "not at all" to "very much so." Respondents were prompted to think about their present feelings while completing these items. The alpha coefficient for this scale was .89 for men and .88 for women at time 1. At time 2, the alpha was .90 for both men and women.

Role Overload   Respondents were given a card containing a 5-point Likert scale ranging from "strongly agree" to "strongly disagree." The interviewer then read a series of 13 items to each respondent, asking the person to think about the last two months as they decided to what extent they agreed with each item. Items include such statements as "There are too many demands on my time" and "I seem to have more commitments to overcome than some of the other people I know." Reilly (1982) first adapted this scale. The alpha coefficient for this scale was .90 for men and .92 for women at time 1, and .90 for both men and women at time 2.

RESULTS

The findings have been organized into two sections. The first section includes a detailed description of formal scheduling, parental leave, and child care policies available to mothers and fathers at the prenatal interview (time 1) and the policies used by both parents at the postnatal interview (time 2). In addition, the dynamic components of participants' work experiences are also described.

The second section explores the relationships between structural and dynamic aspects of work and parents' well-being at time 1 and time 2, using correlational analyses. It also presents the regression analyses conducted to examine the combined effects of structural and dynamic components of work at time 1 on mothers' and fathers' well-being at time 2.

DESCRIPTIVE ANALYSES

Structural Components: Formal Policy Availability and Use   As table 11.1 illustrates, the majority of parents in our sample were provided with only the most basic benefits packages by their employers and often didn't know whether specific benefits were available to them. A full 94 percent of the men responded to at least one benefit or policy option with the response "don't know"; the same is true of 79 percent of the women. Initial analyses explored the types of policies mothers and fathers had available to them at the time 1 interview as well as the policies they had actually used by the time 2 interview.

SCHEDULING BENEFITS   Nearly half of all women and men reported having a flexible daily work schedule. While the question was designed to indicate the presence of structural components that allow all employees to vary their work hours daily, it quickly became clear that the respondents interpreted this item in a different way, responding affirmatively if they were allowed, on an informal basis, to make up hours missed in the morning by working later at night. This problem was a persistent one. Even after retraining interviewers to better explain the concept of formal flexible scheduling policies, some respondents still insisted that they did have flexible schedules.

When asked at time 2 which of these scheduling benefits they had used, all percentages dropped. Although nearly half of the men and women reported the availability of flextime, only a third reported having used this benefit (29% of men and 34% of women). While the option to work a four-day week with longer daily hours was seen as an available option by 25 percent of men and 22 percent of women, only 7.4 percent of men and 10 percent of women made use of this option. A similar pattern appears in terms of the option to work at home. Eleven percent of men and 15 percent of women reported the option to work from home, but only 6 percent of men and 7.4 percent of women had used this option.

TABLE 11.1

STRUCTURAL COMPONENTS AVAILABLE
AT TIME 1 AND USED AT TIME 2

	Time 1 Percent Who Were Offered Benefit		Time 2 Percent Who Used Benefit	
	Men N = 68	*Women* N = 68	*Men* N = 68	*Women* N = 68
Scheduling Benefits				
Flexible daily work schedule	46.6	49.3	29.4	33.8
The option to work a four-day week with longer daily hours	25.0	21.9	7.4	10.3
Job-sharing (one official position shared with someone else)	8.2	16.4	2.9	4.4
Option to work at home	11.0	15.1	5.9	7.4
Leave Benefits				
Parental leave with pay	11.8	38.2	4.4	32.4
Parental leave without pay	58.8	85.3	11.8	48.5
Paid personal/sick days off specifically for family responsibilities, e.g., a sick child	67.1	71.2	32.4	32.4
Child Care Benefits				
Child care information or referral	21.5	11.0	5.9	4.4
Dependent care assistance plan (DCAP)	21.2	24.7	0	2.9
Vouchers to purchase child care or reimbursement for child care expenses	1.5	8.2	0	0
Contributions to a child care center	1.4	2.7	0	0
Child care center at workplace	5.6	8.2	0	0
Employer-subsidized child care center near workplace	6.1	4.1	0	0
Other Benefits				
"Cafeteria style" benefits package (choice of benefits that suit family's needs)	27.4	31.5	11.8	16.2
Part-time work with full-time-employment benefits	9.6	16.4	2.9	8.8
Right to refuse a relocation or transfer with no penalty	30.1	20.5	0	2.9
Job counseling and job-hunting services for spouse if relocated	5.5	11.0	0	0

PARENTAL LEAVE BENEFITS   The most commonly offered benefits among our sample were parental leave without pay and paid sick days specifically for family emergencies. Even these "bare minimum" benefits were unavailable to many—15 percent of women were not offered unpaid parental leave and 28.8 percent couldn't take a paid sick day to care for a child. While only 9 percent of women were offered no parental leave benefits at all, 34 percent of men reported that their companies fell into this no-leave category. Fifty-nine percent of men and 85.3 percent of women reported the availability of unpaid parental leave benefits, while 38.2 percent of women and 11.8 percent of men reported that their companies offered them some kind of paid parental leave benefits.

The length of paid parental leave available to women ranged from 4 weeks, reported by 8 percent of the women, to 12 weeks, which 13 percent of moms interviewed were lucky enough to have available to them. The majority of paid leave benefits (63%) fell in the 6- to 8-week range. For many companies, the type of birth determines the length of the leave—vaginal deliveries are allowed 6 weeks, while cesarean-section births are allowed 8 weeks. An additional 17 percent of women reported that the length of parental leave was determined by more complex methods. Sometimes the rewarding of parental time was based on length of time having worked for the company. For others this leave was calculated in tandem with unpaid time taken or even with spouse's benefits when both work for the same company. When we compared reported availability of paid leave with the leave women actually took, it became clear that some respondents were conflating true paid parental leave with the ability to use one's vacation or sick time to maintain an income.

Only 11 percent of men reported the availability of paid parental leave for themselves. All paid leave reported as available to new fathers was for 1 week or less.

Turning to the time 2 data, we examine the policies parents actually utilized after the birth of their baby. The length of parental leave taken by women ranged from 2 weeks to more than 21 weeks. Only 7 percent of moms reported taking 2 to 4 weeks of leave, and 17 percent took 5 to 8 weeks following the baby's birth. The majority of women took leaves that were longer than the employer standard of 6 to 8 weeks. Thirty-eight percent of women took 9 to 12 weeks, 33 percent took 13 to 20 weeks, and 5 percent took 21 or more weeks off before returning to the labor force.

Women were asked to specify what types of leave they had taken and for how long. The compiling of time can be a complex arrangement. To address numerous problems with our method of collecting parental leave information, a new section was added to the time 2 interview, which required women to specify the official status of each week of their leave from a list that included personal time, sick time, vacation time, parental-leave time, and disability. Similarly, men were asked to specify the status of each day they took off from work for the birth.

Figures 11.1 and 11.2 show the differences in complexity between women's prenatal reports of leave availability and postnatal detailed leave information. As shown in figure 11.1, when asked during pregnancy (time 1) whether their employers offered them paid parental leave, 38.2 percent of the women said yes. When asked at time 2 as part of the same "benefits and policies" questionnaire whether they had used paid parental leave, 32.4 percent of the women responded affirmatively (this data is not shown in graph format). However, once asked to identify their leave arrangements at the newly specified level of detail, the number of women reporting official fully paid parental leave was reduced to 11 percent of the women interviewed.

Only 37 percent of the women in our sample took all of their time off in one benefit area (for example, unpaid parental leave with no vacation). Thirty-five percent used two different types of benefits, and 13 percent of women used a combination of three or four types of benefits. In this way, one could use up vacation, sick, personal, and compensatory time to "create" a paid parental leave. Seventeen percent of the women drew on their paid vacation time, which ranged from 2 to 11 weeks, with an average of 4.42 weeks of vacation time used. Thirteen percent of new moms used some of their sick time—ranging from 1 to 8 weeks but averaging 3.89 weeks—in order to fund part of their leaves. Twenty-three percent of new moms used some disability time. This disability time was fully paid for only 4 percent, partially paid for 10 percent, and unpaid for 9 percent of the women.

Eighty-one percent of the men surveyed took at least 1 day off from work following the birth of their first child. Men's leaves ranged from 1 to 21 days, with a mean of 7 days. Although 58.8 percent of the men were offered unpaid parental leave as provided by the Family and Medical Leave Act (FMLA), only 3 percent of the men used this type of leave. The men who used the unpaid parental leave benefit were also the men with the longest leaves, taking 15 to 21 days off. Most frequently, men took paid vacation time. Forty-three percent of the men used paid vacation time, ranging from 1 to 15 days, with a mean of 7 vacation days taken. Paid sick time and paid personal time were used by nearly equal

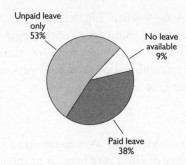

Figure 11.1.   Women's reports of available parental leave benefits at time 1

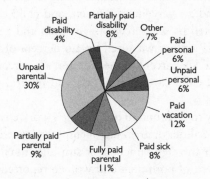

Figure 11.2.   Women's reports of benefits used for parental leave by time 2

portions of the sample (12% and 13%, respectively). Those using sick time took a mean of 5 days off (range 2–10 days), while those relying on personal time took a mean of 3 days (range 1–5 days). Nine percent of the men took unpaid personal time, ranging from 1 to 5 days, with a mean of 3 days taken. Fully paid parental leave was claimed by only three fathers (4%), who reported taking a mean of 6 days, ranging from 4 to 10 days. Two new dads used compensatory time policies to fund their time off by working hours in advance of the birth—one for 5 days and the other for 8 days. Finally, three of the dads reported other strategies for taking time with the baby. One of these dads was a seasonal worker already home on unemployment for the winter. Another was self-employed and could schedule his work around his family's needs. The third dad had been offered a new job, so he planned a 2-week gap between his official end and start dates.

It was much less common for men to use a combination of different benefits than it was for the women. Eighteen percent of the men did use two different benefits, most commonly combining paid personal and vacation time or paid vacation and sick time. Only three of the men used unpaid personal days in combination with paid personal, sick, or comp days. Unlike the women, no men used time from more than two categories of benefits.

CHILD CARE BENEFITS   Men and women reported similar tendencies regarding the availability of child care benefits at the workplace. About a third of the women (36.2%) and men (32.4%) had access to at least one child care benefit. The benefits most commonly available in this group were Dependent Care Assistance Plans (DCAPs), offered to 21 percent of men and 25 percent of women, and child care information or referrals, reported by 22 percent of the men and 11 percent of the women. The DCAP option was used by 2.9 percent of the women and by none of the men. Six percent of the men and 4.4 percent of the women took advantage of child care information and referral services in their workplaces.

Much less likely to be found in our sample's work environments were on-site child care facilities or any kind of employer contributions to child care costs, whether through vouchers or subsidies to child care centers. Less than 10 percent of both men and women reported the availability of these options, and not one person reported having used any of them.

Dynamic Components: Perceptions of Informal Supports

ORGANIZATIONAL COMMITMENT AND SUPPORT   The scale for measuring organizational commitment and perceived support (OCS) ranged from 1 (low commitment) to 4 (high commitment). Men reported a mean of 2.90 at time 1 and 2.82 at time 2, indicating that although their perceptions of OCS had dropped slightly, they still held predominantly positive attitudes about it. While the men's mean score dropped, the minimum scores went up. While at time 1, the lowest OCS score was 1.17, by time 2 the minimum was 1.75. The maximum score for both times was 4. Women's means increased over time from 2.80 at time 1 to 2.87 at time 2. The range for women's scores was from 1.08 to 4 at time 1, and from 1.5 to 4 at time 2.

SUPERVISOR SUPPORT AND COWORKER SUPPORT   On average, both men and women reported a fairly high degree of both supervisor and coworker support. The scale for supervisor support ranged from 1 (low support) to 5 (high support). Men reported a mean of 3.93 at time 1 and 3.69 at time 2. Scores for men fell across the entire range of possible scores from 1 to 5 at both times. Women's mean scores were 3.92 at time 1 and 4.04 at time 2. While the range in women's scores encompasses the full range at time 1, by time 2 the minimum score had risen to 1.4

Support from coworkers also used a scale ranging from a low of 1 to a high of 5. Men reported a mean of 3.94 at time 1, which decreased to a mean of 3.78 by time 2. Men's minimum score increased from 1 at time 1 to 1.25 at time 2, while the maximum score remained stable at 5. Women's scores followed the same decreasing pattern as the men's, with a mean score of 4.01 at time 1 and 3.89 at time 2. Interestingly, women's minimum score decreased from 1.25 at time 1 to 1 at time 2; maximum scores were stable at 5.

INTERPRETIVE ANALYSES

In the following section we move past describing the policies and supports available to families and explore how these are related to parents' psychological well-being. First, the pattern of relationships of structural and dynamic aspects of work with worker well-being at times 1 and 2 is examined. Second, a series of regression analyses explore how both dynamic and structural conditions of employment before the birth predict mental health outcomes once mothers and fathers are back to work full-time after the birth.

Linking Structural Dimensions of Work with Parents' Well-Being
Correlation analyses (not shown) examined how the amount of leave time husbands and wives reported taking after the baby was born was related to mothers' and fathers' psychological well-being. In an interesting twist, results revealed that the more leave time mothers reported, the more role overload they also reported ($r = .39, p < .01$). Moreover, longer maternal leave time was significantly related to husbands' increased anxiety ($r = .35, p < .01$) and depression ($r = .49, p < .001$). Fathers' leave time, measured in days, was unrelated to mothers' or fathers' well-being outcomes.

Linking Dynamic Dimensions of Work with Parents' Well-Being
Correlations were conducted between informal work supports, namely,

organizational commitment and perceived support (OCS), supervisor support, and coworker support, in relation to mothers' and fathers' depression, anxiety, and role overload at time 1 and time 2 (see table 11.2). Correlations between dynamic aspects of work at time 1 and parents' well-being at time 2 were also examined (see table 11.3).

As highlighted in table 11.2, at time 1 the relationships between the dynamic aspects of work and well-being differ by gender. For women, higher levels of OCS, supervisor support, and coworker support are significantly related to lower levels of depression and anxiety. In only one case is role overload related to work dynamics. Specifically, role overload is negatively related to more OCS. The pattern of relationships for men is much weaker. Men's reports of OCS and supervisor support are negatively correlated with role overload. However, no other significant relationships emerge between dynamic components of work and well-being for men at this time point.

At time 2, similar relationships between informal supports and well-being emerge for women. Higher levels of OCS are related to lower levels of depression, anxiety, and role overload. Similarly, supervisor support is negatively correlated with depression, while higher levels of coworker support continue to be significantly related to lower levels of depression and anxiety for new mothers. For men at time 2, OCS and supervisor support are again negatively correlated with feelings of role overload. Most striking, however, is the relationship that emerges for men at this time point between coworker support and psychological well-being. High levels of coworker support are significantly related to lower levels of depression, anxiety, and role overload for these new fathers. Fisher R to Z comparisons reveal that there is significant difference between correlations at time 1 and time 2, suggesting that at time 2 the relevance of coworker support for new fathers takes on new meaning and importance.

Next, we examined possible relationships between dynamic components, or informal supports, at the prenatal time point and psychological well-being at the second time point. The results are shown in table 11.3. For women, two aspects of work at time 1—OCS and coworker support—are significantly correlated with lower levels of depression, anxiety, and role overload at time 2. A less pronounced but still statistically significant relationship exists between supervisor support and depression and anxiety. For men, no significant relationships exist between dynamic components at time 1 and psychological well-being at time 2. As highlighted in table 11.3, Fisher R to Z comparisons were conducted

TABLE 11.2

CROSS-SECTIONAL CORRELATIONS BETWEEN INFORMAL SUPPORTS AND WELL-BEING

	Depression	Anxiety	Role Overload
WIVES			
Organizational Commitment and Perceived Support			
Time 1	−.354**	−.441**	−.253*
Time 2	−.372**	−.374**	−.312*
Supervisor Support			
Time 1	−.242*	−.249*	−.076
Time 2	−.390**	−.257	−.182
Coworker Support			
Time 1	−.315**	−.266*	−.156
Time 2	−.442**	−.368**	−.255
HUSBANDS			
Organizational Commitment and Perceived Support			
Time 1	−.065	−.021	−.280*
Time 2	−.196	−.164	−.265*
Supervisor Support			
Time 1	−.143	−.157	−.306*
Time 2	−.196	−.162	−.218
Coworker Support			
Time 1	−.133	.059	−.112
Time 2	−.524**a	−.415**b	−.429**b

* $p < .05$, ** $p < .01$
R to Z test for significance between correlations: a$p < .01$, b$p < .05$, c$p < .10$

TABLE 11.3

LONGITUDINAL CORRELATION BETWEEN DYNAMIC COMPONENTS AT TIME 1 AND WELL-BEING AT TIME 2

	Depression	Anxiety	Role Overload
Organizational Commitment			
Women	−.535**a	−.490**a	−.419**c
Men	−.027	−.058	−.146
Supervisor Support			
Women	−.307*c	−.327*	−.178
Men	−.075	−.145	−.179
Coworker Support			
Women	−.522**a	−.414**b	−.355**c
Men	−.093	−.108	.091

* $p < .05$, **$p < .01$
R to Z test for significance between correlations: a$p < .01$, b$p < .05$, c$p < .10$
n (time 1) = 70, n (time 2) = 58

to assess whether correlations between workplace dynamics and parents' well-being differed by gender of the parent. Results revealed that in seven out of nine cases, these correlations were significantly different. Conditions of work for a mother at time 1 hold far more implications for her well-being at time 2 than these same conditions do for fathers.

Combined Effects of Structural and Dynamic Components of Work on Well-Being   The next set of analyses examined the hypothesis that multiple dimensions of workplace supports, both structural and dynamic, are related to change in psychological well-being across the transition to parenthood. To test this hypothesis, we constructed hierarchical regression models predicting depression, anxiety, and role overload at time 2 from dynamic and structural aspects of work conditions at time 1. As expected, given the correlation results reported above, no significant relationships were found for male respondents. Results of these regression analyses for women are presented in table 11.4.

Three separate regression models were run, examining depression, anxiety, and role overload independently. The hierarchical models employed had three steps. In step one, the measure of well-being at time 1 was entered into the model to address the question of how change in well-being from time 1 to time 2 is predicted by dimensions of work. In the second step, structural dimensions of work that had been dummy-coded as 0 (no benefit) and 1(at least one benefit) were entered into the model. In this step, only child care benefits (0,1) and scheduling benefits (0,1) were included in the model. Leave time was not included in the model, since at time 1 nearly all women (91%) reported having some leave benefit, so a grouping variable made little sense. In the third step, levels of OCS, supervisor support, and coworker support at time 1 were added to the model. Table 11.4 highlights the findings of these regression analyses.

As expected, assessments of well-being at time 1 are strong predictors of well-being at time 2. In step two, the effects of structural components differed according to the outcome being examined. Structural components at time 1 were unrelated to mothers' depression; however, child care benefits at time 1 were significantly related to less anxiety at time 2. Finally, counter to our hypothesis, the presence of flexible scheduling benefits was related to more overload at time 2 for mothers.

In all three models—for depression, anxiety, and role overload—the inclusion of the dynamic component variables significantly improves the fit of the regression model. Looking at each model, organizational

TABLE 11.4
REGRESSION MODELS PREDICTING MOTHERS' PSYCHOLOGICAL WELL-BEING AT TIME 2

	Depression			Anxiety			Role Overload		
	Step 1	Step 2	Step 3	Step 1	Step 2	Step 3	Step 1	Step 2	Step 3
Time 1 Assessment of Construct[a]	.57**	.57**	.37**	.60**	.68**	.55**	.47**	.46**	.37**
Structural Components									
Flexible schedule		.10	.15		.08	.12		.41**	.46**
Child care benefits		−.04	−.07		−.23*	−.22†		.12	.10
Dynamic Components									
Organizational commitment and support			−.31*			−.13			−.14
Supervisor support			.05			−.05			−.01
Coworker support			−.25†			−.20			−.27*
Adjusted R²	.31**	.30**	.45**	.35**	.37**	.43**	.21**	.39**	.50**
Change in F		.41	5.78**		2.16	2.88*		9.42**	4.85**

† $p < .10$, * $p < .05$, ** $p < .01$

[a] For each regression model, the first independent variable is the time 1 assessment of the construct predicted by the model (i.e., depression for the first model, anxiety for the second, role overload for the third). Standardized beta coefficients are reported.

$N = 58$

support and coworker support were the significant factors related to depression and increased the variance explained in the model by 15 percent. In terms of anxiety, none of the dynamic components of work made a uniquely significant contribution to the model after controlling for structural components; however, the entire step significantly increased the variance explained by 6 percent, and coworker support and OCS were the strongest predictors. Finally, more coworker support at time 1 was significantly related to less role overload for women at time 2.

DISCUSSION

The first aim of this chapter was to describe the availability and impact of family-friendly benefits for couples experiencing the transition to parenthood, with a particular focus on couples in which both spouses were employed in working-class occupations. As expected, these families had few formal "family-friendly" workplace policies available to them. The majority of mothers (62%) had no leave or unpaid leave, while 38 percent reported some type of paid leave. It should be noted, however, that of the women reporting paid leave, the majority achieved this leave by "patchworking" together more traditional structural options, such as sick time and vacation time. This conflation of formal maternity policy with other strategies led to overreporting of family-friendly leave policies among our sample. Similarly, many of the people interviewed felt that they had the option of flextime, since their supervisors would allow them to come in late or make up missed hours when necessary. The issues of policy definition and respondent perception of benefits must be addressed at a high level of detail to avoid such overreporting, especially in studies that rely on participants to complete surveys without an interviewer present to interpret and explain the questions. To be sensitive to the situations of working-class families, future research should use measures of workplace benefits specific enough to distinguish these different grades of flexibility.

An important caveat must be made when interpreting these findings. The availability of benefits to working-class families may actually be inflated in this data set due to our sampling methods. Specifically, people without insurance are less likely to enroll in prenatal education classes, since they must pay for the class out of their own pockets. Since our interviewees were recruited primarily through prenatal classes, they are more likely to have an employer who offered at least some benefits, including health insurance. We are currently modifying our sample recruitment strategies in an attempt to target working families who may not use prenatal classes.

A second goal of this research was to examine the relationships between dynamic and structural conditions of work and employee well-being. While few significant relationships emerged for structural supports, dynamic aspects of work were related to mental health outcomes. In almost every case for women, the more organizational commitment and support, and the more supervisor and coworker support, the less depression and anxiety were reported at time 1 and time 2. For men, on the other hand, at time 1 no dynamic components of work were related to men's depression and anxiety. In terms of role overload, for both men and women at both time 1 and time 2, overload decreased as organizational support and commitment increased.

Of great interest is the change in correlations to coworker support for men from the prenatal time 1 to time 2, when they have become fathers. Specifically, when men became new fathers, coworkers took on a new level of significance: the more supportive coworker relationships were, the less depressed, anxious, and overloaded new fathers were— marking a significant change in this relationship from the time 1 correlations. Perhaps coworkers provide new fathers with a place to talk about their new role, discuss family issues, and problem-solve. Perhaps men don't realize they need coworker support until they're feeling the effects of an "all-nighter" spent with an infant.

There is not much change in the relationship between dynamic aspects of work and well-being for women across the transition to parenthood. However, these results may be related to the timing of the first interview. By the last trimester of pregnancy, women may already be juggling work and family—arranging their schedules around morning sickness, doctor visits, and preparing for parental leave. A prepregnancy measurement of well-being and workplace policies would allow us to determine whether the existing relationships between workplace conditions and women's well-being are preexisting or emerge with the increasing demands of family.

Correlations across times indicate that organizational commitment and support(OCS), supervisor support, and coworker support at time 1 are all significantly and positively related to better reports of psychological well-being at time 2 for new mothers. No similar relationships emerge for fathers. These findings suggest that mothers may bear the brunt of juggling work and family responsibilities and, consequently, that work dynamics are only salient for those managing the juggling act.

It may be the case, however, that women are simply more susceptible to the quality of their work environment, especially during critical life changes such as having a child.

The regression analyses suggest that, in general, the subjective dynamic components of work are more potent indicators of mothers' later well-being than the objective structural aspects of available workplace policies for mothers. Specifically, organizational commitment and support and coworker support appeared to be the most salient indicators of mothers' mental health.

The fact that few relationships emerged between structural or dynamic aspects of work and fathers' well-being is perplexing. It suggests that men's well-being may be impervious to the degree of supportiveness at work. Previous connections between men's employment and their children's outcomes have focused upon dynamic aspects unstudied here—specifically, characteristics of the job itself, such as challenge and autonomy. A next step may be to compare characteristics of the job itself with the support measures used in the present research to see whether any explanatory power is added, or whether men and women are affected by different dimensions of the work experience.

The most perplexing findings are centered on the relationship between maternity and paternity leave and parents' mental health outcomes. Specifically, the more leave time mothers took, the higher their reports of role overload upon return to paid employment. While at first these results appear counterintuitive, further scrutiny suggests that mothers with longer leave time may set up patterns whereby they become the sole child care provider and home caretaker. The longer the pattern persists, the more difficult it is to then add full-time paid employment to the scenario. It may be also harder to enlist father involvement when mothers have longer full-time responsibility for home duties. The fact that longer maternal leave time is related to increases in fathers' depression and anxiety may reflect this same issue. Fathers may have grown accustomed to a full-time at-home spouse, and her transition back to work may make life more complicated. Alternatively, when mothers take longer maternity leaves, the family becomes more stressed financially, and this too may negatively affect fathers' well-being. Since the time 2 interview took place when mothers had been back to paid employment for only one month, it would be important to see if parents' well-being rebounds over time once new patterns have been established. Future research will include visits to each family when the child is one year old, to search for lingering effects of length of leave.

These results also highlight the strong effects of dynamic components in the workplace. Support and understanding in the workplace make a big difference for both parents, especially for pregnant women preparing for the transition to parenthood. While structural policy changes rest in the hands of a few, there is much that supervisors and coworkers can do to help new parents prepare for and adjust to life as workers by treating them with respect and kindness, listening to their concerns, and making it clear that the work they do is valued.

While CEOs and company presidents find themselves under pressure to increase their responsiveness to employees, and while there has been substantial growth in family-friendly policies over the past decade (Bowen 1995), our current data suggest that working-class families are rarely the beneficiaries of such supports. As researchers continue to evaluate the effectiveness of workplace change and innovation on behalf of families, careful attention must be paid to how these policies differentially benefit some employees over others as a function of class, race, or gender.

REFERENCES

Bowen, G. L. 1995. Corporate supports for the family lives of employees: A conceptual model for program planning and evaluation. In *The work and family interface: Toward a contextual effects perspective*, edited by G. L. Bowen and J. F. Pittman. Minneapolis: National Council on Family Relations.

Briggs, Gerald G., Roger K. Freeman, and Sumner J. Yaffe. 1987. *Drugs in pregnancy and lactation: A reference guide to fetal and neonatal risk*. Evansville, Ind.: Mead Johnson Laboratories.

Caplan, Robert D., Sidney Cobb, John R. P. French Jr., R. Van Harrison, and S. R. Pinneau Jr. 1975. *Job demands and worker health: Main effects and occupational differences*. Rockville, Md.: U.S. Department of Health, Education, and Welfare; Public Health Service; Centers for Disease Control; National Institute for Occupational Safety and Health.

Eisenberger, Robert, Robin Huntington, Steven Hutchison, and Debora Sowa. 1986. Perceived organizational support. *Journal of Applied Psychology* 71: 500–507.

Friedman, D. E. 1983. Government initiatives to encourage employer-sponsored child care: The state and local perspective. New York: Center for Public Advocacy Research.

Greenberger, Ellen, Wendy A. Goldberg, Sharon Hamill, Robin O'Neil, and Constance Payne. 1989. Contributions of a supportive work environment to parents' well-being and orientation to work. *American Journal of Community Psychology* 17:755–83.

Hughes, R., Jr., and M. Perry-Jenkins. 1996. Social class issues in family life education. *Family Relations* 45:175–82.

Kanter, Rosabeth Moss. 1977. *Work and family in the United States: A critical review and agenda for research and policy.* New York: Russell Sage Foundation.

Lambert, S., K. Hopkins, G. Easton, J. Walker, H. McWilliams, and M. S. Chung. 1993. *Added benefits: The link between family-responsive policies and work performance at Fel-Pro, Inc.* Chicago: School of Social Service Administration, University of Chicago.

Levine, J. A., and T. L. Pittinsky. 1997. *Working fathers.* Reading, Mass.: Addison-Wesley.

Menaghan, E. G., and Toby L. Parcel. 1995. Social sources of change in children's home environment: The effects of parental occupational experiences and family conditions. *Journal of Marriage and the Family* 57:417–31.

Perry-Jenkins, Maureen. 1993. Working-class women: Negotiating jobs and parenthood. Bethesda, Md.: National Institute of Mental Health. Unpublished proposal.

Perry-Jenkins, M., and A. C. Crouter. 1990. Men's provider-role attitudes: Implications for household work and marital satisfaction. *Journal of Family Issues* 11:136–56.

Piotrkowski, C. S., D. Hughes, J. Pleck, S. Kessler-Sklar, and G. Staines. 1993. *The experience of childbearing women in the workplace: The impact of family-friendly policies and practices (final report).* New York: National Council of Jewish Women, NCJW Center for the Child.

Radloff, Lenore. 1975. Sex differences in depression: The effects of occupation and marital status. *Sex Roles* 1:249–65.

Reilly, Michael D. 1982. Working wives and convenience consumption. *Journal of Consumer Research* 8:407–17.

Spielberger, Charles D. 1972. *Anxiety: Current trends in theory and research.* New York: Academic Press.

U.S. Bureau of Labor Statistics. 1994. *1993 Handbook on women workers: Trends and issues.* Washington, D.C.: U.S. Department of Labor.

U.S. Bureau of the Census. 1988. Household and family characteristics, 1987. *Current Population Reports,* series P-20, no. 423. Washington, D.C.: U.S. Government Printing Office.

CHAPTER 12

Work, Family, and Gender in Medicine

How Do Dual-Earners Decide Who Should Work Less?

Lena M. Lundgren, Jennifer Fleischer-Cooperman, Robert Schneider, and Therese Fitzgerald

INTRODUCTION

Medicine is generally viewed as the prototypical profession, characterized by high status, high professional autonomy, and high pay. The study of work, family, and gender roles in medicine is particularly interesting, considering that the rate of women entering into this traditionally male-dominated profession is one societal measure of gender equality. It is only in the last generation that women have come to represent a significant proportion of physicians, taking on major roles in medicine. Physicians have traditionally made a work-intensive life commitment to their profession, expecting to work long hours, including weekends, and nights. Why, then, as previous studies have shown, do some women in medicine choose an alternative career strategy, that is, working reduced hours? Specifically, why would a two-income couple decide, as our current study shows, that it is the woman physician who should cut back her work hours? This question is the focus of this chapter.

BACKGROUND

Much has been written about the maldistribution of work hours among American employees (Jacobs and Gerson 1997, 1998; Schor 1991).

This work was supported by a grant from the Alfred P. Sloan Foundation.

While many people are working very few hours, others are working very long hours. Employees working very long hours (i.e., 50 or more per week) tend to be highly educated and desirable employees, clustered especially in management and the professions (Jacobs and Gerson 1997, 1998). Indeed, in the United States working very long hours is a sine qua non of the professions. Yet working more than 40 hours has been associated with negative outcomes, including psychological distress (Gutek, Searle, and Klepa 1991; Keith and Shafer 1980; Marshall and Barnett 1993; Parcel and Menaghan 1994; Staines and Pleck 1983). Moreover, most employees are married, and most couples are two-earner couples (U.S. Bureau of Labor Statistics 1997). Because distress is relational, one partner's distress will be reflected in the other partner's distress (Barnett et al. 1993).

One strategy to reduce distress is to reduce work hours. Recent studies indicate that employees who are working very long hours would strongly prefer to reduce their hours by a substantial amount—20 or more hours per week (Jacobs and Gerson 1997; see Gerson and Jacobs, chapter 10 in this volume). This preference was expressed equally by men and women and was unrelated to the presence of young children in the home. Despite this strong preference, relatively few employees actually make the decision to work a reduced schedule. The Bureau of Labor Statistics estimates that in 1994, only 20 percent of the 33 million managers and professionals at work were employed part-time, the large majority voluntarily.

How do couples decide that one partner should reduce his or her work schedule? Specifically, how do couples decide *which* partner will work the reduced schedule? This chapter addresses this question in a sample of married couples in which one member is a physician working a reduced-hours schedule. The chapter first reviews key theoretical frameworks used to explore career decisions and family division of labor. Second, quantitative results are presented on the factors that 126 dual-earner couples considered when deciding that one partner should reduce her or his work schedule.

THEORETICAL FRAMEWORK

Working reduced hours is a non-normative career path in medicine. However, the women who enter that path (and it is largely women who work reduced hours in medicine) are simultaneously taking on the traditional role of working mothers, that is, they decrease their work hours in order to spend more time on family and child responsibilities. There is scant systematic data on what motivates a professional couple to have one spouse work reduced hours. Relevant literature, reviewed here, tends to focus either on the "whether or not to work" decision or on household division of labor decisions. This literature varies greatly on the locus of these decisions. Scholars have argued for a variety of perspectives on this issue, including assumptions that these decisions originate at the individual, the couple, the family, the workplace, or the societal level. The review that follows summarizes some of the key arguments.

THE INDIVIDUAL LEVEL ARGUMENT

The decision to enter into reduced-hours professional or managerial employment is often perceived as the ideal solution for women wanting to combine career and family responsibilities. According to Schwartz (1989), the trend for women to leave a professional career for a number of years or to reduce their work hours (i.e., the "mommy track") is a decision made by women choosing to combine career and family.

In another example, Cardozo (1986) argues that many women in professional careers employ what she calls a "sequencing strategy" in making career decisions. A typical sequence is that women first pursue a professional career, they then raise children full-time, and finally they reintegrate their career and family lives by reentering the labor market. Cardozo argues that sequencing is a positive choice made by women who want to keep both their traditional role as child rearer and their career role. Other analysts point to the negative effects of sequencing for women. Ozawa (1989) and her colleagues, using a "life cycle" perspective, argue that the trend of leaving careers to care for children and elderly parents differentially and negatively impacts the economy of women compared to men. A major limitation with both of these arguments, as well as with other research efforts, including the work of Gerson (1985), is that they view the decision-making process from the perspective of the individual decision maker, that is, as an isolated event in the context of family life.

THE SYSTEMS/FAMILY CONTEXT ARGUMENT

Numerous research efforts have highlighted that the individualized model is not appropriate for examining families and how they make decisions (Burr et al. 1979; Hertz 1991; Lewis 1994; Scanzoni 1980; Thomas 1977). For example, individualistic models do not capture the negotiating processes that take place within the family unit in order to reach decisions about career patterns. These models ignore, as Hertz argues (1986, 12), that dual-earner "partners negotiate, bargain, trade, and occasionally battle in an effort to shape career, marriage and children into a complex but livable arrangement." In other words, these models disregard the fact that most employees live in dyads and that these two-person systems have mutually interactive effects on the system members. Decisions are reached by a process of weighing pros and cons, some of which are rational and objective, others of which are emotional and subjective.

Moreover, systems are fluid and dynamic, and so are the decisions that are made within them. For example, evidence from a study of the transition to parenthood highlights the interdependence of career decisions within couples. According to Cowan and Cowan (1988), some couples become more traditional with their entry into parenthood. Thus, new mothers were more likely to decrease their involvement in the paid labor force and new fathers were apt to increase theirs.

The outcomes of decisions are also evaluated within the system. What is good for one partner may not be good for the other and, as a result, may ultimately not be good for the two-person system. To illustrate, partners may have different expectations for the changes accompanying a reduction in work hours. Failed expectations on the part of either spouse might prompt a reinstatement of the previous full-time pattern. To capture this dynamic and fluid process, one must abandon the individualistic model underlying most research and adopt a systems perspective (see Moen and Wethington 1992 for a full discussion of this point).

THE ROLE OF THE SPOUSE: THEORIES OF
POWER AND GENDER

One model for how couples divide work and family is an economic argument developed by Becker (1981). In this model, decisions about paid employment versus household labor are made based upon economic efficiency, and the partner who has the greatest earning potential outside of the home will be chosen to enter the paid workforce. However, others argue that economics explain only one aspect of how differences in earnings and occupational prestige affect decision-making about work and family. In fact, level of earnings and other measures of occupational prestige interact with the balance of power between spouses and with having traditional gender norms.

Those who focus on the power relationship between spouses generally argue that in traditional, sole-breadwinner families, the male partner often exerts greater authority regarding career decisions due to his general power within the gender stratification system (Blood and Wolfe 1960, Ferree 1991; Zvonkovic et al. 1996).

Traditional gender norms also confound how couples determine the balance of household and paid labor (Hiller and Philliber 1986; Huber and Spitze 1983). For example, Hochschild and Machung (1989) found that even wives who earned more than their husbands performed more housework than their husbands in order to enable the husband to maintain his valued role as breadwinner in the family. In a recent study by Zvonkovic et al. (1996), couples did not consider the option of the wife becoming the breadwinner even when the husband lost his job and the family was faced with economic adversity.

A study conducted by Greenstein (1996) showed that men took on nontraditional gender roles such as increased household labor only in families where *both* spouses adhered to nontraditional gender norms. Potuchek (1992) looked at two groups of employed women, one nontraditional group whom she called the "co-breadwinners," and one group whom she called the "reluctant traditionalists." She found an interaction between occupational prestige and gender-role ideology: the nontraditional "co-breadwinners" were more likely to be clustered in high-paying professional and management jobs and to have spouses with relatively low earnings. The more traditional group had low earnings and spouses with high earnings and career mobility.

In another study on occupational prestige and work/family decisions, Tesch et al. (1992) interviewed full-time employed female physicians who were married to either physicians or other male professionals. The data from this study showed that women who were married to physicians worked fewer hours, were more likely to interrupt their careers for child rearing, and were more likely to have the primary responsibility for child rearing and household tasks than women who were married to non-physician professionals. These results suggest that when gender is controlled for, occupational prestige plays a significant role in determining who will reduce his or her work hours.

Age has also been suggested as a mediating factor in the decision-making process, along with gender and occupational prestige. It appears that younger couples are more likely to engage in mutual decision making than older couples. For example, Tesch et al. (1992) found that the younger female physicians in their study were more likely to partake in an egalitarian decision-making process than the older female physicians. Consistent with these findings are the results of Shelton's (1992) analysis of two longitudinal national data sets, which demonstrated that younger couples had more egalitarian social norms than older couples.

In what ways are these studies relevant to our study of reduced-hours careers in medicine? Specifically, exploring the views of both husbands and wives, this chapter examines whether the choice that the woman physician rather than her spouse should work a reduced-hours schedule is accounted for by individual family preference, specific occupational constraints, or normative expectations. This chapter also examines the interactions between traditional gender norms, level of family income, spouse's occupation (whether or not the spouse was a physician), and number of children at home with factors that suggest that the choice to work less was based on either individual/family preference or external constraints.

SAMPLE

The study "Dual-Earner Families and Reduced-Hours Career Paths in the Medical Profession" is a multiyear research effort funded by the Alfred P. Sloan Foundation. The overall sample of this study consisted of 144 married physicians who work reduced hours and their spouses (N = 285). In this sample, the choice to work a reduced-hours career in medicine was made largely by women who also are parents. Of the 144 primary-respondent physicians, 118 (82%) were women and 26 (18%) were men. It was our original intention to interview an equal number of male and female reduced-hour physicians; however, we had great difficulty locating male physicians who use this working arrangement. The male sample of reduced-hours physicians (N = 26) was not included in the analysis described here.

Working a reduced-hours schedule was defined as working less than the median number of hours worked per week by other physicians of one's own gender—50 hours per week for men and 40 hours per week for women (Yoon 1997). There are a small number of female primary respondents (N = 9) who worked between 40 and 50 hours per week; yet since they considered themselves working a reduced-hours schedule relative to others in their place of employment, they were included in the reduced-hours sample. Moreover, they still worked less than 55 hours per week, the mean number of hours worked by male and female physicians combined (Yoon 1997). Other entrance criteria were: (1) the physician had to consider himself or herself working a reduced-hours schedule; (2) the physician had to have been working the reduced-hours schedule for at least 3 months; (3) the physician had to be married; and (4) the spouse had to be employed, either full-time or part-time.

The mean age of the primary respondents was 42.1 years (SD = 6.5) and the mean age of the spouses was 43.0 (SD = 7.2). All of the respondents were parents; the mean number of children for primary respondents and for the spouses was 1.9 (SD = 0.9) for both groups. The mean number of years in occupation for primary respondents and spouses were 12.8 (SD = 7.1) and 11.7 (SD = 7.1), respectively. Race was not one of the variables we examined, and all of the respondents in this sample were white.

The mean number of hours worked per week was 30.2 (SD = 9.1) for the reduced-hour physicians and 48.7 (SD = 13.2) for the spouses. Hence, on average the spouse worked approximately 18 hours more per week than the primary-respondent physicians, many of whom still worked what is considered a standard workweek, even when working a reduced-hours schedule. The reduced-hour physicians had been working their current schedules for a mean of 47.1 (SD = 46.9) months, indicating that a reduced-hours career path in medicine was not a temporary career pattern.

We used three strategies to develop the sample. First, we used the publicly available registry of the Massachusetts Board of Certification in Medicine, which licenses all physicians who practice in the state, to randomly sample physicians aged 30 to 65 who were working within a 25-mile radius of Boston and, as a proxy for work hours, reported 50 or fewer hours per week of patient care if male, and 40 or fewer hours per week of patient care if female. Although patient-care hours underrepresent work hours to varying degrees, total work hours are not among the data contained in the registry. We also requested nominations from project participants. Finally, we contacted every HMO, hospital, and practice partnership in the area and invited their participation in the project, either by nominating eligible staff physicians or by publicizing the study and asking interested physicians to contact us.

Because it is not possible to compute a response rate for those physicians who contacted us after hearing about the study (N = 22 couples), they are not included in the following calculations. Of the 512 names obtained using the random sampling approach, 203 were determined ineligible. Of the 167 known eligibles, interviews were completed with 82 couples, yielding a completion rate of 49.1 percent. Eligibility could not be determined for 142 cases, but among the 370 cases with known status, the eligibility ratio was 45.1. Thus, we estimate that 62 of the undetermined cases might have been eligible. Dividing the number of completed interviews by the known plus the estimated eligibles gives an overall response rate of 35.5 percent for potentially eligible randomly sampled physicians and their spouses. The cooperation and response rates were better for the nominated sample. Of 109 nominations received, 9 were determined ineligible. Of the 51 physicians known to be eligible, 40 couples were interviewed.

To evaluate the adequacy of our response rate, we compared it to those reported in previous studies of physicians. In one study, in which interviewers made as many as 60 contact attempts, the response rate of 62.7 percent for a 20-minute survey completed by mail or by phone was described as "comparable with or somewhat better than for other physician surveys" (Parson et al. 1994, 763). In another, the authors described their response rate of 64 percent—achieved after up to three mailings of a 145-item survey—as "similar to other physician surveys" (Sobal et al. 1990, 714). In these studies, however, only the physician had to agree to participate, whereas in our study both physician and spouse had to agree. The majority of the physicians in our sample (60.3%) were married to other physicians, with the same notoriously high refusal rates. The probability that two physicians will agree to participate, given likelihoods of independent participation ranging from .60 to .65, is only .36 to .42. These figures approximate the conservatively calculated overall response rates achieved in this study, with cooperation rates substantially higher. It should also be noted that the amount of time required for participation in the present study was considerably longer than for the other studies discussed here (80 minutes vs. 20 minutes in Parson et al. 1994; 550 items vs. 145 items in Sobal et al. 1990) and that the present study required a face-to-face interview rather than a more convenient mail or telephone survey.

PROCEDURES

The survey measures were developed based on a set of initial qualitative in-depth interviews conducted with 22 couples in which one partner was a physician who met our eligibility criteria. The interviews were conducted separately with the husband and the wife and covered many aspects of their lives, including the reasons why the physician reduced her or his hours. The interviews were audiotaped, and the tapes were transcribed. Content analyses of the transcription were conducted to identify the most frequently mentioned reasons for reducing work hours. Based on the qualitative results, we generated several closed-ended quantitative measures that were administered to 144 reduced-hours physicians during the survey phase of the study.

During the survey phase, each physician and spouse was interviewed separately by a trained interviewer. The interviews took approximately one hour and were conducted at a time and place convenient to the participant. Prior to the interview, each participant received a mailed survey, which took about 20 minutes to complete and was collected at the time of the interview. The face-to-face interviews covered the quality of the participants' major social roles (partner, employee, and where appropriate, parent) along with a number of quality-of-life indicators.

RESULTS

The results presented in this section were derived through factor analysis and multiple regression methods. The factor analysis responded to two questions. First, what factors were the most important when deciding that the woman physician and not her spouse should reduce her work hours—external constraints or individual family preferences? Second, did the spouses consider different factors? The multiple regression models responded to the question: Were traditional gender norms, level of income, occupation of the spouse and number of children at home associated with high scores on either "external constraints" or "preferences" in the two samples?

FACTOR ANALYSIS

Many of the survey items were developed from the results of the qualitative interviews with 22 dual-earner couples in which one spouse was a physician who met our eligibility criteria. Specifically, based on these qualitative results, an eight-item closed-ended quantitative measure was developed that asked the question: Why did you and not your spouse (or Why did your spouse and not you) decide to work a reduced-hours schedule? The initial factor analysis of this eight-item measure used an eigenvalue of 1.0 as the default for identifying factors. The resulting factors were rotated with an orthogonal (varimax) rotation. The analysis yielded three factors. Because of the moderately high inter-factor correlation observed in the first analysis, the resulting factors were then rotated using an oblique (promax) rotation.

As table 12.1 indicates, the first factor, "external normative constraints," accounted for 41.3 percent of the variance for the female physicians and 37.5 percent of the variance for their male spouses. The three items that loaded strongly on this factor measured the respondent's agreement with statements that it is more acceptable socially, at your place of work and in your family, for women to reduce their work hours than men. The second factor, "occupational constraint of the spouse," accounted for 17.5 percent of the variance among the women and 17 percent for their spouses. Items with high loadings on this factor measured the respondents' perception that the male spouse would pay a higher career penalty for reducing hours than the woman physician. The third factor, "individual/family preference," accounted for the least amount of variation among physicians (13.0%) and their spouses (13.0%). Items in this factor focused on individual preferences regarding spending more time with children and the relative importance of career to the two respondent groups.

The three factors combined accounted for 60 percent of the variance within the eight items. Reliability measures (Cronbach's alpha) ranged from .62 to .82 and the inter-factor correlations were relatively low, ranging from −.17 to .35. There were no statistically significant differences when the factor scores of the women physicians were compared with those of their male spouses.

MULTIPLE REGRESSION ANALYSIS

The regression analysis examined whether the three factors just described were associated with several independent variables including: (1) having traditional gender role norms, (2) level of family income, (3) whether or not the spouse was a physician, and (4) the number of children at home. As the literature reviewed earlier in the chapter suggests, these are factors that previous research has found to affect decisions about both careers and household labor. It should be noted that our decision to measure spouse's occupational status by whether or not the spouse was a physician, rather than using other occupational data on the spouse, was based both on the findings of previous studies that women physicians married to physicians are more likely to take on traditional gender roles than if they are married to partners with other occupations, and the high likelihood of women physicians being married to other physicians. Indeed, in our sample 60 percent of the women physicians were married to other physicians.

Multiple regressions were run separately for the female physicians and for their spouses. As table 12.2 shows, having more traditional gender norms was associated with the first factor ("external normative constraints") for the women (beta $= .271, p = .01$). However, for their spouses, number of children was the only variable that was significantly associated with this factor (beta $= .253, p = .04$). For both the women physicians and their spouses, none of the variables was significantly associated with the second factor ("occupational constraint of the spouse" [husband]). Analyses for both the female physicians and their spouses found a statistically significant relationship between more traditional gender norms and the third factor, "individual/family preference." In addition, for the women, a higher family income was associated with stating that "individual/family preference" was a key reason behind why they and not their spouses chose to work less.

DISCUSSION

In our study a reduced-hour career in medicine was largely the career pattern of women who were parents. Indeed, our intention to sample an equal number of men and women working part-time proved futile, since the men working reduced hours either argued that they did so in order to build up a full-time practice or for health reasons (Lundgren and Barnett 2000). Results from a qualitative study (Lundgren et al. forthcoming) also support this finding. In the latter study, women described being the ones to work a reduced-hours schedule instead of their spouses, even when objective conditions included the woman physician having a more stable career path and twice the income of her spouse. It should be noted that the large majority of women in our study worked a standard workweek (approximately 35 hours per week) and that other research indicates that women who work a reduced-hour schedule show a higher level of career satisfaction than women who are in academic medicine—the most prestigious, yet demanding, career path in medicine (Barnett and Gareis 1998).

Further, our analysis indicates that this consistent pattern of wives and mothers working less in order to increase time spent on family was

TABLE 12.1

PSYCHOMETRIC DATA ON "REASONS PHYSICIAN REDUCED HOURS RATHER THAN SPOUSE" SCALE

	All (N = 217)	Physicians (N = 109)	Spouses (N = 108)
Factor 1: External normative constraints			
Percent of variance accounted for by factor	39.7%	41.3%	37.5%
Internal consistency (Cronbach's alpha)	.75	.82	.74
Test-retest stability over 1–3 months[a]	.78	.83	.71
Factor loadings for individual items			
It is more acceptable socially for women to reduce their hours than for men to reduce their hours	.87	.86	.88
It is more acceptable at your place of work for women to reduce their hours than for men to reduce their hours	.80	.83	.78
It is more acceptable in your family for women to reduce their hours than for men to reduce their hours	.78	.73	.78
Factor 2: Occupational constraint of the spouse			
Percent of variance accounted for by factor	17.3%	17.5%	17.0%
Internal consistency (Cronbach's alpha)	.79	.68	.75
Test-retest stability over 1–3 months	.68	.65	.76
Factor loadings for individual items			
Spouse would have paid a higher price professionally for reducing hours than physician	−.90	−.91	−.90
Reducing hours would be less detrimental to physician's career than it would be to spouse's career	−.87	−.88	−.84

Factor 3: Individual/family preference

Percent of variance accounted for by factor	13.0%	13.0%	13.0%
Internal consistency (Cronbach's alpha)	.66	.62	.62
Test-retest stability over 1–3 months	.85	.88	.80
Factor loadings for individual items			
The children need more time with physician (mother) than they need with spouse (father)	.82	.84	.79
Spending time with the children/family is more important to physician (mother) than it is to spouse (father)	.85	.81	.82
Spouse's career is more important to him than physician's career is to her	−.66	−.69	.62
Intercorrelations among factors			
External norms with occupational constraints	−.31	−.29	−.29
Externals norms with preference	.35	.35	.31
Occupational constraints with preference	−.18	−.19	−.17

NOTE: Principal components analysis with oblique rotation. Item 2, "career is more important to secondary," loaded onto more than one factor in the overall sample and in the physician subsample. Couples in which both spouses worked reduced hours (N = 20 pairs) did not answer any items from this scale.
ᵃTest-retest sample comprised 55 respondents (31 physicians and 24 spouses).

TABLE 12.2
MULTIPLE REGRESSION ANALYSES: DECISION-MAKING FACTORS FOR FEMALE PHYSICIANS AND THEIR SPOUSES

Independent Variables	External Normative Constraints	Occupational Constraint of the Spouse	Individual and Family Preferences
Female Physicians			
Gender role identity	.271*	−.055	.381***
Family income	.064	−.048	.352**
Number of children at home	.100	−.030	.169
Spouse is a physician	−.078	−.033	.006
R²	.09	.01	.29
Male Spouses			
Gender role identity	.134	.057	4.27***
Family income	.195	−.159	−.96
Number of children at home	.253*	−.177	.46
Spouse is a physician	.177	−.038	−.18
R²	.09	.03	.18

* $p < .05$; ** $p < .01$; *** $p < .001$

not necessarily pursued out of preference. Rather, the study indicates that it is more socially acceptable for women to choose an alternative career path than for men. This view is shared by both the women and the men in our sample. Hence, this would suggest that a framework that emphasizes individual choice/preference in career decisions seems to be the least relevant for explaining the decision to work less.

The differences between the factors that emerged to account for how the couples decided who would work a reduced-hours schedule support our contention that such decisions are made systemically rather than individually or unilaterally. The factor that accounted for the most variance, "external normative constraints," is a macro-level, sociocultural one. It is based upon perceptions of phenomena that occur beyond the boundaries of the couple (e.g., "It is more acceptable socially for women to reduce their hours than it is for men to reduce their hours"). As discussed previously, our analysis shows that this level of influence has the most significant impact on the decision-making process for both men and women, albeit more so for women.

For the women only, having traditional gender norms is significantly associated with scoring high on both preference and external normative constraints. What does this imply? First, this result confirms previous findings that women who follow traditional gender norms generally choose career paths that increase their family participation. Second, it is possible that the women eligible for inclusion in this study because of their career choices are a self-selected group, who may observe more traditional gender norms compared to women physicians who work full-time. Also, in this study higher income indicates a greater likelihood of perceiving that the choice to work less was based on one's own or one's family's preference.

Finally, the analysis suggests that the way that the couples in the study perceived these external normative constraints and occupational constraints not only made it more acceptable for women to work less, but also made it more likely for the couples to conclude that the men would pay a greater penalty if they were the ones who worked less. Familial beliefs regarding gender roles also proved to be important in the decision-making process regarding who should reduce their hours. Although by entering a traditionally male-dominated profession the women in these high-status careers have moved away from the traditional roles that their mothers and grandmothers may have assumed, they continue to be influenced by traditional gender norms about family and caretaking responsibilities. In the face of perceived pressure from society, workplace, and family, both women and men adhere to traditional gender roles when considering the decision to reduce work hours. Men continue to maintain the role of primary breadwinner, while women, no matter how prestigious their position and no matter how much education or advanced training they have acquired, continue to be the ones to take the reduced-hours path.

Both the women and the men in this study agreed that it is more acceptable for women to reduce their hours than it is for men. Their responses indicated that they believed the men had careers that made it more difficult for them to work a reduced-hours schedule. This result may be due to a perception that the workplace views men who choose to work less than full-time more negatively than women who choose this path. Or, early in their careers, men and women may have identified career paths that were more or less flexible with respect to balancing work and family. For example, a medical school dean suggested in an interview (Lundgren and Barnett 2000) that many women enter medical school and choose specialties that are more likely to support reduced-hours schedules; for instance, they become general internists rather than surgeons.

IMPLICATIONS

The results of this study suggest that the weight of traditional gender-role norms creates a widespread workplace model whereby it is more acceptable for women who are parents to cut back on their hours than it is for men. Therefore, even though work/family policies may be offered to parents of both genders on paper, they remain based on an assumption that women will take advantage of these policies while men should continue to be the primary breadwinners, working the number of hours they worked before having children.

Whereas the development of work/family policy will reduce stress and promote family well-being, it is not likely to impact gender equality at home and at work unless underlying norms are addressed by organizations adopting these policies. Further, educational and training institutions need to address these issues early on if we are to see a change in medical students' perceptions of gender roles.

FUTURE RESEARCH

In order to further explore the high level of congruence between gender-role ideology and external norms as well as the consistency of this finding across gender in our sample, couple-level analysis of data—for instance, using hierarchical linear modeling—is needed. This is the next step in our ongoing research effort. Further, there is a clear need for studies that compare factors underlying work/family decisions made by physicians working reduced hours and by their colleagues who work full-time. This type of study would clarify the perceptions of constraints and opportunities in making decisions about work hours. Finally, further research is needed on how to develop family-supportive workplace policy that (1) supports both women's and men's work and family involvement, (2) does not strengthen traditional gender patterns, and (3) does not lead to decreased professional status and prestige for those working fewer hours.

REFERENCES

Barnett, Rosalind C., and Karen C. Gareis. 1998. *A comparison of part- and full-time employed physicians: Selected background characteristics.* Waltham, Mass.: Brandeis University.

Barnett, Rosalind C., Nancy L. Marshall, Stephen W. Raudenbush, and Robert T. Brennan. 1993. Gender and the relationship between job experiences and psychological distress: A study of dual-earner couples. *Journal of Personality and Social Psychology* 64(5):794–806.

Becker, Gary. 1981. *Treatise on the family*. Cambridge, Mass.: Harvard University Press.

Blood, Robert O., and Donald M. Wolfe. 1960. *Husbands and wives: The dynamicsof married living*. New York: Free Press.

Burr, Wesley R., Reuben Hill, Ivan F. Nye, and Ira L. Reiss, eds. 1979. *Contemporary theories about the family*. New York: Free Press.

Cardozo, Arlene. 1986. *Sequencing: Having it all but not all at once: A new solution for women who want marriage, career, and family*. New York: Athenaeum.

Cowan, Carolyn P., and Philip A. Cowan. 1988. Who does what when partners become parents: Implications for men, women, and marriage. *Marriage and Family Review* 12(3/4):105–31.

Ferree, Myra M. 1991. The gender division of labor in two-earner marriages. *Journal of Marriage and the Family* 12:158–80.

Gerson, Kathleen. 1985. *Hard choices: How women decide about work, career, and motherhood*. Berkeley: University of California Press.

Greenstein, Theodore. 1996. Husband's participation in domestic labor: Interactive effects of wives' and husbands' gender role ideologies. *Journal of Marriage and the Family* 58:585–96.

Gutek, Barbara A., Sabrina S. Searle, and Lilian Klepa. 1991. Rational versus gender-role explanations for work-family conflict. *Journal of Applied Psychology* 76(4):560–68.

Hertz, Rosanna. 1986. *More equal than others: Women and men in dual-career marriages*. Berkeley: University of California Press.

———. 1991. Dual-career couples and the American dream: Self-sufficiency and achievement. *Journal of Comparative Family Studies* 22(2):248–63.

Hiller, Dana V., and William W. Philliber. 1986. The division of labor in contemporary marriage: Expectations, perceptions, and performance. *Social Problems* 33(3):191–201.

Hochschild, Arlie, and Anne Machung. 1989. *The second shift: Working parents and the revolution at home*. New York: Viking Penguin.

Huber, Joan, and Glenna Spitze. 1983. *Sex stratification: Children, housework, and jobs*. New York: Academic Press.

Jacobs, Jerry A., and Kathleen Gerson. 1997. The endless day or the flexible office? Working hours, work-family conflict, and gender equity in the modern workplace. Report to the Alfred P. Sloan Foundation.

———. 1998. Who are the overworked Americans? *Review of Social Economy* 56(4):442–59.

Keith, Patricia M., and Robert B. Shafer. 1980. Role strain and depression in two-job families. *Family Relations* 29(4):483–88.

Lewis, Suzan. 1994. *Role tensions and dual-career couples*. London: Paul Chapman.

Lundgren, Lena, and Rosalind C. Barnett, R. 2000. Reduced-hours careers in medicine: A strategy for the professional community and the family. *Community, Work and Family* 3(1):65–79.

Lundgren, Lena, Faith Ferguson, and Jennifer Fleischer-Cooperman. Forthcoming. Negotiating a reduced-hours career path in medicine: Strategies and consequences in the United States. In *Research in the sociology of work: Employment restructuring.* Greenwich, Conn.: JAI Press.

Marshall, Nancy L., and Rosalind C. Barnett. 1993. Work-family strains and gains among two-earner couples. *Journal of Community Psychology* 21(1): 64–78.

Moen, Phyllis, and Elaine Wethington. 1992. The concept of family adaptive strategies. *American Review of Sociology* 18:233–51.

Ozawa, Martha N. 1989. *Women's life cycle and economic insecurity problems and proposals.* New York: Praeger.

Parcel, Toby L., and Elizabeth G. Menaghan. 1994. Early parental work, family social capital, and early childhood outcomes. *American Journal of Sociology* 99(4):972–1009.

Parsons, Jennifer A., Richard B. Warnecke, Ronald F. Czaja, Jan Barnsley, and Arnold Kaluzny. 1994. Factors associated with response rates in a national survey of primary care physicians. *Evaluation Review* 18:756–66.

Potuchek, Jean L. 1992. Employed wives' orientation to breadwinning: A gender theory analysis. *Journal of Marriage and the Family* 54:548–58.

Scanzoni, John. 1980. *Family decision-making.* Beverly Hills, Calif.: Sage Publications.

Schor, Juliet B. 1991. *The overworked American: The unexpected decline of leisure.* New York: Basic Books.

Schwartz, Felice. 1989. Executives and organizations: Management women and the new facts of life. *Harvard Business Review* 67(1):65.

Shelton, Beth Anne. 1992. *Women, men, and time.* New York: Greenwood Press.

Sobal, Jeffrey, Bruce R. DeForge, Kevin S. Ferente, Herbert L. Muncie, Carmine M. Valente, and David M. Levine. 1990. Physician responses to multiple questionnaire mailings. *Evaluation Review* 18:711–22.

Staines, Graham L., and Joseph H. Pleck. 1983. *The impact of work schedules on the family.* Ann Arbor: University of Michigan.

Tesch, Bonnie J., Janet Osborne, Deborah J Simpson, Sara F. Murray, and Joanna Spiro. 1992. Women physicians in dual-physician relationships compared with those in other dual-career relationships. *Academic Medicine* 67(8):542–44.

Thomas, Edwin. 1977. *Marital communication and decision-making.* New York: Macmillan.

U. S. Bureau of Labor Statistics. 1997. *Employment and earnings.* No. 029-001-03260-9. Washington, D.C.: U.S. Government Printing Office.

Yoon, Young-Hee. 1997. Reduced-hours careers in medicine. Unpublished manuscript, Alfred P. Sloan Foundation.

Zvonkovic, Anisa M., Kathleen M. Greaves, Cynthia J. Schmiege, and Leslie D. Hall. 1996. The marital construction of gender through work and family decisions: A qualitative analysis. *Journal of Marriage and the Family* 58:91–100.

CHAPTER 13

From Baby-sitters to Child Care Providers

The Development of a
Feminist Consciousness in
Family Day Care Workers

Heather M. Fitz Gibbon

On the face of it, one might expect family day care providers—women providing home-based paid child care—to be politically conservative and comparatively traditional in their views on gender and family (Fosburg 1981; Nelson 1990). Though engaged in paid work, they are doing so within the home while supposedly continuing to fulfill the obligations of family work; and many of them begin this work because they "feel it is wrong for mothers to leave their children" (Nelson 1990, 54). As such, their work seemingly supports an ideology of caring that locates caring labor within the private sphere and in the hands of women (Abel and Nelson 1990). Indeed, many providers see their work not as an occupation, but rather as an extension of their roles as women and as mothers.

Given these expectations, I was surprised when through the process of interviewing 45 family day care providers in the Midwest, I came to meet a group of remarkable women who through both their actions and their words were expressing what I came to see as a feminist consciousness. All were members of a formal local network of family day care providers. I eventually interviewed every active member of this network—a total of 20 women. These women ranged in age from 21 to 70, and had been providing day care for periods from one month to 26 years. While most were from working-class backgrounds, a few lived in an exclusive part of town, had graduate degrees, and had held professional-level jobs before beginning work in child care. Others had been factory workers, some had received public aid, and some had never worked outside the home. What nearly all of them had in common was a strong sense of professionalism and a passion for their work.

This professionalism led some of these women to construct definitions of self, work, and family that challenged traditional gender expectations. This chapter examines the relationship between professionalism and the development of a feminist consciousness among these family day care workers. I argue that as providers identify themselves as professional caregivers rather than "baby-sitters," and as they come into contact with others doing the same work, they begin to develop a politicized, feminist identity of themselves as workers and as women.

THE DETERMINANTS OF A FEMINIST CONSCIOUSNESS

Much of the literature explaining feminist attitudes has centered on the relative impacts of political ideology and self-interest. In particular, researchers have focused on the effect that direct exposure to nontraditional lifestyles has on attitudes. Klein, for example, proposes that "[w]omen became feminists largely because the day-to-day experiences of a nontraditional lifestyle led them to reject traditionalism and demand equal opportunity" (Klein 1984, 116). From this perspective, the rise of feminist attitudes in the 1970s, for example, can best be explained by structural changes such as the entrance of women into the paid labor force and the increase in divorce. As Banaszak and Plutzer argue, individuals "adopt political attitudes that endorse or reinforce lifestyle arrangements in which they find themselves" (1993, 32).

Togeby (1995) extends this argument by suggesting that not all attitudes are affected by self-interest or everyday experiences. Based on an examination of Danish election data, she suggests that a key variable missing in much of the literature is the nature of the attitude to be explained. Specifically, attitudes that are more direct and immediately salient to us, such as those surrounding workplace policies, are more fully explained by self-interests. Ideology or "symbolic politics" may better explain those attitudes that are more distant from everyday experiences, such as national politics. Thus, measures of feminism that ask respondents only about distant political issues may not capture feminist perspectives on everyday life.

An alternative position is that political attitudes are best explained not by self-interest or everyday experiences, but by an underlying political ideology that predisposes individuals to embrace consonant symbols and perspectives (Reingold and Foust 1998; Sears and Funk 1990; Sears and Huddy 1990). Researchers from this position present empirical evidence that demonstrates how little of the variance in feminist consciousness can be explained by concrete socioeconomic variables (Reingold and Foust 1998, 24). They argue further that the relationship between nontraditional lifestyles and a feminist consciousness might be spurious: while exposure to nontraditional lifestyles may lead to feminist consciousness, it is also likely that people might choose nontraditional lifestyles because of an ideological predisposition.

Most of the studies from both these positions are based on the quantitative analysis of cross-national election data. Because these studies are based on large samples, they do allow us to compare the relative impact of various attitudinal, demographic, and sociostructural variables. Because they provide only snapshots of attitudes at a particular time, however, they do not allow us to understand political consciousness as a complex, sometimes nonlinear process. Out of a desire to remain consistent in their responses, subjects might not choose attitudes contradictory to their stated political ideologies. The effects of contradictory new experiences or emerging self-interest might be difficult to discern from this sort of survey research.

Additionally, studies that assume that feminist consciousness only develops through direct exposure to nontraditional lifestyles fail to address how actors interpret these lifestyles (Klein 1984). While such exposure may be an important catalyst toward changing attitudes, this chapter shows that the determination of a feminist consciousness does not lie in whether an activity is traditional or nontraditional, but rather in the meaning attributed to that activity, and that this meaning arises through interaction with others sharing common experiences.

The recognition of a shared fate marks the beginning of the development of a collective identity. As discussed by Rupp and Taylor (1999, 365), building a collective identity includes three processes. First, the boundaries of the group are defined—members come to see that they share interests and experiences and that as a group they possess unique characteristics. Second, the members of the group develop a consciousness of "distinct and shared disadvantages." Third, the actions and everyday experiences of group members become politicized.

Such a politicized collective identity is suggested by Gerson and Peiss's (1985) distinction between female consciousness and feminist consciousness. Female consciousness entails the recognition that women, by virtue of their status as women, share particular problems and perspectives and are due specific rights. Female consciousness arises as women come to negotiate the boundaries of gender—the female identity—and work to fulfill the expectations of that status. It does not automatically imply, however, a challenge to the status of women as such.

Feminist consciousness, according to Gerson and Peiss, arises as individuals come to challenge the social order. Following the development of female consciousness, as women attempt to achieve the rights due them given their status, they find their efforts blocked. At this point their work often becomes politicized and they may see themselves as part of a larger social movement. This represents the beginning of feminist consciousness.

According to Lerner's historical analysis, feminist consciousness includes

> the awareness of women that they belong to a subordinate group; that they have suffered wrongs as a group; that their condition of subordination is not natural, but is societally determined; that they must join with other women to remedy these wrongs; and finally, that they must and can provide an alternate vision of societal organization in which women as well as men will enjoy autonomy and self-determination. (Lerner 1993, 15)

Though Lerner refers here to the emergence of feminism in particular historical eras, her framework does help us understand the distinction between group consciousness and feminist consciousness. The latter implies not only a collective identity but also the recognition that feminists are involved in social movements and in political action (Rupp and Taylor 1999).

As many scholars suggest, however, feminism is not a dichotomous status that one either occupies or not (Gerson and Peiss 1985; Henderson-King and Stewart 1997; Stanley and Wise 1993). Instead, it is developmental and continuous, changing through contact with women's culture and interactions between men and women. The development of feminist consciousness passes through various stages of embeddedness and commitment, beginning with a more passive perspective and ending with an active commitment to social change (Henderson-King and Stewart 1997, 369). This broader conception of feminist consciousness acknowledges that women may not self-identify as "feminist." Though self-identification is one component of feminist consciousness, it is not the sole component, nor does its absence signify that feminist values and beliefs are not present (Henderson-King and Stewart 1994).

The concept of progression from female consciousness to a feminist consciousness helps to explain the experiences of family day care providers I interviewed. It would be a mistake to believe that because family day care providers are engaged in traditionally gendered work (Murray 1996; Tuominen 1994), or because they don't identify themselves as feminist, they cannot be feminist in their orientations. As the data here demonstrate, many of the women in this study developed a female consciousness through their interactions with other women. Through these interactions, particularly with the mothers of the children for whom they care, they developed a common awareness of the expectations of care giving and the problems associated with these expectations. Mothers and providers may share stories of how they negotiate household duties with their husbands, how they handle the stress of a new infant in the home, or how they can maintain a romantic relationship with their partner after a long day with the children.

At what point do these interactions become politicized? As family day care providers become more professionalized, as their identities shift from being simply baby-sitters to being caregivers, they begin to negotiate further the boundaries of the public and private spheres. Particularly, as family day care providers work together on the project of defining what they do as a profession, their work moves them closer to a feminist consciousness. This chapter explores this progression of providers' identities from baby-sitters to caregivers and its impact on their attitudes toward other providers, other women, and relationships with members of their families.

METHODS

The results reported in this chapter derive from interviews with a subsample of 20 family day care providers in the Midwest who were involved in an organized local family day care provider network. This subsample was drawn from a larger sample of 45 providers. Interviews were conducted in the providers' homes, generally during the children's afternoon nap time or in the evenings, and lasted from one to four hours. I tape-recorded all interviews. Additionally, I attended several meetings and workshops of two support groups for family day care providers. The names used in this chapter are all fictional to protect the women interviewed.

I drew the sample of providers from two general sources. First, I located local networks of providers and contacted all the members of these networks. I also located providers through informal networks of friends, neighbors, and acquaintances who use home day care. The larger sample was almost equally divided between those who were members of a network and those who were not. Similarly, about half of the providers (22) were certified. While it is impossible to know how many providers in any region are certified (or licensed), it is likely that this sample is more heavily weighted toward certified providers than is the general population of home providers.[1]

The time the women in this sample had been caring for children ranged from 1 month to 26 years, with a mean of 7.9 years and a median of 4 years. These numbers are slightly higher than the national average (Nelson 1990), explained most likely by the fact that more of these women were career providers than would be the case in the population as a whole. The women in this sample cared for between 1 and 15 children, with a mean of 4.9 and a median of 5.5. All but 9 of the providers (80%) had school-age or preschool-age children of their own to care for. On average, the women cared for a total of 4 children.

All but one of the providers were white, and only three had four-year college degrees (two of the degreed women also held graduate degrees). Most (over 75%) of the women had worked previously, generally in female-dominated professions. Many had worked in clerical or service jobs (mostly as sales clerks), two had been teachers, and two had previously worked in child care. The average annual income for the providers was $9,000, and the average hourly rate was $2 per hour per child.

Similarly, the providers' husbands were mostly blue-collar workers; most were employed in semiskilled or unskilled labor. Two were engineers, one was a writer, and four were unemployed. The median income for spouses was $27,500.

DEFINING PROFESSIONALISM

The family day care providers I interviewed came from a part of the country where the economy had previously been predominantly man-

1. Compared with many other states, child care in this Midwest state is relatively underregulated. The state does not require providers caring for fewer than six children (including any of their own children under age six) to be registered, licensed, or certified. Through their departments of human services, counties do certify providers who wish to care for children of parents receiving public funds. Certified providers need little training initially but yearly must complete a small number of "in-service" hours of training and pass inspections.

ufacturing. Economic restructuring in this region meant diminishing opportunities in manufacturing for working-class men and increasing but
low-paid work opportunities for women. These changes made balancing
work and family difficult. The women I interviewed had faced two
choices for achieving this balance. They could fully embrace either the
public sector (by working outside the home full-time and hiring others
to care for their children and homes) or the private sector (by staying at
home and not working for pay). Though there is support for maintaining
the separation of spheres within middle-class ideology, neither of these
approaches was financially an option for these women. One solution,
then, was to mediate the two spheres by bringing the public sphere into
the private.

The providers in this sample used one of two strategies for integrating
the public and private spheres. The first was to define their work as an
extension of the caring they provided as wives and mothers. Thus
though being rewarded financially, they did not challenge the notion
that caring is women's work and therefore not work in the true sense.
These women often referred to themselves as "baby-sitters." They were
very traditional in their orientations and often did not pursue day care
as a career. Their work as family day care providers was supplemental
to their primary roles as caretakers for their own children. It was a
financial bridge for them between the time when they had no children
and were free to pursue waged labor outside the home and the
time when their children were out of the home. Those who considered
themselves baby-sitters resisted training and the regulation of their
work. Many feared that increasing regulations would make child care
more of a business and less like a family relationship, and thus less
"caring." Also, since women are "by nature" good caregivers, they
viewed training programs with suspicion—you cannot teach that which
comes naturally.

The second strategy was to define caring as work and to challenge
the assumption that caring remains merely within the private sphere.
These providers, though maintaining the benefits of staying home with
their families, attempted to gain some of the protections of the public
sphere. By recognizing that they were in fact working in the public
sphere, they were aware of many of the contradictions within and between spheres.

Providers undertook a variety of activities that we can call professional and that distinguished them from "baby-sitters." These included

county certification, national certification, subscribing to the local food program for funds for feeding children in their care, participating in a network, previous course work in child development, attending workshops, and finally, the use of a contract. All but the last of these activities required providers to move out of the realm of the home and interact with public institutions. As such, they had to publicly identify themselves as professional caregivers (rather than simply women who help out their neighbors or friends) and embrace the recognition that child care involves specialized skills that need to be nourished and developed. A contract similarly indicates a level of professional power and leads providers to articulate their expectations to both their clients and themselves.

None of these items in isolation is an indication of professionalism. Some women joined the food program simply to gain additional financial support for their work, without seeing themselves as professionals. Providers who were certified with the county had to attend several workshops to maintain their certification, whether or not they saw the value in these programs. Nonetheless, providers who participated in a number of these activities developed a level of awareness of the special skills and duties of a child care provider and a stronger sense of identity as a caregiver. Most important was the interaction with other providers in a formal organization or network. I will focus for the remainder of this chapter on the 20 providers who were part of a network.

PROFESSIONALISM, NETWORKING, AND THE DEVELOPMENT OF A FEMINIST CONSCIOUSNESS

Though many providers began work as baby-sitters, through the course of their work some began to redefine their work as professional caregiving. The primary precipitator of this redefinition was the participation in a formal network of family day care providers, which led to the development of a feminist consciousness in three ways. First, the growth of their professional orientation led providers to redefine the work of caring as employment rather than an extension of themselves as women. Second, through the network women began to renegotiate their relationships at home, thus blurring the boundaries of work and family. Finally, through these critical bonds with other providers and with their clients, they came to understand that they shared common problems and concerns by virtue of their status as women.

THE NETWORK

All 20 women discussed in this chapter belonged to a single organized local network of family day care providers. The network was originally initiated by a local social service agency to serve as a support group for the providers and to give training to family day care providers contracted with the county Department of Human Services. The operation of the network was eventually taken over by the providers themselves and was quite active and vibrant at the time of my interviews. The network met formally once a month and sponsored occasional training workshops for providers across the region. Members talked to me with great pride about the workshops they ran, the community projects they sponsored, and the help they provided one another on a daily basis.

The women came to the network for a variety of reasons and from a variety of backgrounds. For some, the network provided a needed opportunity to escape the isolation of child care work. Others first came to the network only for the training programs but stayed because of the connections they developed with other providers. Members of the network did not differ demographically from women who had not joined the network. At the time they joined the network, they were no more likely to have a college degree, to be certified, or to have a higher family income. It was through the network, however, that many providers first learned about such things as the importance of a contract, the need to be certified, or the value of attending additional training programs.

Developing a professional perspective is difficult for home providers, since they are isolated in their work and often have little contact even with others doing the same work. The network provided that contact and gave providers comparisons by which they could measure the quality and seriousness of their work. Sarah, a caregiver for nine years, described what the network provided for her:

> To know that there are other professionals . . . that there are other women that do the same thing I do and take it seriously. There's a lot of women out there . . . and we're legitimate. . . . We don't have 12 kids in our house, we're not in this to try and . . . knock-down-drag-out each other . . . we're not competitive with each other. If anything we probably scratch each other's back. And I think that's what networking—it'd be like us all going to a job and meeting in the hallways and asking, "How's your day?"

One of the clearest purposes of the network was to build the self-esteem of the women. Workshops run by the network, especially early in the history of the network, contained a section on self-esteem, and it was a topic of discussion in many network meetings. Several participants spoke of learning through the network that others also suffered from low self-esteem or from lack of support from their spouses. Linda, for example, described some of the women she met who do family day care:

> These women are continually dehumanized in their lives. I wonder why a lot of times women won't go to these meetings of the network, but they'll come and they'll say, "My husband won't let me out of the house, won't let me go." They've spent 15 hours locked up in the house and their husbands won't let them go? Once you become a wife then you're diminished, you're much less. They're beaten down because they are wives, they're beaten down because they're mothers, and they're beaten down because they are day care providers. We're lower than illegal aliens; we're lower than janitors. We don't get any kind of recognition or value.

The network also provided practical assistance in meeting the stresses of the work, as well as validation that the women are doing a good job. In referring to the organizer of the network, one woman argued:

> One of the biggest things that made me just feel, like, professional again was connecting up with [the organizer] and just her positive reinforcement when she comes out to the house and will say, "You are doing a good job." Nobody says to a mom, "You are doing a good job." And when the parents, you know, are just so—their lives are just so hectic and they are just trying to get their child and go; they are forgetting to tell you we appreciate what you do.

Through sharing experiences with other providers, those in the network came to recognize that many of their problems were structural rather than personal. After two years of sharing experiences and complaining about parents and governmental agencies that do not respect their work, the women in the network next centered their attentions on political action. Recently, when initiatives on welfare reform in the state senate included cutting state grants for aid in child care and food programs, the women in the network organized other providers and parents to begin a letter-writing campaign. They got children who were in their care to send pictures they had drawn to senators, they signed petitions, and they made phone calls. One provider discussed her frustration with the politics in her city:

> They don't recognize the value of child care. We do, and we can make them aware of how important it is. All these men go to these big think tanks and these executive suites and talk about all these high-level things and all these plans for the future of the city, I wonder if any of them have considered the need for day care? If they want quality business and they want quality

employees and a great majority of their employees are parents, not only has it been proven fact they will work better if they don't have to worry about where their children are; what would they do if we all up and quit?

Judy was quite surprised to find herself becoming politically active. Following a protracted meeting about how providers could get the attention of state agencies to provide stronger child care regulations, she stated:

> My God, I sound like a Democrat. I've always been very conservative in my politics before, but we do need help from the government. And we need their respect. I never saw myself as a political activist before, but I've come to realize that this is really important, and we have to make sure that when the government makes changes, our voice has to be heard.

Thus, the network gave some providers an avenue for political action and was the catalyst in the development of their political ideology. But because of the gendered nature of their work and because this politicization led to a redefinition of their roles as caregivers, women, and family members, this was a feminist political ideology.

REDEFINING CARING

An essential step in the development of a professional identity for these family day care providers was the redefinition of caring for children as work. Many were reluctant to do this at first, fearing that by calling what they do "work" or a "job" they would be diminishing the love and care they felt for the children (Nelson 1990, 52). Rather than subsuming the work into their homes and blending it with the work of caring for their own children, professional providers came to make a clear distinction between their work as mothers and their work as caregivers. This is represented, for example, in the distinct area set aside by many professional providers in their homes for day care. This is often a basement or a back porch area, designed to meet the requirements of certification and to keep their living areas free from the intrusion of their work.

More important, however, these caregivers struggled with convincing others that what they do is work. The most common complaint I heard from providers concerned the issues of respect. These women had decided to pursue day care as a lifelong vocation and were committed to their work. They wanted this commitment to be recognized. Sarah stated that her greatest complaint was with the parents:

Oh, they don't appreciate what you do. They have the attitude that I am
there to serve them. They have a low opinion of what I do, like I sit around
and eat bonbons all day. I am a hard-driven person, and I take my job real
serious. I've had some people say—parents—"Why don't you get a real job?"
That's really hard.

Similarly, Betty discussed the point at which she came to view her
work more professionally:

This is a job. So many times I think other people think—and I thought until
I really got into this—"How great. We can bake cookies and we can make
roasts for dinner. And you can run to the store and do this and that." No.
It took me a couple of years to get it through my head that this is a job. And
until the last child goes out the door, I'm not home. So that was just something I just finally had to say to myself: "You know, from 7:30 until 5:30
you're at work. And if nothing gets done, nothing gets done." And I tend to
just stew all day long. I'll think in the morning—I would get up and I'd
think—"Okay, I want to get the laundry done today and get the vacuum
run," and the laundry wouldn't get done. And finally I just said, "That's it,"
you know, "it won't get done."

Nancy, a former teacher, began the work of day care casually, out of
a desire to be at home with her children. Although she began as a "sitter," for Nancy this work soon became a permanent employment solution. She is now nationally certified and is in the process of trying to
open a day care center in her home.[2] She completely and consciously
redefined her work and her perception of the work:

My business has been in operation for three and a half years. We moved out
here five years ago. Before then I did, quote, baby-sitting when I was having
my children in [former residence], but it wasn't officially a business. Usually
it was by accident that I would wind up watching someone else's child; it
would happen to be someone I knew from church, and their children were
the same ages as mine, so it was—but it was nothing that I ever pursued.

Nancy compared her work, as did many of the providers I spoke with,
to that of a day care center. In her case, however, the purpose of this
comparison was not to emphasize the homelike nature of her work, but
to stress that she is as much a professional as are workers in a day care
center. She stated:

---

2. The state makes the distinction between type B family day care homes and type A
homes. All of the women in my sample operated type B homes. These are homes where
one individual cares for children other than (and perhaps in addition to) his/her own
children in the home. Type A homes are those where an individual administrates day care
in his/her home, hiring others to help with the care. These are rare, with presently only
34 in the state.

> It amazes me that parents will go to a day care, even though admittedly they
> would prefer family day care if they could find it; they'll fork over a $30
> registration fee, an annual fee to cover insurance; they'll pay whether the
> child goes or not, whether the child's ill or not; they'll pay extra for tumbling
> classes. But then when they come to the family day care provider, they're late
> with the fees, and they don't want to pay unless the child comes. And they'll
> admit as soon as they come in that the child's safer and happier and better
> taken care of, and yet by the same token, they have this shortcoming of
> wanting to treat you as someone they can take advantage of. Like you're not
> doing it for money. Just for love [she laughs]. And I would say, "How am I
> supposed to buy groceries? You can't do this to me."

Since her work was home-based, parents considered her wages nones-
sential and the care she provided as less like work. Though they had
contracted for her services on a regular basis, they were not willing to
make a commitment to her as a worker in the same manner as they
would to someone working within an organization.

Professional providers established themselves as professionals by
adopting the methods of other businesses. Anne, for example, talked
about the importance of using a contract:

> I'm here to provide a service for these people, and I want to be treated like
> a professional. The contract really helps. You know what the limits are, they
> know what I expect, and I know what I can expect of them. I know some
> people have a lot of trouble; I really haven't. I've heard one woman talk
> about a family that didn't pay her for a whole month. I don't understand
> that. How can you let that happen? After the first week I would shut the
> door and not let them in. I'm providing a service, and I want to be treated
> like a professional. I'm not just a sitter. When I call people at work, I say tell
> them their home provider called them. I sat when I was 13 years old; that's
> not what I do now.

Similarly, Judy worked hard to develop herself professionally by attending many workshops, both locally and nationally, and by training
other providers. She began working as a child care provider when she
realized that the cost of having her two children in child care was nearly
$200 per week. She wanted to be home with her children, but she needed
the extra income. Unlike some who begin the work gradually, perhaps
caring for one or two children on a casual basis, Judy established her
"day care" as a business from the beginning. She immediately became
certified, joined the network, and worked with county officials to find
clients:

> I'm in this long term too. I didn't get into this with . . . "when my kids get
> into school I'm going to get a real job." I want that respect, but I still find

that society does not accept that. I don't get upset if someone calls me a baby-sitter, but I humor them and say I've never sat on a baby before.

Over the years Judy developed a stronger sense of what it means to be a professional. When a client repeatedly failed to pay her, she sat down with another provider and crafted a detailed contract that she required each of her clients to sign. Two years into her work as a provider she recognized that she needed to establish a separate space in her home for her child care work, so she completely renovated her basement to serve that purpose. Most important, in the course of trying to learn more about the work of child care, Judy heard of a training program in Colorado that provides courses in family day care.[3] She attended the program and, based on that experience, developed workshops for other providers in the network.

Like Judy, over time Nancy became more politically involved in local networks and in national organizations to try to improve the situation for family day care providers. While one of her greatest frustrations was that her work is not valued within U.S. culture, she was perhaps more angered by the less-than-professional women who provide day care illegally and give family day care a bad reputation. Becoming professional, then, involved defining the boundaries between "baby-sitters" and "professionals."

Nancy and other professional providers like her realized that by defining their work as baby-sitting or an extension of motherhood they risk not being recognized as having important skills to offer clients. Thus it is very easy for others to exploit them. Those, by contrast, who saw themselves as professionals were more likely to build in vacation time for themselves, claim their work on their taxes, and require that their clients sign contracts. They gained, therefore, some clear benefits and controls through their professional status.

CHANGING RELATIONSHIPS AT HOME

Redefining their family day care work as a job had an impact on the nature of the providers' relationships at home. When many of these women began family day care, their families expected that the house

---

3. Windflower Enterprises in Colorado offers a Master Provider program that gives extensive training in various child care issues. It also offers a "train the trainer" program, which teaches providers to lead workshops on issues such as child development, business development, self-esteem, and nutrition.

would not be affected in any way by the work. But as they became more professional in their orientations, they began to exert more power in their relationships. Shirley, for example, talked about her husband's change in perspective, which was due not only to a better, firsthand understanding of her work but also to her increased earning power:

> This last September over Labor Day he had a week's vacation coming. So Monday obviously I had no children, but Tuesday, Wednesday, Thursday, Friday I had seven children. Tuesday, Wednesday, and Thursday Bob was home. Bob understands that I don't sit and watch soap operas all day; he knows now why there's always dishes in the sink, why at night I die. So he understands now. He used to be angry, but now that I'm making so much money, he can't say anything.

Of all the providers I interviewed, however, Debbie's relationship with her husband changed the most dramatically through her child care work. I first met Debbie very early in her work as a provider. When I asked her why she began working as a family day care provider, she stated that her husband would not let her work outside the home. His work, however, was sporadic, so they needed the extra income. In her words, he "grudgingly" let her "sit" for a few children in her home.

When I encountered Debbie two years later at a provider network meeting, I saw a fairly dramatic change. She had begun to accept county-subsidized children, and through this contact with the county she had heard about the local network of providers. She had increased her fees, instituted a contract, and was attending night school to take courses in early childhood education. Her ultimate goal was to become an elementary school teacher. Though she was leaving the work of child care, her experiences during the past two years—both in the work itself and through contact with others—had given her more confidence in her abilities and more autonomy at home. Her husband, once reluctant to "let her work," was now proud to see what she had accomplished and encouraged her future career directions.

Not all husbands were as supportive, however. Sarah explained the difficulty some women have in getting respect for their work from their husbands:

> A lot of these women, you hear that their husbands just give them a really hard time—they are not supportive at all. You're part of a marriage . . . I don't understand why these husbands aren't more supportive. Sometimes the women are bringing home $400 a week, and that's all they earn. I know one woman—her husband repairs cars, so she's really the sole income. And I want to tell him, she's earning all the money. My husband is really suppor-

tive. He'll come home, the house is a mess; he'll step over the toys, or maybe he'll pick them up, and come right in and do the dishes. He doesn't mind.

Several years of arguing with people that she is not merely a housewife led Sarah to be quite outspoken about the nature of her work. Sarah wanted to be home with her children when they were young, but she also believed that as a family day care provider she was able to demonstrate to her daughter the value of the work women do. She was sending a powerful feminist message to her daughter:

> My mother-in-law, everyone I've known worked—except for my mother, but that was in the age of the '40s and '50s, where people just didn't work. My mother-in-law is a very powerful person in a company, and she's done quite a lot with herself. I want to be able to show an example to my daughter Lucy of what women can do and what's possible. I want my daughter Lucy to see that I am a professional, that a woman can be more than a mother.

UNDERSTANDING PROBLEMS THAT WORKING WOMEN FACE

As articulated by Lerner (1993), one component of a feminist consciousness is the recognition that women as a group have a lower status and that many of their personal problems are due to membership in a subordinate group. Through participation in the network and through interaction with their clients, many providers come to develop this collective identity. Family day care requires them to come into contact daily with women from many class backgrounds: professional women who are part of a dual-career couple, other working-class women, single mothers, and poor women barely making ends meet. This interaction leads some to recognize the precarious position in which many women find themselves. This "emotional bond" with other women is an important component of a feminist consciousness (Conover and Sapiro 1993).

During our interview, for example, Linda received a phone call from one of her clients. The woman asked Linda if she could bring her child, who was sick, the next day. Linda's husband, Fred, heard the discussion and begged Linda to make the woman stay home with her child.

FRED: Don't let her bring him. Roslyn's responsibility is to say to her boss, "My kid is sick, I can't come in."

LINDA: I don't want to go into that right now. She's not in a position to just tell her boss . . . because this just isn't her boss. She works for a

> company that loans her out to a company. She has no say. They can look at her and say, "You look at me funny and you're fired."

FRED: Then she should get another job.

LINDA: They can't survive on one income. She's already lost one job because of lack of day care. She had a hard time finding this job. It's not easy.

Linda clearly saw herself as an ally and a supporter of this woman in the face of a poor work situation and an abusive husband. She explained to me that the mother had left her husband once, with Linda's emotional and financial help (in the form of a child care fee waiver), but had returned to him a few weeks later.

Several other providers mentioned the difficulties their clients who are single mothers have managing their lives. In part because of these difficulties, some providers refused to take on the children of single mothers. These providers perceived that some single mothers were slow to pay, were less likely to pick up their children on time, or were more likely to bring their children when they were sick. Others, however, were proud to be of help to these women and to provide good care for their children. Paula, for example, discussed some of the clients she got from the county program:

> Well, most do not want to go back on assistance. They are just doing their best trying to scrape by. They'll try to find someone to come and watch the kids, or leave them with the older child, which is not a good thing. That's why they need the county assistance for child care. Before I started this business, I was really against welfare. But now I see what so many of my parents are going through. They need some help. You do what you have to do.

Paula also indicated that since single mothers have to balance so many responsibilities of work and home, they were more likely to be appreciative of the work of the provider.

Nancy, a remarkable home provider for 24 years, was also quite willing to take on children sent by the county. She often found herself acting as a surrogate family member to those for whom she provided care.

> I feel a responsibility to educate them. I don't only feel like I'm raising their kids, but them too. They feel like this home is theirs too—they ask me for aspirin when they have a headache, and things like that.

She felt this responsibility to "educate the parents" most keenly with single mothers. Many of these parents would call her at home for advice with a sick child, or sometimes to discuss their own emotional problems. The responsibility to the families extended, in Nancy's case, to buying clothing for some of the poorer children and providing extra food during the day, knowing there would be little food at home. Additionally, during her "free" evenings she volunteered at the local battered women's shelter.

Providers sympathized not only with the problems of single or working-class women but with the lives of other mothers, regardless of class. Anne, a provider living in an upper-middle-class neighborhood and working mostly with wealthy clients, illustrated this point when she discussed the following difficult situation: While toilet training one of the children in her care, she saw marks on the child that led her to believe that the child was being abused. She subsequently reported the situation to the authorities, who discovered that the husband had repeatedly abused both his children. Here Anne discusses her thoughts after the husband was arrested:

> I looked at Kelly [the wife] differently that day. I started thinking that she must be a battered wife. I stopped by her house to see if she was okay. It was like she was just in the kitchen . . . and it reminded me of Lee [the child] sitting in the corner. Looking at her house I'd never imagined what was going on in there. But I was glad I was able to help her and her children in some way. I kind of look at it like we're all working together.

Through daily interaction with other women trying to manage the expectations of work and family, home providers come to recognize that they share problems common to many women. Family providers are also in a position to watch the interactions between the mothers and fathers of the children they care for. From this "outsider within" position, similar to that of many domestic workers (Collins 1990), providers see status and power inequalities in the families of their clients that the clients themselves may not recognize.

CONCLUSION

Though working in a "traditional" occupation, family day care providers occupy a unique position between public and private spheres. This positioning and their shared experiences with other women often lead them to a surprisingly politicized perspective on their work.

Research on working-class women in general and family providers in particular (Emlen, Donoghue, and LaForge 1971; Nelson 1990) often portrays them as traditional, "willing to accept patriarchal authority, reluctant to work outside the home, and prepared to sacrifice themselves endlessly to family demands" (Ferree 1987, 289). This characterization ignores the reality of most working-class women's lives, that is, that they find rewards and costs in both paid work and family work. Women, like men, support the family through work both within and outside the family. Much as research on men locates their work solely within the public sphere and thus fails to identify the extent to which their paid labor involves a commitment to the family, research on women's work outside the home often fails to capture the sense that this work is also an expression of care for the family.

Working-class jobs for women are difficult and on the face of it unrewarding, but women do reap rewards from their economic contributions to the family. Choosing paid work does not mean that women are denying the value of family, nor does it mean that their work decisions are entirely involuntary. Working-class women often feel a sort of ambivalence toward both sectors of work, because to "develop an unqualified preference for either paid work or housework would require the individual to deny the real problems in the one and the real rewards in the other" (Ferree 1987, 297).

Family day care providers are in a position to feel this ambivalence most clearly. They see the daily guilt of mothers dropping their children off for the day, and they see the exhaustion in these mothers as they come at the end of the day to pick them up. They also, however, recognize the power they feel in earning money to support their own family and the increased self-esteem they feel when they are recognized as child care professionals. As such, they begin to renegotiate relationships in their own home.

Family providers actively mediate the conflicts between the public sphere and the private sphere for both themselves and their clients. As such, they are in a unique position to see that these are clearly not separate spheres, but rather they are part of a social, political, and economic system that limits options for women in all sectors. This position between spheres is a dangerous one, however, for though it provides many of the benefits of each sphere, it provides the protection of neither.

The primary limitation of family day care as an institution is that it is located in the informal labor market, meaning therefore that it is for the most part unregulated. This has severe consequences for both the workers and the children they care for. Though women in family day care certainly establish most of the conditions of their work, these conditions are constrained by the general economic value we as a society place on women's work. Since child care costs are generally seen as taken from the woman's salary, women can afford to pay little for child care. This, combined with the invisible nature of the costs of child care, means that we are not forced to establish coherent public policy about child care (Tuominen 1997).

As providers themselves become more politically aware, they can and should begin to have a voice in the processes of making this policy. Given the traditional nature of family day care providers' work, however, we might not think to look to them for this political change. It is easy to believe that because providers are engaged in caring work with children in their homes, they are not likely to be or to become political—and most especially, not feminist. But by believing this, we perpetuate the ideology that caring is only personal and private and is not linked to work or politics. By understanding that women can develop a feminist perspective in traditional occupations, we recognize more fully that work and family—and politics and caring—are not separate and opposed but are intimately linked. Family day care providers are located in precisely the right place to show us those connections.

REFERENCES

Abel, Emily K., and Margaret K. Nelson. 1990. Circles of care: An introductory essay. In *Circles of care: Work and identity in women's lives*, edited by E. K. Abel and M. Nelson. Albany: State University of New York Press.

Banaszak, Lee Ann, and Eric Plutzer. 1993. The social bases of feminism in the European community. *Public Opinion Quarterly* 57:29–53

Collins, Patricia Hill. 1990. *Black feminist thought*. Cambridge, Mass.: Unwin Hyman.

Conover, Pamela Johnson, and Virginia Sapiro. 1993. Gender, feminist consciousness, and war. *American Journal of Political Science* 32:1079–99.

Emlen, A. C., Betty A. Donoghue, and Rolfe LaForge. 1971. *Child care by kith*. Portland: Oregon State University Press.

Ferree, Myra Marx. 1987. Family and job for working-class women: Gender and class systems seen from below. In *Families and work*, edited by N. Gerstel and H. Gross. Philadelphia: Temple University Press.

Fosburg, Stephen J., Judith Singer, and Nancy Irwin. 1981. *Family day care in the United States: Summary of findings*. Washington, D.C.: U.S. Government Printing Office.

Gerson, Judith, and Kathy Peiss. 1985. Boundaries, negotiation, consciousness: Reconceptualizing gender relations. *Social Problems* 32(4):317–31.

Henderson-King, Donna, and Abigail J. Stewart. 1994. Women or feminists? Assessing women's group consciousness. *Sex Roles* 31:505–16.

———. 1997. Feminist consciousness: Perspectives on women's experiences. *Personality and Social Psychology Bulletin* 32(4):415–26.

Klein, Ethel. 1984. *Gender politics: From consciousness to mass politics.* Cambridge, Mass.: Harvard University Press.

Lerner, Gerda. 1993. *The creation of feminist consciousness.* New York: Oxford University Press.

Murray, Susan B. 1996. "We all love Charles": Men in child care and the social construction of gender. *Gender & Society* 10(4):368–85.

Nelson, Margaret K. 1990. *Negotiated care: The experience of family day care providers.* Philadelphia: Temple University Press.

Reingold, Beth, and Heather Foust. 1998. Exploring the determinants of feminist consciousness in the United States. *Women and Politics* 19(3):19–48.

Rosen, Ellen. 1987. *Bitter choices: Blue-collar women in and out of work.* Chicago: University of Chicago Press.

Rupp, Leila J., and Verta Taylor. 1999. Forging feminist identity in an international movement: A collective identity approach to twentieth-century feminism. *Signs* 24(2):263–86.

Sears, David. O., and Carolyn L. Funk. 1990. Self-interest in Americans' political opinions. In *Beyond self-interest,* edited by J. J. Mansbridge. Chicago: University of Chicago Press.

Sears, David. O., and Leonie Huddy. 1990. On the origins of political disunity among women. In *Women, politics and change,* edited by L. Tilly and P. Gurin. New York: Sage.

Stanley, L., and S. Wise. 1983. *Breaking out: Feminist consciousness and feminist research.* London: Routledge and Kegan Paul.

Togeby, Lisa. 1995. Feminist attitudes: Social interests or political ideology? *Women and Politics* 15(4):39–61.

Tuominen, Mary. 1994. The hidden organization of labor: Gender, race/ethnicity and child-care work in the formal and informal economy. *Sociological Perspectives* 37(3):229–45.

———. 1997. Exploitation or opportunity? The contractions of child-care policy in the contemporary United States. *Women and Politics* 18(1):53–79.

PART FOUR

CHILDREN'S EXPERIENCES

CHAPTER 14

Children, Work, and Family

Some Thoughts on "Mother-Blame"

Anita Ilta Garey and Terry Arendell

"Mother-blame" is the indictment of a group—mothers—for the negatively labeled behavior of individual children as well as for social phenomena that have been constructed as social problems. Mother-blame is based on the assumption that mothers are impaired or inadequate and that their influences on children are determinative and damaging (Thurer 1993). To avoid mother-blame is not to argue that the actions of individual mothers never affect their children negatively, or that all mother-child or adult-child interactions are desirable. Avoiding mother-blame *does* mean refusing to perpetuate the idea that mothers, as a group and a social position, are the cause of individual or social outcomes.

Mother-blame is not a new phenomenon. In the 1940s and 1950s mothers were held responsible for autism (McDonnell 1998), schizophrenia, the emotional breakdowns of young soldiers, and homosexuality (Terry 1998; Thurer 1993). In the 1960s mothers were held responsible for the rebelliousness of youth—for their political protests, drug usage, sexual activity, and fondness for rock 'n' roll. A study of clinical psychology journals published between 1970 and 1982 found that "mothers were blamed for seventy-two different kinds of problems in their offspring, ranging from bed-wetting to schizophrenia, from

This chapter and the need to write it grew out of early discussions about the research we were each beginning at the Center for Working Families, funded by the Alfred P. Sloan Foundation, at the University of California, Berkeley.

inability to deal with color blindness to aggressive behavior, from learning problems to 'homicidal transsexualism'" (Caplan 1998, 135).
Mothers are blamed for children's poor school performance, low self-
esteem, and poverty.

Paula Caplan suggests that the term "momism," coined by Philip
Wylie to describe mothers as overprotective, domineering, and destruc-
tive, should now be used "to label mother-blame and mother-hate ex-
plicitly and succinctly as a form of prejudice as virulent as the other
'isms' [sexism, racism, ageism] are acknowledged to be" (1998, 131).[1]
Mother-blame not only puts a tremendous burden of guilt and anxiety
on women with children (Thurer 1993), it also deflects attention from
social solutions for ensuring the well-being of children. Today, children's
problems—or children as problems—are often linked to the social situations of their mothers (poor mothers, unmarried mothers, divorced
mothers, and employed mothers) rather than to the social and economic
forces that shape their worlds (Arendell 2000; Garey 1999, 29–41;
Smith 1987, 167–75, 1999).

The topic of children's care and well-being as it is currently constructed in the United States is inextricably linked to the conduct of
mothers (Caplan 1998; Hays 1996; Ladd-Taylor and Umansky 1998).
As sociologists, we thus face the problem of whether it is possible to put
children in the center of our research without contributing, even if inadvertently, to the cultural tendency to blame mothers for "child outcomes." How do we study, talk, think, and write about children in the
work/family nexus in ways that are sensitive to the situations of both
children and their parents? How do we confront the oppression of
women within families while also recognizing the importance of the care
that often takes place in the context of family relations? Many feminist
scholars have been concerned with these same issues (see, for example,
Flynn and Rodman 1989; Jacobs 1990; Presser 1995; Thorne 1982,
1993a; Tronto 1989).

Our aim in this chapter is not to further document the existence of
mother-blame, but to discuss how to avoid it in our own research.[2] Our
thoughts on how to approach research about children while avoiding

---

1. Philip Wylie's *Generation of Vipers* (1942) is often quoted as a prime example of a
mother-blaming treatise. See Terry (1998) for an excellent discussion of Wylie's "momism"
and mother-blaming during the Cold War era.
2. For writings that document and critique mother-blame, see Chodorow and Contratto 1982; Garcia Coll, Surrey, and Weingarten 1998; Jacobs 1990; Ladd-Taylor and
Umansky 1998.

the pitfalls of mother-blame are grounded in two often-overlapping literatures: feminist thinking on families and, more generally, sociological thinking that emerges from C. Wright Mills's notion of a "sociological imagination" (Mills 1959). Feminist thought delineates and critiques the material and ideological systems of gender stratification and reminds us to be sensitive to the power relations and differences within situations and relationships, to question the conventional terms of analysis, and to avoid overgeneralization in our analyses. A sociological imagination points us to the patterns that emerge from the intersection of individual lives with the larger social, political, economic, and historical contexts within which they are situated. We separate "feminist thought on families" and "a sociological imagination" in order to talk about their historical roots. However, for us and many other sociologists, these two approaches are inextricably linked in a coherent feminist sociology.

We suggest that we can avoid falling into mother-blaming in our research by drawing systematically on a feminist sociology. Four themes are especially significant. First, families are composed of individuals with both common and diverse interests. Second, our ideas about children and families are historically and culturally situated. Third, families are economically and culturally situated and may vary accordingly. And fourth, the care of children is a public issue that is connected to social and economic forces.

DIVERSE INTERESTS WITHIN FAMILIES

A feminist sociology challenges the idea of a monolithic family and pushes for the recognition that family members occupy different positions within families and hold divergent as well as common interests (Bernard 1998; Hertz 1986; Hochschild and Machung 1989; Morgan 1985; Thorne 1982). Examining the institution of the family from the perspective of its differently positioned members was a breakthrough in the study of family life, and the growing focus on children's social worlds is a significant step in the effort to see children as active agents in their own lives (Briggs 1992; Cahill 1987; Martin 1996; Orellana et al. 1998; Prout and James 1997; Solberg 1997; Thorne 1987,1993b). Bringing children to the center of sociological inquiry is long overdue, and the study of children as players in the work and family nexus has been particularly ignored. Even the large and expanding literature on child care treats children, for the most part, as passive and vulnerable dependents, often as burdens on both parents and employers, and as impediments to the efficiency and productivity of workers, particularly mothers. Can we put children in the center of our research on "children, work, and family" without blaming employed mothers for real or imagined social problems?

To avoid gratuitous or unintentional mother-blame, we suggest that it is essential to consider carefully how "parental care of children" is framed in our research. Our concern with the position and interests of children need not obscure the situatedness of other household members. When we ignore or understate the gendered nature of parenting, we render women's mother-work invisible. Women perform the large majority of the physical and emotional work of providing the hands-on care of dependents (Bond, Galinsky, and Swanberg 1998; Hochschild and Machung 1989). Using the terms "parent" and "parenting," rather than "mother" and "mothering," serves to obscure social reality: "parent" is a neutral term with a differential impact (Fineman 1995). Studies that focus on care of children must be clear and explicit about how various constructions of children's care and needs differentially affect mothers and fathers (Presser 1995). Admonishments to "parents" are, in effect, castigations of mothers. Moreover, when we contribute to the processes of mother-blame, we uncritically accept and even add to the oppression of a group that is already subordinate in a gender-stratified society.

EXAMINING ASSUMPTIONS ABOUT
CHILDREN AND FAMILIES

Conflicting interests among family members are sometimes based on normative ideas about individuals' needs. Women's various activities and identities, most particularly employment and mothering, are repeatedly characterized as being in opposition, rather than as interdependent dimensions of constructed lives (Garey 1999). Employment *does* pull parents away from their children for specified and regularized periods of time. So, too, the educational system pulls children out of their homes and into the public realm. As long as we hold to the notion that children can be nurtured and cared for in healthy and ideal ways only by women engaged in "intensive mothering," women's employment will continue to be framed as conflicting with children's needs (Hays 1996). Where are the fathers in this framework? Where is the organized demand for more family-oriented social policy and structural change aimed at accommodating family care needs (Presser 1995)?

Jerome Kagan argues that in the upheavals of the post–World War II era in the United States the contemporary focus on security and attachment in the child's relation to his or her mother serves a "therapeutic function" by addressing the uncertainty and uneasiness people feel in response to the rapid social changes of the period. Other ideas about children's needs have performed therapeutic functions in other eras (Kagan 1998, 95; Prout and James 1997). Kagan notes that whether or not the idea that a child needs a secure attachment to his or her mother or primary caretaker has some validity—and he questions much of the research in this area—the point is that this idea is historically situated. He argues that assumptions, rather than scientific evidence, underpin the *popularity* of attachment theory (Kagan 1998, 94–96). Research on children, work, and family must examine, from a critical stance, ideas about what children need or what parents should provide (Solberg 1997). We need to take into account the historical specificity and variability of those ideas. One way to avoid mother-blame is to assess the assumption that the sole or primary responsibility for children's care belongs to mothers, or to individual parents, in the first place. Challenging the assumption that it is mothers who are primarily responsible for children opens up new possibilities for meeting the social and developmental needs of children.

DIVERSITY AMONG FAMILIES

In addition to challenging the idea of the monolithic family, feminist scholars, particularly feminists of color, call attention to the diversity of families and assert the need to de-center the norm of the white middle-class two-parent nuclear family (Baca Zinn 1991; Collins 1994; Glenn, Chang, and Forcey 1994). These same considerations belong at the center of our study of children. We must ask, "Which children are we discussing?" Children are not generic; they occupy socioeconomic, racial-ethnic, regional, and other social locations (Orellana et al. 1998; Prout and James 1997). And so do their mothers (Garcia Coll, Meyer, and Brillon 1995; Lamphere et al. 1993).

Sixty percent of American children will spend some time in a single-parent family (Cherlin and Furstenberg 1994; Martin and Bumpass 1989). Most of these families are mother-headed. Nearly half of the children currently living with single mothers are poor, even though most single mothers are employed (U.S. Bureau of the Census 1999). Further, the numbers and proportion of children living in poverty are likely to increase in the wake of the late 1990s implementation of stringent welfare-to-work requirements (Flores, Douglas, and Ellwood 1998). Even as popular discourses lament the loss of childhood and the parental neglect of children, the mothers of poor children confront conditions of increasing economic hardship and material deprivation (Edin and Lein 1997; Sidel 1996). While mothers perform the great measure of the work of child rearing, they do so in conditions typically not of their own making.

Families differ in ways beyond economic and class situation. Children, and families, are culturally embedded—the particular behaviors that meet the needs for appropriate interaction, attachment, trust, and development of self, for example, are dependent on the shared understandings in which that behavior takes place (Orellana et al. 1998; Weisner 1996). Research on the care of children, therefore, must be clear both about which children it is centering and about the culture in which those children are embedded.

Researchers are also culturally situated. The diversity of families and the cultural situatedness of our ideas about families are entwined. That a middle-class child in the United States, for instance, does his or her own laundry may be categorized by a researcher as a deprivation and a lack of maternal care, but the child may experience and understand it as a sign of competency and responsibility. In her research on the meaning of food in children's lives, for example, Elaine Kaplan (1999) found that preparing dinner for themselves or their families had a variety of meanings to the kids she interviewed: reciprocity, giving, competency, and neglect.

Sociologist Anne Marie Ambert cautions that "The Western emphasis on mothering and intense emotional bonding between parents and children results in Western biases in constructs which affect research paradigms" (1994, 529). Research paradigms and findings also affect public law and policy. In her research in southern Africa, for example, Garey found that child support laws in Botswana, which are based on European family law, do not take into account the culture in which Tswana families are embedded. The primacy given to biological paternity in European law has unintended negative consequences in a culture where social fatherhood and links between kin groups are crucial for the social position of children. The law thus intended to help provide for the children of unmarried women actually works against their social well-being (Garey 1996; Garey and Townsend 1996).

PUBLIC ISSUES IN LOCAL AND GLOBAL CONTEXTS

C. Wright Mills noted that "What we experience in various and specific milieux . . . is often caused by structural changes. Accordingly, to understand the changes of many personal milieux we are required to look beyond them" (1959, 10). Specifically, with respect to the study of childhoods and child rearing, we must remember that children are located not only within individual family units and specific cultures, but also within the larger socioeconomic context. Their situations, like everyone's, are influenced continuously by powerful social and economic forces. Therefore, studies that center children and children's agency need to examine more than the dyadic relationship between parent and child. We must examine the connections between the situations of children and the structural arrangements and ideologies of capitalism and patriarchy that are at the very core of our society (Orellana et al. 1998).

The examination of the connections between individual lives and social contexts is an empirical issue. Grounding our research in carefully conducted empirical studies helps us to avoid contributing to motherblame. Too often, social problems are rhetorically linked to social statistics or to changes in social life, as if the mere coexistence of both problem and pattern indicated association, if not cause. In a critique of the literature that purports to describe the "erosion," "disappearance," or "obliteration" of childhood and adolescence, Patricia Lynott and Barbara Logue point out that many of those works locate the source of the problem in rising divorce rates, the resultant increase in single-parent families, and the increasing proportion of mothers employed outside the home (1993, 473). Trends in divorce and women's employment *do* point to major social structural changes but in themselves do not indicate a causal link with other social phenomena. Lynott and Logue found that the literature on the erosion of childhood not only ignores the history of childhood and romanticizes the family of the past, but also ignores the weight of empirical studies that look at children's well-being in relation to divorce, to working mothers, and to child care (1993, 487). The leap to linking public issues of children's well-being with selective structural changes simply assumes the connections it claims to establish. It is vitally important that in our studies of children, work, and family we do not fall into these same well-worn grooves.

Mills posited that public issues arouse in people the feeling that some common value is being threatened and that "often there is a debate about what that value really is and about what it is that really threatens it. This debate is often without focus if only because it is the very nature of an issue, unlike even widespread trouble, that it cannot very well be defined in terms of the immediate and everyday environments of ordinary men" (1959, 8–9), or, we would add, of women or of children. To restrict our research on children to their familial or school-based environments, or to restrict our analyses to the interactions that occur within those environments, is to commit the errors against which Mills and others warned. As Dorothy Smith reminded us: "The determination of our worlds by relations and processes that do not appear fully in them are matters for investigation and inquiry, not for speculation" (1987, 99). We need contextually based empirical studies that do not abstract people from their local and particular situations yet also make the connection between those situations and national and global forces.

We conclude that by incorporating a feminist constructionism (Arendell 1997) and the insights of a feminist sociological imagination (Garey and Hansen 1998), we can achieve a centering of children in our research without contributing to mother-blame. This requires examining our own assumptions as well as the assumptions of the larger culture, paying attention to power dynamics and asymmetry within situations and relationships studied, taking into account differences and diversity between people and groups, situating the people we study in the cultures in which they are embedded, and placing our research in its local and global context. As we strive to do these, we will not only avoid blaming mothers; we will also, in the process, be better able to understand the intersection of children, work, and family. And that, after all, is the point of our research.

REFERENCES

Ambert, Anne Marie. 1994. An international perspective on parenting: Social change and social constructs. *Journal of Marriage and the Family* 56:529–43.

Arendell, Terry. 1997. A social constructionist approach to parenting. In *Contemporary parenting: Challenges and issues,* edited by T. Arendell, 1–44. Thousand Oaks, Calif.: Sage.

———. 2000. Conceiving and investigating motherhood: The decade's scholarship. *Journal of Marriage and the Family* 62:1192–207.

Baca Zinn, Maxine. 1991. Family, feminism, and race in America. In *The social construction of gender,* edited by J. Lorber and S. Farrell, 119–33. Newbury Park, Calif.: Sage Publications.

Bernard, Jessie. 1998. The two marriages. In *Families in the U.S.: Kinship and domestic politics,* edited by K. V. Hansen and A. I. Garey, 450–57. Philadelphia: Temple University Press. Originally published in Jessie Bernard, *The future of marriage* (1981).

Bond, James T., Ellen Galinsky, and Jennifer E. Swanberg. 1998. *The 1997 national study of the changing workforce.* New York: Families and Work Institute.

Briggs, Jean L. 1992. Mazes of meaning: How a child and a culture create each other. *New Directions for Child Development* 58:25–49.

Cahill, Spencer. 1987. Children and civility: Ceremonial deviance and the acquisition of ritual competence. *Social Psychology Quarterly* 50:312–21.

Caplan, Paula J. 1998. Mother-blaming. In *"Bad" mothers: The politics of blame in twentieth-century America,* edited by M. Ladd-Taylor and L. Umansky, 127–44. New York: New York University Press.

Cherlin, Andrew J., and Frank F. Furstenberg, Jr. 1994. Stepfamilies in the United States: A reconsideration. *Annual Review of Sociology* 20:359–81.

Chodorow, Nancy, and Susan Contratto. 1982. The fantasy of the perfect mother. In *Rethinking the family: Some feminist questions,* edited by B. Thorne and M. Yalom, 54–75. New York: Longman.

Collins, Patricia Hill. 1994. Shifting the center: Race, class, and feminist theorizing about motherhood. In *Motherhood: Ideology, experience, and agency,* edited by E. N. Glenn, G. Chang, and L. R. Forcey, 45–65. New York: Routledge.

Edin, Katherine, and L. Lein. 1997. *Making ends meet: How single mothers survive welfare and low-wage work.* New York: Russell Sage Foundation.

Fineman, Martha. 1995. *The neutered mother, the sexual family, and other twentieth century tragedies.* New York: Routledge.

Flores, K., T. Douglas, and D. A. Ellwood. 1998. The children's budget report: A detailed analysis of spending on low-income children's programs in 13 states. Occasional paper no. 14. Washington, D.C.: Urban Institute.

Flynn, Clifton P., and Hyman Rodman. 1989. Latchkey children and after-school care: A feminist dilemma? *Policy Studies Review* 8(3):663–73.

Garcia Coll, Cynthia, E. Meyer, and L. Brillon. 1995. Ethnic and minority parenting. In *Handbook of parenting,* vol. 2, *Biology and ecology of parenting,* 189–210, edited by M. H. Bornstein. Mahwah, N.J.: Lawrence Erlbaum Associates.

Garcia Coll, Cynthia, Janet L. Surrey, and Kathy Weingarten. 1998. *Mothering against the odds: Diverse voices of contemporary mothers.* New York: Guilford Press.

Garey, Anita Ilta. 1996. Imported/imposed categories in family research: Marriage, illegitimacy, and child support in Botswana. Paper presented at the annual meeting of the Society for the Study of Social Problems, New York, August.

———. 1999. *Weaving work and motherhood.* Philadelphia: Temple University Press.

Garey, Anita Ilta, and Karen V. Hansen. 1998. Introduction: Analyzing families with a feminist sociological imagination. In *Families in the U.S.: Kinship and domestic politics,* edited by K. V. Hansen and A. I. Garey, xv–xxi. Philadelphia: Temple University Press.

Garey, Anita Ilta, and Nicholas W. Townsend. 1996. Kinship, courtship, and child maintenance law in Botswana. *Journal of Family Issues* 17:189–202.

Glenn, Evelyn Nakano, Grace Chang, and Linda Rennie Forcey, eds. 1994. *Mothering: Ideology, experience, and agency.* New York: Routledge.

Hays, Sharon. 1996. *The cultural contradictions of motherhood.* New Haven, Conn.: Yale University Press.

Hertz, Rosanna. 1986. *More equal than others: Women and men in dual-career marriages.* Berkeley: University of California Press.

Hochschild, Arlie Russell, with Anne Machung. 1989. *The second shift: Working parents and the revolution at home.* New York: Viking.

Jacobs, Janet Liebman. 1990. Reassessing mother blame in incest. *Signs* 15:500–514.

Kagan, Jerome. 1998. *Three seductive ideas.* Cambridge, Mass.: Harvard University Press.

Kaplan, Elaine Bell. 1999. The meaning of food to kids in working families. Working paper no. 5. Berkeley: Center for Working Families, University of California.

Ladd-Taylor, Molly, and Lauri Umansky, eds. 1998. *"Bad" mothers: The politics of blame in twentieth-century America.* New York: New York University Press.

Lamphere, Louise, Patricia Zavella, Felipe Gonzales, and Peter B. Evans. 1993. *Sunbelt working mothers: Reconciling family and factory.* Ithaca: Cornell University Press.

Lynott, Patricia Passuth, and Barbara J. Logue. 1993. The "hurried child": The myth of lost childhood in contemporary American society. *Sociological Forum* 8:471–91.

Martin, Karin. 1996. *Puberty, sexuality, and the self: Boys and girls at adolescence.* New York: Routledge.

Martin, Teresa Castro, and Larry L. Bumpass. 1989. Recent trends in marital disruption. *Demography* 26:37–51.

McDonnell, Jane Taylor. 1998. On being the "bad" mother of an autistic child. In *"Bad" mothers: The politics of blame in twentieth-century America,* edited by M. Ladd-Taylor and L. Umansky, 220–29. New York: New York University Press.

Mills, C. Wright. 1959. *The sociological imagination.* London: Oxford University Press.

Morgan, David. 1985. *The family, politics, and social theory.* London: Routledge and Kegan Paul.

Orellana, Marjorie Faulstich, Barrie Thorne, Anna-Eunhee Chee, and Eva Wan Shun Lam. 1998. Transnational childhoods: The participation of children in processes of family migration. Paper presented at the Fourteenth World Congress of Sociology, Montreal, July.

Presser, Harriet B. 1995. Are the interests of women inherently at odds with the interests of children or the family? A viewpoint. In *Gender and family change in industrialized countries,* edited by K. O. Mason and A. M. Jensen, 297–319. New York: Clarendon Press.

Prout, Alan, and Allison James. 1997. A new paradigm for the sociology of childhood? Provenance, promise and problems. In *Constructing and reconstructing childhood*, 2d ed., edited by A. James and A. Prout, 7–33. London: Falmer Press.

Sidel, Ruth. 1996. *Keeping women and children last*. New York: Penguin Books.

Smith, Dorothy E. 1987. *The everyday world as problematic: A feminist sociology*. Boston: Northeastern University Press.

———. 1999. The standard North American family: SNAF as an ideological code. In *Writing the social: Critique, theory, and investigations*, 157–71. Toronto: University of Toronto Press.

Solberg, Anne. 1997. Negotiating childhood: Changing constructions of age for Norwegian children. In *Constructing and reconstructing childhood*, 2d ed., edited by A. James and A. Prout, 126–44. London: Falmer Press.

Terry, Jennifer. 1998. "Momism" and the making of treasonous homosexuals. In *"Bad" mothers: The politics of blame in twentieth-century America*, edited by M. Ladd-Taylor and L. Umansky, 169–90. New York: New York University Press.

Thorne, Barrie. 1982. Feminist rethinking of the family: An overview. In *Rethinking the family: Some feminist questions*, edited by B. Thorne and M. Yalom, 1–24. New York: Longman.

———. 1987. Re-visioning women and social change: Where are the children? *Gender & Society* 1:85–109.

———. 1993a. Feminism and the family: Two decades of thought. In *Rethinking the family: Some feminist questions*, 2d ed., edited by B. Thorne and M. Yalom, 3–30. New York: Longman.

———. 1993b. *Gender play: Girls and boys in school*. New Brunswick, N.J.: Rutgers University Press.

Thurer, Shari. 1993. Changing conceptions of the good mother in psychoanalysis. *Psychoanalytic Review* 80:519–40.

Tronto, Joan C. 1989. Women and caring: What can feminists learn about morality from caring? In *Gender/body/knowledge: Feminists reconstructions of being and knowing*, edited by A. M. Jaggar and S. R. Bordo, 172–87. New Brunswick, N.J.: Rutgers University Press.

U.S. Bureau of the Census. 1999. *Civilian employment population, 1998*. Current population survey. Washington, D.C.: U.S. Government Printing Office.

Weisner, Thomas S. 1996. Why ethnography should be the most important method in the study of human development. In *Ethnography and human development: Context and meaning in social inquiry*, edited by R. Jessor, A. Colby, and R. A. Shweder, 305–24. Chicago: University of Chicago Press.

Wylie, Philip. 1942. *Generation of vipers*. New York: Farrar and Rinehart.

CHAPTER 15

The Kinderdult

The New Child Born to Conflict between Work and Family

Diane Ehrensaft

The common assumption about America's middle-class children is that they are hurried—through their daily lives and through childhood itself. Working parents rush their children out the door early each morning and subject them to a long day of child care, education, and after-school activities. When we peer into the homes of middle-class families, it looks as if we have created a generation of miniature adults deprived of play and in the process have transformed children's formative years from a child's garden to a hard labor camp. A member of a Jewish congregation, when invited during a High Holiday service to imagine himself a prophet of the 1990s, shouted out, "Thou shalt not treat children like adults." A public outcry has surfaced that childhood has disappeared[1] and we must do something to save it.

Sam is just such a child. He is four years old. While both his parents work at full-time, highly demanding professional jobs, Sam has been enrolled in an academic preschool, since age two. He has become an early reader, a boy quite capable of spending hours away from his parents with no distress, and most importantly, an outstanding karate student. Because of his skill level, he is allowed to participate in a karate demonstration with seven-year-olds. He handles himself remarkably, able to do everything the seven-year-olds do with aplomb and grace.

---

1. See Neil Postman (1982) for a discussion of this issue.

Until his mother interrupts the entire karate demonstration midstream—it is time to change his diaper.

Sam's story is emblematic of children of the middle class today—and a wake-up call that something is wrong with the picture of the modern child as a miniature adult. In 1998 a study released by the University of Michigan comparing the lives of children in 1981 and 1997 reported that children today have less free time, spend an average of 90 minutes more per week at school, watch less TV on weekdays, and spend more time doing homework. According to the study's researcher, Sandra Hofferth, "Children are affected by the same time crunch that their parents are affected by" (Healy 1998, A6). Less than two weeks before the release of that study, the *Wall Street Journal* printed a piece, "Kids Today Are Growing Up Way Too Fast" (Hymowitz 1998). Sex, drugs, and alcohol have seeped into the lives of not just teens but also preteens, creating a new category of "tweens." A fast-paced culture and a driven generation of workaholic parents have created a technologically savvy, sophisticated cohort of children who have no time or can find no place for childhood.

Yet how could childhood have disappeared when we have literate four-year-olds still in diapers? How could childhood have disappeared when we have entire markets devoted to it? We have children's toothpaste, children's aerobic equipment, even a children's bank in Manhattan. Marketing experts and advertisers devote inordinate amounts of time to campaigns that appeal to the specialized interests of children. Presently, big business both designates and reflects the image of the child as a highly complicated being with distinct needs and desires. If childhood were really disappearing, capitalist enterprise would be in for a big loss.

And how could childhood be disappearing when it actually goes on for more years than ever before? We may be scurrying our sons and daughters through their growing-up years, but then we put on the brakes as they approach the finish line. In contrast to past generations, children's dependency on parents today is prolonged well into young adulthood. Advanced education and training now extend far beyond the high school years for a large number of young men and women, leaving them suspended in a financially dependent status well into the age when their own parents and grandparents had already become mothers and fathers and stable members of the workforce. Even for those high school graduates who do not go on for advanced training, the rising costs of living in this country make it nearly impossible for many young adults to support themselves outside their parents' home.

The story of the miniature adult is just that—a story, in fact a myth. It presents only half the picture of the changing status of childhood in a country where the majority of parents work outside the home and the majority of children have working parents. Childhood has not disappeared. Instead, it has simply taken on a new face: the split image of a child who is half miniature adult, half innocent cherub—Sam as karate expert, Sam in diapers. I have labeled this new child the "kinderdult." Parents and professionals alike are strongly influenced by this image of childhood that is actually a double exposure: the young sophisticate superimposed over the "babe in the woods." The image of the kinderdult embodies wild oscillations between the child as a short-standing autonomous individual moving toward maturity and the child as an innocent, dependent, or primitive young thing in need of care and protection. The image does not fade away, even as our children enter adulthood. We called forth the kinderdult in our descriptions of the twenty-something Monica Lewinsky soon after her affair with President Clinton was made public: Monica Lewinsky, "an ebullient vulnerable 'child'"; Monica Lewinsky, "a despairing, ravaged woman" (Leen 1998, A1).

Lest one feel relieved that we have not robbed our children of their childhoods after all, I argue that the concept of the kinderdult is as problematic as the misperceived *disappearance* of childhood and that a driving force behind the creation of this new child is the stressful conflict between work and family demands. The irresolvable tension between work and family has forced mothers and fathers and the society at large to unwittingly develop a concept of a child who they believe will weather the storms of life with harried working parents, and that concept is the kinderdult.

This brings me to myth number two, that parents today are narcissistic. Shortly before his death, Bruno Bettelheim stated, "I think there is a very self-centered generation growing up because parents don't give enough of themselves to their children—not just their time, but their emotions. Like their own parents, they're self-centered" (cited in Stewart 1988, 11). Yet listen to the words of one of those "self-centered" parents, a single working mother with a small child. "When I first went back to work, I used to count the hours Rachel and I actually spent together, as if I'd hit upon the magic number that would make everything all right. On the way home from the office, I would panic whenever the train made an unscheduled stop between stations. That meant I would have even less time with my daughter" (Dickerson 1997, 155). Hardly enraptured by the time away from her child, this parent is tormented not about what she *will not* give, but what she *cannot* give to her child—more of herself.

Arlie Hochschild's book *The Time Bind* presents a profile of parents who preferred to be at work rather than spend more time with their children, even when given the opportunity: "Life at work was more pleasant or, at least, less painfully disappointing in large part because life at home, at the moment, was a torment. . . . in a cultural contest between work and home, working parents are voting with their feet, and the workplace is winning" (Hochschild 1997, 152, 198–99). Operating from this assumption, that working parents vote with their feet, unsympathetic mental health experts often deliver a message to harried mothers and fathers: "If you can't find a way to raise the children, you shouldn't have had them in the first place." Individuals born in the aftermath of World War II have been tagged the "me" generation growing up in a "culture of narcissism" (Lasch 1977). Once grown, those with children have been condemned as a cohort of parents who put work and their own fulfillment before the needs of their children. Yet as we saw with the mother rushing home to see Rachel, her problem was not putting her own needs before her child's, but desperately trying to juggle the competing demands of her life.

Most middle-class parents today, both men and women, have internalized the premise that parenting is only one of many things they are doing to be a full and well-functioning individual in American society. That means they are doing a lot of things, all of which take time. The term "stay-at-home mom" has become a pejorative label, a role that many such mothers are hesitant to admit to publicly.

Like the new definition of childhood, the new definition of parent is a bifurcated image: the nurturing caretaker, the labor force participant. And even with the movement of work back into the home as a result of electronic communications, for the majority of parents these two roles take place in two different locations—in contrast to the cottage industry or farm life of the past where work and home all came together. The changing definition of parenthood leaves us not with a bunch of raving narcissists but with a whole generation of fragmented parents who cannot fathom how they will do it all.

The portrayal of today's working parents as self-centered and negligent of their children's welfare is as mythological as the portrait of the child as miniature adult. Each definition creates a distorted image, one that illuminates only half the picture. I would like to challenge those myths of both parent and child by addressing the dynamics of the kinderdults and their working parents. My analysis is based on 80 interviews I conducted with working mothers and fathers who share the care of their children; clinical case studies of parents and children; my review of professional and media reports on contemporary child rearing; and my own experience as a participant-observer of family life, both my own and the lives of those around me. While I am specifically addressing the experience of middle-class working parents and their children, I believe the concept of the kinderdult has pervaded all of American society, albeit with variations on the theme. We see its presence in families who can barely make ends meet but allow their teenage children to enter the workforce and spend every penny they earn on consumable goods, rather than contributing to the family income or saving for their own future. We see it in families who deplete their entire paychecks buying Christmas presents for their children, leaving no money in the bank to pay January's rent.

The concept of childhood is not static. Each historical era develops its own image of children to fit the times and culture in which those children must grow. The image of the proud African child who by age five has responsibility for her younger siblings while her parents work in the fields diverges greatly from the concept of the American kindergartner who is a latchkey kid left unattended and therefore neglected while her parents are away at work. The Victorian child, who was to be seen but not heard, has nothing in common with today's child, who is to be actively listened to by all concerned adults.

We can identify two poles that bracket the definition of childhood throughout history. On one end is the child as miniature adult, on the other the child as innocent cherub. We can understand the concept of childhood as sliding along a line between these two poles, the shifts mobilized by a matrix of changing historical conditions—economic, political, social, and scientific. For example, following the industrial explosion at the end of the nineteenth century, children who heretofore worked alongside adults for long hours were now removed from the workplace, enrolled in mandatory education, and sent home to be reared by their mothers. Child labor was replaced by the children's garden, and children were transformed from diminutive adults into delicate, precious little beings consumed with primitive urges in need of taming.

By the end of the twentieth century, however, we could no longer locate the concept of the child on *one* point along the continuum between the two poles. Instead, the postmodern kinderdult shifts wildly back and forth, creating the double exposure of child as both miniature adult and innocent cherub. The child who is expected to fend for herself for three hours after school while her parents work is the same child who is expected to do no tasks whatsoever in the evening hours of quality time when family life revolves around her. The child who is expected to keep the same harried schedule as his frazzled working parents is the same child who is gratified in his every request because little children are not meant to be frustrated. The two-year-old who is allowed to make her own decisions about clothes and breakfast each morning will grow into a seventeen-year-old whose father still makes her lunch every day.

How did our society come to create this minotaurian concept of a child—half adult, half cherub? A central component of the answer lies in the conflicts between work and family, as we consider not just that parents are working, but who those working parents are.

Today's working mothers and fathers have a dearth of time in which to parent. In the 1960s we thought technology would be a time saver and give us a break, both at work and at home. Instead, it has only given us more opportunity to work. Over the past three decades the number of hours required of the American labor force have steadily increased. In just sixteen years, from 1973 to 1988, the average workweek jumped from just under 41 hours to over 47 hours (Schor 1991). Professionals are estimated to work 50 hours a week or more. As weekly work hours have increased, vacation time has simultaneously decreased. And with the advent of home computers, fax machines, pagers, and electronic communications, more work comes home, making work potentially a 24-hour-a-day affair. European nations look at our frenetic pace of work and see a country out of control—the Protestant ethic gone berserk. Many Americans feel the same. Even if they themselves do not or cannot get out of the rat race, they celebrate when someone else does. When it was publicized that an investment superstar quit his high-powered Wall Street job to spend more time with his seven-year-old daughter, he received over a thousand letters of support from the American public (Castro 1991).

For American parents, paid paternity and maternity leaves are virtually nonexistent. Increasing numbers of mothers have entered the workforce, and the majority of children in this country live in families where all adult members work outside the home. As estimated workweeks increase, parents' time with children decreases. Even with the reduction of the number of children per household, accomplishing all the daily tasks of work, family, and personal life becomes a daunting if not impossible challenge for working parents. Particularly for working mothers, who take on the lion's share of the "second shift," their calculated workweeks—incorporating paid work, child-rearing tasks, and household responsibilities—sometimes extend into triple-digit figures. Even when the economy is booming, the constant specter of downsizing can infuse a feeling of disequilibrium if not downtroddenness among American workers at every level, rendering a parent helpless to get off the treadmill with confidence and find a saner balance between work and family. Most likely, the Wall Street investment superstar was able to make his choice to come home knowing he had savings from a six- or seven-digit salary in the bank—hardly the case for the huge majority of working parents.

Parents of the middle class, despite the pressures of unwieldy schedules, have nonetheless internalized the contemporary social mandate that child rearing is an extremely important task into which parents should put all their efforts to create healthy, outstanding children, because parents, not the society around them, are the ones solely responsible for their children's good or poor outcomes. Just as the concept of childhood is marked by two poles, so any particular society's sensibility about child rearing also traverses between two poles: nature on one end, nurture on the other. Although developmental theory and scientific data have provided us sufficient evidence that a child's development is a product of a dialectical tension between the two, societies have a difficult time maintaining that perspective, and instead are drawn to one pole or the other.

In the 1940s the dominant schema in Western culture likened children to plants that simply needed to be watered to grow into healthy adults. Nature was considered the prevailing force in a child's unfolding. By the 1990s the child had been transformed into a precious seed in need of careful, elaborate, and consistent care from informed parents, who could make or break their child's future depending on the fertilizer they added and the soil they provided. Nurture had replaced nature as the perceived dominant force. At present, even when someone attempts to argue that what matters most to children's development are their parents' genes, not their nurturing—as Judith Rich Harris argued in her widely publicized book, *The Nurture Assumption* (1998)—a public outcry ensues in protest. Although *Newsweek* predicted that Harris's "idea will be welcome news to guilt-ridden parents convinced that missing one round of 'Goodnight Moon' will scar a child forever" (Begley 1998, 53), the torrent of responses proved otherwise. A mother wrote to *Newsweek,* "my daughter, Claire, who recently left for her first year of college . . . enumerated and thanked me for all the things I have taught her in her 18 years of life and told me that I was her favorite teacher. I will take her assessment of the value of parents in her life over Harris's views any day" (Berkery 1998, 20). In the words of a pediatrician, "I have practiced pediatrics for more than 20 years and have seen parents make a big difference in the lives of their children. . . . It doesn't 'take a village,' DNA or government-controlled schools to raise children. It takes good parents, the unsung heroes of our society. God bless them all" (Staab 1998, 20).

The recent emphasis on genetics as determinants of personality has hardly made a dent in people's everyday lives as they raise their children. Parents continue to carry the weight of the world on their own shoulders as they perceive themselves to be the prime movers in their children's good or poor outcomes. God may be blessing them, but life is taxing them. Paradoxically, this may be why the diagnosis of attention deficit disorder has spread like wildfire in this country over the past ten years— it is the one syndrome that takes parents off the hook by clearly attributing their child's behavioral problems to a neurological disorder rather than a parenting disaster.

Parents are not just held accountable; they are led to believe that they have the potential to achieve perfection through appropriate interventions. With the right flash cards, their child will be an early reader. With the right music played in utero, their child's chances of being a musical virtuoso will be enhanced substantially. Yet all of this pressure about perfectibility comes not only at a moment when parents have less time to parent, but at a moment when family supports have shrunk as well. Parents often live far away from extended family, and even when they live in close proximity, grandmothers may no longer be available for child care or guidance if they too are busy in the workforce. Government supports for families are minimal and good child care a rarity. If Hillary Rodham Clinton (1996) was correct that it takes a village to raise a child, the only village available to most American parents is the miniature one at their own street address.

Many middle-class parents internalize the notion of child perfectibility and their responsibility for it not just because it is forced upon them by the society around them, but because it resonates with the psyche within them. These parents constitute a generation and a half of people born in the aftermath of World War II with a silver spoon in their mouths and a belief that the world was their oyster. This was a time of great prosperity and optimism. The Great Society of the 1960s was the one they were going to inherit. They went to college in greater numbers than ever before. Life was filled with opportunity and chances to better oneself. The academy and the job market were opened up to women and minorities in ways never seen before, although certainly with a long way to go to reach equality. An assumption of limitless horizons was shared by a generation of youth launched into adulthood with the slogan "Do your own thing" and the hymn "We Shall Overcome" in the background. As they reached the age of parenthood, they merely extended this attitude to their children.

Blind to parents' celebration of the potential perfectibility of their children and the concomitant assumption that they are the ones responsible for shaping it, the workplace still expects employees to prioritize work over family. The story of the parent who requests time off from his or her boss to be with a sick child or attend a child's performance only to be looked at askance as an unreliable employee has become a cliché. Even workplaces that claim to be family-friendly by providing sick child care are weighting productivity over children's welfare as they send strangers into sick children's homes to ensure the parents' attendance at work. While mental health experts may admonish parents for not being realistic about the burdens of raising a child, the bosses chastise the same parents for letting the children interfere with their work productivity. The recent tale of a mother who came to me for consultation is a poignant example. Mary is trying to raise her two troubled teenage children single-handedly in the aftermath of a painful divorce from a man who proved to be a toxic father. She reentered the workforce after years as a stay-at-home mom only to be fired from her secretarial position for receiving phone calls from her children while at work. Although Mary tried to shield her children from the reason for her dismissal, her distraught daughter blurted out, "Mom, it was my fault, wasn't it, for bothering you at work?"

Even though there is no boss to fire them, self-employed parents may experience similar strains and dangers in balancing work and family life, feeling at a loss as to how they will do both simultaneously. A divorced father, a psychologist in private practice, panics because his ex-wife has asked him to take more responsibility for their seven-year-old son during the week, and he does not know how he will pick his son up at school and secure a reliable baby-sitter to care for his son while he dashes back to his office to see patients.

As if trying to be perfect parents to perfect children with a dearth of time in which to do it is not enough of a juggling act, one more ball needs to be thrown in: parents' angst about their child's present and future. A 1999 newspaper article titled "Local Abductions and Slaying Fuel Parents' Fears" articulated this anxiety: "It's not in the dictionary, but it ought to be. Parent (par-ent) n. 1. a worry-wart. To be a parent these days is to obsess about dangers, real and imagined" (Costantinou 1999, C7). *Start* ✓

This generation of parents may have been born with a belief in limitless horizons and may want the same for their children, but as they enter the new millennium they look around and are taken aback by what they see. Children are not a priority in this country. Almost a quarter of the children live in poverty. Education funds are cut while academic performance of American children plummets. Parents see school campuses where children get shot and read about a child abducted from her own bedroom. They learn of rising rates of childhood cancers. They hear statistics of drug and alcohol use among the young and rising levels of mental disease in children and suicide among teenagers. A report from the Carnegie Council on Adolescent Development (1995) revealed that the rate of suicide among young adolescents increased 123 percent between 1980 and 1992. A study in the *Journal of the American Academy of Child and Adolescent Psychiatry* concluded that children's problems had worsened over the past half generation, substantiated by reports from both parents and teachers (Achenbach and Howell 1993). Parents work furiously to accrue the funds to meet the six-digit figure it takes to adequately raise a middle-class child from birth to adulthood, yet worry about what will be waiting for their children at the finish line. They are sobered, if not anxiety-ridden, by recent, although perhaps inaccurate, economic projections that grown children will not be able to achieve the standard of living of their parents. In a doomsday scenario their fantasies begin to spin out of control as they imagine the wrong preschool leading to a college rejection leading to life out on the streets as a homeless person.

The unfortunate consequence of this juggling act between work, family, and angst for the future is parenting by guilt. Guilt as a part of parenting is no new phenomenon. In psychological theory, guilt is defined as an anguished state of mind arising out of an internal conflict. It is a state of mind in which we seek to make reparations, trying to fix what has gone wrong and make it up to anyone we have hurt. In the delicate process of raising a child from infancy to adulthood, any good parents will inevitably run into moments of feeling they must make atonement to their children for a hurtful act, as when a parent turns his back for a moment and his toddler falls from a booster chair. Parental guilt used to be primarily a domain for mothers, who were held solely responsible for the day-to-day care of children. But with the present challenge to traditional gender roles, women are now expected to work outside the home yet remain optimal child-rearers, while men are expected to continue to bring home a paycheck yet become nurturing fathers and share the tasks of the "second shift." So we have tackled mother guilt only by generously extending it to fathers. And we discover a hypertrophied level of guilt in both mothers and fathers, generated by the impossible task of simultaneously accommodating the demands of their children, their work lives, and their own internalized notions of the good-enough, if not perfect, parent.

Why do many parents feel they are not doing a good-enough job of parenting? The same reason an employee would feel she is not doing a good-enough job if given a forty-hour assignment at work and told to finish it, *perfectly,* in a quarter of the time. Although child-rearing and parenting arrangements vary dramatically from culture to culture, there are some universal bottom lines—the time it takes to build a bond with a child, the number of caretakers a young child can tolerate, the daily physical care a child requires. In our society we may have come to the point where we are dipping below the bottom line.

The psychoanalyst E. James Anthony (1982) defines the "essential" child, who exists across cultures, as one who feels well, plays well, works well, eats well, thinks well, copes well, enjoys well, and expects well. Certainly a child enacts these essential activities in the context of socially constructed values and practices, and we now have contradictory ones that create mayhem when it comes to raising children: Fathers should be breadwinners and also nurturers; women's identity now typically includes an integration of work and family roles. But there is no "give" for either men or women to be able to integrate these double expectations. Whereas men are more likely to run away to the workplace and women more likely to quit their jobs to escape the thunderous noise when the competing demands of work and family clash, the vast majority of parents of both genders will hold fast and struggle in the din of their colliding roles. And all the while they will drag their guilt behind them and wonder if they are adequately caring for their "essential" child.

The fields of psychology and child development only exacerbate parents' guilt by prescribing ten good ways to get your child to bed, twelve good ways to get them to cooperate, and four more things you can do to stimulate your child's creativity. Seemingly unaware of the extended amount of time such prescribed interventions require, both fields have simultaneously mustered up the concept of quality time: *how* much time you spend with your child does not matter, as long as it is good time. But working parents know full well that they will never be able to do the ten plus twelve plus four good things to make a better child in the thimbleful of moments available to spend with their child, and they are rendered helpless to achieve their goal of being a good-enough, if not great, parent.

Guilt may be in part what induces parents to rush their children from one scheduled activity to another. The hurried child is not just a mirror of the parents' hurried lives. Rushing children from activity to activity becomes an insurance policy that they will receive the adequate stimulation to become healthy functioning adults. Their children's successes in these activities also serve as a guilt-relieving report card for parents, indicating they are indeed doing a good-enough job.

Fueling the flames of parents' guilt is easy in a society that is quick to blame the parent for any ills found in the children. In the *Wall Street Journal* article "Kids Today Are Growing Up Too Fast," the author reports an alarming trend of teenage behaviors showing up in the "tween" eight- to twelve-year-old cohort, as these youngsters engage in high-risk behaviors, crimes, suicide attempts, sexual activity, and drug and alcohol use. Working parents are targeted as the key variable in the acceleration of their children's childhood: "With their parents working long hours away from home, many youngsters are leaving for school from an empty house after eating breakfast alone, then picking up fast food or frozen meals for dinner. Almost without exception, the principals and teachers I spoke with describe a pervasive loneliness among tweens" (Hymowitz 1998, A22). No mention is made of the lack of publicly funded before- and after-school programs that would decrease these children's loneliness. Instead, the author chooses to cite a quote from a retired middle-school counselor: "The most common complaint I hear is, 'My mom doesn't care what I do. She's never home. She doesn't even *know* what I do'" (Hymowitz 1998, A22).

So where is Mom? According to national statistics, she is more likely to be sitting at her desk at a nine-to-five job than gallivanting around town shopping for shoes while her children remain footloose and lonely rather than fancy-free. But if she should happen to pick up the above-quoted *Wall Street Journal* article on her afternoon coffee break, it might be just after she has dashed to call the children to make sure they arrived home safely from school and have started their homework. Nonetheless, she will learn that her "tween" is "shrugged at by parents," "isolated from family," and suffering from a "loss of family life." What could be a better breeding ground for guilt in a mother who is hardly shrugging but rather painfully agonizing over her children's welfare in her absence and the impossibility of parenting long-distance from a work cubicle in a job with inflexible hours?

Guilt can transform parents from jugglers to trapeze artists. Never feeling they are doing a good-enough job, many working parents become caught on a wild pendulum swing. They spend long hours away from the children attempting to devote themselves fully to the workplace, embracing their role as "worker" or "professional." Their workplace may provide them with a sense of community and social support that fills them with an aura of accomplishment, acceptance, and good feeling—an aura that may be sorely lacking when they return home to the three-ring circus of meal preparation, child care tasks, and spousal demands, not to mention unfinished work from the day. Contradicting the social stereotype of the alienated worker, they throw themselves wholly into their work, wanting to do the best they can for their own sense of well-being, out of their commitment to their work community, and to assure that their job and perhaps even a promotion will be awaiting them tomorrow.

They then return home and with equal intensity embrace their role as parent. Even if they do not attend the cascade of classes or read the myriad of books that promise to make them successful parents to a thriving child, they are aware that parenting has become a professional affair rather than an exercise in "doin' what comes naturally." Alternatively emboldened and burdened by the social message that they are the most important factors in preparing their child for the future, they cross the family threshold each night with a determination to be parent of the year, no matter how fatigued they are from a day at work or how few hours are left in the day to perform this feat.

Their guilt gets the best of them, however, and they find themselves overcompensating for their extended absence from the children by catering to them, granting their every desire and demanding nothing from them. Each day many parents are internally driven by the mantra, "I ask so much of you in my absence (while away at work), how can I possibly ask anything of you in my presence (when I return home)?"

I would argue that this mantra is not only internal but unconscious. At a conscious level parents only know that they are driven to provide quality time for their children and to give them the opportunities to develop the self-confidence, happiness, sociability, and motivation to excel that will mark them as successful by contemporary standards. They are not always aware of the mantra of parenting too much to compensate for parenting too little that runs as a deeper undercurrent.

Working parents are at risk for becoming drill sergeants by day, fairy godparents by night. This duality is not an inevitability, but a likelihood for any parent constrained by simultaneous work and family obligations, and can surface in either extreme or subtle fashion. When it does surface, parents unwittingly and unconsciously create the double image of the kinderdult as a survival strategy. The miniature-adult half of the kinderdult will be the child the parents send out into the world each morning, a child who they must believe can handle all the demands of life without a mother and father in a child-unfriendly world of inadequate day care, failing schools, and unsafe neighborhoods. This image is reflected in the cases we hear of a child with flash cards by age two, dial-911 instructions by age four, and bus passes by age seven, pressured to succeed as a competent little person when there is nobody home to parent. We see it in other children programmed to work so hard that play often drops from the equation. A six-year-old enrolled by her parents in wall-to-wall activities, when asked by her friend's mother if she liked playing with Barbie dolls, responded, "Oh no, I'm much too busy to play Barbie." In the miniature-adult half of the kinderdult, cognition is privileged over creativity, academic achievement over artistic expression. The opportunity to lie back and just "do nothing" is denied, because "nothing" is exactly that, and will get you nowhere.

But as the sun fades so does the image of the miniature adult. For working parents caught in the pendulum swing between drill sergeant and fairy godparent, when night falls the day-shift miniature adult is overshadowed by the night-shift innocent cherub. This is the child who has suffered so much already from the demands of her long day away from her parents that she must now be protected from harm, shielded from any stresses, and indulged in her every wish. This child is in no way asked to contribute to family chores, even as the parents madly rush around trying to get everything done; he has already worked too hard. Furthermore, the parents may be loathe to incur their child's wrath by insisting on such onerous labor, lest the child stop loving them

completely after already having been abandoned for the day. "No" becomes an inoperative word from parent to child, who is instead wor-
shipped as "Your Majesty, the Baby" during those condensed evening
moments of "quality time."

Guilt is the propelling force, and parents' exhaustion is the extra fuel
that may power working parents' impulse to avoid at all costs bumping
heads with their progeny. Raising a child, whether a self-willed toddler,
a hyperenergetic preschooler, an oppositional third-grader, or an iden-
tity-seeking teenager, can be an incredible endurance test for any adult.
It takes patience, calmness, goodwill, and a good night's sleep. These
are exactly the elements that may be in short supply in a parent returning
from a demanding day at work. The last thing one wants to face in such
a frazzled state is confrontation. Little infants do not require the disci-
plining, limit setting, and structuring that older children do. So the image
of the night-shift child as innocent cherub holds the potential of freeing
exhausted parents from the more challenging demands of parenting an
older child—getting the child to brush her teeth, do her homework, go
to bed by a certain time. Instead, work-fatigued parents now have the
option to hang out with their child in a conflict-free nirvana of indul-
gence where "Your Majesty, the Baby" reigns for the night and nobody
has to get into a fight.

Superimposing the kinderdult, the two competing images of the competent trooper and the coddled cherub, on one and the same child is a
very disconcerting experience for a child. In the words of one such child,
the daughter of a divorced working mother, "Sometimes I feel like a
princess who is responsible for nothing and sometimes I have to take
care of everything." We are at risk for creating a child with a split identity. This persists throughout childhood, culminating in a young adult
who may vacillate between feeling confident, competent, successful in
the world and feeling dependent, self-centered, and entitled in relation
to family, friends, and colleagues. I am not suggesting that this split
identity is the inevitable outcome for every child born to hassled working
parents. We have enough evidence that children with working parents,
particularly working mothers, receive many psychological benefits and
much social enrichment from parents who communicate to their children the richness of a life that integrates love and work. At the same
time, we must pay attention to the risk factors when children are raised
with day-shift and night-shift identities that so contradict one another.

The children themselves will most likely not complain to us. Few are
nostalgically longing for a return to an antiquated concept of the child

that does not pertain today. The childhood they have is all that they know. A hurried day followed by a haloed evening is simply accepted as a given. To determine whether the new concept of the kinderdult is putting our children at risk, we need instead to look microscopically at specific stress lines, as when a ten-year-old conducts a sit-down strike because he is overscheduled or a twelve-year-old has no capacity to control herself because she has always been given her way. Simultaneously, we must look macroscopically at the entire cohort of growing children as measured, for example, in their rates of anxiety disorders, identity confusions, diminished capacity for play and creativity, egocentrism, and inability to "contribute" in the larger community.

Work/family conflicts have created a bifurcated experience for both parents and children. Men and women who try to be both perfect parents and productive workers create children who are both confident sophisticates and overgrown babies. The kinderdult, created and fostered by conflicts between work and family, is not a healthy image for either child or parent. In the best interests of our children, we need to substitute the split image of innocent cherub/miniature adult with a working model of a child who slowly evolves along the spectrum of infancy to adulthood with stopping points along the way, rather than wildly swinging from innocent cherub to fully developed adult.

A key factor in replacing the kinderdult with this saner image of childhood is time. Good relationships with children, perhaps more than any other connection, require a fair amount of time, especially in a child's early years. Further, it is not just time per se, but a certain kind of time that will ensure a healthy, evolutionary childhood—relaxed time with chances to stop and smell the flowers rather than time filled with wall-to-wall activities. Working parents with a baby in one arm and a report for tomorrow's meeting in the other are not afforded that kind of open-ended time to spend with their children.

To complicate matters, parents begin to internalize that the time they *are* afforded is a "normal" amount of time to spend with children. They grow to believe it is their personal failing rather than the dearth of time that prevents them from being good parents. Even parents who escape to work to avoid the stresses of home do not feel satisfied with their choice. Escape merely serves as a defensive strategy to dodge the maelstrom of time-pressured family life—a strategy that is unsuccessful in bringing parents peace. One needs only to witness their fretful and frenetic behavior when they return home. Whether jugglers or trapeze artists, life for the working parent inevitably becomes a three-ring circus.

Children agree. When asked in a study conducted by the Family and Work Institute in New York what they thought their children would say if asked how they would most like to change their relationships with their mothers and fathers, parents responded, "They want me to spend more time with them." But when the question was posed directly to the children, the children answered otherwise: "We want our parents to come home less stressed" (cited in Shellenbarger 1994, A1). Both the parents and the children are right. Children do not think like epidemiologists—they are not apt to analyze the structural roots of their family ills. They only know that they have harried parents who need to "chill out" more. Parents, more aware of the underlying virus leading to the "illness" of stress, are better able to accurately target the cause—lack of time.

If we are going to eliminate this virus, a radical shift in social structures is in order, requiring shifts in workplace demands and government policies and increases in family support services. It is not necessary for Americans to work the long hours that they do. And it is not necessary for parents to forfeit their children's basketball games to meet an inflexible 8 A.M. to 6 P.M. schedule demanded at the workplace. Flextime, job-sharing, on-site day care facilities, substantial rather than token family leave polices, and shorter workweeks could all alleviate the pressure-cooker lives of working parents.

Consciousness-raising is also in order. Although the story of the guilt-ridden parent who swings toward parenting too much to compensate for parenting too little is in part a genderless affair, it is no doubt a more troubling experience for women than for men. Women in U.S. society are still held up as the keepers of the hearth, whether they are at home or at work all day. The bifurcated roles of nurturing parent/productive worker are burdensome for men but backbreaking for women, who are fighting for a rightful and equal place in the workforce even while agonizing about the havoc they are wreaking on their children because they are absent "bad" mothers. So we not only have to ensure that parents have more time to parent, but that men as well as women will accept the responsibility for taking that time to parent.

Another form of conscious-raising is also in order. At a personal level, the unconscious must be raised to the level of consciousness. The pendulum swing between parenting too much to compensate for parenting too little operates primarily at an unconscious level. Working parents only know that "there is something crazy in what we're doing" when they show up in clinical offices looking like they have stumbled off a battlefield. If parents can be helped to bring the image of the kinderdult to consciousness, to correct their interactions with their children accordingly, and to feel less guilt-ridden about the parenting they *do* provide and less anxious about irreparable damage to their children, they will take an important step toward challenging the insidious creation of the minotaurian child. Although the world is indeed fraught with dangers to children, our sons and daughters are not as fragile as we have grown to believe. They are not "short adults," but they do demonstrate a tremendous resiliency to get back up when they have been knocked down. Children have the opportunity to right themselves as long as they are in the care of loving and committed adults. It will help parents to remember this.

Public recognition of society's complicity in reinforcing the image of the kinderdult in the undue pressures put on working parents may also be a key factor in fostering attitudinal and structural change, both at a societal and a personal level. Conflict between work and family can be remedied only with an integration of social and psychological changes. The problem exists in the society around us and the psyche within us. Social pressures may push middle-class working parents to "hurry, hurry, hurry" and believe that they can have it all, but parents do not have to buy the message. The "village" will certainly have to do its part in providing working parents more unencumbered time for their children, but parents can also adjust their own psyches. With a change in values, practices, and structures and a reduction of the tension between work and family, we just might be able to stop the pendulum swings between parenting too much and parenting too little and bring the "child" back into "childhood."

REFERENCES

Achenbach, Thomas M., and Catherine T. Howell. 1993. Are American children's problems getting worse? A 13-year comparison. *Journal of the American Academy of Child and Adolescent Psychiatry* 32:1145–54.

Anthony, E. James. 1982. The essential human child and his cultural counterparts: An epilogue for an International Congress. In *The child in his family: Children in turmoil: Tomorrow's parents,* edited by E. James Anthony and Colette Chiland. New York: John Wiley.

Begley, Sharon. 1998. Who needs parents? *Newsweek,* 24 August.

Berkery, Pat. 1998. Letter to the editor. *Newsweek,* 28 September.

Carnegie Council on Adolescent Development. 1995. Great transitions. October.

Castro, Janice. 1991. The simple life. *Time*, 8 April.

Clinton, Hillary Rodham. 1996. *It takes a village: And other lessons children teach us.* New York: Simon and Schuster.

Costantinou, Marianne. 1999. Local abductions and slaying fuel parents' fears. *San Francisco Chronicle*, 17 January.

Dickerson, Regina. 1987. What's the rush? *Working Mother*, November.

Harris, Judith Rich. 1998. *The nurture assumption: Why children turn out the way they do.* New York: Free Press.

Healy, Melissa. 1998. Researchers peek into children's busy lives. *San Francisco Chronicle*, 9 November.

Hochschild, Arlie. 1997. *The time bind: When work becomes home and home becomes work.* New York: Metropolitan Books.

Hymowitz, Kay S. 1998. Kids today are growing up way too fast. *Wall Street Journal*, 28 October.

Lasch, Christopher. 1977. *The culture of narcissism: American life in an age of diminishing expectations.* New York: W. W. Norton.

Leen, Jeff. 1998. Conflicting images of Lewinsky—sweet idealist, spoiled rich kid. *San Francisco Chronicle*, 24 January.

Postman, Neil. 1982. *The disappearance of childhood.* New York: Delacorte Press.

Schor, Juliet. 1991. *The overworked American: The unexpected decline of leisure.* New York: Basic Books.

Shellenbarger, Sue. 1994. Moms and dads are the scariest monsters on any screen. *Wall Street Journal*, 26 October.

Staab, Charles H., II. 1998. Letter to the editor. *Newsweek*, 28 September.

Stewart, John. 1988. Bruno Bettelheim. *San Francisco Chronicle, This World*, 18 September.

CHAPTER 16

Passing between the Worlds of Maid and Mistress

The Life of a Mexican Maid's Daughter

Mary Romero

In the 1959 film remake of Fannie Hurst's novel *Imitation of Life,* the African American live-in maid, Annie, who is raising her daughter in her white employer's home, finds herself rejected by her daughter, Sara Jane, who recognizes the racial hierarchy and chooses to exploit the ambiguous color line and pass as white. Ironically, Sara Jane's access to the white world and her ability to "pass" are largely credited to the opportunities she has gained from her mother's negotiating to permit Sara Jane to live in the household and participate in most of the same activities as the employer's own daughter. However, Sara Jane needs to break all ties with her mother in order to hide her blackness. Unlike the experimental racial passing John Howard Griffin (1961) describes in his autobiographical account, *Black Like Me,* Sara Jane's racial passing is not "an unconscious journey to self-knowledge, a way of discovering the meanings of . . . [her] own . . . racial identity" (Ginsberg 1996, 9). For Sara Jane, passing is a form of censorship. In order to break through the social and legal constraints placed upon her race, Sara Jane denies her racial identity by concealing any traces of blackness. Not only does she restrict her behavior to conform to the norms of "whiteness," but her physical being must not show any sign of blackness. Sara Jane constantly needs to suppress any social or physical evidence that may link her to the African American community. Even the most fundamental

I want to acknowledge the many critical insights I gained from my conversations with Eric Margolis.

bond between mother and child must be denied, which some might say has the effect of placing her mother back in the turmoil of slavery: "Sometimes I feel like a motherless child" (Angelou 1991, xii). The censorship involved in racial passing ultimately destroys family and community.

The first scene that reveals Sara Jane's project to pass for white not only exposes the truth to her mother but also highlights that in order to pass successfully, the bond of mother and daughter must be severed, denied, and eventually purged. A teacher asserts to Annie that her daughter could not possibly be in the class because there are no Black children in the classroom. Then Annie points to her daughter sitting among the white children, revealing to all that Sara Jane has been passing, and Sara Jane runs from the classroom and from her mother. In the next scene, Annie's white employer attempts to comfort her by saying, "Don't worry, Annie. I am sure you can explain things to her." Annie responds, "I'm not sure. How do you explain to your child she was born to be hurt?" In a later scene we learn why Sara Jane has decided to deny her racial identity. When the employer's daughter discovers that Sara Jane has been passing outside the neighborhood as white and is dating whites, Sara Jane explains, "If I have to be colored, I want to die. I want to have a chance in life. I don't want to come in back doors or feel lower than other people or apologize for my mother's color. She can't help her color . . . but I can. And I will!"

In this chapter I want to revisit the social phenomena of passing from the standpoint of a maid's daughter. Updating the script to reflect the current employment of domestics and nannies, the live-in maid is a Mexican immigrant. And rather than a tragic mulatto in New York, the daughter is a Chicana in an exclusive, gated community in the Los Angeles area. This narrative is based on a life-story interview I conducted with Olivia,[1] the daughter of a live-in maid. How Olivia "came out" to me as a maid's daughter is part of the narrative about passing as well as part of the lure that drew me to her story. I met Olivia at a conference after a presentation I made on my research on Chicana domestic workers (Romero 1992). Our discussion about research on women of color employed as domestics was the prelude to Olivia's disclosure of her own history with maids and mistresses. Olivia lived with her mother in the Smith household, where her mother was employed as a live-in maid and simultaneously did day work throughout the gated community. Conse-

1. All the names have been changed.

quently, Olivia was known throughout the neighborhood as the maid's daughter. She confided that she rarely revealed her background to other Chicanos because her complex circumstances raised issues of authenticity when her ethnic and class identity came under close scrutiny. After leaving the world of her mother's white upper-middle-class employers, she had tried to submerge herself in the racial ethnic world she felt she had been denied. She did this by limiting her personal, social, and political activities, including employment opportunities, to Chicano and Chicana issues and to Latino communities.

Reflecting on our first meetings, I recognize that Olivia agreed to do the narrative project with me because she was at a stage in her life where she needed to talk through unresolved issues about her own experiences as "one of the family,"[2] and she now felt far enough away to be safe from the pull back into the world of her mother's employers. Telling her narrative was a search for the equanimity to live by the complex, privileged status that in fact is based on her mother's subservient role as the maid. Her position as the maid's daughter is the context in which Olivia's narrative was constructed. It is where her story begins.

A NARRATIVE OF IMITATING AND PASSING

Olivia's mother, Carmen, was born in Mexico, began a lifelong career in domestic service in Cuidad Juarez, and soon afterward crossed the border to the Country Club area in El Paso. Migrating to Los Angeles with friends in a search for better wages, Carmen sought domestic work through an employment agency. She was placed in an exclusive, gated community. When Olivia was born a few years later, Carmen returned to Juarez with her baby, left the child with her mother and sister, and returned to work in El Paso. At the age of three, Olivia found herself removed from her Spanish-speaking grandmother and aunt in Juarez and went with her mother to Los Angeles. There she was forced to adjust to sleeping in the maid's quarters at night and being surrounded during the day by English-speaking white upper-middle-class Americans.

> I started to realize that every day I went to somebody else's house. Everybody's house had different rules. . . . My mother says that she constantly had to watch me, because she tried to get me to sit still and I'd be really depressed and I cried or I wanted to go see things, and my mother was afraid I was

2. "One of the family" refers to a classic adage in domestic service. Employers are cited as referring to their employee as being just like one of the family.

going to break something and she told me not to touch anything. The kids
wanted to play with me. To them I was a novelty, and they wanted to play
with the little Mexican girl. . . .

I did not want to speak their language or play with their kids or do anything with them. At the Smiths they tried to teach me English. There were
different rules there. I couldn't touch anything. The first things I learned were
"No touch, no touch," "Don't do this, don't do that."

At different houses, I starting picking up different things.

Thus began her life as the maid's daughter.

Olivia lived with her mother in the employer's home until she was
eighteen. Throughout the fifteen years she lived with her mother's employers, the Smiths, Olivia was constantly told she was "like one of the
family" and loved like their own child. As Olivia got older, her mother
increased the hours she worked outside the Smith's residence, leaving
her daughter to spend more time alone with the Smith family. Olivia's
involvement with the family broadened to participation in a middle-class
lifestyle unknown to her own family and relatives, including having dinner with the Smiths' friends and attending the country club. Olivia found
herself passing for "one of the family."

> When it was time to start school, Mrs. Smith took me. I had to take this test.
> I remember getting all dressed up, and Mrs. Smith took me to register for
> class instead of my mom.
>
> At the beginning of the school year, Mrs. Smith took me to buy school
> clothes with the rest of the kids. She paid for them. We went to a place called
> Jack and Jill. It was a real nice store. All the help in the store knew my name,
> just like I was one of the Smiths' kids. We spent hours there. They went kid
> by kid until we got all our clothes. I got five or six new dresses. I went home
> and showed my mom. "Look what I got." Mrs. Smith never charged my
> mom for them. Every year it was always the same procedure.

Enrollment in various private schools in the area; shopping at Jack and
Jill, an exclusive clothing store for children; accompanying Mr. and Mrs.
Smith to golf tournaments; attending parties at the beach home in Santa
Monica—successfully participating in all of these events meant passing
as a member of the upper middle class. Olivia was expected to dress
appropriately, speak middle-class English without a "marked" (e.g.,
working-class or Spanish) accent, and competently carry off the role
behavior expected of one of the Smith children in each social setting.

However, like Sara Jane, Olivia was very much aware of the inequalities of her situation. She knew she did not have a legitimate claim
to the middle-class lifestyle and only received whatever her mother's
employers decided to give her. Consequently, she was always assessing

situations to determine whether her role was as one of the family or as the maid's daughter. Her mother's employers determined when Olivia was to pass as one of them and when she was to be the maid's daughter and act accordingly.

> I never wanted to eat with the Smiths; I wanted to eat with my mom. Like Thanksgiving—it was always an awkward situation, because I never knew up until dinnertime where I was going to sit, every single time. It depended on how many guests they had, and how much room there was at the table. Sometimes, when they invited all their friends—the Carters and the Richmans, who had kids—the adults would all eat dinner in one room and then the kids would have dinner in another room. Then I could go eat dinner with the kids, or sometimes I'd eat with my mom in the kitchen. It really depended.

Unlike the maid's daughter in *Imitation of Life,* Olivia was regularly submerged in her own racial ethnic community, both in the United States and in Mexico. Sundays were frequently spent with the families of Mexican immigrants employed in the garment industry in Los Angeles. However, as Olivia grew older, she found she had less and less in common with their children and shared more interests with other college-bound adolescents.

> My godfather had lots of kids. He had a daughter from another marriage. She was a lot older than I was. My godfather's son was two years younger than me, but I played with them a lot. As I got older, I felt like I didn't have much in common. I just felt different. I had different values than they did. I didn't want to go out and do the things they did. Even their whole interaction was different. I didn't want to sit and watch TV. I wanted to go to the park. I wanted us to do something.

A few members of her extended family worked for short periods as domestics and gardeners in Los Angeles, but her major contact with relatives occurred during her visits to El Paso, Juarez, and Aguascalientes.

> A significant factor in growing up was my summer visits home to Juarez. After school ended, my mother sent me or took me to Juarez. I had grown up there as a child, and my mother's sisters had moved back there. My mother took three-month vacations. All of her employers knew that when Olivia got out of school, "I am going to go back to see my family and Olivia will be with my family. And I will come back." They knew my mom had a passport, social security, and all that stuff. They knew my mother would come back because she said so and because I had to start school. They all knew me. So there was never any fear that my mother would not come back.

Throughout her adolescence Olivia devised various strategies for increasing her daily interaction with other Mexicans, such as dating

Chicanos or attending a Catholic parochial high school rather than the prestigious private high school the employers' children attended.

> I wanted to go to the Immaculate Heart High School, an all-girls school that is racially mixed. There were Chicanas and all different kinds of students there. . . .
>
> I never tried to stay home from school. It just wasn't worth it to me to stay at home. I hated being home so much. I really did. I didn't look forward to staying home from school at all. Even when I was sick I tried to go to school. When I was in high school I stayed out as late as possible. I didn't want to have a lot to do with the Smiths. At school I was totally different. My personality changed. From the minute I got off the bus it was really different. The bus dropped me off right at the gate to Liberty Place. That is where I left this whole different reality. I went into this other little trance. From the gate entrance, I walked about half a mile home. I walked past the guards at the entrance. The guards were always Black or Chicano. I knew their names. I waved and chatted to them. Then I was on my way home. Back to lily-white land. I walked past all these rich houses. I looked at the houses and just thought about my history there. I grew up in everybody's houses. I knew what everybody's houses looked like on the inside. As I walked these eight blocks, I went through a settling-down period. Then I got home.
>
> When I got home, I went upstairs to my room, closed my door, and listened to Mexican music while I did my homework. When Mrs. Smith yelled, "Olivia, dinner is ready," I went downstairs. I ate dinner quickly and went back upstairs until the *novella* started. Then I went into my mom's room to watch the *novella*. Sometimes I helped my mom finish the dishes so we could watch the *novella* together.

Even though Olivia and her mother did not have a home other than the Smiths' house, they were able to maintain a separation between the social worlds of the upper-middle-class white employers and the working-class Mexicans in Los Angeles and in Mexico. The gatherings of Latina maids to share a meal, to watch *novellas,* or simply to catch up on the neighborhood gossip remained concealed from the Smiths, Joneses, Livingstons, and other employers, even though they took place on the employers' properties. In addition, Carmen actively managed the separation between social worlds by controlling the kind and amount of knowledge Olivia shared with the Smiths. She prohibited Olivia from talking about their summer trips to Mexico or offering any information about their "Mexicanness." She also discouraged Olivia from answering Mrs. Smith's questions about their life in Mexico, including the kinds of food they ate, cultural practices at holidays, and Carmen's economic assistance to her family, which included the purchase of property and vehicles.

There were a lot of things that my mother instructed me not to discuss with Mrs. Smith. My mother treated me like I had betrayed her if I brought something up that she told me not to discuss. . . . For instance, my mother was really particular about Mexican food. I remember she didn't like to share Mexican customs. Mrs. Smith would ask me, "So, in Juarez, what does your family eat for Easter?" Then I tried to explain to her what *capiratada* was, and my mother would cut me off. Or Mrs. Smith would ask me, "Well, have you ever eaten goat before in Mexico?" My mother would look at me indicating that she didn't want me to say anything. I just felt like it was so absurd. Here my mother supposedly had this intimate relationship with Mrs. Smith, more than I ever wanted it to be, and she treated *me* like I wasn't allowed to speak except when she wanted me to.

Olivia learned to avoid such conversations or to give vague answers. Like other maids, Carmen appears to have carefully regulated information about her personal life and to have experienced employers' questions "as a form of prying rather than the sincere interest of a friend" (Romero 1992, 108).

As the maid's daughter, Olivia was expected to be different from the other children. She was called upon to do errands, baby-sit, and do other odd jobs in the neighborhood, including walking dogs and providing companionship during trips. At the same time, she was expected to blend with the others—to pass for one of the Smiths' children. Pressure to imitate and be "like one of the family" forced distorted behavior and had a profound impact on the real mother-daughter relationship. A theme that emerges throughout Olivia's narrative is her mother's accusation that Olivia is ashamed of her and really wants to be one of the Smiths' daughters. For instance, during her mother's hospitalization one summer, the Smiths moved Olivia out of the maid's quarters and into a spare room upstairs so she would not have to sleep by herself. She was shifted from her mother's class position within the household—the maid's quarters—and moved above to sleep with her middle-class employers. As a ten-year-old enjoying the freedom of having a room to herself, Olivia refused to move back into the crowded maid's room when her mother returned from the hospital.

My mother was really upset. She got into it with them [the Smiths] and said, "No, I don't want it that way." She would tell me, "No, I want you to be down here. *Que crees que eres hija de ellos? Tu te debes de dormir conmigo.* You're gonna be with me all the time; you can't do that."

Later, when Olivia entered college and attempted to break all ties with the Smiths, Carmen assumed that the motive was to conceal the fact that she worked as a live-in domestic.

I said, "You know, I'm just so sick of the Smiths invading my life. I'm so sick of me not being able to have my own life. I can't even go to college without all these little families [the employers] everywhere."

Then she'd say, "Well you're just embarrassed because I'm a maid."

Carmen was not alone in her feeling of rejection. Olivia too felt rejected by her mother. Olivia frequently accused her mother of preferring the company of the employers and their families to that of her own child. As Carmen worked more Sundays and holidays, Olivia resented the additional time she was forced to be with the Smiths and the fewer opportunities she had alone with her mother. A major source of tension throughout Olivia's narrative is the blurred boundary between employee and employer family. The more the Smiths claimed that Olivia and her mother were "just like one of the family," the more mother and daughter feared losing each other to the employer's family.

My mother used the threat: "I'm gonna tell Mrs. Smith!" Sometimes our relationship was real bad. I don't know if it was normal for my age at the time, as a teenager, but I just remember it being horrible and my mom crying all the time, saying, "You wouldn't treat Mrs. Smith this way. You wouldn't talk to Mrs. Smith this way. You would never say no to Mrs. Smith. I'm gonna tell Mrs. Smith how bad you treat me."

I couldn't understand it—you know—until I was about eighteen, and then I said, "It is your fault. If I treat the Smiths differently, it is your fault. You chose to have me live in this situation. It was your decision to let me have two [sets of] parents and for me to balance things off, so you can't tell me that I said this. You are the one who wanted this."

When I was about eighteen we got into a huge fight on Christmas. I hated the holidays because I hated spending them with the Smiths. My mother always worked. She worked on every holiday. She loved to work on the holidays! She would look forward to working. My mother just worked all the time! I think that part of it was that she wanted to have power and control over this community, and she wanted the network, and she wanted to go to different people's houses.

As an adolescent Olivia began to resist passing as one of the family and to assert her ethnic identity. She began to turn her passing into a form of masquerade that would gain her entrance and inclusion into the employer's social space, so that, like the male transvestite whose interest is in the success of the illusion, she could reveal it as an illusion (Ginsberg 1996). Olivia accepted invitations (and all of the conditions) to join the Smiths in their activities. For example, she agreed to shop with Mrs. Smith to purchase the appropriate attire to accompany the family to Easter dinner at the country club. She then presented herself ready to pass as one of the family. Even with her dark hair, dark eyes, and other physical characteristics that marked her as Mexican, everyone would assume her social identity to be one of the "good" Mexicans and most likely refer to her as Hispanic or Spanish from a good upper-middle-class family, maybe one of the old Californian families. Changing her bodily image by dressing like them—that is, reflecting the same status and acquiring the appropriate bodily mannerisms and actions—allowed her to pass as a guest, as one of them, rather than as one of the Mexicans at the country club who served them. Once entrance was gained into the private club, however, Olivia revealed she was "in drag." Rather than ignoring the Mexican valet and other workers at the country club, she made eye contact and addressed them as equals in Spanish.

> I talked to them in Spanish and it just unnerved everybody. Mrs. Smith looked at me. I let her know all the time that I had this identification with them and that identification was more important. I wanted them to know that they couldn't dress me up and take me to their country club and think that I didn't know who I was.

By breaking the illusion of passing as one of the family, Olivia reminded the Smiths that behind the carefully manicured exterior she really identified with Mexican immigrants and the working class. Having noted the norms governing country club etiquette, she set out to violate the norms that maintain racial and cultural dominance. She spoke Spanish in a social space designated as English-only and in the presence of people who spoke only English. Her verbal interactions with the valet, the workers busing tables, and the restroom attendant crossed the border into the familiar—a familiarity coded not with condescension but with ethnic, racial, and class identity and solidarity. Her social acts of speaking Spanish, knowing the workers' names, touching them, and acknowledging their presence as social equals rather than as low-level service workers were clearly a form of resistance as well as a symbolic reminder to the employers that their interpersonal relationship with their maid's daughter did not dissolve the racial, ethnic, or economic differences between them. Olivia's actions not only increased the discomfort level during these exchanges but also eliminated the employers' ability to hold on to their stereotypes and prejudices about immigrants and people of color while maintaining familial relationships with Olivia and her mother by arguing "but Olivia you are different from the others." As Olivia clearly stated, "I wanted them to know that they couldn't dress me up and take me to their country club and think that I didn't know who I was." Breaking the norms of speech and touch, Olivia's social behavior was aimed at reclaiming identity with the racial, ethnic, and class status of the workers of color. She let the Smiths know that she had this social identification with the workers and that this identification was more important than the one with her mother's employers. At the end of the dinner, however, Mrs. Smith granted Olivia her ethnic and class identity but reminded Olivia that she owed her ability to pass to the employers:

> Mrs. Smith says, "The Fullers have a yacht, and they have a house in Cabo San Lucas. We sailed with them from Tijuana over to Cabo San Lucas one weekend. We got off the boat and there were all these poor little kids with no shoes and hardly any clothes. We came out, and they just came running towards the gringos asking us for money and things. They were all begging us for money. You know what I thought, Olivia? I stopped to think about how lucky you are. I thought how fortunate you are to have these wonderful things. Olivia, you don't realize how lucky you really are."

Having broken the delicate mask of race and class through her resistance, Olivia became the problem. Du Bois described the lingering question ready to be posed to those who are conditionally allowed to pass as "one of the family":

> Between me and the other world there is ever an unasked question: unasked by some through feelings of delicacy; by others through the difficulty of rightly framing it. All, nevertheless, flutter round it. They approach me in a half-hesitant sort of way, eye me curiously or compassionately, and then, instead of saying directly, "How does it feel to be a problem?" they say, "I know an excellent colored man in my town"; or . . . "Do not these Southern outrages make your blood boil?" (1989, 1)

Mrs. Smith's comment was intended to teach Olivia that successfully passing relies on embracing a new identity and escaping the subordination and oppression accompanying her ethnic and class identity as well as her need to access the privileges and status of these identities (Ginsberg 1996, 3). Glenn C. Loury summed up the lesson of passing he learned from discovering that his second cousins had disappeared into the white suburb: "What 'passing' seemed to say about the world was that if one were black and ambitious it was necessary to choose between racial authenticity and personal success" (1993, 3).

Olivia dreamed of the day she would leave the employers' neighborhood and become a full-time Chicana, no longer splitting herself to fulfill the expectations of her mother's employers. Olivia assumed this would happen when she left for college. However, leaving for college posed a new set of circumstances for her. She had not counted on the long-term effects of her childhood socialization among the employers and the degree to which her identity was shaped by the Smiths. Her ethnic identity was tied to her mother and extended family; however, her mother's social world extended to other maids, gardeners, and *their* employers. These social relations had become closely woven together. Olivia's extended family remained working class and immigrant, sharing neither her educational aspirations nor her interests in U.S. ethnic politics.

As she became more involved in Chicano student politics at the university, working closely with Mexican American students from the working class and with white student leaders from the middle and upper middle class, she had difficulty separating her experiences and abilities as she had so carefully divided them while growing up as the maid's daughter. For the first time in her life Olivia became aware of the vast cultural capital she had acquired from her experiences with the Smiths at the Los Angeles country club and the numerous social events that included politicians, entertainers, and corporate executives. Unlike the other Mexican American student officers in MEChA (Movimiento Estudiantil Chicano de Aztlán), Olivia knew the ins and outs of the bureaucracy. She had the connections to make things happen, and she had the experience in the social milieu of the university to stand out as a spokesperson and as a leader. At the same time, she was suspect. How did she know how the structure worked? How was she able to get things done? Where did her cultural capital come from? Olivia knew that to admit to growing up in an all-white upper-middle-class neighborhood raised questions of her "authenticity" as a Chicana—at a point in history when identity politics defined racial ethnic identity as "authentic" on the basis of a specific set of lived experiences as well as genetics. The essentialism underscoring the identity politics of MEChA and the struggle for Latino representation made full disclosure of her experiences as the maid's daughter difficult, if not impossible. Therefore, she suppressed information and feared the day she might find herself confronted by either politically active Chicanos or the white fraternity and sorority members who knew her mom as their maid and claimed Carmen as "one of the family."

> I was real involved with student government. . . . I got appointed to this position in student government. Everybody in student government was like frat boys. I knew half of them from elementary school. Here I was in MEChA and involved in all these Chicano things. I would run into them in class or see them, and they would pretend they didn't know me. I would pretend I

didn't know them. . . . My mother knew the Goldbergs, this one Jewish family. She [Mrs. Goldberg] was a big Democrat running for city council. Her daughter, Marjorie, and I had been friends. I used to go over there and swim. They lived two houses from the Joneses. My mother saw Mrs. Goldberg, who said, "Oh, Marjorie is going to UCLA now." Marjorie actually went to look me up. I told my mother, "Don't encourage these people to go find me." Marjorie found me one day and asked me if I would go have lunch with her. I didn't say no. I went and had a sandwich with her. I asked her about her school. I just avoided the whole topic of my political activity. It was horrible. I had nothing to talk to her about.

After MEChA protested the border patrol theme of one of the fraternity parties as racist, Olivia was confronted by former classmates and employers' children.

These people would come up to me and say Olivia, "What are you doing? Why are you involved in this stuff? We've been friends forever."

I said, "We're not friends. We went to the same school and that has nothing to do with it."

They felt like the rest of these Chicanos were just barbarians. They were just from the barrio. They could understand why they were angry because of the economic inequities. But they couldn't understand why I would side with them because, after all, I had been part of their very social structure.

I sat down and said, "I'm not part of your social structure. I'm not involved with you. My mother was the fucking maid at your house, so don't try to claim I am in the same place."

"Yeah, but you know, the proms and this and that. We were in CCD class together."

"No. We don't have anything in common."

They kept saying that we were at the same intellectual level.

DISCUSSION

Olivia's recollections of growing up in her mother's employer's home capture complex and seldom-explored issues of passing that are tied to culture and class-based identity. Placed in the social world of her mother's employers as the daughter of a Mexican immigrant, she experiences life as a child, student, adolescent, daughter, and eventually as a woman in an environment where survival depends on her ability to "fit in" and to pass as "one of the family." Sometimes these experiences include privileges and status of the upper middle class that are only accessible through her relationship with her mother's employers. In order to occupy this social space, Olivia must function as a competent actor in the employers' home, neighborhood, private schools, and country club. Yet the passing required for her to participate in this white upper-middle-class milieu inhibits Olivia's Mexican and working-class identity.

The identity Olivia wants to claim is stunted by cultural scripts that deny her "difference"—both ethnic and class. Defying these cultural scripts may cut her off from the social and economic resources that her mother has worked so hard to make available to her—and may also hurt her mother. I would argue that passing is an obscene form of salvation[3] because it requires Olivia to deny her early years in Juarez speaking Spanish to her grandmother and aunts, her summers in Juarez and Aguascalientes with her poor and working-class Mexican relatives, her *quincinera* in Juarez, Sunday dinner with Mexican immigrant garment workers in San Fernando, and listening to the maids chatting in the evening in Spanish. Olivia lives with the anxiety of being discovered as the maid's daughter and the fear that her social world—consisting of first- and second-generation Chicanos—will collide with the white upper-middle-class world of her mother's employers, where she learned to pass as one of them.

Throughout her narrative, Olivia's class status remains ambiguous. Economically her mother is clearly engaged in a working-class occupation offering little job security; benefits are rare, if not nonexistent, and working conditions are completely left to interpersonal negotiations between worker and employee. At the same time, her mother's personal relationship with employers has given Olivia access to the best private schools in the area, material objects signifying membership in the middle class (e.g., brand-name clothes, shoes, handbags), and social opportunities to acquire cultural capital. However, Olivia is not exactly middle class. She only owns the "signs" of middle class (speech, clothing, educational aspirations); she does not have an economic foothold there. Her ethnic identity is very class-based; she lacks access to learning about Mexican "high culture." Her ties to the Mexican American and Mexican immigrant community in the United States are entirely working class. Olivia uses her ambiguous class position as a strategy of empowerment. As with other racial ethnics attempting to enter the white middle class, the ability to pass physically for white is not necessary (although it

3. I am borrowing this phrase from Mary Helen Washington's (1987, 164) discussion of the use of "passing" in Nell Larsen's writings.

helps), but to pass for middle class relies on shedding any evidence of poverty or the working class. Can we argue, then, that "dressing for success" and other middle-class markers are only empty signifiers?

CONCLUSION

Positioned as both insider and outsider as the maid's daughter, Olivia develops a double consciousness, allowing her to see her "otherness" and the "otherness" of Blacks and other Mexicans through the eyes of the employers. Even as a child she became aware of the "other."

> It was weird to me that we lived in this private neighborhood. There were gates—huge gates that blocked off the streets so no cars could come in. We went outside the gates. They had combination locks. It was not open to the public. I knew everybody who was there. Nobody came in. You could go out but nobody came in. I remember seeing these kids. On one side was a Black neighborhood, and I would see these Black kids. I knew there was something else that I had no access to. At the same time, I was privy to being able to come in. My mother would undo the combination and we could lock the door. We would lock the door and go out.

Even in her visits to the U.S./Mexico border, Olivia understood the gravity of the differences marking the worlds she passed between.

> I remember times when I stayed with Silvia [a first cousin] in my aunt's apartment. My aunt worked for the El Paso Electric Company and went to work at nights. She would lock us in the apartment so that we couldn't get out. It was one of these run-down apartments; the bathrooms were outside. My aunt would leave like at five, and we were locked in after that and we couldn't leave. . . . It was just a one-bedroom apartment with a little kitchen. My aunt had like a hot plate to warm her food up. It was just one of those electric hot plates. There was just one bathroom for the whole place, and it was horrible—horrible bathrooms. We got the other kids who lived in the apartments to open the door for us. I remember feeling really strange that here at the Smiths I had all this freedom. I used to be really scared that at the Smiths I used to have all this freedom—[to] go outside, I could lock myself in, I could do these things—but with my aunt I was locked in the house. We couldn't leave.

As Du Bois noted, "It is a peculiar sensation, this double-consciousness, this sense of always looking through the eyes of others, of measuring one's soul by the tape of a world that looks on in amused contempt and pity" (1989, 3). Although silenced by her passing in order to fit in, Olivia mentally documents every ethnocentric or racist comment made by the employers and their children. In her memory she records the locking of car doors in Black and Latino neighborhoods; the turning of diamond rings as if to conceal their presence from men of color walking down the street; the body movements used at the country club to make the valets, maids, gardeners, and other low-wage workers invisible; and the Smiths' complaint about Spanish-language forms at the post office. Mentally recording inequalities and racist behavior, as well as her intentional acts of resistance to violate norms, are the ways that Olivia attempts to assure her authenticity.

Passing to avoid racist, sexist, or classist verbal or physical acts is a form of self-censorship, not a journey of self-examination or self-disclosure. The politics of passing are based on the ways censoring structures are organized throughout society and the culture, from entrance into private schools and private clubs to the social acceptance required to be successful in a job interview. When passing becomes part of one's everyday life in order not to draw attention to one's difference—a difference socially constructed as inferior, dangerous, impure—individuals are forced to engage in various and subtle forms of restraint just to gain access to opportunities. They learn to fit in, knowing what not to talk about, what emotions not to express, what language not to speak, what colors not to wear, what jewelry or hairdo would expose an identity one must conceal. Racial and class passing force one into silence, into a state of denial. In an era of identity politics and binary conceptualizations of gender, race, and ethnicity, we fear to claim an authentic self that is multicultural and expands these limitations of class and gender. The act of passing points to the denial of identity's contingency. As in the case of Olivia: she is silenced by her mother's employers, who posit the English-speaking-only, white middle class as the norm and allude, conversely, to the stereotyping of Latinos as high school dropouts, teenage mothers, welfare cases, poor, lazy, hypersexed, potential criminals, or sexual threats.

The rigidity of the cultural script for social mobility in the United States requires assimilation into the mainstream—the white, middle-class, heterosexual, and binary gender-specific norm. For those not born into the mainstream, it means following a desperate path of passing as white, passing as middle class, or passing as a heterosexual male or female. Any deviations from the script are read as inferior, "less than," and a problem. The Smiths' acceptance of Olivia and Carmen as part of the family is framed by the ability of these two women to be cast as "good" immigrants or Hispanics. The cultural script consists of fixed social and racial roles. People are placed in terms of race and class, and they are to stay in these places while maintaining proper class distinctions—do not flirt with waiters or chitchat with the maid. At the same time that Olivia claims to feel loyalty to "the race" and works hard to remain within her own social niche in the Chicano working-class society, contradictions in her behavior reveal that here too she is passing by covering up the middle-class remnants of her life with the Smiths. Mechistas would not allow her to pass back and forth from the Smiths to Chicano politics. The identity politics framing Chicano student activism assumes a world of fixed identities and similar experiences, and leaves few options for a plural identity that crosses class and ethnic boundaries.

Olivia has made different choices than the maid's daughter depicted in *Imitation of Life*. Olivia ultimately does not attempt to pass for white, but struggles with trying to maintain a strong cultural identity. However, like Sara Jane, Olivia finds herself having to navigate between the opportunities and the contradictions presented by the employer's claim that she is "one of the family." She wants to avoid the ascribed status as the maid's daughter. Unlike her mother, Olivia has more options available to her. Although she recognizes the positive aspects of the relation that her mother has established with her employers, she also understands that her mother's status is much lower than the employers'. The employers have enormous power over Carmen's economic conditions, salary, the filing or not filing of benefits, access to health care, and raises. Their demands also determine the time and level of energy that Carmen has for mothering her own child. Like Sara Jane, Olivia wants "to have a chance in life"; she does not want to use back doors or "feel lower than other people," and she does not want to feel a sense of emotional debt and obligation. And like Annie, Carmen finds it difficult to explain to her child the liabilities of her ascribed status as the maid's daughter.

REFERENCES

Angelou, Maya. 1991. Foreword. In *Double stitch: Black women write about mothers and daughters,* edited by P. Bell-Scott, B. Guy-Sheftall, J. J. Royster, J. Sims-Wood, M. DeCosta-Willis, and L. Fultz. Boston: Beacon Press.

Du Bois, W. E. B. [1903] 1989. *The souls of Black folk.* New York: Bantam Books.

Ginsberg, Elaine, ed. 1996. *Passing and the fictions of identity.* Durham: Duke University Press.

Griffin, John Howard. 1961. *Black like me.* Boston: Houghton.

Loury, Glenn C. 1993. Free at last? A personal perspective on race and identity in America. In *Lure and loathing: Essays on race, identity and the ambivalence of assimilation,* edited by G. Early. New York: Penguin Books.

Romero, Mary. 1992. *Maid in the USA.* New York: Routledge.

Washington, Mary Helen. 1987. *Invented lives: Narratives of Black women 1860–1960.* New York: Anchor Books.

CHAPTER 17

Eavesdropping Children, Adult Deals, and Cultures of Care

Arlie Russell Hochschild

Taking great care not to creak, they stole up to the middle of
the stairs. They could hear no words, only the tilt and
shape of voices; their mother's, still so curiously shrouded, so
submissive, so gentle, it seemed to ask questions and to
accept answers. The man's voice was subdued and gentle but
rang very strongly with the knowledge that it was right
and that no other voice could be quite as right; it seemed to
say unpleasant things as if it felt they were kind things to
say, or as if it did not care whether or not they were kind
because in any case they were right, it seemed to make
statements, to give information, to counter questions with
replies which were beyond argument or even discussion and
to try to give comfort whether what it was saying could
give comfort or not. Now and again their mother's way of
questioning sounded to the children as if she wondered
whether something could be fair, could possibly be true,
could be so cruel but whenever such tones came into their
mother's voice the man's voice became still more ringing and
overbearing, or still more desirous to comfort, or both,
and their mother's next voice was always very soft.

James Agee, Death in the Family

Many thanks to Allison Pugh for very astute editorial guidance, to Christopher Da-
vidson for excellent research assistance, and to Bonnie Kwan for typing and for the benefit
of her unusual organizational skills.

In his classic novel James Agee describes how six-year-old Rufus and his younger sister, Catherine, secretly sit on the staircase overhearing a conversation between their recently bereaved mother and Father Jackson, the unpleasant priest who is paying a mysterious visit to their mother. The children hardly need to hear what their mother and Father Jackson say in order to catch the emotional exchange. From the pattern of the two tones of voice the children try to discover the purpose and character of this relationship. The children are deeply engaged in family life, but they are also studying it. They listen to the content of talk, of course, and also use their ears as tuning forks to gauge the emotional tenor of adult talk.[1]

Children often observe their parents when they themselves are not being watched or talked to. In *Sweet Summer,* Bebe Moore Campbell describes ten-year-old Bebe seated on the front steps of her home in Philadelphia watching her mother lean into the car in which her father is sitting, ready to take Bebe for a long summer's visit to her grandmother in the South. Her parents are divorced, but Bebe watches to see how they cooperate in their care of her. She sees her mother lean into the car apparently discussing amicably the details of her upcoming trip, and notices that her parents don't touch. They don't have to be lovers or friends, she concludes, to cooperate in their care of her (Campbell 1991).

Although parents may imagine they are most "parental" when they give full attention to their children during "quality time," children are just as influenced by what they see and hear parents doing during "quantity time." What do children eavesdrop on? Conversations of every sort, of course, but especially conversations in which the eavesdroppers themselves and the deals adults make about who is to care for them are the central topic.

I began to grasp the importance of eavesdropping while mulling over my field notes on two young girls I had come to know as part of a larger research project on the families of employees of Amerco, a Fortune 500 company, reported in *The Time Bind* (Hochschild 1997). The parents of both children worked long hours. But one child fell into what I called a "time bind syndrome," while the other did not. In one family the child resented the parents' long hours and was angry and difficult at dinnertime, which made it all the harder for parents to come home (the time

1. Thanks to Allison Pugh for the metaphor.

bind syndrome). In the other, the child had ceased to look to the parents as exclusive caregivers, didn't seem to feel resentful at their absence, and didn't make it hard for the parents to reenter family life. This difference between the two children's responses to the "same" long hours led me to wonder what might account for the difference. I argue that the nature of the deals adults make about children's care and the underlying deep structure of care that a child comes to sense help to shape a child's response to a parent's long workday. I focus, then, on two issues—*how* children learn and *what* they learn about their care. While I can't provide especially rich data on eavesdropping, I do hope to make the case that it's important for us to know more about it.

PICKING UP THE GIST OF DEEP STRUCTURE

Since eavesdropping is only glancingly discussed in the literatures on the socialization of the child, the development of the child, and the relation of work to family life, let me first say a word about how it might fit in. The first two sets of literature take as their task the development of a theory of the child. Much of the work/family literature, on the other hand, keeps a pragmatic eye on the links between women's work and child welfare. But whether or not we have a theory of the child, we know very little about how a child develops a theory about the arrangements working parents make for his or her care.

Eavesdropping is a commonly acknowledged part of everyone's—maybe especially the sociologist's—life. It allows us to gather information that is not intended for us and is quite possibly secret. Yet, oddly enough, when we think of socialization, we usually don't think of eavesdropping. The image evoked by the literature on socialization is associated with direct, face-to-face or voice-to-voice contact. When we think of a child "being socialized," we often imagine a parent telling a child what to do or how to be. Or, following R. D. Laing's theory of attribution, we think of a parent telling a child how she is. A parent might say, for example, "Sally is a lazy girl" and by this attribution incline the child to identify with "lazy" (Laing 1969; Winnicott 1986). Or we think of a parent showing a child the right way to do something and imagine the child imitating the parent. The very term "socialization of children" suggests that socialization is a process done to and not by the child. As Barrie Thorne (1987, 1993, 1998), Jean Briggs (1998), Gary Fine and K. L. Sandstrom (1988), and Barry Mayall (1994) have all emphasized, children have their own perceptions about what adults want for and from them. They pick what information they want to learn and make from it their own picture of what's going on (Corsaro and Miller 1992; Sheper-Hughes and Sargent 1988; Van Manen and Levering 1996). In the course of putting together their own picture of reality, children look over their parents' shoulders, in a sense, to grasp the broader context of their parents' lives. Thus, socialization goes on when the child is in direct contact with an adult and also when she isn't. It is made up not of messages a parent *sends,* but of those a child *receives*—gleans, inter-cepts, or like Rufus and Catherine, in a manner of speaking, steals. Chil-dren are little sociologists.

The content of socializing messages, therefore, includes not only ges-tures and statements about the direct relationship between parent and child ("I love you") or the parent's characterization of the child ("You are a good boy"), but also indirect statements passed over the child's head about the nature of his care ("I've got coverage 'til 5:00" or "It's your turn"). We often imagine socialization to occur inside the nuclear family, for the cultural spotlight is trained there. But children learn about the tilt of the cultural spotlight, among other things, partly by exploring the world well outside of the family, too—baby-sitters, neigh-bors, relatives, child care center staff.

Three sorts of questions animate the "family research" children do. First, the child wants to know: *Is the person taking care of me now going to still be taking care of me later?* Will this baby-sitter last? Is Aunt Alice going to come to our house often and regularly? How long will I stay in summer camp? Second, the child wants to know: *What are the relationships between one caregiver and another?* Are my parents more afraid of my third-grade teacher or is my third-grade teacher more afraid of my parents? Does the baby-sitter resent my mother or does she like my mother? Is she attached to my dad or only to my mom? Third: *What does that relationship lead my caretakers to feel about me?* Does Aunt Alice like taking care of me or does she resent taking care of me? Is she nice to me but resentful on the phone to my mom? What does that resentment have to do with me, and what of it has to do with my aunt's relation to other adults? These are the kinds of questions that allow a child to guess how loving or predictable her world is. They are questions children need to ask and answer. In a sense, this chapter takes a child's viewpoint on important research by Uttal, Macdonald, and Wrigley on relations between parents and those who care for their chil-dren (Uttal 1993, 1996, 1998; also see Macdonald 1998 and Wrigley 1995).

TWO CHILDREN, ONE TIME BIND SYNDROME

While spending time with their families over the course of three summers in the early 1990s, I became acquainted with two little girls, Janey King and Hunter Escala. Both were four years old (when I first met them), both daughters of two-job couples who worked at Amerco, a company I investigated in the course of researching worker response to family-friendly policies. The two girls had much in common. Both came from loving, intact families. Their two sets of parents spoke appreciatively and knowledgeably about their children. Their parents also worked the same long hours for the same company in the same town during the same period of time. But the two children responded to their parents' work hours in very different ways.

Janey King was the younger of two children born to a fast-rising company executive, Vicky King, and her husband, Kevin, a dentist (Hochschild 1997, 81). Janey's parents both worked long hours, and when I met Janey during the first summer I was there, she was spending from 7:00 A.M. to 5:00 P.M. weekdays in a summer program and sometimes also spending from 5:00 P.M. to 7:00 P.M. with a warm, highly competent college student named Cammy.

Many evenings Janey and her mother fell into a certain "time bind syndrome." The company was exerting on Janey's mother steady pressure to meet its production goals, catching her up in its strong company culture, and extending her work hours. Janey's father was less successful at his work, which was in truth less demanding. But as a matter of pride, he put in the same long hours his wife did. Their work hours were also not overlapping but simultaneous.

In response to her parents' long hours, Janey grew resentful, cranky, offish, and demanding—mainly in the presence of her mother. She refused to report on the events of her day or show interest in anyone else's. This made 6:00 P.M. to 8:00 P.M. into a "witching hour," as Janey's mother put it humorously, and created a "third shift" for her, coping with Janey's resentment about her long day. Janey's crankiness exacerbated the strains of reentry and made it covertly a little tempting to extend time at the office. This was the time bind syndrome.

In another household in another part of town, four-year-old Hunter Escala responded to a working-class version of the same long workday in a very different way. Hunter was the second of three children born to Italian American factory workers. Her mother, Deb, worked a rotating swing shift with some overtime, as her parents had before her. Her father, Mario, worked steady day shifts plus overtime, and boasted of being a "60-hour-a-week man." The three children were cared for at various times by a kindly neighbor, by their two grandmothers, by their father's cousin, and by assorted other relatives who lived in town.

When her parents returned home from work, Hunter seemed excited to see them, and this was the general report her parents gave of the interactions with Hunter at the various endings of their workdays, which could be at 3:00 P.M., 4:30 P.M., 5:00 P.M., or other times. In fact, because her parents' schedules were continually changing, it was hard for Hunter to know from week to week when homecomings were, and she often asked to be told when each parent would be home. But Hunter did not appear to lock into an adversarial campaign, as Janey King did, to win more time from her mother. Instead, she seemed to run around in a pack with her brother and sister, alternately appealing for attention from her mother, her father, and her older sister, Gina, who seemed to both nurture Hunter and boss her around.

Why, we may wonder, did Janey and Hunter respond so differently to situations that seem so similar—at least with regard to parental time? Let's consider some possible explanations. First, the difference between Janey's and Hunter's responses could be due to each child's relationship with her primary caretaker, in these cases their mothers. In psychoanalytic terms, it could be that Janey was insufficiently attached to her mother and that her mother, Vicky, was overly preoccupied with her job, working as she did in a job with a strong, absorptive work culture. Maybe Vicky was not what Winnicott has called a "good enough" mother (Winnicott 1986). But actually, Janey's mother spoke knowledgeably, warmly, and frequently about Janey. She showed herself to be extremely well informed about Janey's life and knew the names of her best friends, her favorite activities, the issues that troubled her. Vicky didn't seem to be depressed or angry. She loved her work, and that seemed to rub off at home. Friends and coworkers spoke admiringly of her as a mother. If anything, it was Deb Escala, Hunter's mother, who seemed to be a bit tired and depressed.

Is the participation of the two fathers the critical factor? If so, the results are again confusing: Janey, who expressed more unhappiness, seemed to get somewhat more attention from her father, Kevin King, a dentist who took great pride in his identity as an involved father. On the other hand, Hunter Escala's dad, a good-natured factory worker, wanted to get out of the house to play baseball at the slightest excuse, although he was, both he and his wife reported, "very involved" with the children when he was with them. So both fathers were involved. Janey's dad engaged her in long conversations, while Hunter's dad roughhoused with her and her sister and brother out in the backyard. Janey's father was deliberate, thoughtful, even-tempered, and project-oriented, although it wasn't clear he had fun being with Janey. By comparison, Mario Escala was more emotionally expressive and playful with Hunter. I find it hard to trace a pattern here between fatherhoods and the time bind syndrome.

How about the children's relations to their siblings? Janey had one sibling; Hunter had two. So Hunter had to share parental attention with one more child than Janey did, even though she accepted her parents' long hours with greater equanimity. We might have expected Hunter to show signs of the middle-child malaise so pronounced in parental folk-lore, but here again, we would seem to be wrong.

Can we also speak of a class- and sibling-related effect here? Janey's older brother worked hard at his schoolwork, came home with A's and B's on his report card, and was encouraged—as Annette Lareau's research suggests is true for upper-middle-class children in general—to focus on individual achievements (Lareau 1998a, 1998b). Meanwhile, Hunter's parents encouraged their children to form strong relations with kith and kin, with less encouragement to focus on individual achievements. Along with gender, class background may help account for the fact that Hunter's sister was a "little mama" and Janey's older brother was not a "little daddy."

Social class could have influenced the girls in another way too. In her classic work, *Worlds of Pain,* Lillian Breslow Rubin (1976) observed that the grown children of the working class forgave their parents for childhoods that were much harder than those of middle-class children, who complained more openly about problems less severe. Maybe Hunter had already concluded that her parents faced difficult circumstances and had forgivingly concluded that "they were doing their best," while Janey King, comparing herself to children of upper-middle-class stay-at-home moms, had concluded that her mother was not doing her best.

Social class may enter in yet again through the relative importance of extended kin ties. In Spotted Deer, the fairly rural company town I studied, an employee's occupational rank was strongly linked to the geographic proximity of kin. The company recruited its managers and professionals from a national pool of applicants, but it recruited its unskilled factory workers from the local community. This meant that most managers lived far from their kin, while most factory workers lived close to theirs. Indeed, Janey King, the manager's daughter, was cared for by a paid baby-sitter and by the personnel at the Amerco child care center. Janey King's mother had moved far away from her parents and siblings, and the couple was estranged from Kevin King's dominating father and disapproving mother, who lived nearby.

Hunter Escala, the factory workers' daughter, was cared for by a neighboring baby-sitter, two sets of grandparents—primarily the grandmothers—and a female cousin of Mario's. The social setting Hunter lived in reminded me of Herbert Gans's *The Urban Villagers,* while Janey's social setting recalled scenes from William Whyte's *The Organization Man,* only with organization women added too (Gans 1962; Whyte 1956). In both cases, the mothers organized and coordinated a series of caretakers. But Janey's care was forged more through market bonds, Hunter's more by kin bonds—though these were undergirded by informal favors and payments as well.

I think there is some truth in each of these pieces of the puzzle. But there is one additional, forgotten piece. This concerns how children observe, even spy on, their parents as they negotiate child care. In the course of my fieldwork, I noticed children noticing their parents making deals about their care. They overheard phone conversations and listened to their parents talk to each other, to baby-sitters, to relatives, or to friends about care. This eavesdropping is a child's version of Erving Goffman's (1959) "glimpsed world," the world one catches the gist of as one hurries by. But the deals children glimpse in passing are the deals that hold their world together.

In *The Private Worlds of Dying Children,* Bluebond-Langer (1978) notes how terminally ill children observe in nurses, doctors, the hospital, and the surrounding scene all that their parents cannot bring themselves to say directly. Healthy children do the same. Janey and Hunter were trying to figure out their cultures of care. How many people could their parents rely on to care for them? (How large was their culture of care?) How often would a care provider not appear and how many anxious phone calls would ensue? (How reliable was their culture of care?) Do the people who care for them know and like each other? (How coherent was their culture of care?) Are care providers paid or not? (Was their care market- or kin-based?)

The girls were probably also gauging their *personal footing* in that culture of care. Who feels grudgingly obliged to care for them and who strongly wants to? Most likely they were cocking their heads to listen for a tone of irritation, the gusto of a laugh, a note of resignation. A

child may notice, too, how a parent later refers back to a given interaction—is it in a cursory or lingering way? In so many ways, the child
is checking the *feeling tone* associated with the deals being made over
her head. They provide evidence, also, for the *basis* on which care is
given. Do adults offer care out of a sense of duty, or what Carol Stack
(1994) has called "kinscription"? Or do they give it mainly out of *desire?*
Or in what measure, both duty and desire? Or do adults offer care out
of a sense of professional obligation and need for money? If so, just how
does professionalism go with a desire to care? What, if anything, is expected in return? These questions define the scope of the research projects of small children.

JANEY AND HUNTER

I interviewed all those who cared for the children in each family. I also
spent time observing each family during the week and on the weekend
and talked for some time to each child, although not about eavesdropping. In the course of my time with them, I observed several episodes of
eavesdropping concerning care, and Hunter eavesdropped on my interviews with her mother.

To begin with, both sets of parents made many phone calls and visits
to people concerning child care. So both children got the message that
child care was a problem; it didn't happen automatically. Spotted Deer
was not a town in Sweden or Norway, where child care is guaranteed
as a public right, readily available and publicly subsidized. So for the
Kings and the Escalas, the topic of child care produced a good deal of
anxious talk.

Beyond this, there were differences between the two homes in systems
of care and in the ways parents arranged it. Janey's care came from
Cammy (a college student taking some time off), child care, and after-
school providers. Hunter's care came from relatives. In one conversation
I saw Janey overhear her mother speaking glowingly of Cammy:
"Cammy is great. She's got great people skills, and she's wonderful with
the kids. I'd like to try to get her a job at Amerco." Vicky had searched
far and wide, Janey knew, to find Cammy. Now that she had employed
her, she was also offering extra kindnesses, including helping Cammy
think about a future career with Amerco. But how did this conversation
seem from Janey's point of view? First of all, Janey's mom didn't say,
"Cammy is great. She's just the person to take care of Janey." The world
of Janey's care was revealed as a sideshow next to the main attraction

of Amerco. Also, Janey knew that her mother paid Cammy to take care of her. And from this conversation she might also conclude that friendly as Cammy was, she wasn't going to be caring for her forever. Since Cammy seemed temporary and her father, though permanent, seemed distracted, Janey figured that her mother was it. So it was toward her mother that Janey directed her strong complaint.

Hunter Escala did not seem to begrudge her mother the long hours she was away. Either Hunter was less upset about the arrangement of her care—I believe this was the case—or she directed fewer of her upset feelings toward her mother. Why was she more content with her mother's work schedule than Janey was with her mother's? I would guess it was due to the fact that Hunter felt surrounded by an extended family-and-friend network—two grandmothers, a series of aunts, a friend/baby-sitter next door. And part of the feeling of being surrounded by this network was overhearing gossip, complaints, and endless stories about the people in this network. In contrast to what Janey overheard, much of the talk on which Hunter eavesdropped had to do with personal relations within this friend-kin network.

For example, Hunter was showing her doll how to scramble an egg and was putting the doll to bed near the couch on which her mother and I were sitting as I interviewed her. At one point in this adult conversation, Hunter looked up, interested, though she said nothing. Her mother, Deb, was confiding reservations about letting Hunter stay in her grandmother's care. "Grandma lets Hunter eat candy before meals and doesn't break it up soon enough when [Hunter's older sister] teases her." Hunter could probably surmise that her mother and grandmother disagreed on these issues but that their relationship was not on the line over them. The deal about sweets might change, but the deal about grandma's care would last.

When a child eavesdrops on conversations about deals parents make concerning their care, the child learns specific facts (Mommy is going to get Cammy a different job; Grandma gives me too much candy). But the child also gets the gist of a deep structure of care. By "deep structure of care" I mean the tacit "social wiring" of care. There are many different kinds of care, and like adults, a child can distinguish between market care and kin-friend care and all the many mixes of the two. For example, a child can distinguish between market care by a neighboring friend, market care by an esteemed professional acquaintance, market care by the "only one I could find," non-market care by a resentful overburdened relative, and non-market care by kin as loving friend.

In market care, a parent pays money to a care provider in exchange for a specific service to be rendered within a relatively short period of time. In kin-friend care, a parent may ask a favor and expect a favor in return—but within an extended time frame. In market care, the limits of the exchange are up front and clear. In kin-friend care, the limits are tacit and diffuse. In market care, the acts of care are less symbolically loaded; in kin-friend care, they are more so. When a parent complains of market care, the complaint refers to expectations established by professional standards or by a formal understanding as to what service deserves what fee ("This isn't what I paid for"). On the other hand, when a parent asks a relative to sit for a child, the request appeals to a prior sense of kin obligation, and a complaint refers to assumptions about what a kinsperson owes ("That's not being a good sister"). Similarly, if a friend cares for a child, a complaint might refer to a prior notion of what a friend should want to give ("That isn't how a friend should act"). Eavesdropping offers scraps of evidence about a deeper structure of care.

Since 1970, the proportion of preschool children in paid care has increased while the proportion cared for by relatives has declined. Thus in the future more children are likely to be in Janey's situation and fewer in Hunter's. In my sample and in the nation at large, it is also true that middle-class children, like Janey, are more likely to be in paid care and working-class children, like Hunter, in kin care.

At this writing, I don't know of research that compares parents' relative satisfaction with care offered by kin versus friends. Despite the current tendency to romanticize family and community, many middle-class working parents of a four-year-old would prefer to pay for an exciting Montessori preschool experience (if only they could afford it) than for the care of a crotchety and unimaginative Aunt Matilda. Still, relatives are relatives, and the move to market care is likely to remain a source of some concern.

As the research of Lynet Uttal has shown, parents and baby-sitters negotiate many different kinds of deals—some based on the idea that mothers are giving over part of their responsibility to the child care provider and some based on the idea that she's sharing it. Many parents, Uttal notes, are redefining child rearing from a private to a public (or social) activity (Uttal 1998, 575). Uttal is on to something important here. But just how does a parent make this transition? How private is private? How public is public? What deeper "social wiring" undergirds each notion of care?

Parents don't take "market" and "kin" deals ready-made. They actively shape them. For example, Hunter's parents tried to culturally expand the relationship between themselves and their baby-sitter, Melody. They paid Melody, just as Janey's parents paid Cammy. But Hunter's parents tried to "friendify" this market bond. Melody had lived across the street from the Escalas a long time and was known as a neighbor and the mother of Hunter's pal long before she took Hunter into her family day care. So it didn't seem a big step to exchange gifts at Christmas and birthdays and to share some ritual occasions such as Easter egg hunts or Halloween visits. The Escalas didn't celebrate Melody's birthday, but they crossed the street to celebrate Melody's daughter's birthday. In the grammar of these exchanges, the Escalas were saying, "You're like kin to us."

In contrast, the King family treated Cammy as a college student and future professional, someone who was great with the kids for now but was just passing through. Thus, Janey found herself spending long hours with a baby-sitter she clearly knew would be temporary, and she knew this by eavesdropping on enough conversations to get the gist of the whole scene, just as Rufus and Catherine Follet did as they overheard their mother talk to Father Jackson in the passage at the beginning of this chapter. With an emotionally absent father, a highly individuated and competitive sibling, and a nice but clearly temporary baby-sitter, Janey concluded that Mom was it—and Mom wasn't there. Hence the time bind syndrome. Had Janey's whole scene been structurally organized more like Hunter's, with a maternalized sister, a "kinified" baby-sitter, and relatives on all sides, perhaps Janey would have experienced her mother's absence differently.

If it is indeed true, as the saying goes, that it takes a whole village to raise a child, we can ask what kinds of villages these two children lived in, urban or rural? Indeed, in modern America, children like Janey and Hunter live in contexts that are villages in function but not in structure. This was more true for Janey than for Hunter. Janey's day care teacher, her playmates at day care, her baby-sitter, her brother, her parents, her swimming teacher, her grandmother and grandfather, and the child of her grandparents' neighbor all functioned as her village. But these villagers often didn't know each other, nor did they otherwise cohere as a community. Janey did not live in a self-contained, cohesive, hierarchically ordered Geertzian tribe or Durkheimian social circle. She lived in an urban village and wanted to know what kind of deals it depended on. Hunter's "village" had more different pieces, but they fit together better. The pieces of Janey's village were fewer in number but more discrepant.

In the end, we learn that Janey and Hunter, like Rufus and Catherine, caught from the surface of overheard talk a gist of the deeper, tacit premises concerning who owes how much to whom. And this offers a lesson for parents struggling to free themselves of a time bind syndrome. Part of the answer clearly lies in shorter, more flexible hours. But part of it, too, lies in the ways we weave our cultures of care.

REFERENCES

Agee, James. [1936] 1968. *Death in the family.* New York: Avon.

Bluebond-Langer, M. 1978. *The private worlds of dying children.* Princeton: Princeton University Press.

Briggs, Jean. 1992. Mazes of meaning: How a child and a culture create each other. In *Interpretive approaches to children's socialization* (New directions for child development, no. 58), edited by W. A. Corsaro and P. J. Miller, 25–49. San Francisco: Jossey-Bass.

———. 1998. *Inuit morality play: The emotional education of a three-year-old.* Cambridge, Mass.: Harvard University Press.

Campbell, Bebe Moore. 1991. *Sweet summer: Growing up with and without my dad.* New York: Ballantine Books.

Chodorow, Nancy. 1990. Individuality and difference in how women and men love. In *Feminism and psychoanalytic theory.* Berkeley: University of California Press.

Corsaro, W. A., and P. J. Miller, eds. 1992. *Interpretive approaches to children's socialization.* New directions for child development, no. 58. San Francisco: Jossey-Bass.

Fine, Gary, and K. L. Sandstrom. 1988. *Knowing children: Participant observation with minors.* London: Sage.

Gans, Herbert. 1962. *The urban villagers: Group and class in the life of Italian Americans.* New York: Free Press.

Goffman, Erving. 1959. *The presentation of self in everyday life.* New York: Doubleday Anchor.

———. 1979. Footing. *Semiotica* 25(1/2):1–29.

Hochschild, Arlie Russell. 1997. *The time bind: When work becomes home and home becomes work.* New York: Metropolitan Books.

James, Henry. 1879. *What Maisie knew.* Chicago: H. S. Stone.

Laing, R. D. 1969. *The politics of the family.* Toronto: Canadian Broadcasting Corporation.

Lareau, Annette. 1998a. Class and race differences in children's worlds. Paper presented at the annual meeting of the Eastern Sociological Society, Philadelphia, March.

———. 1998b. Embedding capital in a broader context: The case of family-school relationships. In *Social class, poverty, and education,* edited by B. Biddle and P. Hall. New York: Garland Press.

Lareau, Annette, and E. M. Horvat. 1999. Moments of social inclusion: Race, class, and cultural capital in family-school relationships. *Sociology of Education* 72:37–53.

Macdonald, Cameron Lynne. 1998. Manufacturing motherhood: The shadow work of nannies and au pairs. *Qualitative Sociology* 21(1):25–53.

Mayall, Barry, ed. 1994. *Children's childhoods: Observed and experienced.* London: Falmer.

Rubin, Lillian B. 1976. *Worlds of pain: Life in the working-class family.* New York: Basic Books.

Sheper-Hughes, Nancy, and Carolyn Sargent, eds. 1988. *The cultural politics of childhood.* Berkeley: University of California Press.

Stack, Carol. 1974. *All our kin: Strategies for survival in a black community.* New York: Harper and Row.

Stack, Carol, with Linda M. Burton. 1994. Kinscripts: Reflections on family, generation, and culture. In *Mothering: Ideology, experience and agency,* edited by E. N. Glenn, G. Chang, and L. R. Forcey, 33–45. New York: Routledge.

Swidler, Ann. 1986. Culture in action: Symbols and strategies. *American Sociological Review* 15:273–86.

Thorne, Barrie. 1987. Re-visioning women and social change: Where are the children? *Gender & Society* 1:85–109.

———. 1993. *Gender play: Girls and boys in school.* New Brunswick, N.J.: Rutgers University Press.

———. 1998. Selected bibliography on the sociology of childhood. Unpublished manuscript. Center for Working Families, University of California, Berkeley.

Uttal, Lynet. 1993. Shared mothering: Reproductive labor, childcare and the meanings of motherhod. Ph.D. thesis, University of California, Santa Cruz.

———. 1996. Custodial care, surrogate care, and the coordinate care—employed mothers and the meanings of child care. *Gender & Society* 10:291–311.

———. 1998. Communities of care. Paper presented at the Work and Family Conference, Boston, November.

Van Manen, Max, and B. Levering. 1996. *Childhood secrets: Intimacy, privacy, and the self reconsidered.* New York: Teachers College Press.

Whyte, William H. 1956. *The organization man.* New York: Simon and Schuster.

Winnicott, D. W. 1986. The theory of the parent-infant relationship. In *Essential papers in psychoanalysis,* edited by E. P. Buckley, 233–53. New York: New York University Press.

Wrigley, Julia. 1995. *Other people's children.* New York: Basic Books.

CHAPTER 18

Pick-up Time at Oakdale Elementary School

Work and Family from the Vantage Points of Children

Barrie Thorne

As more and more mothers enter the paid labor force, children are becoming key signifiers and symbols of "family." But the presence of children in the study of work and family is mostly passive, framed by their economic and emotional dependence, by their need for adult labor and time, and by "developmental outcomes" correlated with various child care arrangements. Each of these framings is useful, but none of them attends to children's active participation in the everyday lives of families and communities. Nor does the literature on work and family pay sufficient attention to the ways in which the growing up, and the raising, of children is organized within varied social class and cultural circumstances.

In this chapter I argue that a more capacious view of children, alert to their agency, informed by theories of care, and attentive to the specific

The California Childhoods Project was sponsored and funded by the John D. and Catherine T. MacArthur Foundation Research Network on Successful Pathways through Middle Childhood in a grant to Barrie Thorne and Catherine Cooper. Further support for research in Los Angeles and in Oakland was provided by the Institute of Human Development at the University of California, Berkeley, and by the Sloan Foundation through the Berkeley Center for Working Families. Special thanks to my co-researchers at the Oakland site—Hung Thai, Wan Shun Eva Lam, Allison Pugh, Eileen Mears, Nadine Chabrier, Gladys Ocampo, Ana Gonzalez, and Erindera Rueda—for their many contributions; and to Marjorie Faulstich Orellana, Hanne Haavind, and Arlie Hochschild, who are invaluable intellectual and personal companions on this journey.

contexts and relationships through which their growing up is organized, can provide fresh perspectives on the study of work and family. This approach, developed through collaborative fieldwork on children's daily lives in two urban areas of California, situates families and jobs within larger ecologies of institutions and resources. It also turns attention to the range of beliefs and practices through which particular childhoods take shape.

I begin by sketching the economic, political, and demographic changes that are altering the contours of children's lives in contemporary U.S. society. These changes provide the backdrop for the case study that informs my argument: an ethnography of childhoods in a mixed-income, ethnically diverse area of Oakland, California. The daily pick-up scene at the public elementary school that anchors this research site reveals varied arrangements for the care and raising of children in this com-munity, with patterns loosely related to economic circumstances, im-migration histories, and culture, including different philosophies of child rearing. After mapping these patterns, I discuss the moving dialectic of child and adult agency involved in the process of growing up, and I use the concepts of *caring projects* and *reading signs of care* to analyze the coordination of effort, the differing orbits of practice and meaning, and relations across these lines of difference in a locally situated mosaic of childhoods. In the conclusion I critique the fragmenting assumptions that have guided much research on work and family, and I argue that a broader approach to children and childhoods, and the use of theories of care, can help re-vision this field of study.

THE CHANGING CONTOURS OF CHILDHOOD, WORK, AND FAMILIES

When I moved to California in 1988, I became interested in learning more about the effects of large-scale economic, political, and demo-graphic changes on the everyday lives and experiences of children who are differently positioned by social class, ethnicity, immigration, age, and gender. The literature on work and family brings into focus some of these changes, such as the rising employment rates of mothers and their continuing, disproportionate responsibility for the "second shift" of housework and child care (Hochschild 1989); expanded use of child care arrangements outside the home, with variation by social class and culture; a widely experienced speed-up and a felt shortage of personal and family time; and the diversification of household types and meanings of "family."

All of these changes are linked to major structural transformations that have received far too little attention in the study of family and work (see Gross, chapter 9 in this volume). Global economic changes have set migration streams in motion, with California as a prime destination for immigrants to the United States. A third of all California children now speak a language other than English at home, and the juxtaposition of many cultures in areas like Oakland has further diversified an already wide array of household types, kinship and family relations, and ideas and practices of child rearing. In recent decades social class divisions have also widened, with a dramatic impact on the circumstances of children who live in lower-income families. Cutbacks in state provisioning for social welfare have also pushed more children below the poverty line; in Oakland, well over 20 percent of children now live in poverty. Over the last three decades the contexts of child rearing have also been reshaped in Oakland, as in many urban areas, by the deterioration of public schools, parks, libraries, and transportation systems, and by the unraveling of neighborhoods and voluntary organizations like Scouts and Campfire Girls.

In an age-segmented twist of the commodification of everything, the decline in public provisioning for children has been accompanied by the growth of markets in child products and services. The result is an array of private schools, preschools, day care centers, after-school programs, tutoring centers, lessons, camps, housekeepers, nannies and au pairs, as well as paid domestic workers, household "organizers" (who will tidy up closets and drawers), birthday-party planners, and taxi and van companies willing to move kids across long distances. In short, a marketized infrastructure of child-rearing services has consolidated, with access and quality depending on one's ability to pay (the less expensive versions of paid after-school care tend to be primarily custodial). The lives of affluent and, to some degree, middle-class Oakland children, especially from nonimmigrant families, are increasingly organized through these markets, while lower-income families depend on deteriorating public services, family, neighbors, churches, and children's self-care. The economic and social distance between childhoods in the Oakland "hills" and those in the poorest parts of the "flats" is a microcosm of a social class bifurcation that is deeper now in the United States than at any time in the twentieth century.

METHODS OF INQUIRY

My colleagues and I are examining the shifting configuration of contemporary childhoods through ethnographic case studies of children's daily lives in two urban areas of California (one in Oakland, the other in inner-city Los Angeles) that differ in social class and ethnic composition and in histories of immigration.[1] We have done fieldwork in elementary schools, PTA meetings, homes, neighborhoods, after-school programs, public libraries, fast-food restaurants, and other child-related sites in each locale. We have also interviewed teachers, aides, and other child care workers, as well as children and parents from the range of economic and cultural groups living in each community; and we have invited children to draw, take photographs, and write about their lives. Information from local archives, the census, and school-district and city records has deepened our understanding of the political economy and history of each of our research sites.

This chapter focuses on our Oakland site: the official intake area for Oakdale Elementary School (a pseudonym, as are all names in this chapter). This area of the city, about six miles in radius, includes highly affluent, middle-class, and low-income neighborhoods. In 1996–97, the first and most intensive of our three years of fieldwork, the 465 Oakdale students were 50 percent African American, 17 percent Asian, 14 percent Hispanic, and 13 percent white (these official school-district categories gloss enormous ethnic variation due, in part, to the arrival of many immigrants from Asia, Mexico, and Central America over the last two decades). In 1996–97 about a fourth of Oakdale students transferred into the school from outside the intake area, mostly from lower-income neighborhoods. About half of all the Oakdale students qualified for free or reduced-cost lunch; the rest of the students were more middle class. (To reach across the full range of socioeconomic groups living in the Oakdale intake area, we have interviewed middle- and upper-middle-class parents and children who have "gone private" or else transferred to other public schools.)

This is a school—and a geographic area—"where peoples meet," and thus a fruitful site for exploring a range of contemporary childhoods,

---

1. Our study of contemporary childhoods began in the Pico Union area of Los Angeles, a low-income community of immigrants from Mexico, Central America, and Korea (Marjorie Faulstich Orellana has taken primary responsibility for research in that site). This chapter draws on data gathered between 1996 and 1999 in our second site, the intake area of a public school in a mixed-income, ethnically diverse area of Oakland.

the processes through which they are created (processes that involve, but extend far beyond, contexts of work and family), and the dynamics through which lives divide, and also interrelate, across socially constructed lines of age, social class, gender, racialized ethnicity, and immigration status. This variation comes into view each day at pick-up time, when the elementary school dismissal bell rings and the separate worlds of school, work, family, and out-of-school arrangements briefly converge.

PICK-UP TIME AT AN URBAN PUBLIC ELEMENTARY SCHOOL

It's 11:18 A.M. on a Tuesday morning at Oakdale Elementary School. Bits of litter from morning arrivals—a crushed juice box, the cellophane wrapper from a granola bar, a crumpled list of spelling words, a permission form with a parent's signature—are scattered on the wide concrete steps that lead up to the two-story building. Two white mothers wearing jeans, with younger children in stroller and in tow, converse by the front entrance. A few feet away, an elderly grandfather, an immigrant from China, unzips his tan cotton jacket as he settles onto a low cement wall. A Latina mother, wearing jeans, moves up the stairs, her slow and uneven pace set by the climbing toddler whose hand she is holding.

The dismissal bell for morning kindergarten rings at 11:20, and the heavy front door with a dangling metal chain swings open. The first child out the door is an exuberant five-year-old girl wearing a white blouse and navy jumper; she holds out a drawing as she runs to greet her mother and toddling little brother on the stairs. After hugs and brief talk, they begin the descent down the stairs and the half-mile walk home. As adults (most of them women) continue to arrive, more children burst out the door, pulling on sweaters and jackets, and jostling with one another as they hold on to drawings and the blue flyers that they are supposed to give to their parents. One of the children calls out a greeting in Cantonese as he pushes past a teacher and settles next to his grandfather on the low wall, beginning a two-hour wait for the boy's older brother, a second-grader in the Early Bird reading group. When the brother gets out, the threesome will walk together to the city bus stop and take the bus home, where the grandmother is waiting.

When the second dismissal bell rings at 1:30 P.M., another shift of adults, each of them connected to an Early Bird reader, converges at the school. A Mexican immigrant father who works for a local delivery service has scheduled a late lunch break to coincide with his second-grader's dismissal time. Several months before, when his daughter was switched from a late to an early reading group, he negotiated a change in his own work schedule so that he could continue to pick her up after school, take her home for lunch, and then bring her to the restaurant where her mother is employed as a food server. The mother has little spatial mobility during the workday; on the other hand, her job site is a fixed and safe location, with leeway for the temporary presence of a child. Knowing that this makeshift arrangement depends on the good-will of the restaurant owner and that her parents have no other options, the daughter sits unobtrusively on a chair near the kitchen, doing a bit of homework and watching the restaurant scene, waiting for her mother to get off work so they can go home together on the bus.

The last Oakdale dismissal bell rings at 2:40 P.M. By that time many cars have pulled up, some double-parked, with drivers leaning over to crank down side windows so they can catch the attention of the particular children they have come to transport. Some drivers get out and stand on the curb, snatching quick conversations with one another as they scan the front entrance. The owner of a family-based day care center has parked her van right in front of the building so that the four kids she has come to gather up, including her daughter, can easily find her. An African American father, wearing a suit and on a break from his job as an office manager in a state agency, hurries up the stairs, hoping that the third-grade teacher has let out her class, and thus his eight-year-old son, on time. He also hopes that the boy's grandmother will be at home when they pull up for the drop off and that it will be possible to get back to the office in time for a 3:30 meeting. A Filipina woman wearing the uniform of a security guard, a laminated photo tag clipped to her front shirt pocket, comes up the stairs to look for her two nieces. As an "emergency person" (a term in their family vocabulary), the aunt makes an effort to help with transportation when the girls' mother can't do the pick-up.

More and more adults arrive on foot, including a young white woman who will lead about ten kids into the school cafeteria for a privately run after-school program, which begins with "homework time" and lasts until 6:00 P.M. If parents are late picking up their children, they have to pay a fee. "Kids' Kamp," the other, less expensive, formal after-school program available in the Oakdale area, is run by the city recreation department and is based at a nearby park. An African American staff member with a whistle dangling from his neck stands in his regular spot at the foot of the stairs, waiting for the kids whose names are on his clipboard. When everyone who has signed up is accounted for, they'll walk together to the park.

The last wave of students spills out of the school door, heading for waiting cars or agreed-upon outposts near the curb. Older kids who are responsible for getting their younger siblings home safely look around for their charges with the searching and slightly anxious look also worn by adults doing pick-up duty. Some kids begin to walk toward home or to the city bus stop several blocks away. Others head for midway destinations like the public library, an uncle's dry cleaning business, a video store owned by a family friend, or, as one boy explained, "the house of a lady from church" to wait until a relative or neighbor arrives to complete the transport home. Over the years Oakdale students have established preferred routes for walking to and from the school, with way stations like a McDonald's and a mini-mart. The most-traveled routes lead from the middle-class neighborhood of the school across the freeway and into "the flatlands," the lower-income area of Oakland. Very few children walk in the other direction, toward "the hills," which is the upper-middle-class area of the city. Nearly all of the parents who live in that part of the Oakdale intake area have enrolled their children in private schools or arranged transfers to "hills" public schools.

By 3:15 the school entrance, stairs, and curb are nearly empty. A fourth-grade girl comes back into the hallway of the building to use the pay phone and find out if her auntie is on the way. Several parents have called the office to say that they'll be delayed. In the late afternoon the school janitor comes out to pick up the day's deposit of children's litter, including an afternoon layer of crumpled homework assignments written in pencil and corrected in red pen, a half-empty brown lunch bag, a dried-up curled orange peel, and several copies of the blue flyer announcing a PTA meeting. As the school day closes, the varied lives that have converged during pick-up time carry on in other venues.

THE PICK-UP SCENE AS A WINDOW ON WORK, FAMILIES, AND EVERYDAY LIFE

The after-school scene is a transitional time and place where seemingly set-apart worlds meet, and where one can glimpse different patterns of everyday life and the way these patterns are stitched together. The pieces of everyday life don't come with fixed and agreed-upon labels, as suggested by categories (e.g., "mother in child's home," "relative in child's home," "paid group care," "nonrelative in another home," "child home alone") used in surveys of after-school care. Where in that list would one locate the video store, the public library, or an hour spent standing in front of the school or waiting in a restaurant until a mother wraps up her work shift? Although they make it possible to specify larger statistical patterns, surveys pull away from context and meanings. By staying closer to the ground, ethnographic methods open insight into complex variation and into the processes and relationships that link varied institutional contexts.

Although they reside, work, and go to school in geographic proximity, Oakdale families organize their lives and the raising of children in a variety of ways. After-school arrangements vary not only by age range and other basic characteristics, such as whether a child is blind or has sight, but also in relation to household composition and income; the availability (and unavailability) of public resources such as access to quality public schools, bus transportation, and state-subsidized recreation programs; and the location and scheduling of jobs. Cultural beliefs and practices also enter into the configuration of after-school arrangements, including definitions of family and relations of obligation and reciprocity that may extend across households and to neighbors and friends; divisions of labor and ideologies of motherhood and fatherhood; and assumptions about the needs and capabilities of children, with variation by age and sometimes by gender.

Some arrangements for the transport and out-of-school care of children are organized entirely through networks of kith and kin, with occasional money transfers, as when a grandmother or a neighbor, who regularly does after-school care, is "paid a little something" by the child's mother to smooth out uneven patterns of indebtedness. Children from lower-income families are more likely than middle-class children to walk long distances on their own and to ride by themselves on the city transit system. (Perpetually strapped for funds, the Oakland school district no longer runs its own bus system, except for students with severe physical disabilities.) The children of immigrants, who come from more than eleven different countries at this culturally diverse school, are the most likely to be transported and cared for by extended kin—like the Chinese grandparents who migrated from Hong Kong to help out their daughter, who works long hours in a garment factory, and their son-in-law, who is employed as a cook in two different restaurants. Families with limited income rely not only on networks of relatives, friends, and neighbors but also on government-subsidized resources, such as recreation programs, buses, and the public library—which some parents regard as a safe and beneficial place for children to be on their own after school, although librarians occasionally protest the use of the facility for "child care."

Middle-class nonimmigrant families whose children attend Oakdale Elementary School tend to be small and self-contained, relying irregularly, if at all, on the help of relatives or friends. Some middle-class mothers, especially those with preschool-age children, do not have paid jobs; they are more likely than other adults to arrive at the school early and to visit with one another while they wait for the dismissal bell to ring. Other mothers work part-time or on night shifts so that they can pick up and care for their children after school. Compared with lower-income parents, middle-class dual-earner couples (a few are lesbians) and middle-class solo parents (a few of them are fathers) are more likely to have the means to shop in the local market of after-school programs, home care providers, lessons, organized sports activities, and summer camps. Paid care providers who will also handle after-school pick-ups are especially favored, and parents who are oriented to the child care market swap information about costs of and experiences with available options.

None of the upper-middle-class children who live in the Oakdale intake area attend the "neighborhood public school." Their parents rely almost entirely on markets to organize their children's time outside the home, and some drive long distances so their children can enroll in a particular private school, play a specific sport, or have access to specialized lessons in music, art, or science. One prestigious private school, which goes from kindergarten through high school, offers on-site after-school programs and activities for every grade level, in effect providing one-stop shopping, at premium prices.

The Oakdale pick-up scene offers a glimpse not only of diverse arrangements for the transport and after-school care of children, but also of the daily routines and practices of different households. Objects that travel between home and school—lunchboxes, backpacks, homework, notes—give clues to daily life within these somewhat private domains. An archaeology of school-ground and lunchroom litter reveals diverse approaches to feeding and eating, with patterns related to ethnicity, income, and orientations to the market. (In children's lunchtime culture at this elementary school, as in the Bay Area middle school that Elaine Bell Kaplan [2000] has studied, prepackaged commercial items are the prestige food, lunches made and carried from home have middling status, and the state-subsidized school lunch is the least valued and may even be stigmatizing.) Other types of litter, such as notes, permission forms, homework assignments, newsletters, flyers, and report cards reveal written patterns of communication between parents and teachers, which, as both parties lament and the litter testifies, are contingent on not-always-reliable child couriers. These artifacts also reflect the demands for labor and time that schools make on families, with varying degrees of success (Smith and Griffith 1990).

Many of the adults who converge when the school dismissal bells ring feel pressed by the time binds that Arlie Hochschild (1997) has insightfully analyzed, and some children seem to feel buffeted by parents' schedules, rushed by quick pick-ups and drop-offs, or bored by long waits in front of the school or at a relative's place of employment. As the after-school scene makes clear, demands for adult time and for being on time extend not only from jobs and from home, but also from schools, after-school programs, and other organized activities (Berhau and Lareau 1993; Lareau 2000; Thorpe and Daily 1999), and from the schedules and contingencies of neighbors, friends, and other caregivers. Oakdale parents often complain about collisions between the time orders of the school and of their places of employment, and when there is a "minimum day" or a weekday with no school, fragile arrangements (e.g., a father who can transport children only during a lunch break, or a neighbor available only after 3 P.M.) may fall apart. When the school system has placed children from the same household into different temporal tracks, the pick-up challenge may be daunting. (See Orellana and Thorne [1998] for further analysis of the ways in which school schedules may exacerbate collisions between work and family time.)

CONCEPTUALIZING CHILDREN: DEPENDENCE, PARTICIPATION, AND PROCESSES OF CARE

Having mapped the contours of childhood in this part of Oakland, I will now bring conceptualizations of children and processes of growing up and raising children into closer focus. The literature on work and family frames children primarily by their economic and emotional dependence and their demand for adult labor, as in socialist-feminist theories of reproductive labor and in time-budget research on the hours adults spend doing child care (although this literature doesn't explore actual processes and experiences of care). The limitations of these frameworks become apparent when one studies older children. As children grow, they are increasingly able to assume the tasks lumped under the rubric of "child care," such as getting themselves dressed, organized, and transported to and from school, and taking care of themselves when adults are not around. As they get older, children also gain in the capacity to care for others and to do forms of paid labor that in industrialized societies are usually relegated to adults. Defining children in terms of economic dependence and the more or less passive stance of "being socialized" within the protected spaces of home, school, and play makes it difficult to see the work that they may do (Solberg 1990). Conventional frameworks also obscure the ways in which children's practices may help sustain, and even alter, a range of institutions (Thorne 1987, 1993).

The pick-up scene offers glimpses of children actively constructing and negotiating everyday life, including divisions of labor within and extending beyond households. Kids take responsibility for locating younger siblings and getting them home; they organize themselves into groups to head for after-school destinations; they make phone calls to check up on adults who are late; they carry messages between school and home. In addition, kids sometimes help out on adult job sites—for example, by sorting dry cleaning at an uncle's store or by helping a mother clear tables in a restaurant. Children also contribute to housework—an area of activity with especially wide variation in practices, meanings, and patterns of negotiation across Oakdale households.

Recognizing that children contribute as well as receive labor gives them a more complex presence in knowledge. But theories of labor are not designed to grasp the moving dialectic of child and adult agency or the array of emotions and experiences bound up in the processes of "growing up" and "bringing up" a child. These paired terms allude to a mix of daily, cyclical time (get up, get dressed, eat breakfast, pack lunches, head for school and work) and the sweep of cumulative time entailed in the passage from child to adult.

Hanne Haavind (1987; Haavind and Andanaes 1992; also personal communication) grasps this complexity by theorizing child development as a highly contextual and relational process. In a qualitative study of Norwegian mothers and their four-year-old children, Haavind shows how everyday practices (such as suggesting that a child pack her own lunch) may embed varied goals and strategies (not only the goal of getting out the door more quickly, but also helping the child learn skills needed for access to a wider social world). Haavind uses the metaphor of a "running wheel" that turns in the minds of mothers and other engaged caregivers as they mentally record how a child is doing, both now and with an eye to the future, and as they adjust their daily practices with these assessments in mind. Children also monitor their own changing capacities, sometimes refusing to "go forward" or trying to accelerate the pace or attempting to pursue goals other than those that their parents or teachers have in mind for them. Growing up/bringing up is a guided but open-ended and highly contingent process, involving conflicts of will and desire, and struggles over autonomy and control (Brannen and O'Brien 1996; Polatnick 1999; Solberg 1990).

Haavind's theorizing of "the tasks of growing up" brings children's vantage points into conjunction with an insightful literature on the ideologies, practices, and experiences of mothering (e.g., Glenn, Chang, and Forcey 1994; Ruddick, 1982). A particular construction of motherhood (such as the full-time intensive mothering embedded in dominant family ideologies [Hays 1996] or the more collective and shared conception of mothering that is associated with African American culture [Collins 2000]) is also a construction of the "nature" and needs of children. Bringing up a child is a long-range process involving "bundles of tasks" (Hughes 1971) that are continually negotiated and redefined. In the dominant U.S. culture, mothers are given primary responsibility for organizing the raising of children—and major blame if it goes awry. But as more and more mothers enter the labor force, with more extensive use of out-of-home child care arrangements, and as family patterns diversify (for example, with grandparents migrating from China in order to take care of their grandchildren in the United States), the participation of other actors has become increasingly visible, as have efforts to adjust and rework ideologies of motherhood (Garey 1999; Macdonald 1998; Uttal 1996).

To bring the process of growing up/bringing up and the coordination of varied actors and contexts into broader view, I have found it useful to think of child rearing as a shared *caring project* that is undertaken with a sense of purpose and guided by varied conceptions of the "good." I like the word "project" because it conveys (in Haavind's words) the "directed but open-ended" quality of child rearing, as well as efforts to coordinate shared activity across an array of people and contexts. Raising a child may variously resemble the producing of a movie, the building of a house, or the moment-by-moment improvisation (including the missteps and uncertain cadences) of a dance. The "project" metaphor should be qualified, however, since the "object" of the activities of child rearing is another sentient being who participates in the production, building, or choreography both in the everyday and over longer spans of time. Children often prefer to dance or to build, at least in part, according to their own designs. Furthermore, parents vary in the degree to which they try, or even think it is possible, to shape a particular kind of adult (Hallden 1991; Lareau forthcoming).

All of the Oakland parents we have interviewed express long-range goals, hopes, and worries about the children they are raising. Some parents detail remarkably specific blueprints for their children, as in the purposive, ends-oriented approach described by a white college-educated mother, who is a part-time graduate student and whose husband works long hours managing a small business. This couple lives near Oakdale Elementary School but transferred their daughter to a "hills" public school in a more affluent part of the city. Speaking in a mode of both dreaming and determination, the mother said that she wanted her daughter (then seven years old) to attend Stanford University on a soccer scholarship and then go to graduate school at either Stanford or Berkeley. (This kind of close and even vicarious identification with one's child suggests another meaning, and pronunciation, of the word "project"—the psychodynamic process of projection, which is also relevant to parent-child relations.)

Oakdale parents more often talk about their orientations to child rearing in general terms, for example, saying that they hope to raise a child who will finish high school, perhaps go to college, and end up in a "decent" job. A college-educated African American mother who works, as does her husband, in an administrative position in a state bureaucracy, stressed "academics," homework, and going to college as central preoccupations of her child rearing. She actively shops for affordable lessons, recreation programs, and summer camps as a way of keeping her children out of trouble and headed toward securely middle-class lives.

Some parents use ethical language when they describe the goals that guide their child rearing. For example, a mixed-ethnic middle-class couple who are active in local politics said that they want their daughter to be able to get along with and respect "different people from different backgrounds" in a world that is increasingly diverse. They had this end in mind when they chose to live in a mixed-income, racially diverse "flats" neighborhood and to enroll their daughter in Oakdale Elementary School. Another sort of moral orientation—ensuring that their children will grow up with a firm attachment to Islam and to extended kin—

guides the collective caring project of a family from Yemen, whose thickly knit relations extend across national boundaries (Orellana et al. 1998). The mothers in this extended family express fear that their children might start to smoke, use drugs, or become interested in sex (teenage dating culture looms large in their horizon of worry). Other Oakdale parents, especially those who are scrambling for economic survival and who live in dangerous neighborhoods, also talked about what they do *not* want their children to do or become; "I'm not raising my son to be a gang-banger," an unemployed African American father said with determination.

Lower-income immigrant parents often frame their children's trajectories as part of the economic survival and potential mobility of the family as a whole, musing about how it is to raise a child here compared with in their countries of origin. For example, a Mien mother, a refugee from Laos, said that her family would "have a life here" if the children "do good in school." But she feared that as recent immigrants, Mien parents "haven't gotten the experience to raise their children here." She continued:

> I think a lot of children are getting bad because their parents do not know how to deal with it yet. Because the way we raise our children in our own country is different. Like when children get older . . . they just go out and work in the field, and when their parents tell them what to do, they just go and do it. Parents don't have to go out and watch them every day.

The Mien mother also spoke of the shame she would feel if any of her children turned out "bad."

In short, caring projects encompass longer-range goals, hopes, and fears, *and* keen awareness of the "here and now," including the immediate challenges of organizing children's daily lives, keeping them safe and out of trouble, and juggling these efforts with other activities. Sometimes long-term goals are eclipsed by the demands of the present, such as scrambling for economic survival or coping with illness, death, or being evicted from yet another apartment. Both navigating present circumstances and efforts to shape a hoped-for future involve mobilizing networks and resources, and coordinating lines of action. These dimensions are sometimes at odds, as when parents like the Mien mother or the unemployed African American father are overwhelmed by present contingencies and lack resources to actively promote a desired end.

The metaphor of "project" and the related images of building and producing point to the labor involved in child rearing. But metaphors of work don't adequately grasp the range of experiences that child rearing may entail; thus my added image of child rearing as a dance, evoking pleasure and a sense of play. Theories of *care,* understood as a practice guided by concern for the well-being of another, tap into the domain of work; but they also encompass other dimensions of experience, especially the quality of relationships and orientation to meeting others' needs (Hochschild 1999; Ruddick 1998).

Joan Tronto (1994) theorizes care as a social process with four phases: (1) *caring about,* that is, attending to and being aware of the need for caring (akin to the "running wheel" of consciousness that Haavind describes); (2) *caring for,* or taking general responsibility for meeting the needs of another; (3) *caregiving,* that is, the material meeting of a need for care (a parent may take responsibility for organizing the care of a child but delegate much of the hands-on care to others); and (4) *care-receiving,* a dimension that highlights the relational nature of care (recipients, including children, may be grateful or dissatisfied; they may feel controlled but not cared for; they may try to command particular kinds of care). As Tronto observes, caring processes may be fragmented; needs may be misrecognized or approached in ways more harmful than helpful. Parents may care about and take responsibility for their children but lack the means to give adequate care. In short, care should not be romanticized, but rather should be used as a lens for understanding complex relationships and interactions that unfold over time.

READING SIGNS OF CARE

I do not know even know if it matters, or if it explains
anything. . . . All that compounds a human being is
so heavy and meaningful in me.
         Tillie Olsen, "I Stand Here Ironing"

These poignant words from a short story express the mix of love, responsibility, guilt, and nagging uncertainty that lies at the heart of mothering, and of deeply felt caring projects more generally. The process of raising and caring for a child is laced with uncertainty about what the child needs in order to flourish, and about the adequacy of the care she or he is receiving. When the process of care is guided by long-range goals, such as securing family loyalty and an attachment to Islam or ensuring that one's child will go to college, the uncertain connection of present actions to future outcomes magnifies feelings of anxiety. So also does the participation of many different people, not necessarily of one's choosing or under one's control, in the process of raising a child (Tillie Olsen's story beautifully conveys this theme).

Some parents opt for home schooling as a strategy for limiting outside influences and more tightly integrating the phases of care. Dual-earner couples may work split shifts not only because they can't afford to pay for child care, but also as a way of retaining more control over the caring process. Mobilizing relatives and friends to provide care may also reduce anxiety. Immigrant parents often want their children to play with siblings and cousins rather than with friends from families whom they do not know, and they prefer relatives as caregivers, partly because these are people they feel they can trust. Upper-middle-class parents who pay for private schools rely on selective admissions to shape the company their children keep, as well as to ensure that their children are on track for admission to elite colleges.

To cope with these many sources of uncertainty, including the fact that no strategy or formula for child rearing yields guaranteed results, parents and other caregivers continually look for signs and portents. Like fortune-tellers reading tea leaves, they scan children's faces, bodies, pockets, and possessions, looking for signs of how the child is doing and whether trouble is afoot.[2] Sign reading, at its best, is a form of "attentive love" (Ruddick 1982), part of the running wheel of noticing and responding to another's needs. But sign reading may also become surveillance, diminishing the sense of autonomy and self-determination that may be important for the well-being of a growing child.[3] This ambiguity seems to be intrinsic to processes of care, especially when caregivers have much more power than care-receivers.

Sign reading is a collective process that moves across institutional sites

2. People caught up in fateful but unpredictable situations often engage in collective efforts to reduce feelings of uncertainty. Thus, parents coping with the uncertainties of child rearing have something in common with patients in a TB sanitorium who look for clues that might predict the course of an unpredictable disease (Roth 1963), and with people in situations of war and internment who circulate rumors to try to fill gaps in information (Shibutani 1966).

3. After the spring 1999 high school shooting rampage in Littleton, Colorado, the news media reverberated with questions about why the parents of the two killers didn't pick up signs that their sons were in trouble. How did seemingly "normal" (white, middle-class, married, suburban) parents raise teenagers steeped in fantasies of violence and capable of murder? Littleton has become a symbol of the painful uncertainty of caring projects, the connected themes of threat and victimization that permeate contemporary representations of children and teens, and the ambiguous line between healthy parental vigilance and excessive snooping and efforts to control.

and frameworks of interpretation. Schools produce systems of signs (grades, test scores, suspensions) whose meanings are continually negotiated and sometimes contested. Many of the Oakland parents and children whom we interviewed spoke of "good grades" as a prime symbol that a child is "on track." (Grades, of course, are more than symbols; in and of themselves, they have the power to open or shut down opportunities.) Homework is another much-discussed sign, loaded with information because it regularly travels between home and school. When homework is not turned in or is poorly done, teachers may assume that parents don't care about their child's education. Parents may also read homework for signs of whether or not, and how much, a teacher can be trusted to care about a child. For example, a Mexican immigrant mother observed that her nine- and eleven-year-old children, who were in the same split-grade classroom in Oakdale Elementary School, routinely came home with identical homework assignments. "If they bring the same homework and do the same thing, then who is advancing, and who is falling behind?" the mother asked, suspecting that the teacher didn't care.

Details of comportment and appearance, such as a child's hair, style of dress, or attitude, are less stable in their positioning as signs, and interpretations are less stylized. When parents, teachers, day care workers, and other participants in caring projects get together, they pick up seemingly small details and weigh them for larger significance (e.g., "Her hair is always tangled when she comes to school; I think that there may be trouble at home." "That first-grader has been waiting in front of the school for half an hour; do you think his baby-sitter is unreliable?" "He's getting hyper; is there something wrong at Kids' Kamp?" "You've been late coming home every day this week; are you getting an attitude?").

The sharing and negotiation of signs are the stuff of parent-teacher conferences, conversations between parents and child care workers, casual chitchat among adults who are waiting to pick up children after school or who meet on the sidelines of soccer games. Sign reading may lead to heart-to-heart talks between parents and children; and, moving to especially consequential domains, reading signs of care is a central activity of social workers, police, and other professionals who are charged with investigating disputes over child custody or investigating reports of child neglect or abuse.

The process of reading signs of care is central to the orchestration of caring projects, especially when different actors, contexts, and gaps of information are involved. When mothers anguish about whether or not to seek employment, switch jobs, or change paid caregiving arrangements, they often scan their children for signs of possible impact. The search for a baby-sitter, day care center, school, or after-school program may also involve looking for and interpreting signs of care. One mother decided not to enroll her daughter in kindergarten at Oakdale Elementary School, which is near their home, because the girls' bathroom was dirty on the day she visited. She and her husband decided to request a transfer to a "hills" school in part because the bathroom was cleaner. But another mother who pondered a similar transfer decided against it because she thought the kids in the "hills" school looked too "rich," which would make her daughter feel marginal. Thus goes the contested world of sign reading, interpretive frameworks, assumptions about well-being, and the improvisational and generally uncertain nature of the caring projects through which lives, and childhoods, take shape.

SIGN READING ACROSS LINES OF CLASS AND CULTURE

Sign reading is part of the building, producing, dancing of specific caring projects, or styles of child rearing, moving through time. The process also enters into the juxtaposition and interrelationship of multiple caring projects within a neighborhood, school, or community. Adults and children read signs of care across cultural and class divides, as well as across differences in child-rearing philosophies. Some middle-class Oakdale families actively engage with the world of lessons, sports, camps, and other scheduled out-of-school activities. But others, who find that approach "too structured," believe that good care entails giving children time to "just hang out and be a child" (Lareau 2000). Cross-project readings may be conducted with idle, ambivalent, or appreciative curiosity; a wish to reach out and find common ground; suspicion and self-protection; or with the intent of reaffirming stereotypes and distancing one's self, and one's children, from a socially distant Other. Practices of sign reading help constitute and regulate social relations across lines of social class, racialized ethnicity, and gender.

Children's autonomous use of public space—a highly visible sign of family caring practices—is a staple item in menus of parent talk. For example, a white middle-class mother commented in an interview that she thought a Yemeni family was neglectful because they let their six-year-old boy walk to and from school by himself. But the boy's mother saw no problem in letting her young son walk alone along the safe and much-traveled few blocks between home and school. Boys in the Yemeni extended family help out in the family liquor store when they are as young as seven, and a certain amount of spatial autonomy is a routine part of their upbringing. Yemeni girls, on the other hand, are more closely watched and protected.

The question of how much spatial autonomy a child should have, and at what age, is an especially fraught subject because it taps into concerns about safety and about how to reconcile the contradiction between children's need for protection and their need for self-determination. In our group interviews with fifth- and sixth-graders we heard many stories of negotiation and conflict over after-school arrangements. For example, some kids thought it was "babyish" to be picked up, but others found it a burden that they had to walk or take the bus long distances; one pushed to go to Kids' Klub rather than to his grandmother's apartment after school; several found it scary, although perhaps a family necessity, to be home alone after school, while others begged for the opportunity. (For insightful research on children's negotiations of autonomy, see Solberg [1990], essays in Brannen and O'Brien [1996], and Polatnick [1999].)

Kids who walk on their own and/or who take care of themselves at home after school can often recite specific family rules governing these activities, such as "I have to be home by four or I get in trouble"; "My mom says that I have to walk this certain route"; "I kept telling my mom I was too old to be picked up—now she lets me walk home if one of my friends is with me"; "When I get home, I have to keep the door locked, and I can't use the stove"; "I can't answer the phone unless it rings twice and stops and then rings again—that's a signal that my dad or someone else from his job is phoning to check on me." Kids sometimes use their knowledge of the practices of other families to justify claims for expanded autonomy ("But Ben's mother lets him stop at McDonald's on the way home . . .").

Living in a culturally and economically diverse community sharpens awareness not only of variation in child-rearing practices but also, in effect, of childhood as a social construction. Awareness is also enhanced by the dramatic differences, spontaneously mentioned by many of the parents we have interviewed, between the circumstances in which children grow up now and the parents' memories of their own childhoods (the contrast is especially vivid in the accounts of immigrants from rural parts of Mexico or Asia). Everyone agrees that growing up now is much riskier than in the past, with dangers like child kidnapping, sexual abuse, street crime, drugs, gangs, the availability of guns, media violence, and consumer culture. The sheer uncertainty of the future in a rapidly changing world compounds the worry.

CONCLUSION

In this chapter I have argued that a broader approach to studying children, attentive to their agency and informed by theories of care, can not only enrich but also provide leads for re-visioning the study of work and family. The study of work and family is a hybrid field that is narrowly framed and in need of more theoretical integration. Note the telling vocabulary and syntax that organize this area of research: two nouns linked by a hyphen and by an array of other words signaling connection ("work-family nexus," "relations between work and family," "balancing work and family," "juggling work and family"). The paired terms "work" and "family" still carry baggage from the nineteenth-century gendered ideology of "separate spheres," although there has been considerable progress in challenging this ideology and in theorizing the changing dynamics of gender.

What is work? What is family? Most of the literature on work and family takes these categories to be self-evident, using them in ways that gloss complex, contradictory, and shifting realities even as the categories continue to order perceptions of the world. Dorothy Smith (1993) has insightfully discussed the use of self-referential "ideological codes" that draw on commonsense typifications in an unexamined way (see also Bourdieu 1996). A good example is the use of the term "working families" to stake out and draw boundaries around a terrain of study. The term, as Loic Wacquant (1999) has argued, is haunted by the lives it excludes—"non-working," "non-families," i.e., the stigmatized "underclass." Other terms, such as "middle-class dual-earner families," have also been artificially fixed, reified, and sliced from relational and historical contexts. The connecting, hyphenating "linkage" vocabulary of research on work and family, including the circus imagery of individual performers "juggling" and "balancing," signals a field that has been cut off from its historical and contextual moorings.

How can one move beyond this problematic framing? First, by using concepts in a more self-reflective way, alert to underlying assumptions and the realities they may obscure, as well as the realities they may help constitute and reproduce. Another strategy is to define research topics informed by larger historical, social, and cultural contexts. Dramatic structural transformations (such as global economic shifts and cutbacks by the state) that are reshaping work, family, and the rest of social life should be brought to the forefront of this area of study.

Finally, the study of work and family can be re-visioned by breaking with the "linkages" framework and pursuing research topics with more solid theoretical grounding. Some of the most fruitful topics illuminate social processes that don't necessarily stop at the pre-specified boundaries of "work" or "family," such as changing divisions of labor, trade-offs between time and money, patterns of reciprocity and obligation, the dynamics of consumerism, quests for economic and physical security in an increasingly unstable world, and the giving and receiving of care. Theories of care provide especially generative leads for studying children and for framing a wide range of topics that move beyond the limiting discourse of work and family (Hochschild 1999). By highlighting relations of interdependence and by raising questions about human needs, theories of care can also provide critical perspective on the instrumental values that permeate much of the literature on work and family.

REFERENCES

Berhau, Patricia, and Annette Lareau. 1993. Beyond the work-family divide: Developing family portraits across class, race, and gender. Paper presented at the annual meeting of the Society for the Study of Social Problems, Miami, August.

Bourdieu, Pierre. 1996. On the family as a realized category. *Theory, Culture, and Society* 13:19–26.

Brannen, Julia, and Margaret O'Brien, eds. 1996. *Children in families*. London: Falmer Press.

Collins, Patricia Hill. 2000. *Black feminist thought*, 2d ed. New York: Routledge.

Garey, Anita Itta. 1999. *Weaving work and motherhood*. Philadelphia: Temple University Press.

Glenn, Evelyn Nakano, Grace Chang, and Linda Rennie Forcey, eds. 1994. *Mothering: Ideology, experience, and agency*. New York: Routledge.

Haavind, Hanne. 1987. *Liten og stor: Moedres omsorg og barns utviklings-muligheter* (The big one and the little one: The organization of care by mothers and possibilities for development in children). Oslo: Scandinavian University Press.

Haavind, Hanne, and Agnes Andenaes. 1992. Care and the responsibilities for children: Creating the life of women creating themselves. Unpublished manuscript. Department of Psychology, University of Oslo, Norway.

Hallden, Gunilla. 1991. The child as project and the child as being: Parents' ideas as frames of reference. *Children and Society* 5:334–46.

Hays, Sharon. 1996. *The cultural contradictions of motherhood*. New Haven: Yale University Press.

Hochschild, Arlie Russell. 1997. *The time bind: When work becomes home and home becomes work*. New York: Metropolitan Books.

———. 1999. Working families and the quiet crisis in care: A research map. Working paper. University of California, Berkeley, Center for Working Families.

Hochschild, Arlie Russell, with Anne Machung. 1989. *The second shift: Working parents and the revolution at home*. New York: Viking.

Hughes, Everett C. 1971. *The sociological eye*. Chicago: Aldine.

Kaplan, Elaine Bell. 2000. Using food as a metaphor for care: Middle-school kids talk about family, school, and class relationships. *Journal of Contemporary Ethnography* 29:474–509.

Lareau, Annette. 2000. Social class variation in the everyday lives of U.S. children. *Childhood: A Global Journal of Child Research* 7 (2).

———. Forthcoming. *Contours of childhood*.

Macdonald, Cameron L. 1998. Manufacturing motherhood: The shadow work of nannies and au pairs. *Qualitative Sociology* 21:25–54.

Olsen, Tillie. 1960. I stand here ironing. In *Tell me a riddle*. New York: Dell, 1–12.

Orellana, Marjorie Faulstich, and Barrie Thorne. 1998. Year-round schools and the politics of time. *Anthropology and Education Quarterly* 29 (4):446–72.

Orellana, Marjorie Faulstich, Barrie Thorne, Wan Shun Eva Lam, and Anna Chee. 1998. Transnational childhoods: The participation of children in processes of family migration. Paper presented at the Fourteenth World Congress of Sociology, Montreal, July.

Polatnick, Rivka. 1999. Too old for child care? Too young for "self-care"? Negotiations between preteens and their employed parents. Working paper. University of California, Berkeley, Center for Working Families.

Rainwater, Lee, and T. M. Smeeding. 1995. Doing poorly: The real income of American children in a comparative perspective. Luxembourg Income Study, working paper no. 127.

Roth, Julius. 1963. *Timetables: Structuring the passage of time in hospital treatment and other careers*. Indianapolis: Bobbs-Merrill.

Ruddick, Sara. 1982. Maternal thinking. In *Rethinking the family: Some feminist questions*, edited by Barrie Thorne, with Marilyn Yalom, 76–94. New York: Longman.

———. 1998. Care as labor and relationship. In *Norms and values: Essays on the work of Virginia Held*, edited by Joram C. Haber and Mark S. Halfon, 3–25. Totowa, N.J.: Rowman and Littlefield.

Shibutani, Tamotsu. 1966. *Improvised news: A sociological study of rumor*. Indianapolis: Bobbs-Merrill.

Smith, Dorothy E. 1993. The standard North American family: SNAF as an ideological code. *Journal of Family Issues* 14:50–65.

Smith, Dorothy E., and Alison Griffith. 1990. Coordinating the uncoordinated: Mothering, schooling, and the family wage. In *Perspectives on social prob-*

lems, edited by Gayle Miller and James Holstein, 25–43. Greenwich, Conn.: JAI Press.

Solberg, Anne. 1990. Negotiating childhood: Changing construction of age for Norwegian children. In *Constructing and reconstructing childhood,* edited by Allison James and Alan Prout, 126–44. London: Falmer Press.

Thorne, Barrie. 1987. Re-visioning women and social change: Where are the children? *Gender & Society* 1:85–109.

———. 1993. *Gender play: Girls and boys in school.* New Brunswick, N.J.: Rutgers University Press.

Thorpe, Kate, and Kerry Daly. 1999. Children, parents and time: The dialectics of control. In *Contemporary perspectives on family research,* vol. 1: *Through the eyes of the child: Re-visioning children as active agents of family life.* New York: JAI Press.

Tronto, Joan. 1994. *Moral boundaries: A political argument for an ethic of care.* New York: Routledge.

Uttal, Lynet. 1996. Custodial care, surrogate care, and coordinated care: Employed mothers and the meaning of child care. *Gender & Society* 10:291–311.

Wacquant, Loic. 1999. What work, whose family? The ideology of "working families" in the age of liberal paternalism. Workshop presentation at the University of California, Berkeley, Center for Working Families, April.

About the Contributors

MICHELE ADAMS is a doctoral candidate at the University of California, Riverside. She has published in the areas of family and gender and is involved in research on the cultural understandings of marriage, cohabitation, and alternative family forms.

TERRY ARENDELL is Professor of Sociology at Colby College. In 1998–99 she was a Senior Research Fellow at the University of California Center for Working Families. She is the author of *Mothers and Divorce: Legal, Economic, and Social Dilemmas* and *Fathers and Divorce*, and the editor of *Contemporary Parenting: Challenges and Issues*. She has also published in various scholarly journals, including *Signs, Gender & Society, Family Science Review*, and *Qualitative Sociology*. One of her current research projects involves the study of middle-class mothers with elementary-school-aged children.

AMY ARMENIA is a graduate student in the Sociology Department at the University of Massachusetts, Amherst. Her current research explores the predictors of family leave taking after the passage of the Family and Medical Leave Act.

SCOTT COLTRANE is Professor of Sociology, Chair of the Department of Sociology, and Associate Director of the Center for Family Studies at the University of California, Riverside. He is the author of *Family Man: Fatherhood, Housework, and Gender Equity* and *Gender and Families* and coauthor (with Randall Collins) of *Sociology of Marriage and the Family: Gender, Love, and Property*.

CYNTHIA H. DEITCH is Associate Professor of Women's Studies and of Sociology at George Washington University. Selected publications include "Manufacturing Job Loss among Blue Collar Women: An Assessment of Data and Policy" in *Gender Differences: Their Impact on Public Policy* (1991); "Gender,

Race, and Class Politics and the Inclusion of Gender in Title VII of the 1964 Civil Rights Act" (*Gender & Society* 1993); and "How U.S. Radiologists Use Their Professional Time: Factors Affecting Work Activity and Retirement Plans" (*Radiology* 1995).

DIANE EHRENSAFT is Professor of Psychology at the Wright Institute, Berkeley, and a faculty member of the Psychoanalytic Institute of Northern California. She is the author of *Parenting Together: Men and Women Sharing the Care of Their Children* and *Spoiling Childhood: How Well-Meaning Parents Are Giving Their Children Too Much—But Not What They Need*. She is on the editorial board of *Gender and Sexuality* and has had a clinical practice in Oakland, California, for the past 20 years. She is presently working on a project addressing reproductive technology, family, and child development.

THERESE FITZGERALD is Research Coordinator at the Center on Work and Family at Boston University. Her areas of research interest include work/family consequences facing the low-income family and program evaluation.

HEATHER M. FITZ GIBBON is Associate Professor of Sociology at the College of Wooster. Her past research examined the work of family day care providers. Currently she is conducting a study on the career and family decisions of recently laid-off white-collar workers.

JENNIFER FLEISCHER-COOPERMAN is Research Assistant at the Center on Work and Family at Boston University. She has coauthored (with Len Lundgren) articles on the career consequences of working an alternative career path.

ELLEN GALINSKY is President and Co-founder of the Families and Work Institute, a Manhattan-based nonprofit organization conducting research on the changing family, workplace, and community. She is the author of over 20 books and reports, including *Ask the Children: The Breakthrough Study That Reveals How to Succeed at Work and Parenting*, and more than 100 articles in academic journals, academic books, and magazines.

ANITA ILTA GAREY is a sociologist and Assistant Professor of Family Studies at the University of Connecticut. In 1999 she was a senior research fellow at the Center for Working Families at the University of California, Berkeley. She is the author of *Weaving Work and Motherhood*, which received the 2000 William J. Goode Award from the American Sociological Association, and coeditor of *Families in the U.S.: Kinship and Domestic Politics*.

KATHLEEN GERSON is Professor of Sociology at New York University. She is the author of *No Man's Land: Men's Changing Commitments to Family and Work* and *Hard Choices: How Women Decide about Work, Career, and Motherhood*. Her current research includes examining trends in working time and their consequences for conflict between work and family and exploring how the "children of the gender revolution" are responding to growing up in nontraditional families during an era of rapid, pervasive work and family change.

HARRIET E. GROSS is Professor Emeritus of Sociology at Governors State University in University Park, Illinois. She taught for twenty-five years before her recent retirement. Her current research interests center on work and family policy. She is a former member of the Balancing Work and Family Committee of the Governor's Commission on the Status of Women in Illinois.

HEATHER-LYN HALEY is a graduate student in the Sociology Department at the University of Massachusetts, Amherst, where she is a research assistant for the Work-Family Transitions Project. She is currently studying stability and change in the social networks of working-class couples as they experience the transition to parenthood.

SHIN-KAP HAN is Assistant Professor of Sociology at the University of Illinois at Urbana-Champaign and faculty associate at the Cornell Employment and Family Careers Institute. He is the coauthor (with Phyllis Moen) of "Clocking Out: Temporal Patterning of Retirement" (*American Journal of Sociology* 1999). He is currently at work on two projects, one on coupled careers and the other on the network structure of the decision-making process in the U.S. Supreme Court.

ROSANNA HERTZ is Professor of Sociology and Women's Studies at Wellesley College. Presently she is Chair of the Women's Studies Department. She is the author of *More Equal Than Others: Women and Men in Dual-Career Marriages*. Her edited books include *Reflexivity and Voice, Qualitative Sociology as Everyday Life* (with Barry Glassner), and *Studying Elites Using Qualitative Methods* (with Jonathan Imber). For the past nine years she has been the editor of *Qualitative Sociology*. She is presently working on a study of single mothers by choice.

ARLIE RUSSELL HOCHSCHILD is the author of *The Time Bind: When Work Becomes Home and Home Becomes Work; The Second Shift: Working Parents and the Revolution at Home;* and *The Managed Heart: The Commercialization of Human Feeling.* Professor of Sociology at the University of California, Berkeley, and Co-director of the Center for Working Families there, she is working on a book of collected essays, *The Commercialization of Intimate Life and Other Essays.*

MATT L. HUFFMAN is Assistant Professor in the Sociology Department at the University of California, Irvine. His recent publications investigate the earnings penalty associated with female-dominated jobs and occupations, and organizational influences on the gender composition of managerial positions. His current work explores the links between job search and recruitment strategies and gender inequality.

JERRY A. JACOBS is Professor of Sociology and Chair of the Graduate Program in Sociology at the University of Pennsylvania. He has studied a number of aspects of women's employment, including authority, earnings, working conditions, part-time work, and entry into male-dominated occupations. His current research projects include a study of women in higher education and a study of working time and conflict between work and family.

MARCIA BRUMIT KROPF is Vice President of Research and Information Systems at Catalyst, a nonprofit research and advisory organization working with business to advance women. Most recently she served as the principal researcher at Catalyst for *A New Approach to Flexibility: Managing the Work/Time Equation* and *Two Careers, One Marriage: Making It Work in the Workplace*. Currently she is responsible for all of Catalyst's research and also leads the Catalyst Award Evaluation Committee, an interdepartmental committee that examines best practices for advancing women in corporations and professional firms.

LEON LITCHFIELD is the Director of Research at the Boston College Center for Work and Family. As a quantitative research specialist, his research interests include a variety of topics within the work/life field, including measurement issues, manifestation within small businesses, work and family issues for women at midlife and beyond, and the impact of specific work/life initiatives, such as flexible work arrangements and on-site child care centers.

LENA M. LUNDGREN is Assistant Professor of Welfare Policy in the School of Social Work and Director of the Center on Work and Family at Boston University. Her present research examines work/family integration and reduced-hour careers in medicine and their consequences for the professional, his or her spouse, and the health care organization.

NANCY L. MARSHALL is Senior Research Scientist and Associate Director of the Center for Research on Women at Wellesley College. She is the author of "Combining Work and Family" in *Health Care for Women: Psychosocial, Social, and Behavioral Influences;* "The Changing Workforce: Job Stress and Psychological Distress" (*Journal of Occupational Health Psychology* 1997); and numerous other chapters and articles on working conditions and work/family issues. She is presently working on a study of employment among women and men over 50.

PHYLLIS MOEN is Ferris Family Professor of Life Course Studies at Cornell University as well as Founding Director of the Bronfenbrenner Life Course Center. She is also Director of the Cornell Employment and Family Careers Institute. She is the author of *Women's Two Roles: A Contemporary Dilemma* and *Working Parents: Transformations in Gender Roles and Public Policies in Sweden.* Her edited books include *A Nation Divided: Diversity, Inequality, and Community in American Society; The State of Americans: This Generation and the Next;* and *Examining Lives in Context: Perspectives on the Ecology of Human Development.* She is presently studying the career paths, strategies, and experiences of two-earner middle-class families and the retirement planning of the baby-boom generation.

MARK NIELSEN is a graduate student at the University of Chicago where he is a Predoctoral Fellow in the Alfred P. Sloan Working Families Center on Parents, Children, and Work. His research interests include family structure; intergenerational transmission, and decision-making.

MAUREEN PERRY-JENKINS is Associate Professor of Psychology at the University of Massachusetts, Amherst. She has published recently in the *Journal of Marriage and the Family* and the *Journal of Family and Economic Issues* on challenges faced by working-class families. She is the principal investigator on a five-year NIMH project on the transition to parenthood and the transition back to paid employment for working-class couples.

MARCIE PITT-CATSOUPHES is Assistant Professor at the Boston College Graduate School of Social Work. She is a co-U.S. editor for the international journal *Community, Work, and Family* and coedited "The Evolving World of Work and Family: New Stakeholders, New Voices" (*Annals of the American Academy of Political and Social Science* 1999). She is currently a member of a research team studying the work and family experiences of women at midlife and pre-retirement. She is also the principal investigator for the Alfred P. Sloan Work-Family Researchers Electronic Network Project.

MARY ROMERO is a sociologist and Professor in the School of Justice Studies, College of Public Programs, at Arizona State University. She is the author of *Maid in the USA*. Her edited books include *Women's Untold Stories: Breaking Silence, Talking Back, Voicing Complexity* and *Challenging Fronteras: Structuring Latina and Latino Lives in the U.S.* She is currently working on a book based on the narrative of the maid's daughter.

LILLIAN B. RUBIN is Senior Research Fellow at the Institute for the Study of Social Change, University of California, Berkeley, and is also a practicing psychotherapist. She is the author of nine books, including *Worlds of Pain: Life in the Working-Class Family; Intimate Strangers: Men and Women Together; Families on the Fault Line: America's Working Class Speaks about the Family, the Economy, Race, and Ethnicity; The Transcendent Child: Tales of Triumph over the Past;* and most recently, *Tangled Lives: Daughters, Mothers, and the Crucible of Aging.*

ROBERT SCHNEIDER is Research Assistant Professor at the Center on Work and Family at Boston University. He is also a psychologist for Harvard Vanguard Medical Associates. He has published over 20 articles on work/family well-being and employee assistance programs.

BARRIE THORNE is Professor of Sociology and Women's Studies, and Co-director of the Center for Working Families, at the University of California,

Berkeley, She is the author of *Gender Play: Girls and Boys in School* and the coeditor of *Feminist Sociology: Life Histories of a Movement; Rethinking the Family: Some Feminist Questions;* and *Language, Gender, and Society.* She is the U.S. editor of *Childhood: A Global Journal of Child Research.* Her current research focuses on the organization and daily lives of children in a mixed-income, ethnically diverse area of Oakland.

LINDA J. WAITE is Professor of Sociology at the University of Chicago where she codirects the Center on Parents, Children, and Work, an Alfred P. Sloan Working Families Center. She also directs the Center on Aging at the University of Chicago. She is the coauthor (with Frances Goldscheider) of *New Families, No Families: The Transformation of the American Home,* which received the Duncan Award from the American Sociological Association. She has recently completed *The Case for Marriage* (with Maggie Gallagher), which focuses on marriage as a social institution and the benefits it produces for individuals.

Index

Text: 10/13 Sabon
Display: Sabon
Composition: Binghamton Valley Composition
Printing and binding: Maple-Vail Book Manufacturing Group